Spectrum of Terror

R. Hrair Dekmejian
University of Southern California

CQ PRESS

A Division of Congressional Quarterly Inc.
Washington, D.C.

CQ Press
1255 22nd Street, NW, Suite 400
Washington, DC 20037

Phone: 202-729-1900; toll-free, 1-866-4CQ-PRESS (1-866-427-7737)

Web: www.cqpress.com

Cover design: Malcolm McGaughy
Cover photos: AP/ Wide World Photos
Composition: MacPS

♾ The paper used in this publication exceeds the requirements of the American National Standard for Information Sciences— Permanence of Paper for Printed Library Materials, ANSI Z39.48-1992.

Printed and bound in the United States of America

11   10   09   08   07   1   2   3   4   5

Library of Congress Cataloging-in-Publication Data

Dekmejian, R. Hrair
   Spectrum of terror / R. Hrair Dekmejian.
      p. cm.
   Includes bibliographical references and index.
   ISBN-13: 978-1-933116-90-7 (alk. paper)
   ISBN-10: 1-933116-90-0 (alk. paper)
   1. Terrorism. 2. Terrorism—History. I. Title

HV6431.D436 2007
363.325' 12—dc22

                                                    2006101717

Dedicated to
the multitudes fallen victim to terrorism, genocide,
and other forms of strategic violence
and
to my many students at USC who dream of a peaceful future

Contents

c h a p t e r o n e
The Spectrum of Political Violence 1

PART I: VIOLENCE AGAINST THE STATE

c h a p t e r t w o
Assassins versus the State 25

PART II: VIOLENCE BY THE STATE

c h a p t e r   s e v e n

State Terrorism, Politicide, and Genocide   203

c h a p t e r   e i g h t

The Armenian Genocide and the Jewish Holocaust   227

Tables, Figures, and Boxes

Tables

Figures

Boxes

Preface

THIS BOOK IS A LABOR not of love but of obligation for one seeking to uncover the causes of political violence. It is my hope that through the pursuit and dissemination of such knowledge, future instances of violent behavior may be prevented or at least contained.

Despite my passionate devotion to the professoriate, I long resisted teaching courses on political violence, a depressing topic by any measure. However, with the upsurge of violent conflicts in the aftermath of the Cold War, I began offering Political Science 366: Terrorism and Genocide—a course on unconventional forms of political violence. I have now taught the course for seventeen years to more than 4,000 University of Southern California students. The structure and content of this book reflect the organization and analytic framework of that course as it developed and expanded over the years in keeping with the dynamics of emerging conflicts and cataclysmic events.

In planning and writing *Spectrum of Terror* I was determined that it not become yet another generic, primarily descriptive book on "terrorism" to crowd the shelves of bookstores and libraries. Instead, I took a more comprehensive and dynamic approach to the conceptualization of political violence in its nonconventional forms. I sought to approach the subject of terrorism in a more systematic, analytical fashion. Thus, this book places violent conflicts between states and nonstate entities along a single continuum—the spectrum of political violence. This spectrum ranges from micro-level acts of terrorism like assassinations, bombings, and violence perpetrated by individuals or small, domestically focused groups; to transnational violence such as that perpetrated by al-Qaida, to macro-level state-sponsored atrocities, massacres, and even genocides. The fundamental rationale for this approach is the inexorable interactive dynamic that connects the micro and macro types of political violence between nonstate entities and nation-states. In other words, political conflicts between states and ethnic, religious, and ideological subgroups usually begin at the micro-level, and if left unresolved, quickly evolve toward more violent and deadly episodes of genocidal proportions.

This evolutionary process is why violent interactions between state and society should be depicted along a single continuum. To that end, the case studies in this book represent each category of political violence and show how they could—or did—evolve either toward peaceful resolution or mass killing. This depiction of state-society relations along a continuum of intensity—from low to high level—emphasizes the interactive and interdependent nature of violent conflicts. To fully understand a particular situation of conflict, one needs to analyze it as an interaction—violence against the state and violence by the state—an analysis that many books on "terrorism" fail to offer. The case studies in this book show that unless conflicts within states and society are resolved in their infancy, they are likely to degenerate into state terrorism en masse—the destruction of whole groups and communities. In other words, one needs to understand why individuals, groups, and states engage in violent behavior and what the consequences of such behavior are. To focus on the interactive and strategic nature of unconventional political violence, I adopted a modified and simplified game-theoretic framework, which is easy to understand and helps illuminate the interactions between actors in political violence. My objective was to identify on a case-by-case basis the strategic rationale of violent actions by conflicting groups as shaped by historical, psychological, cultural, and situational determinants.

I have applied this conceptual framework to the sixteen case studies in the text—from the IRA, ETA, LTTE, and the Chechen rebels; to Aum Shinrikyo, Kashmiri separatists, Hamas, and Hizbullah; to U.S. militia groups and Sendero Luminoso; to al-Qaida; to the genocides of Armenians, Jews, Kurds, and Tutsis—thus representing the entire breadth of the spectrum of political violence. In each chapter, I systematically present the historical and cultural backgrounds of the various conflicts; take readers through the phases of the conflict, while paying close attention to the parties' strategic interactions; and typically conclude with an assessment of the current situation and a discussion of the prospects for continuing violence or conflict resolution. The book's concluding chapter, in particular, provides an overview of the future prospects for terrorism in the world, with a look at the specific determinants of violence, and then turns to address what may be the most pressing emerging global threats. The chapter ends with what I hope are some "antidotes" to political violence.

To help readers keep track of the book's typology and approach, I have constructed a series of tables that show where each case falls along the spectrum and created numerous timelines that crystallize sequences of events so that readers can easily trace the dyadic nature of the conflicts. In addition, in the appendices I provide a master table showing the main characteristics of each case in the spectrum, a master timeline for all major events discussed in the book, and a list of invaluable Web-based resources for further research.

Acknowledgments

For the successful completion of this ambitious project I was privileged to have the support and assistance of many colleagues, friends, and students. I am deeply grateful to over two dozen individuals without whose assistance this book would not have been possible. I am especially beholden to my teaching assistants—Michelle Flores, Som Chounlamountry, Louis Gordon, and Zaid Eyadat—who helped in different ways in my teaching, research, and many revisions of the manuscript. Michelle Flores deserves special thanks for her all-around assistance and critical insights on many theoretical and substantive issues without which this book would have been so much poorer. I greatly benefited from Som Chounlamountry's exceptional computer skills and research assistance and Louis Gordon's bibliographical support and critical help on the Holocaust chapter. Aimee Hernandez read the manuscript in its entirety. A special word of gratitude goes to Anush Der Baghdasarian and Nayri Jilizian for their secretarial assistance, editorial work, and multifaceted support for bringing the book into fruition while keeping my office in operation.

Among the colleagues I wish to thank are Professors Gideon Doron of Tel Aviv University and Zaid Eyadat of the University of Jordan, whose comments on the game-theoretic framework were most helpful. I am also indebted to Professor Don Miller, director of USC's School of Religion, for his yearly lectures in my class on the Rwandan and Armenian genocides that helped deepen and sharpen my knowledge and perceptions of those two tragic episodes. Similarly, my students and I greatly benefited from the time-tested practical wisdom of former U.S. Assistant Secretary of Defense and Naval Secretary Paul Ignatius, during his frequent visits to his Trojan alma mater. Another valued friend, film producer Robert Kline, has been a regular guest speaker in my terrrorism course, which we cotaught at its inception. His six-part documentary, "Terrorism—A World in Shadows," which I coproduced, closely parallels the conceptual scheme used in this book. Drawing on his successful career in the Marine Corps, Lt. Col. Dr. Ken Graham shared with my classes his unforgettable firsthand experiences with the tactics and weaponry of violent subnational groups.

Eight reviewers provided invaluable and constructive criticism on the initial drafts of this book. I am indebted to Professors Navin Bapat of Pennsylvania State University, Miriam F. Elman of Arizona State University, Jennifer Holmes of University of Texas–Dallas, Karl Kaetenhaler of Rhodes College, Brian Lai of University of Iowa, Carol Sholy of University of Missouri–St. Louis, Frank Tachau of University of Illinois–Chicago, and one additional anonymous reviewer.

I would be amiss not to acknowledge the multifaceted contributions and support of many colleagues and friends—Charly Ghailian, Vatche Mankerian, and Harut Sassounian of the University of Southern California Institute of Armenian Studies, and Dr. Jack Lewis, director of the IBEAR program in the Marshall School of Business and his assistants, Diana Kurdian and Ivonne Castillo. Harut Sassounian, in particular, read parts of the manuscript and provided bibliographical support. I am especially thankful to Professor Ann Crigler, chair of the department of political science, and her staff—Veronica Pete, Paul Kovich, Gerlonda Battles, Wanda Johnson, and Brandee Pierce. Last, but not least, I remain deeply indebted to Dean Peter Starr of the University of Southern California College of Letters, Arts, and Sciences for granting me research funding, a lighter teaching load, and plenty of wise counsel. Also, I owe many thanks to the college's development staff, in particular, Diane MacGillivray and Susan Redfield.

Words are inadequate to express my gratitude to my family, who bore the heaviest burden of my anxieties and the demands on my time that writing this book required—my wife, Anoush; sons Gregory, Armen, and Haig; my sister, Mary Kassabian; brother-in-law, Dr. John Kassabian; and sister-in-law, Alice Hagopian. USC Chaplain, Fr. Vazken Movsesian, was a constant source of strength and inspiration; his insights gained during a recent visit to Rwanda with Dr. Miller helped frame my understanding of genocide. The staff at CQ Press were true professionals in offering sound editorial advice, continuous encouragement, and timely assistance—the best I have seen in the publishing business. Charisse Kiino, Elise Frasier, Anna Socrates, and Anne Stewart worked diligently to keep me on track and on schedule.

While expressing my profound thanks to all of my devoted helpers, I remain solely responsible for the contents of this modest opus.

R. Hrair Dekmejian
University of Southern California
January 2007

The Spectrum of Political Violence

HUMANS HAVE USED VIOLENCE to achieve political objectives since the beginning of time. Political conflict, marked by the interaction between and among individuals, groups, and governments, is a hallmark of the human condition. In political conflicts, each of the contending parties, unequal in power, will seek to maximize their self-interests in the pursuit of their respective goals. The clash of competing interests often produces violent outcomes, unless conflicts are resolved through bargaining and negotiation. Although political violence takes many forms—the most conventional and most commonly studied being revolutions and wars between states—the central aim of this book is to systematically study political violence in its nonconventional manifestations—the conflicts between states and nonstate entities.

A compelling reason for focusing on nonconventional forms of violence is that the contemporary nation-state system has seen few wars between states in contrast to dramatic increases in violence between states and nonstate entities. In 2001 there were over forty major and minor groups operating against governments in twenty-eight countries.[1] Among the nonstate entities that have challenged state authority are three categories of subnational and transnational groups—ethnic, religious, and ideological—each pursuing interests detrimental to the national interests of states. When the clash of these interests turns violent, countries become destabilized, economies are ruined, and the interactive terror claims hundreds, thousands, or even more victims. Therefore, the study of these nonconventional forms of violence is crucial to acquire a comprehensive understanding of the global political environment, to determine the causal factors responsible for their occurrence, and to identify the conditions and mechanisms that can bring about their peaceful resolution.

Conflicts between states and nonstate entities occur along a wide spectrum, reflecting various forms and magnitudes of violent behavior. To analyze these encounters, this book depicts political violence along a five-fold continuum ranging from micro-level acts of violence against the state by individuals, subnational groups, and transnational organizations to state-sponsored violence and mass murder—genocide. This classification of the agents and types of nonconventional violence provides a comparative explanatory framework for the case studies presented in later chapters.[2] It facilitates comparative analysis, while heightening the dynamic relationship between the five categories. Thus, the underlying logic of viewing political violence along a single continuum is the ominous possibility that some conflicts between states and nonstate entities pass through stages of escalation—i.e., what begins as micro-level, low intensity terrorism could well evolve into genocide.

Political Physics and Game Theory

The study of political violence challenges scholars and students because it requires a high degree of objectivity and dispassionate analysis. Indeed, even the most earnest scholars often have difficulties in maintaining impartiality when contemplating the human victims of these violent contests. In striving for a degree of objectivity, this book will employ a modified game theoretic framework to analyze the case studies. At each step, this approach seeks to explain why the antagonists choose to use violent methods in order to achieve their objectives.

A useful way for students to conceptualize game theory is to view conflictual situations in terms of "political physics." This approach to the analysis of different forms of political violence is guided by three fundamental attributes or laws of human behavior. First, people behave rationally. Individuals and unitary groups act to obtain what they perceive to be in their interest, and their interests can be expressed as ordered preferences—that is, each party logically and consistently ranks its preferences for one outcome over alternative lower-ranked outcomes. Second, relations between two individuals or groups are usually interactive, in that each party reacts to the other's actions. Third, neither party is likely to "turn the other cheek" to what it sees as a wrongful act committed by the other side. Simply stated, most individuals or groups are unlikely to forgive and forget what they consider unfriendly or injurious acts toward them despite age-old religious and ethical injunctions to the contrary.

These interactive laws of human relations assume special significance in the realm of politics, where power is the primary element. Hence, it is possible to posit a dynamic model of "political physics" in which two antagonists of unequal power engage in a dialectic of conflict often leading to violence in response to each other's actions. Yet the participants in this interactive model are not simply motivated by the psychological compulsion to take revenge, but by rational calculations about the strategic utility of their choice of action, its costs and consequences. Thus, each party enters the conflict in pursuit of its own perceived self-interests and order of preferences, aiming to prevail over the other side in order to fulfill its political objectives. In such contests of violence, three different outcomes are possible:

1. A victory by one of the parties, leading to an imposed solution by the winner over the loser.
2. A resolution of the conflict if the parties decide not to pursue their maximal or first preferences and make sufficient mutual concessions as incentives to obtain a peaceful equilibrium because of changed circumstances, external pressures, or the high costs of continuing the conflict.
3. A continuation of interactive violence if both parties are willing and capable of bearing the costs of the conflict, and each is determined to achieve dominance or strengthen its relative power position before pursuing a negotiated solution.

The foregoing conceptualization of dyadic conflicts—also known as two-person games—based on the principles of causality and reciprocity, is a first step toward developing the rational choice/game theoretic schema used to analyze the case studies in this book. The basic elements of game theory are summarized as follows:

1. The parties to a conflict, A and B, are strategically interdependent in that the decisions or choices of each side depend to some extent on those made by the other side.
2. In their strategic interaction, A and B are motivated to maximize their respective perceived self-interests.
3. Each side is cognizant that their strategic decisions will result in payoffs—either rewards or penalties.
4. In making strategic decisions, each side will anticipate the other's likely choices by placing itself in the opponent's circumstances. Thus, at each decision point the behavior of A and B will depend on their perceptions of each other's preferences. Each side identifies the possible outcomes and ranks its own as well as its opponent's preferences.
5. The decisions and preferences of the contending sides are limited by uncertainties arising from incomplete or asymmetric information that distorts their perceptions of each other's choices of action.

6. Once the strategic interaction is enjoined, the unfolding moves in the game will produce a "learning curve" as both sides update their preferences according to the past behavior of the other side and their perceptions of how it will behave in the future.

7. Strategic interactions may produce either zero-sum or non–zero-sum outcomes. A zero-sum game occurs when gains for one side result in losses for the other. A non–zero-sum game involves mutual gain or loss and has greater potential for leading to a mutually satisfactory and hence stable agreement.

8. The two antagonists may reach a Nash Equilibrium—a stable outcome—when neither side wants to alter its strategic choice because each side knows that changing its strategy may not necessarily result in the anticipated gains. An example of a Nash Equilibrium occurs in situations known as the "Prisoner's Dilemma" where A and B have to decide whether to cooperate to achieve a common objective. Because each party does not trust the sincerity of the other, both reject cooperation resulting in a Nash Equilibrium which persists unless a new factor—an internal shift or an external agent—forces the antagonists to cooperate.[3] Box 1.1 illustrates the outcomes of the prisoner's dilemma.

Prisoner's Dilemma Games and Conflict Resolution

If both antagonists have the resources and the will to sustain the interactive violence over time, they will reach an "equilibrium of terror" in which neither side backs down and the conflict continues. If neither party can decisively win, however, there are two possible ways to bring about resolution of the conflict: reordering of the actors' preferences or external intervention. The first, reordering of preferences, takes place when, as the violence drags on, the antagonists realize that they cannot unilaterally arrive at their most preferred outcome—defeating their opponent. Recognizing the magnitude of the costs of continued violence, they may be prompted to accept a lower ranked preference and bring the conflict to "equilibrium of peace."[4] The second, external intervention, occurs when a third party emerges to mediate the conflict. A modified form of the prisoner's dilemma game illustrates the dynamics in this case. Unlike the classic prisoner's dilemma situation outlined in Box 1.1, the jailer mediates and transmits messages between the two "prisoners." This redefinition of the jailer's role to include a "brokerage" function makes the prisoner's dilemma model more applicable to real political situations. Thus, the jailer emerges as a third party pursuing its own self-interests as it attempts to impose its will upon the two rivals. Its success in bringing about an equilibrium of peace is contingent upon its ability to force both sides to stop fighting by accepting lower-ranked preferences.[5]

Box 1.1
Prisoner's Dilemma Games: A Simple Example

The following is an example of a prisoner's dilemma game: in the wake of a terrorist attack, two suspects are apprehended at the airport after attempting to use false documents to board an airplane. After being taken into custody, they are interrogated separately by a jailer who seeks to determine culpability so as to get a conviction for the unresolved bombing. Each prisoner has two choices—confess to the attack or deny involvement. Both of them have been told separately that if one confesses, the confessor walks free while the other suspect receives a twenty-five year sentence, and if both confess, each will receive a ten-year sentence.

In the absence of any other evidence that would lead to a conviction for the bombing, if neither confesses, they will both be convicted on false documents charges and be given a three-year sentence. Based on the inducements offered by the jailer, four outcomes are possible:

1. Both confess and receive ten-year sentences.
2. Prisoner A confesses and goes free while prisoner B receives a twenty-five year sentence.
3. Prisoner B confesses and goes free while prisoner A receives a twenty-five year sentence.
4. Neither confesses and both receive a three-year sentence.

Given these outcomes, Prisoner A ranks the above outcomes in order of preference as follows:

$$2 > 4 > 1 > 3$$

Similarly, prisoner B's preferences are as follows:

$$3 > 4 > 1 > 2$$

If both prisoners act strategically—that is, according to their interests and in consideration of each other's preferences—both will choose to confess and receive ten-year sentences. Seeking to maximize their interests, both sides ultimately achieve their third preference! How does this rational behavior lead to what seems, from the perspective of the prisoners, to be an irrational outcome?

Consider the perspective of prisoner A: if prisoner B confesses and prisoner A also confesses, they will both receive ten-year sentences. If prisoner B confesses and prisoner A does not, then prisoner A will receive a twenty-five year sentence. Thus, if prisoner B confesses, then it

Box 1.1 continued

is better for prisoner A to confess. However, if prisoner B does not confess and A confesses, then A will go free. If prisoner B does not confess and A also does not confess, then A will receive a three-year sentence. So if prisoner B does not confess, then it is better for A to confess. Thus, when prisoner A considers prisoner B's possible course of action, it is clear that prisoner A is better off confessing regardless of prisoner B's choice. If prisoner B makes the same calculations then both will choose to confess, and both will be stuck with their third-ranked preference. In such cases, despite being rational, both players play their dominant strategy (to confess) even when they are fully aware that this is likely to lead to suboptimal outcomes.

Expanding the Model

The eight elements of basic game theory described on pp. 3–4, along with the application of the prisoner's dilemma game to conflict resolution, serve as a foundation to build an expansive framework to analyze strategic violence. This basic foundation is the "thin" version of rational choice analysis, where the preferences of the two sides are derived from their respective self-interests, perceived as the maximization of material gains. However, some game theorists argue persuasively that calculations of self-interest are not the product of material rationality alone, but are further constructed by psychological, situational, cultural, and historical factors that are unique to different individuals, groups, and social settings.[6] In the "thick" game theoretic model, these factors must be included to explain how each side defines its interests—that is, the ranked preferences which determine how the game will be played. The rationale for including these factors in the "thick" model is as follows.

Psychology. In strategic interactions, the actors base their decisions or "moves" on the information they have about each other and their estimation of each other's intentions. In principle, the greater the amount of accurate information, the clearer are their mutual perceptions and the lower is the level of uncertainty about each other's intentions. Yet in real situations, decision makers analyze informational data through their individual perceptual prisms and "operational codes" that color and distort their views of each others' intentions and preferences.[7] Thus, the action of each side is, to some degree, the product of psychologically determined calculations of self-interest, a dynamic that applies to any bargaining situation, such as negotiations, and to cases of interactive violence among states and between states and nonstate entities.[8]

Psychological factors in gaming situations are especially salient in explaining the behavior of leaders and their constituents. The scholarly literature on political psychology includes a wealth of case studies on the often-decisive impact of personality on political leaders' strategic calculations and behavior.[9] By revealing their belief systems and motivational factors, psychological profiles of leaders can provide remarkably accurate explanations of leaders' preferences in conflictual situations. Indeed, psychological factors are critical in explaining the German kaiser's preferences in World War I, Hitler's and Stalin's actions during World War II, bin Ladin's compulsion to attack the United States on September 11, 2001, PLO leader Yasser Arafat's apparent misperceptions in negotiating with Israel in 1996 and 2001, and Shoko Asahara's motivation to unleash poison gas in the Tokyo subway in March 1995. Paranoia, suicidal tendencies, schizophrenia, narcissism and other psychological pathologies distort leaders' preferences and assessments of the risk involved in the choices they make and the meaning of the outcomes.[10] Further examples of psychologically conditioned violent behavior include assassins, suicide bombers, and sundry terrorists engaged in "martyrdom operations."

Milieu. Preferences and decisions of individual leaders or cohorts of leaders are also influenced by the social forces and networks prevailing in their immediate milieu, defined as the "spirit of the times"—*zeitgeist*—and the "spirit of the people"—*volksgeist.* In times of crisis, a leader might face a situation of mass psychosis, popular expectancy of peril, calls for revenge against an enemy, or challenges from internal rivals or factions. Consequently, the social-psychological interaction between the leader's personality and the social milieu could shape his or her calculations in taking action against an antagonist.[11]

Culture and History. Individual and collective decisions are ultimately shaped by the cultural and historical imperatives that determine the beliefs, experiences, and memories of a given collectivity, factors that transcend the immediate milieu. Patterns of culture—ethnic, religious, and ideological—are constructed and reinforced by collective memory and help form the psychopolitical orientations of both leaders and their constituencies, as well as constrain how decisions are made vis-à-vis an opposing party. Thus, consideration of the cultural and historical factors is crucial in shaping antagonists' preferences and calculating the amount of costs they are able to bear in contests of strategic violence.[12]

Summarizing the Model

The foregoing section outlined the key building blocks of an expansive or "thick" dyadic model to explain the logic and dynamics of political violence initiated by one or both conflicting parties. The first step was to posit a game theoretic model of strategic interaction—the "thin" model—based on the rational calculations of actors in conflict pursuing their self-interests. In order to understand how those interests are shaped in situations of violent political conflict, however, a number of additional factors had to be considered in the formation of the preferences that determine the outcome of the game. Thus, to account for the psychological peculiarities of the contending decision makers, personality was introduced as the second factor in the calculation of self-interest. Milieu was added as the third element because decisions are not made in a vacuum, but within the context of countervailing social forces, rivalries, and popular expectations. Finally, culture and history were incorporated to help illuminate the causal factors, modalities, and patterns of violent behavior and the conditions that determine its continuation or cessation. The explanatory and predictive power of this "thick" rational choice model, illustrated in Figure 1.1, will be demonstrated by focusing on a range of critical questions in analyzing cases of political violence:

1. Historical Background: What preexisting conditions shaped the self-interests and preferences of the antagonists that led to violent outcomes?
2. Causal Factors: What specific triggers led one or the other side to initiate the use of violence?
3. Psychocultural Factors: How and to what extent did the psychological and cultural predispositions of leaders or parties on either side shape the ordered preferences of that side?
4. Preferences: What objectives did both sides seek to achieve prior to the start of violence?
5. Strategic Calculations: What were the calculations and expected payoffs that led one or both antagonists to decide to use violent means?
6. Dominant Strategy: To what extent was the protracted nature of interactive violence prompted by the leaders' dominant strategies to perpetrate the conflict?
7. Internal Divisions: To what extent did internal divisions and rivalries within one or both contending parties lead to the use of violence?
8. Tipping Point: What factors led the two sides to abandon their first preferences and participate in negotiations?
9. Cataclysmic Loss: If one of the parties suffered a cataclysmic defeat or genocidal loss, how was it able to revive its contestation using violent and/or non-violent means?
10. Cyclicality: Did certain instances of interactive violence follow cyclical patterns and if so, what determined the ebb and flow of interactive violence?
11. Third Parties: What role did third parties play in contributing to the continuation of violence or in pushing the antagonists toward a peaceful outcome?

FIGURE 1.1 Strategic Interactions: An Expansive Game Theoretical Model

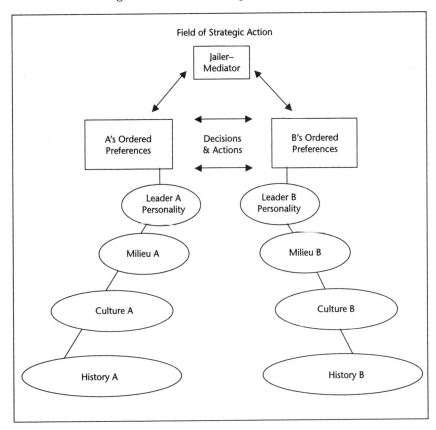

12. Audiences: To what extent did the need or desire to influence specific domestic constituencies and international public opinion determine the behavior of the two sides?

The expansive game theoretic model above provides a general analytic framework for the case studies of various forms of political violence in the chapters to follow. The case study narratives will raise implicitly or explicitly the twelve critical questions above in tracing the anatomy and life cycle of each conflict from its historical origins, causes, leaders, strategies, and cyclical evolution to the changes in preferences, external intervention, and the factors determining the outcomes—peaceful resolution, continuing violence, oppression, or genocidal destruction.

FIGURE 1.2   The Spectrum of Political Violence

Direction of violence	Anti-State				State
	←				→
Magnitude	Micro				Macro
Type	Individual terrorism	Subnational terrorism	Transnational terrorism	State terrorism against domestic and transnational opponents	Politicide and genocide
Perpetrators	• Assassins • Bombers	• Ethnic nationalists • Religious militants • Ideological radicals • Hybrid organizations	Transnational terrorist organizations and states	• Secret police • Special forces • Military • Paramilitaries • Other state-sponsored groups	• Secret police • Special forces • Military • Paramilitaries • Other state-sponsored groups

A Typology of Political Violence

Scholars use typologies to organize information using various criteria of classification. Typologies help clarify and structure complex phenomena by providing a conceptual framework for the selection and comparative analysis of case studies.

Figure 1.2 presents a typology of the agents and types of political violence, a spectrum ranging from micro-level terrorism against the state to macro-level acts of repression and mass terror by the state. The guiding criteria are the type of agent, the amount of violence used, and its consequences in human losses. Moving left to right on the spectrum, from individual terrorism to genocide, the dominant trend is toward quantum increases in the magnitude of violence and the number of its victims.

The spectrum in Figure 1.2 divides political violence into two general categories according to the role of the state in the conflict—either as target (violence against the state) and or as perpetrator (violence by the state). Perpetrators of anti-state violence include those actors listed on the bottom row of Figure 1.2 such as assassins and bombers, subnational groups, and transnational organizations. Acts of violence perpetrated by the state range from suppression of domestic dissidents and insurgencies, targeting transnational terrorist organizations, initiating clandestine foreign operations, and using mass terror of genocidal proportions against specific population groups. Clearly, transnational terrorism presents a unique type of political violence in which the state, as perpetrator or target, is involved in unconventional conflict beyond its borders.[13]

Anti-state Violence

In the five-fold classification of the participants in dyadic conflicts in Figure 1.2, the central player is the state as it interacts with different types of nonstate actors. Indeed, in the contemporary international system, nation-states are the main repositories of power, sovereignty, and legitimacy. As such, states claim the right to have a monopoly of coercive power and to use it within and even beyond their sovereign boundaries against any real or perceived antagonists. In addition, the international system strongly favors structural stability over the instability engendered by nonstate entities. Consequently, there exists an inherent asymmetry in the balance of power and legitimacy between states and their subnational and transnational challengers. Given the growing preponderance of state power resulting from modern technological capabilities of control and coercion, most nonstate entities begin their contestation with state authority at a significant disadvantage because of their relative weakness, and the illegitimacy of their cause under international legal norms and in the arena of public opinion.

Individual Terrorism versus the State

The category of "individual terrorism" consists of persons who individually commit acts of violence against the state through assassinations, bombings, and any other means of sabotage and disruption available to them. Assassins and various *agents provocateurs* have been prime agents of anti-state violence since ancient times. Among the perpetrators of individual terrorism are the "lone wolves" who attack on their own initiative, acting independently of anti-state organizations. Their choices of methods and targets of attack represent highly individualistic manifestations of opposition to state power in pursuit of their personal political agendas. With recent advances in technology, suicide bombings and remote-controlled explosive devices have replaced traditional techniques of killing leaders and leadership cadres. These innovations have greatly increased the effectiveness, scope, and reach of terrorist attacks by individuals against human and institutional targets. The category of individual terrorism does not include agents who are dispatched by subnational or transnational organizations or states to carry out specific missions as a part of an overall strategic plan.

Subnational Terrorism versus the State

The next category of anti-state violence denoted in Figure 1.2 consists of subnational dissident groups and organizations. When disgruntled individuals come together around a unifying cause, they are able to pursue collective action against the state more effectively than as individual terrorists. Such organized collective action can increase both the scope of terrorist activities and the magnitude of their lethal impact.

Since the end of World War II, over one hundred subnational groups have used violence to challenge state authority. The emergence, endurance, and demise of these groups depend on six factors: (1) the popularity of their cause, (2) the effectiveness of leadership and organization, (3) changes in their objectives, (4) the strategic rationale for violent actions, (5) the nature of state responses ranging from negotiated settlement to repression, mass killing, and genocide, and (6) the role of external powers and world conditions. Although some of these groups have short life cycles of interactive violence with states, others continue to endure for decades or reemerge after periods of decline and quiescence. A logical and analytically consistent method of classifying these diverse groups is to focus on the nature of their cause, which defines their motivations and objectives, and provides self-justification for engaging in anti-state violence. Subnational terrorists can be classified under three broad categories—ethnic, religious, and ideological—in keeping with the causes they pursue.

Ethnic Nationalists versus the State. Violence perpetrated by ethnic nationalist groups against states has been a persistent occurrence during and after the breakup of empires in the twentieth century. Ethnic terrorism usually occurs as a reaction to state policies that are considered detrimental to an ethnic group's basic interests and aspirations, such as physical security, political independence, cultural integrity, or economic well-being. Among the causes of ethnic terrorism are oppressive state policies, forceful subjugation of one ethnic group by a regime controlled by another ethnic group, and ethnic aspirations that cannot be realized within a state's political framework. The objectives of ethnic terrorism could range from the quest for civil rights and economic equality, to autonomy or independence.

Major examples of interactive terrorism between ethnic nationalist groups and states are: Irish Republican Army versus Great Britain, Basque Homeland and Freedom versus Spain, Liberation Tigers of Tamil Eelam versus Sri Lanka, and Chechens versus Russia.

Religious Militants versus the State. Religious belief has long been a powerful force in providing the motivation and justification to commit acts of political violence. Groups that have engaged in anti-state religious terrorism include cults, sects, and chiliastic offshoots of mainstream faiths that are propelled by fundamentalist zealotry into the political arena to reshape it through violence. A representative sample of groups manifesting the dynamics of religious violence includes: Aum Shinrikyo versus Japan, Hizbullah versus Israel and United States, Kashmiri separatists versus India, and Hamas versus Israel.

Ideological Radicals versus the State. Terrorist groups that define themselves and their objectives in ideological terms represent the two opposite ends of the political spectrum, from left to right. Both leftist and rightist ideological groups aim to overthrow the ruling order to establish a new regime committed to the transformation of society according to the dictates of their specific political creeds. The leftists claim to fight for the interests of the economically and politically disadvantaged classes that are exploited and repressed by governments controlled by the capitalist class. In pursuit of these revolutionary objectives, leftist groups borrow from the ideological maxims of anarchism, socialism, and communism and its Maoist and Castroite variants. In sharp contrast to the leftists' focus on class interests, rightist groups derive inspiration from fascist and Nazi ideologies. Right-wing terrorists aspire to take power in order to establish an autocratic state based on doctrines of national or racial supremacy. Examples of leftist and rightist terrorist groups include: *Sendero Luminoso* versus Peru and White supremacist groups such as the Ku Klux Klan, the Aryan Nations, and the Militia Movement versus the United States.

Transnational Terrorism against States

Reaching beyond their domestic origins, anti-state terrorist groups can also develop a transnational outreach. Some subnational terrorist groups confronting a regime make a strategic choice to transnationalize their operations against that regime's embassies, diplomats, soldiers, or even citizens located in other countries. By shifting the arena of violence from the national to the transnational level, these terrorist groups seek to maximize their coercive leverage, heighten the target country's vulnerability and insecurity, and increase its costs, while creating an international forum for propagating their cause. Among the subnational groups that have periodically engaged in transnational terrorism are the Irish Republican Army, factions of the Palestine Liberation Organization (PLO), and the Sikhs of India. Another category of transnational terrorism consists of groups with a multinational following united under a common political, religious, or ethnic ideology. These groups seek to further their objectives by attacking ideologically defined foes, usually governments, but also corporations and other nongovernmental organizations. The most well-known transnational terrorist organization of this type is Osama bin Ladin's al-Qaida.

State Terrorism

As the recognized repositories of power in the international system, states have always sought to legitimize and assert their monopoly over the use of coercive force. The use of various forms of terrorism by states against internal and external opposition groups, although common throughout history, has increased in the modern context. In fact, the frequency, magnitude, and destructiveness of violence perpetrated by governments far exceed those authored by anti-state terrorist organizations.

State-sponsored Terrorism: Transnational Targets

In addition to conventional warfare, states often engage in acts of violence in foreign countries and occupied territories. This type of state-sponsored terrorism represents the projection of coercive force overtly or covertly across territorial boundaries in order to annex territory, establish friendly regimes, subvert unfriendly regimes, assassinate or capture enemy leaders, or destroy terrorist bases and cells.

Among the countries that are known to have practiced state-sponsored terrorism are Libya, Iran, Iraq, Chile, Algeria, Pakistan, Turkey, Syria, Sudan, Israel, Britain, Russia, and the United States. Although illegal under international law, some of these states have justified transnational violence as necessary and legitimate acts of self-defense.

State-sponsored Terrorism: Domestic Targets

In its most common form, state violence occurs as counterterrorism to fight subnational opposition groups. Although states often use excessive force against dissidents, most democratic regimes refrain from the forceful suppression of nonviolent individuals and groups opposed to the state. As distinct from counterterrorism, state-sponsored domestic violence often involves the imprisonment, torture, physical displacement, or destruction of a regime's real or perceived enemies. Among the many examples of the use of repression by states are Egypt's crackdown on the Muslim Brotherhood, Argentina's "dirty war," and Pinochet's atrocities against civilians in Chile.

Genocide and Politicide

The use of violence by the state or its allied militias with the intent to destroy, in whole or in part, a targeted population is defined as genocide—the ultimate terror. Genocidal acts by governments in the twentieth century have claimed millions of lives, many more than the total number of deaths by all other types of anti-state and state-sponsored terrorism. Despite rhetorical pronouncements of "never again," the international community has repeatedly failed to prevent mass murder by governments. Five case studies of genocide are selected for detailed analysis: Khmer Rouge versus Cambodians, Ottoman Empire versus Armenians, Third Reich versus Jews, Turkey and Iraq versus Kurds, and Rwandan Hutu versus Tutsi.

Problems of Definition: What Is Terrorism?

In the quest for a scientific study of politics, political scientists have long faced the problem of finding appropriate terminology to describe and classify the actors and actions involved in the political processes within and across countries and cultures. This task has proven particularly daunting in the study of political violence, especially regarding use of the terms "terrorist" and "terrorism" to describe specific perpetrators and acts of violence.

In the wake of the cataclysm of September 11, 2001, the debate over the use of the words terrorist and terrorism intensified with inconclusive results. Scholarly discourse by academics was mostly replaced with rhetoric from a motley crew of politicians, pundits, journalists, lobbyists, and intelligence analysts who obfuscated the meaning of terrorism, in keeping with their individual perceptions and political agendas.

Clearly, the word terrorism lacks precision and objectivity from a scholarly point of view, yet there is no escape from its incessant use in political discourse, articles, books, and the media. Although some scholars refrain from using terrorism as a descriptive category, others have sought to refine its meaning, or have preferred to substitute the more neutral term "political violence."

The origin of the words terror and terrorism harks back to the French Revolution of 1789, and the Jacobin Reign of Terror that triggered mass executions of revolutionary leaders and followers by the guillotine or gun. In the French revolutionary context, terrorism involved both violence against the state and violence perpetrated by the state. In the nineteenth century, the word terrorism appeared in descriptions of the anti-Tsarist violence of the *narodniki* and the Social Revolutionary Party. The cyclical violence of Stalin's purges from the 1930s onward was characterized as mass terror because of similarities to the Jacobin killings. Since the 1960s, the terrorism label has gained increasing currency mostly to describe anti-state violence by subnational groups in the context of the Cold War and the rise of ethnic, ideological, and religious insurrectionary movements. In modern parlance, violence committed by the state is often labeled "state terrorism" or "state terror," and even "reign of terror," a revival of the old Jacobin term now used to describe gross human rights violations such as crimes against humanity, genocide, politicide, and ethnocide.[14]

Some scholars criticize the negative characterization of violent dissident groups as terrorists because in this context the label upholds the legitimacy of the use of violence by states only and denies the legitimacy of cause to anti-state groups that use violence. In response, such groups use the terrorist label to describe the state's violent suppression of their activities. This reciprocal characterization of each other's violent actions as terrorism is an attempt by both antagonists to justify their conflicting causes and uses of violence in the political arena. In such contests of interactive violence, the attribution of terrorism becomes a matter of perspective depending on the observer's values and loyalties, hence the adage, "one person's terrorist is another's freedom fighter." However persuasive, this formulation has been challenged on legal and moral grounds. Some writers differentiate between the legitimacy of large-scale insurgencies and guerrilla wars against despotic regimes and the illegitimacy of attacks by small bands against democratic states. In this perspective, broad-based insurgent movements are accorded a degree of legitimacy of cause despite their use of terrorist tactics, while smaller dissident groups are classified as terrorists because they are said to lack popular support and use violence against a legitimately constituted state, i.e., a democratic regime. Yet, even this definition is flawed because it assumes that all states, including democracies, always rule justly over all segments of the population under their control. What if some democracies become corrupt or control populations within and outside their territories who resort to violence because their human rights or aspirations for independence have been forcefully suppressed? Moreover, there are disagreements as to which countries are truly democratic as distinct from quasi-democratic or democratizing regimes.

A more persuasive attempt to distinguish between guerrilla organizations and terrorist groups is based on the differences in their power and methods of fighting. While both groups have the common goal of regime change, guerrillas and insurgents usually occupy some territory and fight according to the conventions of war, while terrorists intentionally target civilians in a clandestine manner.[15] Yet it can be difficult to distinguish terrorists from guerrillas because they employ similar tactics and identify themselves as a part of revolutionary and liberation movements. Sometimes there could even be an overlap between the two when a terrorist group grows into a guerrilla organization leading an insurgency, as in the case of the Tamil Tigers in Sri Lanka and *Sendero Luminoso* in Peru. Like guerrillas, terrorists are idealists, fighting for what they believe to be a noble cause. According to Bruce Hoffman, the terrorist is unlike a violent lunatic or common criminal because he is an "altruist," a "violent intellectual," prepared to shed blood in pursuit of his organization's self-defined objective to achieve a greater good.[16]

The task of defining terrorism has also involved various U.S. government agencies. According to the U.S. State Department and Title 22 of the United States Code, Section 2656f(d), terrorism is defined as:

> ... premeditated, politically motivated violence perpetrated against noncombatant targets by subnational groups or clandestine agents, usually intended to influence an audience.[17]

The operative phrase in the State Department's formulation is "noncombatant targets" which denotes unarmed civilians—men, women, children—as well as buildings and infrastructural targets serving the civilian population. The State Department's definition of noncombatant targets also extends to off-duty military personnel and military personnel not engaged in conflict. Also instructive are the definitions of terrorism adopted by the Federal Bureau of Investigation and the U.S. Department of Defense, both emphasizing the unlawful nature of such violence:

> ... the unlawful use of force or violence against persons or property to intimidate or coerce a government, the civilian population, or any segment thereof, in furtherance of political or social objectives.[18] (FBI)

> ... the unlawful use or threatened use of force or violence against individuals or property to coerce or intimidate governments or societies, often to achieve political, religious or ideological objectives.[19] (U.S. Department of Defense)

Clearly, there is no consensus on the definition of terrorism and the debate is far from resolved. In an attempt to reach consensus, Alex P. Schmid and Albert J. Jongman made a concerted systematic effort to parse over one hundred definitions of terrorism.[20] Although a consensus has not been reached, Schmid has continued his quest to create a cogent conceptual scheme by viewing terrorism from five analytic perspectives: terrorism as crime, terrorism as politics, terrorism as warfare, terrorism as communication, and terrorism as religious fundamentalism.[21]

Terrorism as Crime

Terrorism is considered a crime under international law. The prevention and suppression of international terrorism are addressed in twelve conventions and protocols that outlaw airplane hijacking, attacks on ships and ports, targeting diplomatic personnel, hostage-taking, bombings, endangering nuclear materials, and financing terrorist groups.[22] The UN Ad-Hoc Committee on Terrorism defines terrorism as a criminal act in which an individual intentionally causes:

a. death or serious bodily injury to any person; or
b. serious damage to public or private property, including a place of public use, a state or government facility, a public transportation system, an infrastructure facility or the environment; or
c. damage to property, places, facilities, or systems referred to [above], resulting or likely to result in major economic loss, when the purpose of conduct, by its nature or context, is to intimidate a population, or to compel a government or an international organization to do or abstain from doing any act.[23]

Terrorism as Politics

Most analysts define terrorism as a form of political violence. In the competition for control of the state, political parties or groups sometimes use terrorism as part of their political strategy. The conflicts between the state and opposition groups can be viewed as an interactive process, with an asymmetry of power favoring the state. In some cases, violence by the state will be countered by nonviolent campaigns either because the opposition is too weak to use violence or it desires to hold the moral high ground and garner international support. However, in other instances, the opposition may choose to use terrorism. As interactive violence continues and both sides escalate their violent face-off, the moral distinction between the two sides tends to erode. Counterterrorism measures could result in state terrorism or even escalate into massacre, internal war, ethnocide, politicide, or genocide.[24] Terrorism, like war, may be regarded as a continuation of politics.[25]

Terrorism as Warfare

Acts of terrorism occur both in times of peace and war. Wars of aggression are criminal acts under international law and even in legitimate wars, the laws of war are often breached by the intentional killing of noncombatants, captives, and innocents. These are terrorist acts justly classified as war crimes committed by soldiers. Similarly, when opposition groups attack civilian targets as part of a deliberate strategy to influence state policies, they are engaged in committing war crimes. Hence, anti-state terrorism can be appropriately equated with war crimes, the killing of civilians in violation of the laws of war and moral constraints that bind conventional armies and guerrilla outfits. Although terrorists view themselves as "soldiers," in their attacks on civilians, they are more like soldiers who have committed war crimes. Yet in some situations, the distinction between soldiers and terrorists can become obfuscated. To the extent that some wars have become more terroristic—targeting predominately civilians rather than military opponents—the moral difference between the conduct of soldiers and terrorists has grown smaller.[26]

Terrorism as Communication

Terrorism is not only an act of violence but an instrument of political communication. In committing violence, terrorist groups are signaling to four distinct constituencies: members of the group, the targeted regime, the citizenry, and the international community. At each level, the terrorist group propagates its cause forcefully to promote internal cohesion, to capture public attention, coerce opponents, and win converts. Since the onset of modern terrorism after the mid-nineteenth century, when dynamite, the telegraph, and mass circulating newspapers became available, anarchists and leftist revolutionaries were quick to utilize the propaganda potential of violent acts.[27] The advent of television and other types of electronic media in the twentieth century provided potent venues for terrorist propaganda. By staging dramatic acts of violence through bombing, kidnapping, or hostage-taking, terrorist groups expose the state's impotence in protecting its citizens while at the same time gaining continuous media coverage for extended periods. Thus, terrorists can readily use the media to manipulate target audiences such as editors and reporters who may unwittingly become accessories to murder.[28] The dynamic relationship between terrorism and propaganda has been well understood by both theorists and practitioners of political violence, from the anarchist prince Pyotr Kropotkin, to the Brazilian urban guerrilla Carlos Marighela, to bin Ladin and his jihadist followers.

Terrorism as Religion

The religious perspective on terrorism is unique in its focus on sacrifice and martyrdom. Religious suicide terrorists engage in the sacrificial killing of their innocent victims as well as themselves in order to assert their belief in a divine will.[29] Although all mainstream religions preach peace and nonviolence, their extremist off-shoots have periodically engaged in acts of terrorism and slaughter of innocents which are justified as salvational acts for a transcendent purpose. Among the causes of religious terrorism are poverty, social injustice, humiliation, state repression, military defeat, and foreign domination.[30]

Conclusion

Taken together, Schmid's five conceptual frameworks—terrorism as crime, politics, warfare, communication, and religion—provide a comprehensive approach to understanding terrorism. Notably, Schmid defines anti-state terrorism as a criminal act under international law. While this definition favors the state, Schmid also recognizes the dynamic linkage between terrorism against the state and terrorism by the state. He emphasizes that counterterrorism measures could bring about state terrorism ranging from atrocities to massacres and genocide. The logic of this linkage, viewing political violence by anti-state entities and states as a dynamic process over a single continuum, guides the structure of this book. According to this rationale, a general definition of terrorism covering political violence against and by the state can be framed under the umbrella of international law. UN conventions and protocols outlaw and criminalize anti-state terrorism, as well as prohibit acts of state terrorism though instruments such as the UN Declaration of Human Rights (1948) and the UN Genocide Convention (1948). An inclusive definition of terrorism thus logically covers the entire spectrum of political violence outlawed under international law:

> The strategic use of force or the threat of force, beyond the bounds of international law, against human and material targets carried out by any individual, subnational group, transnational organization, or state to achieve a political objective in pursuit of its perceived self-interest.

Thus, under this overarching definition, which is used in this book, all types of political violence that are outlawed by international law would constitute terrorism. The obvious strength of this formulation is that all perpetrators of terrorism are treated as equally culpable under international law. However, contending sides, neutral observers, or scholars could raise the following questions in applying this definition to specific cases of political violence:

1. Should there be moral equivalence between states and nonstate actors using violence?
2. At what point is it justified for a state to use violence against a nonstate challenger? After a public demonstration or riot? To preempt a likely attack? In response to an attack?
3. At what point is it justified for a nonstate entity to use violence against the state? In response to political and economic injustice? In response to acts of oppression by the state? In response to atrocities perpetrated by the state?
4. Are attacks against the military forces of an occupying power considered terrorism?

5. Does a military attack by the state on a hostile nonstate target which results in collateral damage—the killing of civilians—constitute an act of terrorism?

6. What can be done when states and nonstate perpetrators of violence choose to disobey the norms of international law?

In seeking answers to these fundamental questions, students are invited to read the case studies and draw their own conclusions. In the end, what is and what is not terrorism may be a matter of perspective for each reader, except in cases of state terrorism of genocidal proportions where questions of moral equivalence would violate universal maxims of ethics, civility, and humane behavior.

By investigating conflicts from a game theoretic perspective students could also raise the following questions: What strategies brought victory to one or the other party? What strategic mistakes caused one party to lose or led both sides into cycles of protracted bloodshed? Could the antagonists have made certain strategic choices that might have prevented or minimized bloodshed? What attributes of an effective third-party mediator could have moved the antagonists toward a peaceful resolution?

As students consider these crucial issues and critically evaluate each case of interactive violence, they should keep in mind three key factors. First, in order to make an intelligent judgment about a specific conflict, one needs to identify its causal origins and resulting patterns of interactive bloodshed. Second, only through detailed study is it possible to identify the necessary and sufficient conditions and elements to move a violent conflict toward a peaceful resolution. Finally, only by careful study of previous and ongoing political conflicts is it possible not to repeat them. There can be no better way of preventing future bloodshed than by learning the hard lessons of humanity's bloody past.

Notes

1. Nils Petter Gleditsch, Peter Wallensteen, Mikael Eriksson, Margareta Sollenberg, and Havard Strand, "Armed Conflict 1946–2001: A New Dataset," *Journal of Peace Research* 39, no. 5 (2002): 629–635; Lotta Harbom and Peter Wallensteen, Appendix 2A, *SIPRI Yearbook 2006* (Stockholm, Sweden: International Peace Research Institute, 2006), 5–6.

2. Although revolutions are considered an unconventional form of political violence, they are not studied in this book because they merit comparative study in a separate framework as examples of successful mass collective action against a government.

3. On the fundamentals of rational choice and game theory see Todd Sandler, *Economic Concepts for the Social Sciences* (Cambridge: Cambridge University Press, 2001), 33–55; Gideon Doron and Itai Sened, *Political Bargaining* (London: Sage, 2001), 1–17; and James D. Morrow, *Game Theory for Political Scientists* (Princeton,

NJ: Princeton University Press, 1994).

4. In these situations, the antagonists can be said to be in a "satisficing" mode of behavior as explained by Herbert Simon, *Models of Man* (New York: Wiley, 1957).

5. R. Hrair Dekmejian and Gideon Doron, "Changing Patterns of Equilibria in the Arab-Israeli Conflict," *Conflict Management and Peace Science* 5, no. 1 (1980): 41–54.

6. On the logic of combining rational choice theory with cultural, historical, situational, and psychological modes of analysis see Robert H. Bates, Rui J. P. de Figueiredo Jr., and Barry R. Weingast, "The Politics of Interpretation: Rationality, Culture, and Transition," *Politics and Society* 26, no. 2 (1998): 221–256; Rose McDermott, *Political Psychology in International Relations* (Ann Arbor: University of Michigan Press, 2004), 13, 52, 271–273; and Robert H. Bates, et al., *Analytic Narratives* (Princeton: Princeton University Press, 1998).

7. Alexander George, " 'The Operational Code': A Neglected Approach to the Study of Political Leaders and Decision-Making," *International Studies Quarterly* 13, no. 2 (1969): 190–222.

8. On the relationship between strategic rationality and psychology as determinants of collective terrorist behavior see the debate between Martha Crenshaw and Jerrold M. Post in Walter Reich ed., *Origins of Terrorism* (Baltimore: Johns Hopkins University Press, 1998), 7–40.

9. James David Barber, *The Presidential Character* (Englewood Cliffs, NJ: Prentice-Hall, 1992); McDermott, *Political Psychology in International Relations*, 1–75; and Erik Erikson, *Gandhi's Truth: On the Origins of Militant Nonviolence* (New York: Norton, 1969).

10. Walter Langer, *The Mind of Adolf Hitler* (New York: Basic Books, 1972); Harold Lasswell, *Psychopathology and Politics* (Chicago: University of Chicago Press, 1930); James David Barber, *The Presidential Character* (Englewood Cliffs, NJ: Prentice-Hall, 1992); Alexander George and Juliette George, *Woodrow Wilson and Colonel House: A Personality Study* (New York: Dover Publications, 1964).

11. R. Hrair Dekmejian, "Charismatic Leadership in Messianic and Revolutionary Movements," in *Religious Resurgence*, R. Antoun and M. Hegland, ed. (Syracuse: Syracuse University Press, 1987), 78–107.

12. Robert H. Bates, Rui J. P. de Figueiredo Jr., and Barry R. Weingast, "The Politics of Interpretation: Rationality, Culture, and Transition," *Politics and Society* 26, no. 2 (1998): 221–256.

13. For other typologies of terrorism see Cindy Combs, *Terrorism in the Twenty-First Century*, 4th ed. (Upper Saddle River, NJ: Prentice-Hall, 2006); and Brigitte Lebens Nacos, *Terrorism and Counterterrorism: Understanding Threats and Responses in the Post 9/11 World* (New York: Pearson/Longman, 2005).

14. Patricia Marshak, *Reigns of Terror* (Montreal: McGill-Queen's University, 2003.)

15. Boaz Ganor, *Defining Terrorism,* www.ict.org.il/articles/define.htm.

16. Bruce Hoffman, *Inside Terrorism* (New York: Columbia University Press, 1998), 43.

17. Alex P. Schmid and Albert J. Jongman, *Political Terrorism* (New Brunswick, NJ: Transaction Publishers, 2005) 32.

18. *Ibid.*

19. *Ibid.*, 33.

20. *Ibid.*, 1–38.

21. Alex P. Schmid, "Frameworks for Conceptualizing Terrorism," *Terrorism and Political Violence* 16, no. 2 (2004): 197–221.

22. *Ibid.*, 198.

23. *Ibid.*, 199.

24. *Ibid.*, see Table 1, 201.

25. *Ibid.*, 201–202.
26. *Ibid.*, 204–205. See also David Rappoport, "The Politics of Atrocity," in Y. Alexander and S. M. Finer, eds., *Terrorism: Interdisciplinary Perspectives* (New York: John Jay Press, 1977), 47.
27. Schmid, "Frameworks for Conceptualizing Terrorism."
28. *Ibid.*, 208.
29. *Ibid.*, 210–221.
30. *Ibid.*, 212.

Further Reading

Combs, Cindy C. *Terrorism in the Twenty-First Century,* 4th ed., Upper Saddle River, NJ: Prentice-Hall, 2006.

Hoffman, Bruce. *Inside Terrorism.* New York: Columbia University Press, 1998.

Laqueur, Walter. *The New Terrorism: Fanaticism and the Arms of Mass Destruction.* New York: Oxford University Press, 1999.

McDermott, Rose. *Political Psychology in International Relations.* Ann Arbor: University of Michigan Press, 2004.

Morrow, James D. *Game Theory for Political Scientists.* Princeton, NJ: Princeton University Press, 1994.

David C. Rapoport. *Terrorism: Critical Concepts in Political Science.* New York: Routledge, 2006.

Reich, Walter, ed. *Origins of Terrorism: Psychologies, Ideologies, Theologies, States of Mind.* Baltimore: John Hopkins University Press, 1998.

Sandler, Todd. "Terrorism and Game Theory." *Simulation and Game Theory* 34, no. 3 (2003): 319–337.

Schmid, Alex P. and Albert J. Jongman. *Political Terrorism.* New Brunswick, NJ: Transaction Publishers, 2005.

Whittaker, David J. *Terrorists and Terrorism in the Contemporary World.* New York: Routledge, 2004.

Assassins versus the State

THE MURDER OF GOVERNMENT leaders and officials is the oldest form of political violence. Among those who have fallen victim to the assassin's dagger, poison, bullet, or bomb are Roman tribunes, Arab caliphs, Ottoman sultans, European monarchs, U.S. presidents, and scores of prime ministers and leading public figures. All such assassinations, even those without a political motive, constitute acts of political violence because they have political consequences that alter the course of history. Although assassinations represent a micro-level technique of violence against state power, their impact often transcends the state to affect the international order.

A logical method of classifying assassins is to focus on their diverse motivations and social milieu. The motivation to kill a head of state or other political leader can range from psychological pathology or personal vengeance, to a carefully considered rational act to achieve a personal political objective or one dictated by a conspiratorial group. In each of these cases, assassins respond violently to their feelings of victimhood and strategize according to their perceived interests. A summary of the case studies discussed below is found in Table 2.1 at the end of the chapter.

Pathological Assassins

Pathological assassins target leaders or other symbols of authority as an expression of their individual pathologies such as paranoia, identity crisis, cognitive disorders, and feelings of inferiority, helplessness, rejection, or marginality. In Erik Erikson's formulation, such persons are in a state of "patienthood" that must be remedied through some "medium of salvation."[1] Because of their inability to resolve their personal crises, these assassins will project their individual patienthoods upon society and, in their attempt to universalize their personal pain, could focus on the destruction of a leading figure or monument. The basic motivation of such individuals may or may not be political, as they are driven to violence because of total desperation, profound anger at society, or a quest for fame and glory. Thus, the very act of assassination brings purpose to a meaningless life in a dramatic resolution to a life-long identity crisis. In one blow, the murder of a powerful figure lifts the assassin from obscurity to immortality, from nothingness to allness, from abject weakness to supreme power, consummated at the moment of attack.

The quest of "little men" to gain recognition and glory through violence is commonly known as the "Herostratos Syndrome"—a brand of self-motivated terrorism that has been traced back to the destruction of the Temple of Artemis in Ephesus in 350 B.C. by the arsonist Herostratos,[2] Recent U.S. examples of Herostratic terrorists are Arthur Bremer, Samuel Bych, and John Hinckley Jr. Bremer shot Governor George Wallace in May 1972, leaving Wallace paralyzed for life. Bych was killed as he attempted to hijack a plane on February 22, 1974, intending to crash into the White House and kill President Richard Nixon; and Hinckley severely wounded President Ronald Reagan on March 30, 1981, who survived the ordeal after surgery. These men shared psychological illness, troubled childhoods, and failure to secure respectable niches in society. They were "marginal men" whose psychological disorientation and social deprivation propelled them to seek revenge not only to settle a personal account but also to compensate for their powerlessness by striking at symbols of authority that would ensure them fame and notoriety. While the basic motivation of such individuals was not purely political, had their actions been fully successful, they could have had profound political consequences.

The category of pathological assassins also includes those who kill for vengeance. As symbols of authority, leaders often generate intense anger and hatred among individuals who feel personally victimized by the ruling order and its representatives. These individuals translate their deeply-held feelings of victimhood and alienation into a determination to take revenge on those at the apex of power. The loss of a personal stake in power or fortune becomes converted into a compulsion to strike at the figures of authority who are seen as responsible for that loss.

Three of the best-known cases of assassination motivated by personal loss and vengeance are Count Jacob Johan Anckarstrom's assassination of King Gustav III of Sweden on March 16, 1792, John Bellingham's killing of British prime minister Spencer Perceval on May 11, 1812; and Charles J. Guiteau's assassination of President James Garfield on July 2, 1881. A captain in the royal regiment, Anckarstrom had developed an intense hatred of the king after Anckarstrom's wrongful arrest and trial for slandering the sovereign. A failed business-man, Bellingham was infuriated by the British government's refusal to help him win compensation for his unjustified imprisonment in Russia under charges of impropriety as a merchant broker. An infamous pla-giarist, Guiteau volunteered to campaign for Garfield and claimed sole credit for the president's victory. When his demand for an ambassador-ship was ignored, Guiteau became furious and shot the president.

Political Assassins

The most common type of assassination is primarily motivated by political causes. Some political assassins operate as "lone wolves" or with a few accomplices, making themselves the self-appointed embodiment of a political cause to justify targeting authority figures. Although their primary motivation is political—based on ideology, ethnicity, or reli-gion—psychological infirmity also can play a role in an assassin's com-pulsion to kill. Lone wolf type assassins often adopt a cause without any connection to an organization representing that cause.

In game theoretic terms, pathological assassins and vengeance killers have a single overwhelming preference—the murder of a specific leader in order to settle a personal account. In contrast, the ultimate preference of political assassins is to cause major harm to the ruling or-der by targeting its leading personage. Here the logic of assassinating an all-powerful monarch, president, prime minister, or party leader is to undermine the political system by promoting instability or even rebel-lion.

The political cause that nurtured the violent aspirations of many lone wolves during the nineteenth century was anarchism.[3] Fueled by revolutionary fervor, anarchism became an infectious inspiration for free-wheeling assassins dedicated to the overthrow of the capitalist po-litical and economic order. The overriding aim of anarchist terrorism was to transform anti-state "propaganda by word" into "propaganda by deed" to demonstrate to the exploited masses the vulnerability and weakness of the political order by murdering heads of state and other leading figures. According to the anarchists' strategic logic, killing lead-ers would trigger ever-escalating cycles of interactive violence in which growing levels of regime repression would result in a mass uprising.[4]

Russia's precarious internal situation in the nineteenth century provided a fertile soil for anarchist groups such as *Narodnaya Volya*—The People's Will. Inspired by the writings of Pierre-Joseph Proudhon (1809–1865), Mikhael Bakunin, (1814–1876) and Prince Pyotr Kropotkin (1842–1921), the Russian anarchists assassinated high-rank-ing government officials, culminating in the murder of Tsar Alexander

II in March 1881. As anarchism spread outside its Russian epicenter, it became a disorganized movement, which nevertheless provided a powerful ideological venue for many disgruntled individuals fervently dedicated to fighting state repression in the name of the people. Between 1894 and 1900, Italian anarchists operating individually killed French president Marie-Francois Carnot (1894), Spanish prime minister Canova del Castillo (1898), Austrian empress Elizabeth (1898), and King Umberto I of Italy (1900).

Although anarchist terrorism failed to trigger mass rebellions, it had an impact on the political landscape of the countries that experienced its murderous reach. More importantly, the anarchists established a precedent in the use of assassination as a political tool that would be revived in the subsequent decades of the twentieth century.

The most infamous lone wolves who changed the course of U.S. history were John Wilkes Booth, Leon Czolgosz, Lee Harvey Oswald, James Earl Ray, and Sirhan B. Sirhan. Booth plotted with three Confederate sympathizers to cause the collapse of the Union government by targeting its top leaders—President Abraham Lincoln, Vice President Andrew Johnson, and Secretary of State William Seward. On the night of Good Friday, April 14, 1865, Booth killed President Lincoln in Ford's Theater in Washington, D.C., although Johnson and Seward escaped death. Another presidential assassin, Leon Czolgosz, inspired by Emma Goldman's anarchist writings, killed President William McKinley on September 6, 1901 in Buffalo, New York. There would be no more assassinations of U.S. presidents for another sixty-two years.

This salutary hiatus was broken on November 24, 1963, by Lee Harvey Oswald's assassination of John F. Kennedy in Dallas, Texas. A communist loner with an unsettled family life, the precise nature of Oswald's motivation remains unknown because, two days after killing the president, he was shot dead by Jack Ruby, a nightclub owner. Kennedy's assassination was only the first in a turbulent decade. As Americans faced the dual challenges of civil rights and Vietnam, two other political murders darkened the horizon. On April 4, 1968, James Earl Ray, a white supremacist, struck down the Rev. Martin Luther King Jr.—the foremost leader and advocate of nonviolence in the African American struggle for civil rights. Two months later, Sen. Robert F. Kennedy was killed in Los Angeles by Sirhan B. Sirhan, a young Palestinian angered by the senator's support of Israel in the June 1967 war.[5]

Outside the United States, the Cold War years witnessed the assassinations of four world leaders, for which lone wolf terrorists bore personal responsibility. On January 30, 1948, Nathuram Godse assassinated Mahatma Gandhi, the saintly exponent of the Indian movement of nonviolent civil disobedience against British rule. Although a member of a Hindu right-wing group, Godse acted alone in killing Gandhi, blaming him for the partition of the subcontinent into the states of India and Pakistan. A similar act of political revenge targeted Prime Minister Indira Gandhi, the daughter of India's first prime minister, Jawaharlal Nehru, one of Mahatma Gandhi's original disciples. Indira Gandhi's Sikh bodyguards, Beant and Satwant Singh, shot the prime minister on October 31, 1984, in retaliation for ordering the attack on Sikh militants occupying the holiest Sikh temple in Amritsar. In killing Mrs. Gandhi, the two bodyguards were not acting on behalf of Sikh militant organizations; they were simply doing what they saw as their personal duty as Sikhs to avenge the Indian Army's desecration of the Golden Temple.

In a classic case of regicide, the quest for vengeance also claimed the life of the venerable King Faisal bin Abdul Aziz of Saudi Arabia. The king's policies of incremental modernization had provoked opposition from Islamist conservatives led by Prince Khalid ibn Musaid, who was killed in August 1965, in a clash with security forces. Ten years later, on March 25, 1975, a U.S. educated loner, Prince Faisal bin Musaid, assassinated King Faisal to avenge his older brother's death.

In contrast to regicides for revenge, the killing of Israeli prime minister Yitzhak Rabin was motivated by the assassin's religious objective to abort the Israeli-Palestinian peace process. On November 4, 1995, Yigal Amir assassinated Rabin after a Tel Aviv peace rally, because of his belief that the prime minister's plan to withdraw from the Palestinian lands was contrary to God's messianic promise to the Jews. The destabilizing regional developments since Rabin's murder testify to the success of this lone extremist's strategy to undo the 1993 Oslo Accords, in an act that has had significant regional and international consequences.

Assassination as Collective Action: Historical Antecedents

As distinct from assassinations of leaders planned and carried out by one or a few loners, history is replete with acts of regicide or tyrannicide by cabals or larger political organizations. In these instances, the planning and execution of political murder is a collective act implemented as part of an organized conspiracy hatched within or outside a leader's entourage. In contrast to assassinations by disgruntled lone wolves, such conspiratorial killings represent the well-reasoned strategic objectives of oppositional groups seeking to replace those in authority in order to achieve the groups' political agendas.

Roman Empire. Three classic cases of conspiratorial assassinations stand out from the bloody pages of Roman history. The best-known example is the murder of Julius Caesar on the steps of Pompey's Theater on March 14, 44 B.C. The assassins, Marcus Junius Brutus and Gaius Cassius Longinus headed a senatorial conspiracy to kill Caesar because he had assumed dictatorial powers at the expense of the Senate. However, the assassins failed to achieve their strategic goal of empowering the Roman Senate because the Senate could not sustain its legitimacy after Caesar's death. Mark Antony and Caesar's nephew Octavian filled the resulting power vacuum. More compelling cases of tyrannicide were the assassinations of Emperors Caligula and Commodus, two of Rome's most despotic and deranged rulers. As part of a plot involving a cabal of senators, Cassius Chaerea, the Prefect of the Praetorian Guard, killed Caligula, his wife Caesonia, and their infant daughter on January 15, 41 AD. A similar plot organized by Prefect Quintus Aecilius Laetus led to the strangulation of Commodus on December 31, 192 AD, a day before his planned march into the Senate chamber to be proclaimed consul.

Zealots: Sicarii. In the Roman context, assassination was a form of collective action involving struggles for power among cliques within the narrow confines of the ruling class. Meanwhile, another form of collective action was being used by the Zealots against Roman rule during the Jewish Revolt in Judea (66–71 AD). These religious militants sought to achieve freedom from Rome through a mass revolt that required the grassroots mobilization and unity of the Jewish community, including the elite classes who opposed challenging Roman power. In order to neutralize the pro-Roman Jewish elites, the militants unleashed the Sicarii, or dagger men, expressly sent to assassinate their opponents in public places in order to maximize the psychological horror of their grisly deeds.

Islamic Rule. The history of Islam after the death of the Prophet Muhammad was punctuated by a series of assassinations that generated sectarian and political divisions persisting until the present. Of the four "Rightly Guided Caliphs" who succeeded to the Prophet's mantle, only Abi Bakr, the first successor, died naturally. All three caliphs who succeeded Abi Bakr were assassinated—a manifestation of the struggle for power among competing factions at the center of an expanding empire. The second caliph, Umar, a powerful charismatic figure, was killed by the poisoned dagger of a Persian slave on November 3, 644 AD in the midst of his own congregation. The selection of the third caliph, Uthman, symbolized the ascendance of the Umayyad aristocracy over the faction of Abi Bakr and Umar, known as the "Emigrants," a group of 200 early believers who had made the trek to Medina where Muhammad established the first Islamic state. A pious old man, Uthman was too weak to check the power of his Umayyad kinsmen who had taken charge of administering the state. Amid charges of nepotism and corruption, an insurgency broke out, supported by the tribal relatives of the Prophet and the Emigrants. A group of assassins, led by the son of the first caliph, Abi Bakr, killed Uthman on June 17, 656 AD as he read the Quran. Seven days later, Ali ibn Abi Talib was proclaimed the fourth caliph to preside over a far-flung empire wrought with competing conspiratorial groups. The succession to the Prophet Muhammad had become a great chess game that had claimed many victims; Ali would be no exception.

Ali's ascendance represented the return to power of the Prophet's family, for Ali was Muhammad's first cousin, the husband of Muhammad's favored daughter, Fatimah, and father of his two grandsons. Because of his family ties to the Prophet and distinguished personal attributes, Ali commanded the loyalties of a significant faction known as *shiat Ali*, that regarded him as the only true legitimate successor to the Prophet. After Ali defeated his challengers, he was tricked by the stratagems of Muawiya, the rebellious Umayyad governor of Syria who succeeded in dividing Ali's partisans, which led to an abortive revolt by the Kharijites, who opposed both Ali and Muawiya. On January 24, 661 AD a Kharijite killed Ali with a poisoned saber. The resulting power vacuum was filled by Muawiya, who established the Umayyad caliphate in Damascus, an empire based on hereditary rule. What began as a struggle for leadership solidified into a sectarian split within Islam, between the dominant Sunni majority and Ali's partisans, the Shiite minority. Beyond the Sunni-Shia divide, the basic social units that have continued to shape the power interactions among the Arabs and some Muslims are tribal and kinship groups, which act according to their specific calculations of collective self-interest based on group solidarity, *asabiya*. These sectarian and tribal factions have continued to play a dynamic role in the Muslim countries until the present.

As a movement of permanent opposition to successive Sunni Muslim empires, Shiism evolved into several subsects, some politically quiescent, others committed to the overthrow of Sunni caliphs by subversion, terrorism, and insurgency. One such insurgent group, the secret order of Assassins, had its ideological roots in the Ismaili branch of Shiism. The Ismaili revolutionary doctrine, which used an esoteric system of secret organization and propaganda to subvert and destroy the Sunni Abbasid caliphate of Baghdad, fueled the Qarmatian communistic insurrection that challenged the caliphate during the ninth and tenth centuries. After the defeat of the Qarmatian state, its Ismaili doctrine of strategic terror was taken up by the Assassins, a secret movement founded by Ibn al-Sabbah in 1090 at the mountain fortress of Alamut in Persia. As Grand Master of a tightly structured militant order, Ibn al-Sabbah dispatched his *fidaiyin* to terrorize the Muslim world by raids and assassinations. The *fidaiyin* used the dagger with great virtuosity to carry out suicidal missions as "self-sacrifices"—targeting men in power, such as Nizam al-Mulk, the brilliant vizier of the Seljuk sultanate in 1092. In the late eleventh century the Assassins had captured hill fortresses in Northern Syria, from where their master, Rashid al-Sinan (d. 1192)—known as "The Old Man of the Mountain"—spread terror among the medieval Crusaders. According to Marco Polo's account of

Alamut (1271–1272), before the *fidaiyin* embarked on suicidal missions, the Grand Master was said to have hypnotized them with *hashish,* hence their description as *hashish* takers —*Hashshashin,* latinized as "Assassins." The Assassin fortresses in Persia and Syria were finally destroyed in the 1250s by the Mongol and Mamluk invasions.[6]

Assassination as Collective Action: The Interwar Period

The twentieth century has been properly characterized as "the age of conflict," marked by wars, revolutions, collapsing empires, and recurring genocides. This persistent instability set the stage for the emergence of numerous subnational organizations pursuing political objectives defined by their ethnic, ideological, or religious interests. In their difficult struggle to match the state's overwhelming power, these rebellious groups found assassination to be an irreplaceable weapon.

Ethnic nationalism was the principle motivation for one of the century's most consequential assassinations. On June 28, 1914, Gavrilo Princip, one of seven Serb conspirators, killed Austrian archduke Franz Ferdinand and his wife Sophia at a procession in Sarajevo. The assassins were members of Serbian ethnic nationalist groups, Young Bosnia and the Black Hand, which advocated Bosnia's unification with Serbia. The archduke's killing ultimately triggered World War I.

There was no let-up in targeting leaders in the two decades of relative peace after World War I. Ethnic nationalism, mixed with revenge, remained a motivating factor in assassinations with victims ranging from British officials to the defeated leaders of the Ottoman Empire. On June 22, 1922, two members of the Irish Republican Army shot to death Field Marshall Sir Henry Wilson in London, in response to the conflict over Northern Ireland. The attack may have been ordered by Michael Collins, the leader of the Irish rebellion, who was later assassinated by Irish extremists for making peace with Britain, without incorporating Northern Ireland into the Irish Free State.

The series of assassinations of former Ottoman Turkish leaders by Armenian revolutionaries is a prime example of terrorism as "the weapon of the weak." The victims of the first genocide of the twentieth century, 1.5 million Armenians perished in 1915–1922 in a systematic campaign of mass killing organized by the Young Turk leadership of the Ottoman Empire. At the war's end, the survivors had nothing left to fight with except the determination to bring to justice the leading perpetrators of the genocide. This quest for justice became known as "Operation Nemesis," a plan coordinated by the Armenian Revolutionary Federation (Dashnaks) to assassinate the top ranks of the Young Turk regime who had escaped after the Ottoman defeat in 1918 to live in exile under disguise. Between March 1921 and August 1922, young survivors of the Armenian genocide assassinated Mehmet Talat Pasha (Berlin, March 15, 1921), Said Halim Pasha (Rome, December 5, 1921), Behaeddin Shakir and Jemal Azmi (Berlin, April 17, 1922), and Jemal Pasha (Tiflis, July 25, 1922). These assassinations represented retributive justice against the members of the former Ottoman regime. As such, the killings did not materially serve the equalizing goal of empowering the small Armenian state against the Turkish Republic, both of which had emerged out of the ruins of the Ottoman Empire.

Conflicting leftist and rightist ideologies motivated another category of assassinations in the interwar period. Among the victims of rightwing terrorism was the first president of newly independent Poland, Gabriel Narutowicz. His election by a parliamentary coalition of left, center, and Jewish deputies enraged the National Democrats, who accused the president of having Jewish sympathies. While attending an art exhibition on December 16, 1922, Narutowicz was shot to death by Eligiusz Niewiadomski, a modernist painter with strong right-wing affiliations. An ideological murder of greater consequence was the assassination of Austrian chancellor Engelbert Dollfuss on July 25, 1934, by a group of Austrian Nazis led by Otto Planetta. This abortive coup d'etat signaled the beginning of the nazification of Austria that ended in the Anschluss of March 1938.

On the communist side of the ideological spectrum, the killing of Leon Trotsky stands out as an early example of the transnational assassination of an ousted leader by a country's secret services—a technique that would be used by some governments during the Cold War. One of Lenin's most prominent disciples, Trotsky had been forced into exile in 1929 after losing to Joseph Stalin in the struggle for leadership of the Soviet state and the world communist movement. As founder of the Fourth Communist International to challenge Stalin's supremacy, Trotsky had become a prime target of the Soviet NKVD and took refuge in Mexico City. Having survived an attack on his home in May 1940, Trotsky died from wounds inflicted by an ice pick driven into his head on August 20, 1940, by Ramón Mercader, a Spanish communist agent. With Trotsky's brutal murder, Stalin sent a clear signal to his foes in the world communist movement about the global reach of his totalitarian power and the futility of opposition to his supreme will.

Assassination as Collective Action: Post–World War II

The assassination of leaders as a product of collective action persisted in the six decades after World War II. However, there were important changes in the type of organizations sponsoring this type of terrorism. In addition to dissident ethnic and ideological groups, an increasing number of religious extremist organizations as well as governments became sponsors of assassinations during and after the Cold War.

Many of the ethnically motivated assassinations were generated by the Arab-Israeli conflict, the Catholic-Protestant "Troubles" in Northern Ireland, Basque separatists in Spain, and the Tamil-Sinhalese struggle in Sri Lanka. In the Middle East, prominent victims of group-sponsored assassination were Count Folke Bernadotte and King Abdullah I of Jordan. A distinguished Swedish diplomat, Bernadotte had saved thousands of Jews from Nazi concentration camps during the war. As UN mediator in the 1948 Arab-Israeli war, the count had arranged a cease-fire and advanced a partition plan that was rejected by both sides. On September 17, 1948, the Jewish extremist group, LEHI, assassinated Bernadotte in Jerusalem, fearing that his peace plan would favor the Arab side. As the world condemned the Count's murder, the Israeli government forced LEHI to disband; three decades later, however, one of its leaders, Yitzhak Shamir became prime minister of Israel. Bernadotte's failure to impose a UN cease-fire and Israel's subsequent capture of more Arab territory exacerbated the situation of the Palestinian population, many of whom had become refugees. After the Arab-Israeli cease-fire of 1949, the West Bank and Arab Jerusalem were incorporated into the Kingdom of Jordan under King Abdullah's rule. A British-appointed monarch, Abdullah had little legitimacy among the Palestinians, who suspected him of planning to sign a separate peace with Israel jointly with Lebanon, without the participation of the other Arab states that had fought in the 1948–1949 war. On July 20, 1951, the King was shot dead by Mustafa Shukri Usho as he entered the Al-Aqsa Mosque in Jerusalem to eulogize at the funeral of the Lebanese prime minister Riyad al-Sulh, who had been assassinated in Amman four days earlier. The Palestinian assassin, a Jerusalem tailor, had fought the Israelis as a member of the Arab Dynamite Squad, and belonged to a larger conspiracy involving leading Palestinian figures.

At the height of its campaign against British rule, the IRA used assassinations strategically to increase the costs of the conflict to Britain, demoralize the enemy, and to strengthen esprit de corps among its members. One prominent victim was Lord Mountbatten, the former viceroy of India. Although Mountbatten played no role in the Northern Ireland conflict, he and his wife died in the explosion of their yacht at County Sligo on August 27, 1979, targeted because he was Queen Elizabeth's uncle. Among the IRA's other victims was Airey Neave, the British shadow representative for Northern Ireland, assassinated in London on March 30, 1979, and several British officials killed in the bombing of the Grand Hotel in Brighton on October 12, 1984, where the ruling Conservative Party was meeting. Prime Minister Margaret Thatcher, the main target of the bombing, escaped unhurt.

The Basque separatist group, ETA, has routinely targeted government officials during its 70-year struggle against Spanish rule. As the only group to seriously challenge Generalísimo Francisco Franco's fascist rule, the Basques had enjoyed great respect among all Spanish opposition elements. In their most notable feat, Basque operatives killed Prime Minister Admiral Carrero Blanco in December 1973, whom Franco had appointed as heir apparent. Since Franco's death in 1975, ETA's extremist wing has continued targeting Spanish police, magistrates, and high-ranking officials.

The ethnic separatist group that pioneered the use of suicide bombers to assassinate leaders is the Liberation Tigers of Tamil Eelam (LTTE), also known as the Tamil Tigers. As a primary weapon in their armed struggle against the Sinhalese-controlled Sri Lanka government, the Tamil Tigers have used suicide bombers to kill many officials and even wounded and partially blinded President Chandrika Kumaratunga on December 18, 1999. Their most prominent victim was Indian prime minister Rajiv Gandhi, killed by a female LTTE suicide bomber, Thenmuli Rajaratnam, on May 21, 1991. Rajiv Gandhi's assassination, during a campaign visit to the Indian state of Tamil Nadu, was prompted by LTTE's fear that he would dispatch the Indian army to Sri Lanka, as in 1987, to suppress the Tamil struggle for independence.

Two leftist terrorist groups in Europe resorted to killing leaders before their suppression by the authorities. The Red Army Faction of West Germany, popularly known as the Baader-Meinhof Gang, assassinated Deutsche Bank president Alfred Herrhausen in 1989 in a futile effort to mobilize a leftist revolutionary movement to undermine the German liberal democratic state and its central position within the NATO alliance. Meanwhile, Italy had to confront the Red Brigades, an ideological twin of Baader-Meinhof. In the pursuit of radical revolutionary objectives, the Red Brigades were more lethal than their German counterpart in the use of terror by assassination. At the height of their insurrectionary cycle in the 1970s, the Red Brigades assassinated a slew of government officials, judges, and police officers. Their most notable victim was former prime minister Aldo Moro, who was abducted and killed after abortive negotiations between the terrorists and top Italian officials. On December 17, 1981, the Red Brigades succeeded in abducting U.S. Brigadier General James L. Dozier as part of their campaign against U.S. and NATO bases in Italy. After a month in captivity, the general was freed in a raid by Italian commandos. In retrospect, the targeting of leaders by both the German and Italian terrorists was dysfunctional because the killings brought down upon them the full coercive force of the Italian and West German governments at a time when mass support in Europe for leftist revolutionary causes was in precipitous decline.

Beginning in the 1960s, religious extremism emerged as a powerful causal factor of political violence. Among early examples of killings sponsored by extremist religious groups were the assassinations of Malcolm X and Egyptian president Anwar al-Sadat. In the 1960s, Malcolm X had emerged as a charismatic leader of the Nation of Islam, one of the groups comprising the Black Muslim movement. A disciple of Elijah Muhammad, the founder of the Nation of Islam, Malcolm X left the group in March 1964 to embrace mainstream Islam. Malcolm's defection seriously undermined the Black Muslim movement. On February 21, 1965, he was assassinated during a speech in Audubon Hall in New York City by Talmadge Hayer, Norman 3X Butler, and Thomas 15X Johnson, all members of the Nation of Islam.

In the Middle Eastern context, the assassination of Egyptian president Anwar al-Sadat represents a foremost example of religious terrorism by an extremist Islamist organization. While reviewing a military parade on October 5, 1981, President Sadat was gunned down by five members of Tanzim al-Jihad, led by Lt. Shukri al-Islambuli. The three reasons cited in the *fatwa*, the religious edict, which authorized the president's killing were making peace with Israel at Camp David, jailing and mistreating Muslims, and taking political actions that diverged from Islamic laws.

Conclusion: Strategic Utility and Prospects

The assassination of leaders is one of the oldest forms of individual and collective violence against those in authority. Yet this ancient modality of terrorism has retained its political utility through the centuries, to assume even greater lethal potential in the modern context. Indeed, during the course of history, the assassins' political logic has remained unchanged, while their instruments of violence have evolved under the impact of modernization—from swords and poison, to guns and explosives triggered by remote control, to suicide bombings. In this sense, assassins have sought to raise their threat potential by upgrading their modalities and technologies of killing to keep pace with the immense scientific strides in lethal power achieved by governments.

From a game theoretic perspective, there are several reasons why assassination will remain an important method of terrorism in the future. Killing political leaders constitutes a powerful means of communication in signaling a terrorist group's lethal potential to the government while having a dramatic impact on public opinion and marshalling the support of sympathizers. Moreover, assassinations force the state to engage in the interaction with the terrorist group by escalating the cost of inaction. As a weapon of the weak, assassinations provide a relatively

TABLE 2.1   Assassins versus the State: Typology and Examples

Type	Perpetrator	Victim	Date	Country
Pathological Assassin	John Bellingham	Prime Minister Spencer Perceval	May 1812	Great Britain
	Charles J. Guiteau	President James Garfield	July 1881	United States
	Arthur Bremer	Governor George Wallace	May 1972	United States
	John Hinckley, Jr.	President Ronald Reagan	Mar. 1981	United States
Political Assassin (Lone Wolf)	John Wilkes Booth	President Abraham Lincoln	Apr. 1865	United States
	Leon Czolgosz	President William McKinley	Sept. 1901	United States
	Nathuram Godse	Mahatma Gandhi	Jan. 1948	India
	Lee Harvey Oswald	President John F. Kennedy	Nov. 1963	United States
	Prince Faisal bin Musaid	King Faisal bin Abdul Aziz	Mar. 1975	Saudi Arabia
	Yigal Amir	Prime Minister Yitzhak Rabin	Nov. 1995	Israel
Political Assassin (Collective Action)	Marcus Junius Brutus and Gaius Cassius Longinus (Roman Senate)	Julius Caesar	Mar. 44 B.C.	Rome
	Abd al-Rahman ibn Muljam (Kharijites)	Ali ibn Abi Talib	Jan. 661	Arabia
	Gavrilo Princip (Young Bosnia/ Black Hand)	Archduke Franz Ferdinand	June 1914	Austro-Hungary
	Soghomon Tehlirian (Dashnaks)	Mehmet Talat Pasha	Mar. 1921	Germany
	Mustafa Shukri Usho (Arab Dyna-mite Squad)	King Abdullah ibn Hussein	July 1951	Jerusalem
	ETA bombers (ETA)	Admiral Carrero Blanco	Dec. 1973	Spain
	IRA bombers (IRA)	Lord Louis Mountbatten	Aug. 1979	Ireland
	Shukri al-Islambuli (Tanzim al-Jihad)	President Anwar al-Sadat	Oct. 1981	Egypt
	Thenmuli Rajaratnam (LTTE)	Prime Minister Rajiv Gandhi	May 1991	India

cheap means for a terrorist group to impose great harm on the state by heightening its vulnerability, polarizing the public, and forcing it to re-assess its strategy in the conflict. The choice of assassination is a strate-gic gamble for the terrorist group in terms of risks and payoffs—it may either force the regime to bargain or provoke it to intensify its coun-terterrorism efforts. In turn, a quantum increase in counterterrorism could result in the short-term debilitation of the terrorist group, but could also lead to the delegitimization of the regime should it resort to mass violence or "dirty war."

Beyond building up their coercive capabilities, governments have taken extensive counter-measures to defend against potential assassins including surveillance of suspect individuals and groups, imposition of high-tech security cordons around leaders during public appearances, and using ruses and stratagems to distract and confuse potential assas-sins. While these measures have been effective, they also place a heavy burden on police and security personnel, as well as the personages who are being protected. The net political effect of these preventative mea-sures is the growing isolation of leaders from the citizenry—a serious problem in democracies where leaders are expected to remain in per-sonal touch with the people beyond their appearances on television.

Notes

1. Erik Erikson, *Young Man Luther* (New York: Norton, 1958).
2. Albert Borowitz, *Terrorism for Self-Glorification: The Herostratos Syndrome* (Kent, OH: Kent State University Press, 2005).
3. Colin Ward, *Anarchism: A Very Short Introduction* (Oxford: Oxford University Press, 2004).
4. Walter Laqueur, *The New Terrorism* (Oxford: Oxford University Press, 1999), 14–18.
5. James W. Clarke, *American Assassins: The Darker Side of Politics* (Princeton, NJ: Princeton University Press, 1982).
6. W. B. Bartlett, *The Assassins: The Story of Islam's Medieval Secret Sect* (Stroud, UK: Sutton, 2001).

Further Reading

Bartlett, W. B. *The Assassins: The Story of Islam's Medieval Secret Sect.* Stroud, UK: Sut-ton, 2001.
Borowitz, Albert. *Terrorism for Self-Glorification: The Herostratos Syndrome.* Kent, OH: Kent State University Press, 2005.
Clarke, James W. *American Assassins: The Darker Side of Politics.* Princeton, NJ: Prince-ton University Press, 1982.
Hitti, Philip K. *History of the Arabs.* London: MacMillan Press, 1970.
Ward, Colin. *Anarchism: A Very Short Introduction.* Oxford: Oxford University Press, 2004.

Ethnic Nationalists
versus the State

VIOLENT INTERACTIONS BETWEEN ETHNIC GROUPS and nation states have occurred persistently in the contemporary state system. The problem arises out of the reality that the populations of most nation states are heterogeneous, constituting a mosaic of groups with distinct identities defined by a shared history, culture, and vision of their collective self-interests.

Even before the breakup of the polyglot Austro-Hungarian and Ottoman empires during World War I, there had been an upsurge of nationalism among the many ethnic minorities living under imperial rule; hence, President Woodrow Wilson's call for self-determination of subject peoples that went unheeded by his British, French, and Italian wartime allies. After World War II, the issue of national self-determination once again came to the forefront of world politics with the progressive dismemberment of the French, Italian, Portuguese, Spanish, Dutch, Belgian, and British empires, culminating in the demise of the Soviet Union in 1991. These imperial powers created ethnically diverse successor states by drawing borders, which divided ethnic groups between two or more national sovereignties. The multiethnic makeup of these newly independent states was a recipe for conflict, because their governments had adopted the integrationist model of nation-building pioneered by the Western European countries, which sought to dissolve ethnic identities into a single national identity as defined by the cultural norms of the dominant group. The unitary nation state, even in democratic countries, lacked mechanisms to accommodate diverse ethnic interests or promote inter-ethnic coexistence, as done in Switzerland and Belgium under consociational federalism. Instead, in many instances, the ethnic group that gained power used the state apparatus to repress the less powerful ethnic groups, setting the stage for interactive violence.

The demands of ethnic nationalist groups resorting to anti-state violence range from outright independence, to political or cultural autonomy within the state, to basic civil rights to live as full-fledged citizens. In every case of ethnic-state relations, history weighs heavily on the shoulders of both sides in shaping their interactive behavior.

Each ethnic group defines itself in a distinct way, not often shared by states or the world community. Yet, the most politically relevant is the group's definition of itself as a distinct social entity in terms of its members' shared historical memory, language, religion, race, tribe, social status, or some combination of these sociocultural characteristics. The self-defining elements of an ethnic group's identity will shape its behavior toward the state authorities, who may or may not accept the group's self-definition and the legitimacy of its cause to pursue its self-determined interests.[1] Other factors contributing to a group's behavior and efficacy include membership size, ordered preferences, leadership type, and tactics. Table 3.1 encapsulates several key aspects of the four major ethnic nationalist groups discussed in this chapter. These groups were chosen because of their diversity in terms of geographical setting, tactics, strategies, and interactions with the state. Furthermore, each case represents a different phase in the evolution of the conflict: the Irish-British case is an example of a conflict nearing resolution; the Basque-Spanish case appears to be entering the beginning stages of a negotiated peace; the Tamil-Sri Lankan conflict continues to be in a heightened stage of interactive violence; and the Chechen-Russian struggle has entered a dormant phase with clear potential for resumption of violence.

Irish Republican Army (IRA) versus Great Britain

Northern Ireland is one of the last remnants of the now-defunct British Empire, which once controlled all of Ireland. In fact, Ireland was one of Britain's first colonial acquisitions, predating its global hegemony over vast territories acquired in the eighteenth and nineteenth centuries. Therefore, the violence that characterized Irish-British relations in the twentieth century was the legacy of imperial domination with deep roots going back to the twelfth century.

Historical Background, 1170–1914

England's first incursion into Gaelic Ireland occurred in 1170, and by 1177 it had conquered Ulster, one of the four original Irish provinces. In the fifteenth century English control extended to Dublin,

TABLE 3.1 Ethnic Nationalists versus the State

Name of Group	Target State	Date Founded	Group Membership	Group's First Preference	Leadership Type	Key Leaders	Tactics	Killed in Interactive Violence
Irish Republican Army (IRA)	Britain/ Unionists	1919	2,000	Unification with Ireland	Collective	Gerry Adams	Assassinations, bombings, marches, hunger strikes	3,500
ETA	Spain	1959	300	Independence	Collective	Alvarez Txillardegi	Bombings, assassinations,	800
LTTE	Sri Lanka	1976	8,000	Independence	Charismatic	Velupillai Prabhakaran	Bombings, suicide attacks, assassinations	64,000
Chechens	Russia	1994	800	Independence	Charismatic	Aslan Maskhadov, Shamil Bashayev	Bombings, assassinations, suicide attacks, hostage taking, airplane hijacking	100,000

and further colonization during the sixteenth century triggered several Irish revolts that were all crushed. The seventeenth century marked the start of large-scale settlement—"The Plantation of Ulster"—by Protestant English and Scottish colonists. In response to Irish rebellions in the 1640s, Oliver Cromwell reconquered Ireland and exacted revenge by mass atrocities and forced deportations, which would fit the definition of genocide under present-day international law. Another disaster that befell the Irish was the defeat of the Catholic King James by the Protestant King William of Orange at the Battle of the Boyne on July 12, 1690, opening the way to the imposition of Penal Laws in the 1700s placing economic and religious restrictions upon Catholics. The lands of the Catholic Irish aristocracy were turned over to Protestant settlers who emerged as an upper-class minority protected by British power. These confiscations resulted in two uprisings led by Wolfe Tone (1798) and Robert Emmet (1803), both of which were brutally crushed, signifying the hopelessness of the Irish Catholic cause. The Irish status of subservience to Great Britain was formalized in the Act of Union of 1800, which created the United Kingdom of Great Britain and Ireland. Given Ireland's strategic proximity and agricultural productivity, it was unthinkable for Britain to make any concessions to Irish nationalists at the height of its imperial power in the nineteenth century. Yet Irish nationalists could not remain unaffected by the rise of ethnic nationalist movements against the imperial powers, which led to the Rebellion of 1848. The potato famine of 1845–1851 fueled Irish discontent, as starvation and emigration caused a significant decline in Ireland's population. In 1857, the Irish Republican Brotherhood was established, but its uprising was defeated ten years later, despite the support extended by Irish American groups, known as the Fenians.[2]

At the dawn of the twentieth century, the prospects for Irish emancipation were bleak against the backdrop of 800 years of interactive violence without any real gains. The establishment of the Sinn Féin—"Ourselves Alone"—movement in 1906 marked the onset of a renewed quest for independence as the world hurtled toward war. This climate of international conflict provided new opportunities for the Irish cause.[3]

Recent History, 1915–1965

The parties engaged in the struggle over Ireland were designated by different names that defined their objectives and preferences. The Catholic majority represented by Sinn Féin and its military wing, the Irish Republican Army, sought "Home Rule" leading to a fully independent republic over the whole of Ireland. These "Republicans" confronted the British government and its "Unionist" allies, representing the Protestant minority concentrated in Ulster, which strongly supported continued union with Britain.

Sinn Féin's growing agitation prompted Unionist Sir Edward Carson to form the Ulster Volunteer Force in 1912, which later fought in the war in France as part of the British Army. The opening gambit that transformed the political face-off into an armed struggle was the 1916 Easter Rising, when Irish rebels seized the Dublin post office building. The rebellion was quickly put down and seventeen of its leaders executed in a demonstration of British strength despite the exigencies of the war in Europe. If the Republican aim in the post office seizure was to trigger an immediate general uprising and capitalize on Britain's wartime weakness, it was a gross miscalculation. However, the brutality of Britain's response created an atmosphere of popular revulsion and defiance that fueled the IRA's guerrilla campaign in 1919 under its charismatic leader, Michael Collins. The conflict ended in 1921 with a treaty that partitioned the island into a Catholic-dominated autonomous Irish Free State and a Protestant-controlled self-governing Northern Ireland, consisting of the six Ulster counties. This compromise solution split the IRA because it ceded Ulster to Britain, while failing to gain full independence for the Irish Free State. The ensuing civil war saw the defeat of IRA's extremist faction, leading to the establishment of the Irish Free State in 1923, although its founding leader, Michael Collins, was assassinated. In 1949, the Irish Free State left the British Commonwealth and became the fully independent Republic of Ireland.[4]

Northern Ireland: A Time of Troubles, 1966–1972

In signing the 1921 treaty, Collins was forced to forego the Republicans' first preference of a united independent Irish state. However, IRA's maximalist objective remained alive among many Irish nationalists both in the Republic of Ireland as well as in Northern Ireland, where a 60 percent Protestant majority ruled over the Catholics. The nationalist cause in Northern Ireland found especially fertile soil because of the crisis conditions besetting the Catholic minority. In the decades after acquiring self-rule in 1920, the Unionist Protestants had monopolized power in Northern Ireland and imposed a regime of political and economic discrimination on the Catholic minority. Not only were the minority Catholics economically marginalized, but they had been rendered politically impotent as second-class citizens. The polarization between the rulers—Protestants— and the ruled—Catholics—was exacerbated by the constant reinforcement of the two conflicting identities through ethnic and religious socialization based on clashing historical memories. The conflict reached a tipping point in the late 1960s under the impact of external influences such as the mass student demonstrations engulfing France and West Germany and the civil rights movement in the United States. In response to the vehement opposition to reforming the system from Rev. Ian Paisley's extremist Unionists, a civil rights movement emerged in 1967 led by John Hume and other Catholic moderates, with support from some Protestants. What came to be known as the "Troubles" began on August 7, 1969, when the Catholics defied the ban on public marches imposed by the Protestant-led government. The ban was particularly repressive in light of the frequent parades and marches that the Protestants had freely carried out for centuries.[5] On that day, as Catholics rallied to march from Londonderry to Belfast singing "We Shall Overcome," they were beaten and gassed by the Royal Ulster Constabulary (RUC). Meanwhile, armed Protestant mobs threatened the Catholic enclaves in Londonderry and Belfast, triggering large-scale inter-communal violence. Shocked by the magnitude of destruction, Prime Minister Edward Heath sent in the British Army to maintain order. What had started as a peaceful quest for social and political equality was transformed into inter-ethnic violence, reverting to the historical pattern of the British-Irish struggle.[6]

Prisoner's Dilemma: Phase I

In game theoretic terms, Britain's direct intervention changed the structure of the conflict from a two-party game to a triangular game. As a third party intervening into the conflict as peacekeepers, the British assumed the role of "jailer" in a modified "prisoner's dilemma" situation, that would enable them to use their superior power position to offer incentives to the warring sides to move them toward peace. In the end the British failed to meet the challenge despite the favorable circumstances. At the onset, both sides welcomed the British—the Unionists saw them as old allies, while the Catholics hoped that they would protect them from the Unionist forces and vigilantes. Guided by inexperience and blinded by history, the British Army joined the Unionist RUC to oppress the Catholic population. The resulting Catholic helplessness sparked the IRA's renaissance in 1969, after four decades of relative quiescence, as its Provisional wing (Provos) took up the struggle not only to protect the Catholics but also to pursue the greater Republican cause of a united Ireland.[7] Thus, the British Army's failure in its peacekeeping mission had two consequences: the reversion of the tripartite game to a two-party interactive struggle between the Catholics and the Unionist/British coalition; and the change of Catholic objectives/preferences from self-defense and civil rights, to the IRA's ultimate preference to achieve a unified Irish state.

The conflict escalated as the British forces became an army of occupation that imposed harsh measures such as the internment of hundreds of IRA suspects without trial in August 1971, as the Unionist Ulster Volunteer Force joined the onslaught against the Catholics. On January 30, 1972, known as "Bloody Sunday," British soldiers killed thirteen Catholics during mass demonstrations in Londonderry. In a belated attempt at a more balanced policy, Prime Minister Edward Heath abolished the Unionist regime in Belfast in March 1972, and imposed direct rule over Northern Ireland from London. While the Unionists felt betrayed by the British action, the IRA declared a temporary cease-fire, and several of its leaders, including Gerry Adams, were secretly flown to London for ultimately unproductive negotiations. On July 21, 1972, the IRA exploded twenty-six bombs, killing nine people in Belfast. This attack, known as "Bloody Friday," was in apparent retribution for the British Army's "Bloody Sunday."[8]

From the IRA's reemergence in December 1969, to Bloody Friday in July 1972, the basic fact pattern of interactive violence conformed to the laws of political physics. This dynamic of terror and counter-terror would persist until the Good Friday Agreement of April 10, 1998. The ebb-and-flow of violence in the intervening twenty-six years was marked by cease-fires, changes of leaders, strategies and objectives, and attempts by extremist groups on both sides to overturn all attempts at a peace settlement.

Cycles of Interactive Violence: An Outline, 1972–1986

After its abortive attempt (1971–1972) to push the antagonists toward an equilibrium of peace, Britain revived its role as "jailer-mediator" in January 1974 by establishing a power-sharing executive that would include both Catholic and Irish Protestant members. Election of the executive would be based on a quota system. In February 1974, the Conservatives in Britain were defeated by the Labour Party, which was less supportive of the Unionists. The Labour government further expanded Britain's role as "jailer-mediator" by legalizing Sinn Féin and the Ulster Volunteer Force (UVF), secretly negotiating a cease-fire with the IRA, and ending the internment of IRA prisoners without trial. This British attempt to revert to a tripartite prisoner's dilemma game was disrupted in May 1974 as Loyalist (Unionist) paramilitaries expanded the conflict into the Irish Republic with a series of bomb attacks, killing 31 people in Dublin and Monaghan. After Protestant strikes and protests in Northern Ireland, the power-sharing executive was abolished and direct rule from London was reestablished.[9] In response to Britain's cancellation of the power-sharing agreement and the Unionist bombings in the Irish Republic, in October and November 1974 the IRA expanded its operational reach into England by carrying out several bombing attacks on pubs, killing twenty-one people in Birmingham. A year later, it

FIGURE 3.1   IRA versus Britain/Unionists: Interactive Violence, 1979–1985

Mar. 1979	IRA splinter group, the Irish National Liberation Army (INLA), kills Airey Neave, Conservative MP and shadow Northern Ireland Secretary
May 1979	Margaret Thatcher becomes prime minister
Aug. 1979	Lord Mountbatten assassinated by IRA at Sligo; two bus bombings and 18 British soldiers killed
1980–1981	Hunger strikes in Maze Prison by IRA prisoners demanding political prisoner status; Bobby Sands and nine others fast to death, triggering mass riots
Dec. 1982	INLA bombs a pub in County Derry, killing seventeen
Dec. 1983	IRA bombs the Harrod's department store in west London, killing five people
Oct. 1984	IRA bombing of Brighton Hotel during Conservative Party's Annual Conference, resulting in five deaths; Prime Minister Thatcher survives
Nov. 1985	Agreement signed between Britain and Irish Republic

was the Unionists' turn to upset British attempts to keep the peace by dispatching the Ulster Volunteer Force (UVF) to carry out a series of attacks that killed twelve and injured forty-six people. As a result, the UVF lost its legal status.

There was a notable decline in interactive violence during 1976–1977. However, the violence resumed in February 1978 and intensified after hard-line conservative Margaret Thatcher's election as prime minister in May 1979 and continued until November 1985, as the timeline in Figure 3.1 shows. In November 1985, Britain and the Irish Republic signed an agreement to decide Northern Ireland's future by majority vote.[10]

Protracted Violence: Prelude to Negotiations, 1987–1994

Although the November 1985 agreement benefited both Britain and the Republic of Ireland, it did not provide sufficient incentives or punishments to the Unionists and the IRA to cease violence, and as such, it was rejected by both sides. Britain agreed to recognize the Irish Republic as a partner in the search for a settlement in Northern Ireland, in return for Dublin's promise to crack down on the IRA's activities in the areas bordering Ulster. The British were likely calculating that the 1985 agreement would weaken the IRA and give Prime Minister

Thatcher's government a free hand to crush its terrorist potential. This calculation proved false, as the two sides became entangled in an eight-year period of heightened interactive violence, marked by the expansion of the conflict beyond Northern Ireland's borders. The timeline in Figure 3.2 depicts the escalation of violence by both sides as increases in British force evoke corresponding IRA attacks against both civilian and military targets not only in Northern Ireland, but in Britain itself. The IRA's attacks in London and other targets in Britain were attempts to heighten Britain's vulnerability by exploiting its weaknesses. The interactive violence between the IRA and its British and Unionist adversaries continued after John Major succeeded Thatcher as prime minister until the signing of a peace declaration by the prime ministers of Great Britain and the Irish Republic in December 1993.[11]

The United States Enters the Game: Prisoner's Dilemma, Phase II

In February 1994, Sinn Féin leader Gerry Adams was finally granted a visa to visit the United States by President Clinton in a move to start the peace process. This created a new prisoner's dilemma situation, as the United States entered the game for the first time in history with British and IRA consent. Clinton's move, supported by Irish Americans, empowered and legitimized the Sinn Féin/IRA as a negotiating partner. As a result, in August 1994 the IRA announced the cessation of all violence in order to help the peace process, and in October 1994 the Unionist Military Command also announced a cessation of hostilities.[12] In December 1995, President Clinton visited Northern Ireland and shook hands with Gerry Adams, signaling the start of peace talks.

The U.S. strategy as "jailer," "arbiter," or "mediator" was to press both the British and Sinn Féin/IRA to negotiate. As the stronger party, Britain insisted that Sinn Féin make the first conciliatory move. Sinn Féin complied by declaring a "total cease-fire," expecting a British willingness to negotiate. But the British refused, insisting that the IRA first give up all its weapons before negotiations could begin. Prime Minister John Major's relatively hard-line position on the IRA's disarmament was shaped by a two-level strategy: first, to force the IRA to give up its "threat power," making it impossible for the IRA to revert to terrorism if the talks proved unsatisfactory; and second, to assuage Conservative Party hardliners, particularly its traditional Unionist allies in Parliament, as Britain prepared for the 1997 elections.

Consequently, John Major refused to change his position despite pressure from former U.S. Senator George Mitchell, chairman of the International Commission on Disarmament in Northern Ireland, who favored negotiations before disarmament. In response, the IRA refused

FIGURE 3.2   IRA versus Britain/Unionists: Interactive Violence; 1987–1994

May 1987	Fighting breaks out between IRA and British Special Air Services (SAS), killing eleven IRA members
Nov. 1987	Britain intercepts the *Eksund,* a ship full of Libyan arms for IRA
Nov. 1987	IRA bombs Enniskillen, killing eleven
Mar. 1988	Three IRA members killed in Gibraltar, suspected of planning attack on British garrison
Mar. 1988	Loyalist gunman kills three Catholics
Mar. 1988	Two British soldiers abducted and killed
Sept. 1989	Eleven British army bandsmen killed in Deal, Kent, by IRA bomb
July 1990	Conservative MP Jan Gow, strong Unionist supporter, killed by IRA bomb in Sussex
Nov. 1990	Prime Minister John Major succeeds hardline Margaret Thatcher
Feb. 1991	IRA mortar lands near the office of the new Prime Minister John Major; no one hurt
Feb. 1992	IRA kills seven Protestant workers in County Tyrone
Apr. 1992	IRA bomb near Baltic Exchange building in London, killing three
Mar. 1993	IRA bombs in Warrington, Cheshire, killing two children
Apr. 1993	IRA's Bishopsgate bomb at N.W. Tower in London, killing one
Oct. 1993	Loyalist gunmen kill eight people in a bar in Greysteel County, Londonderry
Oct. 1993	IRA bombs Shankill fish shop, Belfast, killing ten
Dec. 1993	Joint Declaration of Peace signed by Irish and British prime ministers.
Feb. 1994	Sinn Fein leader Gerry Adams visits United States
Aug. 1994	IRA cease-fire
Oct. 1994	Loyalist cease-fire

unilateral disarmament because of its conviction that giving up its threat power would remove any real incentive for the British/Unionist side to make real concessions at the negotiating table. On February 9, 1996, the IRA ended its seventeen-month cease-fire, with a series of high profile attacks on British and Unionist targets, signaling its ability and willingness to restart and even expand its terrorist reach. A series of attacks ensued until the May 1997 election in which the Labour Party took power

FIGURE 3.3   IRA versus Britain/Unionists: Interactive Violence, 1996–1999

June 1996	IRA bombing destroys Manchester's Arndale Center
July 1996	Unionist Orangemen march at Drumcree sparks clashes between Catholics and Protestants
July 1996	Bombing of hotel in Enniskillen, many injuries
Oct. 1996	IRA bomb at Lisburn Barracks, killing one soldier
Feb. 1997	IRA sniper shoots British soldier in Armagh
April 1997	IRA bomb hoaxes cause havoc on Britain's highways
May 1997	Tony Blair of Labour Party elected, defeating Conservative John Major
July 1997	Second IRA cease-fire
Sept. 1997	All-party peace talks begin
Apr. 1998	Good Friday Agreement signed after negotiations and violence
May 1998	Referendum in Northern Ireland and Irish Republic approves the Good Friday Agreement
1998	Disagreement on timetable for decommissioning IRA's weapons; attacks by "Real IRA" and other extremist IRA splinter groups
Sept./Nov. 1999	U.S. Senator Mitchell is asked to reenter the peace process
Dec. 1999	Power is devolved from London to the Northern Ireland Executive, based on a power-sharing agreement between Protestants and Catholics

and Tony Blair became prime minister.[13] Figure 3.3 illustrates this series of events.

Good Friday Agreement: Peace at Last?

Tony Blair's election on May 1, 1997, with a large Labour Party majority reopened the path to a settlement. Unlike the Conservatives, the Labourites were not beholden to Unionist MPs for support in Parliament. Also, there was greater trust toward Blair by the Sinn Féin leadership, as the prime minister showed willingness to drop John Major's precondition regarding IRA's disarmament prior to peace talks. Hence, IRA's move to reinstate its cease-fire on July 19, 1997, followed by a British invitation to Sinn Féin to join the peace talks which began on September 15, 1997. After months of mostly Unionist violence and acrimonious bargaining, the Good Friday Agreement was concluded in April 1998, and passed by an all-Ireland referendum on May 21, 1998. The next eighteen months were marked by persistent disputes and deadlock over IRA's promise to participate in the decommissioning of arms. Once again Senator Mitchell was called upon to rescue the peace process, as the Unionist-Republican standoff reverted to a classic prisoner's dilemma situation. On November 18, 1999, the senator succeeded in breaking the deadlock, allowing the implementation of a power-sharing government.[14] On December 1, 1999, power was devolved from London to the new Northern Ireland government in Belfast.[15] The peace process had been saved from breakdown, but peace was not yet at hand over a year later when President Clinton paid his third and final official visit to Ireland and Northern Ireland. However, for the first time, external intervention had succeeded in imposing a consociational regime on Northern Ireland based on shared power between the Unionist Protestants and the Republican Catholics.[16]

Two-Level Games

A key variable affecting the resolution of conflict is the number of players involved in it—the larger the number of players, the more difficult it could be to reach a settlement.[17] The conflict over Northern Ireland involved no less than six key players, not counting outside actors such as the United States and other international mediators. To reach a settlement, the interests of all six parties needed to be at least minimally satisfied. As two of the major participants, the Irish and British governments welcomed the Good Friday settlement, because it would remove a primary issue of contention between them, which had serious domestic repercussions in both countries.[18] However, the contending sides in Northern Ireland faced an infinitely more complex situation because neither the Unionists nor the Republicans were internally united. In fact, during the long years of the Troubles and negotiations, the game was being played by four parties—Unionist moderates and hardliners versus Republican moderates and hardliners. The hardliners on each side represented a persistent threat to the moderates by vetoing any concessions and disrupting the peace process through terrorism. Consequently, the trick for the Sinn Féin's Gerry Adams, the Ulster Unionist Party's David Trimble, and the British and Irish governments was how to neutralize the hardliners so as to save the peace process. Both Adams and Trimble were repeatedly challenged by hardline organizations within their respective constituencies during the half-decade after the devolution of power in 1999. These challenges included communal rioting, violent clashes, and terrorism by dissident paramilitary groups such as the Real IRA (Catholic) and the Red Hand Defenders (Protestant). The difficult task for Gerry Adams was convincing his IRA constituency to disarm at a time when the Unionist paramilitaries were still active, the British Army continued to maintain a presence in Northern Ireland, and the Catholic minority remained vulnerable to Protestant vigilante attacks. The Unionist hardliners were alarmed at the prospect of sharing power with the hated Republicans and separating from Britain's protective umbrella. Although distrustful of the Unionist/British side, Adams adopted an incrementalist strategy on disarmament in an attempt to retain a role in the peace process, while minimizing defections of IRA's hawkish factions. It was agreed that IRA's disarmament would take place in stages under the Independent International Decommissioning Commission (IIDC), led by Canadian General John de Chastelain, and two independent weapons inspectors—former Finnish president Martti Ahtisaari and prominent South African official Cyril Ramaphosa.[19] Under the IIDC's supervision, significant batches of IRA weapons were placed "beyond use" in October 2001 and April 2002. Meanwhile, the split among the Unionists widened, with hardliner challenges to David Trimble as internecine fighting erupted among factions of the Ulster Defense Association. The IRA's insistence on incremental disarmament made good sense from the strategic perspective of two-level games. The IRA's refusal to disarm unilaterally was useful in safeguarding its threat potential at a time when the Unionists' Loyalist paramilitaries still kept their weapons. Internally, Sinn Féin's choice of gradual disarmament made sense by keeping most IRA hardliners in check, many of whom might have resisted wholesale disarmament without equivalent action on the Unionist side. By advocating careful gradualism on the disarmament issue, Gerry Adams succeeded in maintaining a high degree of discipline in IRA ranks, unlike the disorder among the Unionist/Loyalist factions.

In the end, however, Gerry Adams could not fully accommodate the conflicting demands of his external partners (Britain/Trimble) and internal constituents (IRA's hardliners). In refusing British/Unionist calls for precipitous total disarmament, Adams preferred to accommodate his internal constituency rather than David Trimble, whose position as first minister of Northern Ireland and Ulster Unionist Party leader were under grave challenge by Protestant hardliners. The IRA's position seriously undermined Trimble, leading to his party's defeat by the Democratic Unionist followers of hardliner Rev. Ian Paisley in May 2005, who refused any dealings with Sinn Féin.

In an attempt to start a peace offensive in July 2005, Gerry Adams declared the ending of the IRA's armed campaign with finality, and called upon its members to pursue the Republican goal of uniting Ireland by peaceful means. Although Tony Blair welcomed Adams' statement, he now faced the difficult task of bringing together an increasingly moderate Sinn Féin with its most implacable antagonist, the Unionist leader Rev. Ian Paisley. If a deal could be struck between these traditional foes, driven by strong popular sentiments for peace and a flourishing economy, then there could be a good chance that an enduring peace will prevail, ending a thirty-six-year struggle that has cost over 3,500 lives. However, any settlement would have to involve the peaceful cohabitation of two groups with conflicting objectives—Sinn Féin will continue to pursue its goal of a united Ireland by political means, while the Unionists will refuse unity with the Irish Republic and integration into its Catholic majority. Meanwhile, the demographics of Northern Ireland favors the Catholics, who are expected to become a majority over the next two decades, because of their higher birth rate.

Despite Paisley's recalcitrance, however, it would appear that for the time being the two sides have reached a Nash equilibrium. To be sure, it would be unacceptable for either side to upset this equilibrium by changing its preference to violence because of the high cost such behavior would entail.

Basque Homeland and Liberty (ETA) versus Spain

The Basque struggle for independence is rooted in the multicultural mosaic of peoples that were unified under the Spanish monarchy after the 1492 Christian reconquest of the Iberian peninsula that ended eight centuries of Arab/Muslim rule. Unlike other parts of Spain, the Basque region was relatively untouched by Islamic cultural influences.

The Basques are an ancient people with a unique language and culture that predate the rise of Europe's contemporary nation-state system. While sharing the Roman Catholic faith with the rest of Spain, the Basques speak Euskera, a non-Latin language that forms a main pillar of their identity and solidarity. This linguistic distinction is reinforced by specific cultural attributes and ethnic historical narratives.

Historical Background

The origins of the Basque quest for independence go back to the founding of the Basque Nationalist Party (PNV) by Sabino Arana in 1895, in reaction to Spain's abolition of regional autonomy charters known as *fueros* and the arrival of non-Basque mineworkers from other regions of the country. The Spanish newcomers were seen as an existential threat to the cultural integrity of the Basque country—Euskadi, where Euskera was spoken. Thus, to the Basques, the only way to preserve Euskadi and the integrity of their cultural identity was to become independent of Spain.[20]

In 1936, the Basque Nationalist Party took the fateful decision to join the leftist Spanish Republican government because it accorded the

Basque region full autonomy. In the ensuing Spanish Civil War (1936–1939), Generalísimo Francisco Franco's Fascist armies, with German and Italian military support, overthrew the Republican regime. The war had disastrous consequences for the Basques. In April 1937 the German Luftwaffe attacked the Basque city of Guernica, leveling the city, and killing and wounding over 2,000 people. The first president of the autonomous Basque regime, Jose Antonio Aguirre, escaped to France and organized a government in exile as 275,000 Basques were forced into dispersion. The Franco regime executed and imprisoned thousands of Basque soldiers and nationalists, and forbade the use of Euskera. Pablo Picasso's famous painting, "Guernica," immortalized the brutal oppression visited upon the Basque homeland by Franco.[21]

Despite the fervent hopes of Basques and many Spaniards for freedom, the Franco regime survived the defeat of Nazi Germany and Fascist Italy in World War II. Although supporting the Basques during the war, the Allied powers led by the United States and Britain decided to keep Franco in power as a bulwark against communism. A pact concluded in 1953 provided Spain with economic aid in return for U.S. military bases. The support of the West empowered the Franco regime, dampening the prospects for democracy in Spain and the revival of the Basque nationalist cause. Meanwhile, the Basque presence was further diluted by a new wave of immigrant workers needed to service the expanding industrial economy in the Basque region. These crisis factors created tensions within the Basque nationalist movement leading to a split in PNV and emergence in 1959 of Euskadi ta Askatasuna (ETA)— Basque Homeland and Liberty. Representing the younger and more activist members of PNV, ETA rejected PNV's first preference for Basque autonomy within Spain to assert its own first preference for an independent and united homeland, comprising the seven Basque provinces in Spain and France.[22]

ETA's first actions against the state were an abortive attempt to derail a train in July 1961, and a string of failed robberies that brought the full force of Franco's repressive regime upon its inexperienced members.[23] After the mid-1960s, ETA was beset by several splits involving ideology, tactics, and goals. Some factions favored a Marxist-type class based struggle, while nationalist groups wanted to take up violence to pursue Basque liberation. A critical strategic issue was whether to join other anti-Fascist groups to overthrow the Franco regime or to fight for Basque independence from Spain. But how could the ETA sustain an effective campaign against Franco when half of the population of the Basque provinces in the 1960s was of immigrant or mixed origin? Despite the illogic of the situation, ETA's lead strategist, Jose Luis Alvarez Enparantza, "Txillardegi," succeeded in purging the pro-Spanish faction with help from young party activists, to pursue the armed struggle for the ultimate goal of Basque independence.[24] This radical faction of young activists, which in subsequent years came to be known as ETA-V, and later as ETA-M, took the lead in challenging Franco's oppressive regime with violence. Indeed, the radicalization of the Basque cause grew in direct proportion to the terrorism of the state and the revolutionary milieu of the 1960s, marked by student rebellions in France and West Germany, the civil rights and anti-war movements in the United States, the struggle for freedom in Czechoslovakia, and the Catholic quest for equality in Northern Ireland.

Armed Struggle and Mass Mobilization: Phase I, 1968–1975

The onset of interactive violence began with the accidental shooting of a member of the Guardia Civil, Spain's military police force, by ETA activist Xabier "Txabi" Etxebarrieta who himself died in June 1968 in a police action. The killing of Etxebarrieta made him a martyr and a rallying symbol for the ETA and the traditional Basque nationalists. As the cycle of mass demonstrations and regime repression intensified, the ETA assassinated Melitón Manzanas, a notorious police chief, in August 1968. The regime declared a state of emergency amid mass arrests and repression that widened ETA's support and enabled it to launch more armed attacks against the police. In December 1970, six ETA members were sentenced to death, triggering mass demonstrations backed by large segments of the population, including the Spanish labor movement, mainstream Basque parties, and the Catholic Church hierarchy. The ETA had succeeded in mobilizing a mass movement that focused world attention on Franco's totalitarian regime, symbolized by the ETA prisoners awaiting death at Burgos prison. To dampen the escalating violence, Franco commuted the death sentences. For the first time in the history of Fascist Spain, the ETA had instigated a broad-based challenge to Franco that laid bare the regime's weaknesses and vulnerabilities.[25]

Yet at the moment of its triumph, the ETA remained internally divided. While many ETA leaders favored a strategy of mass agitation, a minority of activists, mainly with ETA-V, continued the armed struggle for the achievement of their first preference—Basque independence from Spain—that most anti-Franco non-Basque Spaniards did not support. Despite its losses of personnel and internal disarray, in December 1973, ETA-V delivered a heavy blow to the regime by bombing the car carrying Prime Minister Admiral Luis Carrero Blanco, Franco's designated successor. The assassination triggered a two-year wave of state terror—the first "Dirty War"— targeting ETA activists both in Spain and in the French Basque provinces.[26] While ETA's killing of Blanco had facilitated Spain's transition to democracy after Franco's death in November

1975, the organization's factionalism would continue to mar the Basque collective quest for a united front.

Truce, Elections, and Violence: Phase II, 1976–1981

After Franco's death, Spain quickly took the path of democratization under King Juan Carlos, as the new government of Adolfo Suarez negotiated with the opposition groups to ensure their participation in the country's first democratic elections in June 1977.[27] The ETA agreed to a truce and the government released hundreds of ETA prisoners under two amnesties. These dramatic events found the Basques divided and their objectives contradictory, which eroded Basque bargaining power in gaining concessions from the post-Franco regime. Since ETA's split in 1974, its two main factions were at odds. ETA-PM, the larger group, agreed on a truce in exchange for the release of its prisoners, while the smaller ETA-M, including remnants of the ETA-V, refused to negotiate with the regime and called for abstention from the elections. In response to the government's willingness to consider devolution of power to the provinces, ETA-PM constituted itself into a political party within a larger Basque coalition—Euskadiko Ezkerra (Basque Country Left)—that won seats in the 1977 elections. ETA-PM's electoral success prompted ETA-M to establish its own political coalition—Herri Batasuna (Unity of the People)—to participate in later elections. This decision marked the start of ETA-M's dual strategy, in direct emulation of the Republicans of Northern Ireland. ETA-M, like the IRA, would be the military wing, while Herri Batasuna, like Sinn Féin, would function as the political face of the movement.[28]

In the four years after Franco's demise, the Basques confronted some hard choices in dealing with the Spanish state. Essentially the interaction between the Basque community and the Spanish state involved two internally split contestants, enormously complicating the bargaining process. The splits within the ETA and the larger Basque community were matched by major fault lines in the Spanish constituency and the state itself between the Socialist Party's moderates and right-wing Falangist descendants of Franco's regime. Clearly, there were "red lines" which neither side dared to cross.

The regime's maximum offer to the Basques was a high degree of political and cultural autonomy anchored to an elected regional parliament as outlined in the Basque Autonomy Statute (1979). Although autonomy was not the first preference of most Basques, a large majority was prepared to accept the regime's offer as a second preference, at least for the immediate future. Thus, the mainstream segments of the population, represented by the Basque Nationalist Party (PVN) and ETA-PM's Euskadiko Ezkerra, participated in the March 1979 general elections and the April 1979 local elections for a Basque Assembly, leading to the formation of a regional government with Carlos Garaikoetxea as president. This was a momentous event because the Spanish government had succeeded in coopting the Basque mainstream, while seeking to isolate the ETA-M in order to either coopt it or destroy its terrorist capability. Neither strategy succeeded as ETA-M went on to disrupt Spain's democratic evolution in the name of its ultimate goal of Basque independence.[29]

ETA's escalating violence in the late 1970s triggered greater levels of state violence from hardliners left over from the Franco regime. At the height of its carnage in 1980, ETA killed 110 policemen, military officials, and suspected spies, which provoked the takeover of the newly elected parliament in February 1981 by Colonel Antonio Tejero's rebellious Guardia Civil. This rightist coup d'état, backed by the military, was aborted by King Juan Carlos, and the conspirators were brought to justice by Prime Minister Leupoldu Sotelo. Notably, interactive terrorism declined under Sotelo's brief premiership because of his negotiations with the Basque parties and controls imposed over the state's coercive apparatus.

Equilibrium of Terror and the Illogic of Vengeance, 1982–1985)

A new cycle of heightened violence began after the October 1982 election of Socialist prime minister Felipe Gonzales. Gonzales tightened civilian control over the military, while taking strong measures against ETA after the failure of peace talks. Meanwhile, ETA operatives were using the Basque region in France to attack targets in Spain without much interference from the French Socialist government. In its impotence to contain ETA's violence and fearing a right-wing coup d'état, the Gonzales government resorted to extreme measures with the formation of GAL (Grupos Antiterroristas de Liberación), a secret paramilitary group of mercenaries, to conduct a "dirty war." GAL's killings and kidnappings in France and Spain claimed many innocent victims, which alienated moderate Basques from the Gonzales government, while driving ETA to more brutal acts of vengeance. Because both parties to the conflict were internally split, the hardliners on each side were able to leverage their influence to polarize and intensify the conflict. GAL was disbanded in mid-1985, as France agreed to cooperate with the Spanish authorities in controlling ETA activities along their mutual border.[30]

There was a decline in ETA's terrorism from 1985–1995, because of the reduction of state violence after GAL's closure and the success of the Basque experience in self-rule that undercut ETA's base of support. Meanwhile, the ongoing violent interaction between ETA and the government had discredited both sides among different segments of the Spanish electorate. While the rightists accused the Gonzales regime of being soft on ETA activists, the Basques and leftists saw the government as practicing state terrorism in unleashing GAL's "dirty war," consisting of extra-judicial killings and torturing Basque prisoners, as documented in March 1997 by the Council of Europe.[31] While the regime's brutality alienated the Basque and leftist constituencies, ETA's attacks had weakened the Gonzales government and helped to elect in March 1996 ETA's least preferred government— the right-wing Partido Popular led by José María Aznar. Ironically, Aznar, a target of an ETA assassination attempt in 1995, stood for a strong centralized Spanish state as opposed to more Basque autonomy, and had promised "to eliminate" the Basque problem.

What rationale could account for ETA's continued violence against the Gonzales regime—a move that would bring to power ETA's worst enemy? Perhaps ETA calculated that the Aznar government would regress to the extreme brutality of its Francoist forebears toward the Basques, a policy that would generate popular opposition and even a rebellion in the Basque provinces. A simpler explanation for ETA's masochistic behavior is the collective emotional compulsion to take revenge—an irrational act that would hurt the group if Aznar tried to "eliminate" the ETA, but also a rational act that would bring a sense of vindication to its members and reinforce the group's identity and solidarity. In the end, Prime Minister Aznar's response to ETA was not too different from that of the Gonzales government, as the ebb-and-flow of interactive violence persisted for another decade while the Spanish polity continued its transition to democracy.[32]

Cease-fires and Changing Preferences, 1996–2005

In 1996 ETA proposed a "Democratic Alternative" outlining its minimal demands—if Spain recognized the territorial integrity of the Basque country and the right to self-determination, ETA would commit to a cease-fire and let the Basque people decide their future through a democratic process. Although this proposal represented a softening of ETA's stance, the government rejected it, refusing "to talk to terrorists," but also fearing that a plebiscite could result in Basques voting for independence. In response, ETA started targeting the ruling party's politicians, such as City Councilman Miguel Angel Blanco, whose kidnapping and killing unleashed massive demonstrations and sparked popular outrage. In a crackdown in December 1997, the government jailed twenty-three leaders of Herri Batasuna for collaborating with ETA. Amid continuing violence, ETA was pressured by the Basque mainstream parties and European public opinion to stop the violence. The signing of Northern

Ireland's Good Friday Agreement by Sinn Féin also had an impact because of its influence on ETA.[33] In September 1998, ETA declared an indefinite cease-fire for the first time that led to meetings between ETA and the Aznar government in May 1999 in Zurich, Switzerland. Although the negotiations failed, the Zurich conclave was a milestone, because for the first time both parties had made concessions—Prime Minister Aznar's right-wing regime had finally consented to sit down with ETA "terrorists" and ETA had taken the unprecedented step of declaring an indefinite truce.[34]

In November 1999, the ETA signaled a return to separatist violence by announcing the end of its fourteen-month cease-fire, ushering in a four-year cycle of interactive terror briefly interrupted by the March 2004 train bombings in Madrid by al-Qaida's Islamist cells. The ETA used two effective tactics to send its message—the assassination of politicians and judges and explosions of car bombs in key cities. These tactics aimed at maximizing fear and ruination, while minimizing collateral damage to humans by serving prior notice in emulation of the IRA's practice in recent years. For its part, the regime used mass arrests of ETA members and suspected supporters, banned the Herri Batasuna party, and outlawed a Basque youth group and newspaper. These tough measures, in coordination with French and international police action, dealt the ETA heavy blows in 2001–2003, in the context of changing circumstances. As a part of the European Union (EU), Spain had become a crucible of globalization and economic development that militated against Basque terrorism. In June 2004, the ETA declared a cease-fire in Spain's Catalonia region, while making secret contacts with a leftist Catalonian party. The ETA aimed to form an alliance between Basque and Catalan groups seeking independence from Spain, to increase the threat level to the regime in compensation for the ETA's weakened potential to wage terrorism.

Despite early evidence of Islamist authorship, the Aznar government initially blamed the ETA for the attacks of March 11, 2004, on Madrid trains. In blaming the ETA and misleading the public, the Aznar regime had hoped to win the elections by hiding the possible causal connection between its unpopular decision to send troops to Iraq and the Islamists' decision to target trains in the Spanish capital. Incensed at Aznar's duplicity, the Spanish voters elected the Socialist Party led by Jose Luis Zapatero, who proceeded to withdraw the Spanish forces from the U.S.-led coalition fighting in Iraq.

The carnage of March 11 in Madrid briefly eclipsed ETA's violent record, which is detailed in Table 3.2. The threat of further Islamist terrorism and the installation of the dovish Zapatero regime seemed to open new prospects for peace with the ETA, which had suspended its attacks for five months after the March bombings. These expectations

TABLE 3.2   ETA versus Spain: Strategic Interactions, 1936–2006

Date	Actor and Type (or Event)	Target	Place	Death Toll/ Outcome
July 1936– Apr. 1939	General Franco defeats the Republicans and occupies Basque land		The Basque provinces	300,000+ killed; 250,000 displaced
July 1959	ETA founded	Franco regime		
1961	ETA attempts train derailment	Train carrying Spanish politicians		110 ETA members imprisoned and tortured; 100 tortured
Aug. 1968	Assassination (gunshot)	Melitón Manzanas	At his house in San Sebastian	1 killed
Dec. 1973	Assassination (car bomb) in retaliation for execution of Basque militants	Admiral Luis Carrero Blanco	Madrid	1 killed
Sept. 1974	Bombing	Cafeteria	Madrid	12 killed
Nov. 1975	Franco dies; King Juan Carlos frees 15,000 political prisoners			
Apr. 1978	ETA political party, Herri Batasuna, founded			
1979	Basque Autonomy Statute approved/ratified			
July 1986	Car bombing	Civil Guards on a microbus	Madrid	12 killed; 50 injured
June 1987	Car bombing	Supermarket	Barcelona	21 killed; 45 injured
Dec. 1987	Car bombing	Civil Guard	Zaragoza	11 killed; 40 injured
May 1991	Car bombing	Civil Guard	Barcelona	10 killed; 28 injured

TABLE 3.2 cont.   ETA versus Spain: Strategic Interactions, 1936–2006

Date	Actor and Type (or Event)	Target	Place	Death Toll/ Outcome
Apr. 1995	Assassination attempt (car bomb)	José María Aznar		One bystander killed
Dec. 1995	Car bombing	Military van	Madrid	6 killed
July 1997	Kidnapping and assassination; six million Spaniards demonstrate against the ETA	Miguel Angel Blanco		1 killed
Sept. 1998	ETA announces cease-fire			
May 1999	Meeting between Spanish government and ETA		Zurich, Switzerland	Negotiations fail
Aug 2000	Car bombing	Unknown	Bilbao	4 killed
Mar.–Nov. 2001	Series of car bombings and assassinations	Various	Various	<50 killed
Dec. 2001–Mar. 2003	Government crackdown on ETA, including arrests, financial seizures, ban on Herri Batasuna, newspaper closure			
May 2003	Car bombing	Police officers	Navarre	2 killed
Nov.–Dec. 2003	Thirteen ETA members captured by Spanish and French police			
Mar. 2004	Madrid train bombings blamed on ETA			
Dec. 2004	Bombs in gas stations, bars, cafes, and other public areas (planned as to prevent injuries and killings)	Infrastructure	Throughout Spain	No injuries
Nov. 2005	56 ETA members on trial			
Feb. 2005–Mar. 2006	Series of ETA bombs (planned so as to prevent injuries and killings)	Infrastructure	Madrid	No injuries
Mar. 2006	ETA declares a permanent cease-fire			

proved illusory as the ETA and the regime restarted the cycle of violence in August 2004. ETA made a new bid for talks in January 2005 that triggered a fierce debate between the Socialist government and the rightist opposition. Despite anti-ETA demonstrations, in May 2004 the government announced its readiness to meet with the ETA if it denounced violence, which prompted an ETA promise not to attack elected officials. In March 2006 after carrying out a series of bombings in connection with a general strike, ETA declared a permanent cease-fire.[35]

Costs of Conflict and Scenarios of Peace

After a seventy-five-year struggle, the Basque quest for independence remains unfulfilled. The human and economic costs of the conflict have been immense, ranging from the genocidal policies of Franco's Fascists toward the Basques to the ETA's more than 800 victims since 1959 and the brutality of successive right-wing and socialist regimes. The economic costs of the conflict in the last decade have exceeded 8 billion Euros. After forty years of interactive violence, neither the ETA nor the Spanish state has succeeded in achieving their first preferences: for the ETA, Basque independence; and for the Spanish state, defeat of the ETA and forging a united and stable country. Given ETA's inability to achieve Basque independence through violence and Spain's inability to neutralize Basque militancy while facing new Islamist threats, a settlement could be possible if both sides moderated their preferences. At least two possible scenarios of peace are possible.

Scenario I: Greater autonomy accorded to the Basque region, inclusive of Navarre province, while postponing a referendum on independence for twenty-five years.

Scenario II: Greater autonomy for the Basque region, without Navarre, that would empower the Basque provincial regime to regulate non-Basque immigration into the Basque region in order to ensure the cultural homogeneity and identity of the Basque community. The sides would negotiate a date for a referendum after three decades of peace.

As the Basque country is one of Spain's most productive regions, it would be extremely hard for any government to agree to a referendum that could lead to full separation, especially when Catalonia and other regions of Spain also aspire to independence. Yet it would be similarly difficult for a democratic Spain to reject the Basques' popular will, should they eventually choose to vote for independence. Hence, postponing that moment of truth could make good sense, if only to have several decades of peace, as the Basques and Spain's other communities have a chance to experiment with coexistence as part of the EU. There is a possibility that the Spanish state and the ETA have reached a point of "shaky equilibrium" that could be stabilized should the two sides moderate their preferences according to scenarios I or II. The antagonists during their four decades of interactive terrorism might have undergone a learning process that could promote mutual tolerance. ETA's frequent cease-fires may be prompted by recognition of its declining potential as a terrorist organization. Also, by these cease-fires, ETA could be signaling its willingness to abandon its first preference of Basque independence if given certain incentives by the Zapatero government. However, the regime might be unable to provide such incentives due to public anger and opposition from hardliners in the Partido Popular. Unfortunately, the Basque case is unlike the Irish, as there is no strong outside agent to act as "jailer-mediator" in a prisoner's dilemma situation. The United States has no direct self-interest to play a role in the Basque-Spanish conflict by pressing the antagonists toward peace. Should Europe's integration continue unabated, the EU could provide an integrative framework and serve as a mediating agency to move the ETA and the Spanish state toward peaceful coexistence.[36]

Liberation Tigers of Tamil Eelam (LTTE) versus Sri Lanka

A tropical island of great beauty, Sri Lanka has witnessed thirty years of bloodshed in an armed struggle between the government and the Tamil minority. An estimated 64,000 people have died in the conflict in a country of 19.5 million people.[37] The roots of violence are found in the effects of British rule, the historical dynamics of migrations, and the economic and political patterns of inter-ethnic relations.

Historical Background: The Burdens of History, 1815–1972

Sri Lanka's population consists of Sinhalese (74 percent), Tamils (18 percent), and smaller groups of Veddas, Muslims, and Burghers.[38] As a distinct ethnic group, the Sinhalese are mostly Buddhist, speak Sinhala, and populate the southwest. The Tamils are mostly Hindu and speak the Tamil language, in keeping with their South Indian ancestry. Historically, most Sri Lankan Tamils have lived in the north and east of the island, while a smaller group of the Indian Tamils is concentrated in south-central Sri Lanka.

The religious and linguistic separation that defined the two major ethnic groups was further reinforced by Britain's imperial presence and the island's geopolitical proximity to the Indian subcontinent. In 1815

Britain took control of Sri Lanka—Ceylon, as it was known—and established a plantation economy that relied on the importation of Indian Tamils, as distinct from the long-established Sri Lankan Tamils who were native to the country. The ethnic affinity between the Tamils of Sri Lanka and the millions of Tamils living in the Indian state of Tamil Nadu represented a cultural and political threat to the Sinhalese majority and its strongly Buddhist identity. Exacerbating the problem, the British gave a disproportionate number of top civil service positions to Tamils because they had a more modern education. Under the 1931 Donoughmore Constitution, the British introduced limited participatory democracy.[39] In 1948, Ceylon became independent and governed by the United National Party (UNP), a coalition of different groups.[40] In 1956, the democratic framework of inter-ethnic accord began to unravel due to the rise of Sinhalese nationalism and the Tamil assertion of their rights within the system. The election of Solomon Bandaranaike in 1956 led to communal riots and the killing of 150 people, mostly Tamils, as Sinhala was declared the official language. As leader of the Sri Lanka Freedom Party (SLFP), Bandaranaike championed the Buddhist religion and the aspirations of the Sinhalese middle class to displace the Tamils in business, civil service, and the professions. In an ironic twist Bandaranaike was assassinated in 1959 by a Buddhist monk, and his widow Sirimavo became prime minister. In the 1965 elections, the UNP returned to power and sought to deemphasize Sinhalese chauvinism, while taking a moderate stance toward the Tamils. Yet, UNP could not resist the growing fervor of Sinhalese nationalism; in 1972, it agreed to change the official name of the country from Ceylon to Sri Lanka and make Buddhism the primary religion of the state.[41]

Changing Preferences, 1972–1983

The unmistakable trend since independence in 1948 was toward growing polarization between the Sinhalese-dominated government and the Tamil minority. By the early 1970s, it was clear that the Tamils would have to accept second-class status to the Sinhalese—a prospect that provoked radicalization in Tamil ranks and a change in their political preferences. At a minimum they would be willing to accept a federal state with autonomy for the Tamil-populated areas. But in the face of Sinhalese recalcitrance, the Tamils' preference for a federal solution gave way to the demand for an independent state, which they referred to as "Tamil Eelam." This demand was put forth by a coalition of mainstream parties—the Tamil United Liberation Front (TULF)—that won all the seats in Tamil areas during the 1977 elections.[42]

Among the half-dozen extremist Tamil groups that emerged in the 1970s, the Liberation Tigers of Tamil Eelam (LTTE), also known as the

Tamil Tigers, stood out for its large size, internal discipline, and lethal effectiveness. The core of these militant groups consisted of Tamil youth, marginalized by the government's favoritism for the Sinhalese in providing employment and educational opportunities. These youthful rebels were also angry at their elders who controlled the mainstream Tamil parties and opposed the use of violence against the regime.

The LTTE, founded in 1976, was one of the first groups of young militants calling for independent Tamil statehood as a first preference. In the early 1980s, the group emerged as the most potent Tamil force fighting the government. Meanwhile, LTTE had neutralized its many Tamil rivals in brutal intra-ethnic combat. Under its maximum leader, Velupillai Prabhakaran, LTTE was organized as a centrally controlled to-talitarian movement, with a widespread grass-roots membership fully in-doctrinated and committed to carrying out the leader's will without dis-sent.[43]

The Tipping Point: July 23, 1983

The early phases of the confrontation between the regime and the Tamil minority were characterized by political infighting mixed with a low-level of interactive violence. Notably, both parties to the conflict were internally divided into multiple factions, each seeking to upstage the others to gain political advantage. On the government's side there were rival Sinhalese political parties and politicians belonging either to the politically dominant Goyigama caste or the lower ranking but more numerous Vahumpura caste. A different caste system existed on the Tamil side with Indian Tamils belonging to lower castes than Sri Lankan Tamils, who are themselves divided into castes. Also, the Tamils were split along generational lines between the elder politicians of the TULF coalition and the younger militants favoring armed resistance. Thus, the internal conflicts among moderates and hardliners on each side fueled the escalation of the Sinhalese-Tamil struggle, culminating in the out-break of inter-communal violence in July 23–31, 1983. The mayhem was triggered after LTTE fighters on the Jaffna peninsula killed thirteen Sin-halese soldiers. In an outburst of revenge, Sinhalese monks killed hun-dreds of Tamils in the capital city of Colombo and elsewhere as the re-gime's security forces mostly abstained from stopping the massacres and an extremist faction of the ruling UNP actually contributed to the Tamil blood bath.

What was the rationale for LTTE's killing of Sinhalese soldiers on July 23, 1983? Reportedly this attack came as a surprise, given the vul-nerable situation of thousands of Tamils in Colombo and other Sin-halese areas who were virtual "hostages" in the hands of an increasingly oppressive regime. Did the LTTE leadership lose control of its young extremists who carried out the killings on their own? Or perhaps the leadership miscalculated by not foreseeing the enormity of the Sinhalese reaction, and the regime's inaction or inability to restrain the marauding mobs. Lastly, it could be that LTTE leader Prabhakaran authorized the killings for the express purpose of radicalizing the situation in order to expand the scope of the conflict into an insurgency and even a full-scale civil war. Whatever intentions LTTE might have had, the Tamil massacres of July 1983 brought about a parting of the ways that would be difficult to reverse. In the ensuing interactive communal violence, the Sinhalese "lion" faced the Tamil "tiger"—symbolizing a fight to the finish.

India, An Abortive Prisoner's Dilemma: Phase I

As the cycle of violence intensified, President J. R. Jayawardene convened a conference of all political parties in January 1984 to agree on a devolution plan to give the Tamils local autonomy. The moderate Tamil leaders rejected the government's proposal because it did not provide full autonomy over the entire expanse of Tamil-populated areas, at a time when LTTE and other extremist groups were fighting for independent statehood. Indeed, the autonomy plan never stood a chance of approval because it was opposed by the Sinhalese nationalist parties and the Buddhist clerical hierarchy, which were ready to sabotage any accord that gave concessions to the Tamils.[44] The hardliners' rejectionist stance was reinforced when in May 1985 LTTE gunmen killed 146 Sinhalese at the Buddhist holy shrine at Anuradhapura—a terrorist action that assured the failure of the first attempt at peace talks held in Bhutan two months later.

President Jayawardene's impotence in dealing with the conflict prompted him to ask India to act as an outside mediator. Indian prime minister Rajiv Gandhi readily consented to play such a role because of domestic and geopolitical reasons. Historically, there were close ethnic ties between the Indian state of Tamil Nadu and the Sri Lankan Tamils, over 100,000 of whom had taken refuge in India to escape the military's brutal crackdown on the island. Also, the Indian government and the Tamils in India were providing military and financial support to the LTTE and other militants fighting the Sri Lankan army.[45] Prime Minister Gandhi could not remain indifferent to the Tamils' plight and its repercussions among the 55 million Tamils of the Tamil Nadu state. Gandhi was also concerned that Sri Lankan attempts to seek military support from outside powers such as Pakistan and China would challenge India's geopolitical supremacy in the region.

Despite India's overwhelming power and the sound strategic logic of its involvement, Gandhi's task proved to be extremely risky and costly, with disastrous outcomes for all three parties. As a "jailer" in a prisoner's dilemma situation, Gandhi had to walk a tightrope, balancing between the two sides, and providing a mix of incentives and punishments as necessary to move them toward a settlement. However, India had little influence on the Sinhalese nationalists who regarded the Gandhi government as being partial to the Tamils. For their part, the Tamils, especially extremist factions like LTTE, expected India to support their cause and were disappointed at Gandhi's attempts at impartiality.[46]

In 1987 the Sri Lankan government attempted to tip the balance of power by unleashing a major military offensive that pushed the Tamil Tigers into Jaffna City and created great hardship among the Tamil population. In April 1987 a massive LTTE car bomb killed over 100 people in Colombo as India threatened military intervention for humanitarian reasons and its air force began drops of supplies to the Tamils besieged in Jaffna. In July 1987, India and Sri Lanka signed an accord that provided for an autonomous Tamil province in the north and east, as part of a united Sri Lanka; the accord would be enforced by an Indian Peace-Keeping Force (IPKF). Although LTTE reluctantly supported the agreement, it was unwilling to disarm, fearing another government offensive. Meanwhile, opposition Sinhalese left-wing and nationalist parties rejected the accord's concessions to the Tamils. For the next two years the Indian army was caught in an impossible quandary, as it was unprepared to face LTTE terrorist tactics. In 1989, the new Sri Lankan government of President Ranasinghe Premadasa called for the withdrawal of Indian forces and resumed peace talks with the LTTE in Colombo. After fourteen months of negotiations between the LTTE and the regime, there was a resumption of violence, although Premadasa had succeeded in breaking the LTTE-Indian alliance. Prime Minister Rajiv Gandhi ordered the withdrawal of his forces in May 1990; a year later he was assassinated during a campaign stop in Tamil Nadu by a female LTTE suicide bomber.[47]

Cycles of Interactive Terrorism, 1991–2000

The decade of the 1990s witnessed three cycles of escalating violence interrupted by abortive peace talks, as the regime and the LTTE sought to use new tactics to increase the costs of the conflict for each other. Having brought about India's departure as mediator and peacekeeper in 1990, the two sides were left alone to engage in interactive bloodletting and periodic negotiations that were bound to be inconclusive because of deep mutual distrust, internal divisions between moderates and hardliners, and changing preferences in ultimate objectives. Sinhalese hardliners continued to push for the total annihilation of Tamil resistance through massive military deployment and occupation

of the Tamil areas. In response, the Tigers employed a mix of terrorism, assassinations, guerilla attacks, and even conventional warfare in
times of their enemy's weakness. The specific targets and brutal tactics
employed by both sides tended to favor the dominance of hard-line
leaders and factions. This causal dynamic could have been due to miscalculations on the part of the combatants. A case in point was the assassination of President Ranasinghe Premadasa in May 1993 in an
LTTE suicide bombing. A relative moderate, Premadasa was succeeded by Chandrika Kumaratunga, a young woman, who managed to
stay in office for over a decade by cynically manipulating the inter-ethnic conflict as a hardliner. Reminiscent of British prime minister Margaret Thatcher's confrontation with the IRA, Kumaratunga's bloody
face-off with LTTE followed a predictable pattern with no end in
sight.

Taking office in 1994, Kumaratunga promised to end the war by engaging LTTE in peace talks, which collapsed, triggering a major army offensive in 1995 that resulted in the capture of Jaffna from the Tamils.
Having lost ground, LTTE unleashed a bombing campaign that extended into Colombo, killing hundreds of soldiers and civilians. Another government offensive in May 1997 failed to break the Tigers who
bombed Sri Lanka's holiest Buddhist shrine in January 1998 and recap-
tured Tamil areas in the north in a major offensive. In 1999 Kumaratunga was wounded in an LTTE bombing, which ironically ensured
her reelection as president. In April 2000, the Tigers captured the Ele-
phant Pass, a strategic point in the north, signifying a renewed determination and ability to challenge the regime.[48]

Equilibrium and Prisoner's Dilemma: Phase II, 2000–2004

The confluence of several developments made the year 2000 a
turning point in the conflict. After seventeen years of fighting, both
sides had been badly hurt by human and material losses and neither side
had been able to prevail in a decisive manner. The standoff clearly indicated that the regime's and LTTE's hardliners had failed to achieve
their respective first preferences. The government had failed to crush
the Tamil insurgency and the Tigers had failed to defeat the regime and
establish an independent Tamil state. The outcome indicated that the
two sides had reached a point of equilibrium that could presage another
attempt at peace if the antagonists could be brought together by an impartial outside agent. In February 2000, Norway consented to act as mediator, as the contest returned to a tripartite prisoner's dilemma situation ten years after India's departure. However, as mediator, Norway
could be far more impartial than India, although it lacked the latter's
leverage over the antagonists.

In November 2000 the top LTTE leader, Prabhakaran, proposed "unconditional" peace talks, which were unwelcome by Kumaratunga due to the shaky position of her minority government in parliament. A year later, the Tigers declared a one-month cease-fire, as Prabhakaran shifted Tamil preferences from independence to autonomy, in a strategy calculated to influence the outcome of the December 2001 elections. The Tamil moves may have contributed to the victory of the UNP coalition of Ranil Wickremesinghe over President Kumaratunga's hawkish party. Two months later Prime Minister Wickremesinghe and Tiger leader Prabhakaran signed a Norwegian-mediated agreement to stop the hostilities. In July 2002 peace talks began in London under Norwegian auspices and continued in different locations until October 2003, the central issue being the Tamil demand for maximum autonomy within a federal structure. The Wickremesinghe government, however, was unable to grant regional autonomy under Tamil administrative control because of pressure from hard-line parties and President Kumaratunga, who was ever ready to manipulate the situation to her advantage.[49] In January and February 2003 the Sinhala nationalist JVP staged mass demonstrations against the government as the Tigers toughened their stance and killed some moderate Tamil leaders to discourage defections. In November 2003, Kumaratunga declared a short-term emergency and accused her prime minister of permitting the Tigers to gain strength. She also postponed the peace talks, followed by Norway's suspension of its role as facilitator.[50]

Constitutional Crisis and Split Coalitions, 2004–2005

President Kumaratunga's unilateral decision in June 2004 to extend her tenure for two years caused a constitutional crisis, culminating in the elections of April that gave her UPFA coalition the largest number of seats, just short of a majority. However, Kumaratunga's winning coalition was inherently unstable since it included the JVP, which had opposed the peace process. Yet internal dissent within the ruling coalition was matched by major splits in the Tamil ranks, and within LTTE itself, which led to internecine bloodshed. Indeed, LTTE's primary objective during 2004 was to sustain its monopoly in representing the Tamil cause vis-à-vis the government and outside parties supporting Norway's peacemaking role such as Japan, India, United States, and the United Nations. As the government secretly sought to deepen the splits within the Tamil minority, LTTE's leadership was attempting to consolidate its power by assassinating pro-regime and moderate Tamil politicians and suppressing its dissident factions, particularly one led by Colonel Karuna Amman based in Batticaloa and Amparai.[51] In May 2004 Kumaratunga broadened the ruling coalition by expanding her cabinet, only to lose the support of JVP nationalists and face violence in parliament perpetrated by Buddhist monks. In an ominous development, LTTE's Black Tigers carried out a suicide bombing in July 2004, the first such act since the October 2001 cease-fire. Amid communal clashes between Sinhala and Tamils, Prabhakaran threatened to break the cease-fire, while Norway called for restraint on both sides. The inexorable pull toward interactive violence was suddenly halted on December 26, 2004, by the massive tsunami that hit Sri Lanka, claiming over 25,000 lives and causing mass devastation of the land.

Shocked by the calamity, both the regime and the Tigers made conciliatory moves, and in January 2005 Norway began a new push for peace. After lengthy negotiations, the Tigers and Kumaratunga agreed to joint efforts to distribute tsunami aid. While the regime was beset by opposition from hard-line JVP and Buddhist monks, factional fighting continued among the Tamils.

Civil War and Prisoner's Dilemma: Phase III, 2005–2006

Six months after the tsunami there were new indications of interactive terror, signifying the failure of both sides to learn from the past and update their preferences toward mutual accommodation. In August 2005, the Tamil foreign minister of Sri Lanka was assassinated, presumably by LTTE for his service to the regime. In November 2005, Mahinda Rajapakse was elected president with the support of Sinhalese nationalists opposed to making concessions to the Tamils. Once again, hardliners had come to dominate the game, triggering a new wave of terror between the Sri Lankan military and LTTE that claimed hundreds of lives and an exodus of Tamil refugees to India across the Palk Straights. By mid-2006, the shaky equilibrium reached after the 2002 truce agreement had been effectively overturned as the situation degenerated into low-intensity warfare, although neither side wished to officially end the cease-fire. In the face of the looming human disaster that could once again draw in India, a Western coalition of countries launched a new peace initiative to supplement and strengthen Norway's efforts. The Western intervention represented a third prisoner's dilemma attempt at resolving the Sri Lankan conflict, except that now India and Norway had been replaced by a coalition of four "jailer-mediators"—the United States, the EU, Britain, and Canada. Despite the coalition's powerful political and economic muscle, its members resisted deep involvement in the quagmire, obviating a peaceful outcome. In May 2006, the coalition partners threatened both sides with a cut-off of foreign aid if they did not end the fighting and begin serious negotiations. The coalition members' pressure on the Sri Lankan regime to make concessions for Tamil autonomy was balanced by their classification of LTTE as a

TABLE 3.3   LTTE versus Sri Lanka: Strategic Interactions, 1948–2006

Date	Actor and Type (or Event)
1948–1956	Ceylon (Sri Lanka) gains independence from Britain; Sinhalese majority monopolizes power
Apr. 1956	Elections followed by communal violence; 150 killed (mostly Tamils)
July 1957	Prime Minister Bandaranaike to recognize Tamil as minority language
Sept. 1959	Prime Minister Bandaranaike assassinated by Buddhist Monk opposed to Tamil recognition
Mar. 1965	Elections—moderate UNP takes power
June 1970	Hardline Sri Lanka Freedom Party (SLFP) takes power and limits education for Tamils and Sinhala/Buddhism given priority in the constitution
1971–1976	Militant Tamil youth organize attacks and bank robberies; TULF pushes for an independent Tamil Eelam
1976	LTTE founded
July 1977	UNP wins election; TULF forms the opposition; anti-Tamil violence breaks out; hundreds killed
1979	Mass arrests, extrajudicial killings, and "disappearances" of Tamil youth
1983	LTTE militants challenge TULF's moderate policies
July 1983	LTTE ambush kills 13 soldiers in Jaffna; anti-Tamil riots kill hundreds of Tamils and displace over 200,000
May 1985	LTTE massacre of 146 Sinhalese worshippers at a Buddhist shrine in Anuradhapura
July 1985	Indian mediated peace talks in Bhutan fail
1987	Sri Lanka Army pushes LTTE into Jaffna; Indian peacekeepers (IPKF) arrive
Mar. 1990	Failing in its mission, IPKF withdraws from Sri Lanka
June 1990	LTTE ends ceasefire killing hundreds of police officers and Muslims as regime allies with other Tamil groups in fighting LTTE; hundreds are killed and over 120,000 displaced
May 1991	LTTE suicide bomber assassinates former Indian prime minister Rajiv Gandhi
1991–1994	Ongoing war between government and LTTE marked by massacres, assassinations, bombings, and ambushes; thousands are killed
May 1993	LTTE suicide bomber assassinates President Ranasinghe Premadasa
Aug. 1994	President Kumaratunga takes power and opens peace talks with LTTE

1996–1997	LTTE fights back, attacking soldiers and bombing Colombo; state of emergency declared
1997–1998	Government carries out major offensive against LTTE and war escalates; LTTE bombs Temple of the Tooth, Buddhism's holiest shrine, and commercial areas in Colombo
Dec. 1999	President Kumaratunga injured in assassination attempt
Apr. 2000	Norway enters as a mediator to the conflict and LTTE captures strategic Elephant Pass
July 2001	LTTE bombs airport, killing 12 people and destroying 13 airplanes
Dec. 2001	Wickremesinghe of UNP becomes prime minister advocating peace talks
Feb. 2002	Government and LTTE sign a permanent cease-fire with Norway's mediation
Sept.–Dec. 2002	LTTE abandons first preference of an independent Tamil state for autonomy in Tamil regions of the north and east
Apr. 2003	LTTE suspends peace talks citing unfair treatment
Nov. 2003	Kumaratunga suspends parliament over opposition to PM's stance in peace talks with LTTE
Mar. 2004	LTTE splits as Colonel Karuna Amman takes troops underground
Dec. 2004	Over 25,000 killed in tsunami; government and LTTE agree to share $3 billion in aid
Nov. 2005	PM Rajapakse becomes president; Tamils mostly abstain from voting
Feb. 2006	LTTE and government meet in Geneva to reaffirm support for 2002 cease-fire
Apr.–Aug. 2006	Interactive violence restarts after rioting breaks out in Trincomalee; both sides join in land and sea battles with government carrying out air strikes and the Tamils undertaking bombings and other violence; hundreds are killed, tens of thousands are displaced

terrorist organization, which angered and alienated the Tamils. Given the depth of enmity between the Sinhalese and Tamils, demonstrated by the interactive violence outlined in Table 3.3, the prospects for a peaceable future appear dim unless the four-state coalition is prepared for a long-term and comprehensive involvement in partnership with India and other regional powers.[52]

Chechens versus Russia

The Chechen quest for independent nationhood has become one of the more intractable ethnic problems confronting the Russian Federation since the demise of the Soviet Union. After two costly wars, the Chechen insurgency has persisted as a dangerous threat to the stability of the North Caucasus and the security of Russia's southern borders. Chechnya's geostrategic position is reinforced by its petroleum resources and its location as a transit point for oil pipelines connecting the Caspian region to consumers in Europe.

Historical Background: Imperial Rule and Identity Formation, 1830–1957

The modern identity of the Chechens is shaped by their distinct language, practice of Sufi mysticism within Sunni Islam, social organization based on clans, and a history of persecution and rebellion. The Chechens were pagans and Christians until the sixteenth century, but Islam gradually became the majority faith under the control of the Khanate of Crimea, an ally of the Ottoman Empire. In an attempt to secure its southern borders, Russia periodically invaded Chechnya, and in 1781 succeeded in gaining acceptance of its jurisdiction by Chechen elders. A rebellion by Chechen leader Shaikh Mansur in 1784 was followed by a protracted insurgency led by Imam Shamil. As a religious leader, Shamil used his authority to rally the disparate Chechen clans against Russia and to establish an Islamic state. Despite his defeat and capture in 1858, Imam Shamil became a heroic symbol of the Chechen resistance to Russian control. Another quest for independence after the Russian Revolution ended in Chechnya's reoccupation by the Bolshevik forces and the formation of the Chechen-Ingush Autonomous Republic in 1936 as an integral part of the Soviet Union.[53]

Although all Soviet citizens suffered under Joseph Stalin's totalitarian rule, the Chechens were destined for especially brutal treatment during World War II. During the brief German occupation of parts of the Chechen-Ingush Republic, the Soviet government accused the Chechens of cooperating with the Nazis in return for independent statehood. After the Red Army's reconquest in 1944, Stalin deported thousands of Chechens, Ingush, and other suspected Nazi collaborators to Central Asia. Over a quarter of the Chechen people perished during the deportations and exile. In 1957, four years after Stalin's death, the Chechen-Ingush Republic was reestablished and 25,000 deportees were permitted to return home.[54]

A Clash of Preferences, 1990–1991

President Mikhail Gorbachev's policies of decentralization after the mid-1980s provided the impetus for the Soviet Union's minorities to seek greater autonomy or independence from Moscow's control. At the breakup of the Soviet Union in 1990–1991, Chechen nationalist sentiment was already growing as represented by the newly formed First Chechen National Congress. During the chaotic transition of power from Soviet president Gorbachev to President Boris Yeltsin of the Russian Federation, the Chechens were faced with a choice between two competing preferences—full independence from Russia, or political autonomy as a "republic" within the Russian Federation. Given the divisions on this issue among the Chechen people and their leaders, there was a clear need for an orderly referendum to determine majority sentiments. Yet there was no such procedure in place, nor even an opportunity for orderly debate. In the end, a military leader employing brute force made the choice.[55]

The split within the Chechen leadership between hardliners calling for independence and moderates favoring autonomy was prompted primarily by calculations of self-interest. Chechens holding leadership and business positions under Gorbachev and Yeltsin tended to support autonomy. This position was supported by Ruslan Khasbulatov, the Chechen speaker of Russia's parliament. The separatist hawks were led by Dzokhar Dudayev, a former Soviet air force general, whose charismatic pretensions could only be fulfilled by becoming the head of an independent state. In September–October 1991, Dudayev's National Congress faction aggressively moved to fill the power vacuum created by the crumbling Chechen-Ingush communist regime. Despite warnings of bloodshed from pro-autonomy, religious, and public figures, Dudayev's armed guards took over the parliament building, as his faction proclaimed him president after an "election" from which over 20 percent of the population had chosen to abstain. On November 1, 1991, Dudayev declared independence over the Chechen part of the Chechen-Ingush Republic, after the Ingush voted to remain within the Russian Federation.[56]

Escalating Violence: Phase I, 1991–1996

Dudayev's declaration of independence and its rejection by the Yeltsin government set the stage for a long-term conflict that resulted in Chechnya's total devastation and significant losses to the Russian military, undermining its geopolitical capability to fight insurgencies. At the outset, the Yeltsin government refrained from direct intervention due to its tenuous position in Moscow after the meltdown of the Soviet state apparatus. Yet increasingly, Russia felt compelled to deal with the Chechen situation because it threatened to destabilize the whole North Caucasus region where several dozen ethnic and religious minorities lived in an unstable state of coexistence. What began as covert aid to a coalition of Chechen groups fighting Dudayev, ended in the deployment of Russian forces, which in November 1994 occupied the Chechen capital, Grozny. The ensuing two-year struggle represented a classic case of interactive violence between a conventional army and an insurgency using terrorist tactics. Although the Russians quickly occupied the open river valleys of northern Chechnya, the insurgents fought a guerrilla war in the mountainous southern regions that prompted Yeltsin to seek an exit strategy, at least on a temporary basis.[57] As Yeltsin declared a unilateral cease-fire, the Chechens sought to heighten their opponent's vulnerability by taking 1,500 hostages in June 1995 from a hospital in the Russian city of Budyonnovsk. This attack, led by Shamil Bashayev, was a turning point because the Chechen struggle against the Russian military in Chechnya was transformed into a terrorist campaign targeting civilians in various locations in the Russian Federation. In April 1996, a precision-guided Russian rocket killed Dudayev, and four months later the Russian military withdrew from Chechnya after signing a cease-fire, but no attempt was made toward a negotiated settlement. Even as Aslan Maskhadov assumed the Chechen presidency, there was a three-year standoff due to Yeltsin's indecision, Russia's military impotence, and splits within the Chechen opposition.[58] These factors were not conducive to the resolution of the conflict through peaceful means.

Escalation and Expansion: Phase II, 1997–1999

Because of the inconclusive outcome of phase I of the conflict, its resumption was inescapable for both sides, which refused to modify their respective maximal preferences. The ignoble departure of the Russian military in 1996 provided dramatic evidence of the declining capabilities of the former superpower. From the Russian perspective, the failure to subdue the Chechens would send a clear signal of weakness to both outside powers and to the restless minorities who could choose to follow the Chechen example of secession. Clearly, Russia felt compelled to return to Chechnya in force to demonstrate that it possessed the necessary power and will to defeat the rebels. If Russia was to survive as a multinational state spread over two continents, it had to resurrect its military might and test it successfully in Chechnya.

The Russian view of the Chechen insurgency as an existential challenge was matched by many Chechens who had come to see Moscow's domination as a threat to their survival as an ethnic group. To match the upgrading of Russia's military power, the Chechens expanded their coalition by reaching out to Chechen expatriates, Muslim states, and militant Islamist groups seeking opportunities to wage jihad against the Russian "infidels" as they had done successfully in the 1979–1989 Afghan war. The emerging alliance between the Chechen nationalists led by Maskhadov and Islamist Chechen and foreign fighters was a fateful development for both the Chechens and Russia.[59] On the one hand, the Islamist involvement greatly increased the costs of the conflict to Russia by strengthening the Chechens' lethal potential and expanding the insurgency to neighboring Muslim republics. On the other hand, the Chechen-Islamist alliance also heightened the divergence of objectives between Maskhadov's nationalists fighting for Chechen self-determination and the Islamists seeking to trigger a mass insurgency among the Muslim minorities against the Russian Federation.[60]

The Second Chechen War, 1999–2002

Russia's refusal to negotiate with Chechen president Aslan Maskhadov and the latter's inability to control various Chechen warlords and Islamist militias set the stage for intensified conflict within and outside the Chechen homeland. Meanwhile, Chechnya had been devastated by the first Chechen war (1994–1996), and with its economy in ruins, people were pushed into desperation and radicalization, providing a ready pool of recruits for the nationalist and Islamist militants.

The next phase of interactive violence was initiated in August 1999 by Chechen attacks on Russian forces in Daghestan, a multiethnic republic located east of Chechnya. Although Maskhadov denied complicity, the incursion into Daghestan appeared to be an Islamist attempt to expand the Chechen conflict into a larger anti-Russian insurgency.[61] Bombings of apartments in Moscow in September 1999 were also blamed on Chechen separatists, prompting the newly appointed prime minister Vladimir Putin to order the reoccupation of Chechnya by federal forces. After the Russian reconquest of the river valleys, a pro-Moscow Chechen regime was installed in Grozny under Ahmad Kadyrov, a former insurgent leader, as the separatist bands went underground or retreated into the mountains to carry on the struggle. To be sure, the Chechen response represented a classic case of matching Russia's superior conventional power with multifaceted terrorist tactics. This approach aimed at destabilizing the pro-Moscow Chechen regime, while demonstrating the vulnerability of the Russian side with strategic attacks on both military and civilian targets in different parts of the Russian Federation. The insurgents' tactics included hostage taking, guerrilla attacks, and suicide bombings—a new modality of terror bearing the Islamist imprint, as practiced by the Palestinian Hamas and al-Qaida affiliates, except that the Chechen suicide bombers were mostly women. These suicide bombers, known as "Black Widows," were recruited from among women whose husbands had been killed during the war.[62]

Ethnic Struggle to Pan-Islamist Rebellion?

The progressive radicalization of the Chechen-Russian struggle since the Soviet Union's demise was fueled by clashing first preferences—the Russian opposition to Chechen separatism and the Dudayev faction's insistence on full independence. While no Russian leader could agree to the federation's dismantling, Putin's determined toughness helped him win two presidential terms and strengthened the centralized power of the Russian state. On the Chechen side, Maskhadov was not strong enough to accept a lesser preference than full independence, given Putin's refusal to negotiate with him, Russia's brutal tactics in Chechnya, and the growing challenge from rival Chechen warlords and Islamist extremists who sought to use Chechnya as a stepping stone for a general jihadist uprising. Given the pursuit of a zero-sum game by both parties, the human losses were enormous—up to 100,000 Chechens and 10,000 Russians killed and 400,000 Chechens displaced.

In June 2000, Russia appointed the Chechen religious leader Ahmad Kadyrov to administer Chechnya.[63] Peace talks held in November 2001 between the Chechen rebels and Russia ended in failure. A referendum held in March 2003 formalized Chechnya's inclusion in the Russian Federation and in October 2003 Kadyrov was elected president. In a protracted campaign to negate the legitimacy of the new Chechen constitution and the effectiveness of the pro-Moscow Kadyrov regime, Chechen and Islamist guerrillas launched a series of devastating attacks against civilian and military targets. In December 2003, suicide bombers attacked a passenger train in southern Russia, killing forty-four. In a separate bombing, six people were killed near the parliament building in Moscow. In February 2004, another suicide attack in the Moscow subway system claimed forty-one lives. And in May 2004, a massive explosion in Grozny killed President Kadyrov and seven others. In August 2004, two female suicide bombers brought down two airliners, killing ninety people. Even more gruesome was the death of 330 children and teachers during the September 2004 assault on a Beslan school in North Ossetia. In February 2005, a call for peace talks by insurgent Chechen leader Maskhadov was rejected and a month later he was killed in a bombing, in an apparent revenge for Kadyrov's assassination.

The fact pattern of the Chechen-Russian interactive violence until mid-2005 reflected the disruptive capabilities of the Chechen fighters despite increasingly lethal Russian military attacks. Several conclusions can be drawn from the events described in Table 3.4.[64]

TABLE 3.4   Russia versus Chechens: Strategic Interactions, 2003–2006

Date	Actor and Type (or Event)	Target	Place	Death Toll
May 2003	Suicide truck bomb	Chechen government building	Chechnya (North)	59
May 2003	Two female suicide bombers	Chechen president Kadyrov (unhurt)	Chechnya	16
June 2003	Female suicide bombers	Military base	Mozdok, N. Ossetia	20
July 2003	Two female suicide bombers	Rock festival	Moscow	15
Aug. 2003	Truck bomb	Military hospital	Mozdok	50
Dec. 2003	Suicide bomb	Passenger train	S. Russia	44
Dec. 2003	Female suicide bomber	Near Russian Parliament	Moscow	6
Feb. 2004	Suicide bomber	Subway	Moscow	41
May 2004	Bomb	Ahmad Kadyrov	Grozny	7
June 2004	Ingush/Chechen assault	Russian forces	Ingushetia	Dozens
Aug. 2004	Two female suicide bombers	Two airlines	South Russia	90
Sept. 2004	Assault/hostage taking	School	Beslan, North Ossetia	330
Feb. 2005	Event	Maskhadov's call for peace talks rejected by Russia and Chechen regime in Grozny		
Mar. 2005	Bomb	Maskhadov killed	Chechnya	1
June 2005	Bomb	Russian soldiers	Daghestan	10
July 2005	Bomb	Chechen police	Grozny	10
Oct. 2005	Assault	Government buildings	Nalchik, Kabardino-Balkaria	Dozens
Nov. 2005	Parliamentary election	Won by pro-Russian Chechens		
Mar. 2006	Election	Ramzan Kadyrov elected prime minister		

1. After 1995, the anti-Russian coalition evolved from a mainly Chechen ethnic nationalist insurgency to a joint Chechen/Islamist insurrection. This pattern of violence points to the possibility that this conflict could develop into a multiethnic rebellion of Chechens, Ingush, Daghestani,

and other North Caucasian minorities united under the banner of militant Pan-Islamism.

2. Despite the Russian commitment of increasing military and financial resources to the Chechen imbroglio, in 2003–2005 the insurgency intensified in lethality and expanded in geopolitical parameters. Using a variety of terror tactics, Chechen and allied Islamist fighters demonstrated their ability to attack Moscow as well as local government and civilian targets in at least four of the republics of the North Caucasus, while exporting Chechen fighters to join al-Qaida cells in Europe, Central Asia, and the Middle East. Despite a decrease in the number of attacks and progress achieved in stabilizing Chechnya in 2005–2006, the Chechen conflict has the potential to threaten the security of southern Russian, as well as the other countries targeted by al-Qaida's multiethnic affiliates, which recruit expatriate Chechens and neighboring minority fighters for the jihadist cause. According to this logic, Chechnya and the larger North Caucasus region could become the crucible to train and indoctrinate future Islamist combatants not only to fight Russia, but for export to other target countries, much like the role played by Afghanistan in 1980–2002 as a center for the training of Islamist terrorist cadres.

3. The Chechen-Russian conflict has been exceptionally costly in lives and property, as a result of the indiscriminate use of violence by both sides. Much of Grozny and the Chechen countryside were destroyed and the heavy handed tactics of the Russian military, combined with pervasive hopelessness among the Chechen population, fueled and expanded the insurgency, radicalizing its members and driving some to adopt the nihilistic ideology of jihadism which could have serious long-term consequences for Chechnya and the Russian Federation.

4. The Islamist drift of the Chechen insurgency and its expansion to nearby regions dramatically increased the costs of the conflict to the Russian side. If the Chechen cause is monopolized by the Islamists seeking a larger conflagration, then both sides will be playing a zero-sum game with all of its ominous consequences.

The strengthening of the Russian state under President Putin, reinforced by oil-driven economic development in the mid-2000s, provided an opportunity for the Moscow authorities to stabilize Chechnya by combining counterterrorism measures with coopting the Chechen population by offering economic incentives. There were clear indications that the Russian government was investing heavily in strengthening its Chechen allies and rebuilding Grozny. Pro-Russian Chechens won the November 2005 parliamentary elections and in March 2006 Ramzan Kadyrov was elected prime minister of Chechnya in a sign of continuity with his late father's legacy in accepting republican status within Russia as a first preference.

A Tipping Point? 2006 –

Several events during summer 2006 signified a possible tipping point in favor of Russia. In June the separatist president, Abdul Halim Saidullayev was killed, followed in July by Shamil Bashayev, the preeminent exponent of Chechen terrorism within and beyond Chechnya's borders.[65] Bashayev's killing was significant because for eleven years he was the mastermind of attacks on military as well as civilian targets, from Budyonnovsk hospital and the Moscow subway to airlines and the school in Beslan. Also, Bashayev embodied the convergence between the Chechen nationalists and the Islamist jihadists, as well as the strategy to expand the Chechen separatist struggle into a Pan-Islamist insurrection throughout Russia's Muslim republics.

Clearly these losses considerably degraded the Chechen insurgency and demonstrated the success of Russian president Vladimir Putin's hard-line strategy of counterterrorism. Only the passage of time will tell whether Russia's economic incentives of rebuilding Chechnya, in tandem with the effectiveness of Kadyrov's administration, will be sufficient to subdue the terrorist threat and change the ordering of Chechen preferences to forego independence and settle for autonomous status within a Russian multiethnic federal system. Now that Russia appears to have the upper hand, it would be wise for President Putin to initiate peace negotiations with the new separatist president, Doku Umarov and his foreign minister Ahmad Zakayev, who are known as nationalists lacking close connections to the Islamists or Bashayev's followers. Such a strategic move would divide the Chechen fighters and perhaps win over enough of the nationalists to join a coalition government with a high degree of autonomy under a loose Russian confederation. However, given the vagaries of Russia's domestic situation and the Islamists' intrusive role, it would be too early to say whether a tipping point has been reached where the equilibrium of terror is replaced by an equilibrium of mutual accommodation.

Ethnic Nationalists versus the State:
A Comparative Overview

Four case studies of conflict between ethnic nationalists and states have been presented, focusing on interactive political violence viewed from the perspective of game theory. A comparative analysis of the four cases helps reveal important similarities and differences, which are instructive in understanding the anatomy and the evolutionary stages of ethnic nationalist challenges to state authority as well as the forces and circumstances shaping preferences, strategic shifts, and outcomes.

Stages of Evolution. In terms of the onset and duration of violence, the case studies represent two distinct time periods and stages of evolution. The Irish and Basque cases turned violent in the 1960s, while the Tamil struggle began in the 1970s and Chechnya in the 1990s. As relatively older conflicts, the Irish and Basque have evolved out of their violent nascent stages and have experienced cycles of terrorism and the costs of mutual bloodshed. These costly and painful experiences have eroded the influence of hardliners on both sides of the conflict, opening up opportunities for moderates to reorder preferences and push for a peaceful settlement. In contrast, the Sri Lankan and Chechen conflicts are of more recent origin and are stuck in intense equilibria of terror where serious consideration of second-level preferences by both sides is only in the formative stage.

Determinants of Interactive Terrorism. The comparative analysis of the patterns of violence reflects a high degree of strategic behavior on the part of both governments and ethnic insurgents. Both sides choose gradations in the use of violence depending on each other's actions; they target each other's leaders and other vulnerabilities and they impose maximal losses to effect attrition of power and morale. These strategies are intended primarily to prevail in the given conflict, and secondarily, they aim to satisfy internal hardliner or moderate factions as well as external actors and constituencies. However, during periods of protracted violence, strategic decision-making sometimes gives way to acts of blind interactive vengeance both by ethnic terrorists and government counterterrorists.

Leadership Role. In all cases of interactive terrorism, the respective role of leaders is crucial in understanding the life cycle of such conflicts. As discussed in the modified game theoretic model in Chapter 1, leaders on both sides make decisions based on their calculations of self-interest and perceptions of the enemy's strategic intentions. In some cases, a single leader plays a dominant role, while in other situations the leadership role is more diffuse, involving a small group of leaders engaged in collective decision making.

In the conflict over Northern Ireland, several leaders played decisive roles in shaping the ebb-and-flow of violence. On the British side, Prime Minister Margaret Thatcher's hardliner stance exacerbated the conflict, while under her successors, John Major and Tony Blair, a move toward accommodation became possible. Clearly, Thatcher's hard-line policy preferences toward the IRA were determined largely by her particular personality traits rather than the objective national interests of the United Kingdom. In the case of the IRA/Sinn Féin versus the Unionists there was no single dominant leader on either side, thus necessitating collective decision-making in a slow process to reach consensus. In the end, Gerry Adams (Sinn Féin) and David Trimble (Unionist) were consensus leaders representing the majority of moderates on both sides seeking an equilibrium of peace. This equilibrium was threatened by the election of Rev. Paisley, whose refusal to cohabit with Sinn Féin reflected his long-term personal hostility toward the IRA and the Catholics of Northern Ireland.

In the conflict between the Basques and Spain, neither side was led by dominant personages after Franco's death in 1975. However, single leaders did play dominant roles in the Sri Lankan and Chechen conflicts. The authoritarian personality of Prabhakaran clearly shaped LTTE's totalitarian structure and the extent and modalities of his group's violent tactics and style of negotiations. Moreover, the Sri Lankan–Tamil conflict was exacerbated by President Kumaratunga's controlling personality and her determination to demonstrate toughness toward the LTTE within the competing male-dominated Sinhalese factions of the ruling elite. In the Chechen case, General Dudayev's personal quest to become the leader of an independent state had a formative impact, as did the subsequent rise of Vladimir Putin to Russia's presidency after Boris Yeltsin's failed presidential tenure.

Prisoner's Dilemma. Real opportunities for external mediation were available only to the Irish and Sri Lankan cases. The Basque conflict was too localized to invite serious external interest and the Spanish government was generally disinterested in a mediating role for the EU or the UN. Similarly, all European efforts to play a mediating role in Chechnya were angrily rejected by the Russian authorities, while the Chechens welcomed such external involvement. In sharp contrast, there were repeated attempts at external mediation in the Irish and Sri Lankan cases with the agreement of the conflicting parties, producing prisoner's dilemma situations involving tripartite negotiations. The decisive U.S. diplomatic role, supported by Britain, appears to have succeeded in Northern Ireland, while India's military intervention, followed by Norway's diplomatic initiatives, failed in Sri Lanka. Conflict resolution by third parties is a highly complex task that does not guarantee success and sometimes could contribute to failure such as in Lebanon (1983), Rwanda (1994), and Darfur (2005).

Notes

1. For further reading on ethnic politics see Rajat Ganguly and Raymond C. Taras, *Understanding Ethnic Conflict: The International Dimension* (New York: Longman, 2006), especially chapters 1, 2, and 5. Also see Tedd Robert Gurr and Barbara Harff, *Ethnic Conflict in World Politics* (San Francisco: Westview, 1994).

2. For historical details see Sean Cronin, *Irish Nationalism* (New York: Continuum, 1981), 1–113.
3. For a chronology of Anglo-Irish relations see http://news.bbc.co.uk/2/hi/events/northern_ireland/history/default.stm.
4. Richard English, *Armed Struggle: The History of the IRA* (New York: Oxford University Press, 2003), 3–78.
5. For more on the "Troubles" see http://www.bbc.co.uk/history/recent/troubles/.
6. English, *Armed Struggle,* 8–108.
7. Cronin, *Irish Nationalism,* 189–215.
8. Alfred McClung Lee, *Terrorism in Northern Ireland* (New York: General Hall, 1983), 177–186.
9. In addition to the Provisional IRA, there were smaller Catholic militias fighting the Unionist/British authorities such as the Official IRA (OIRA) and the Irish National Liberation Army. English, *Armed Struggle,* 174–179.
10. For a more detailed chronology see http://www.bbc.co.uk/history/recent/troubles/.
11. For a more detailed chronology see http://www.bbc.co.uk/history/recent/troubles/.
12. English, *Armed Struggle,* 285–298.
13. For a more detailed chronology see http://www.bbc.co.uk/history/recent/troubles/.
14. Andrew Reynolds, "A Constitutional Pied Piper: the Northern Irish Good Friday Agreement," *Political Science Quarterly,* 144, no. 4 (1999): 613–637.
15. Sean Byrne, "Consociationalism and Civic Society: Application to Peace-Building in Northern Ireland," *Journal of Peace Research,* 8, no. 3 (2001): 327–352.
16. Michael Kerr, *Imposing Power-Sharing* (Dublin: Irish Academic Press, 2005), 87–111.
17. Robert D. Putnam, "Diplomacy and Domestic Politics: The Logic of Two-Level Games,"*International Organization,* 42, no. 3 (1988): 427–460.
18. English, *Armed Struggle,* 297–303.
19. For more on the developments of the IIDC see www.nio.gov.uk/index/key-issues/decommissioning.htm, and English, *Armed Struggle,* 327–336.
20. On Basque nationalism see Daniele Conversi, *The Basques, the Catalans, and Spain* (Reno: University of Nevada Press, 1997), 44–79, and Ludger Mees, *Nationalism, Violence, and Democracy: The Basque Clash of Identities* (New York: Palgrave MacMillan, 2003), 5–20.
21. Conversi, *The Basques, the Catalans, and Spain,* 73–83.
22. On the establishment of the ETA see Mees, *Nationalism, Violence, and Democracy,* 21–24.
23. For a more detailed chronology of ETA's key events see http://news.bbc.co.uk/2/hi/europe/545452.stm
24. John Sullivan, *ETA and Basque Nationalism: The Fight for Euskadi, 1890–1986* (London: Routledge, 1988).
25. For a more detailed chronology see http://news.bbc.co.uk/2/hi/europe/545452.stm. On the decline of Franco's regime, see Mees, *Nationalism, Violence, and Democracy,* 1–119.
26. For more details on the "Dirty War" see Paddy Woodworth, *Dirty War, Clean Hands: ETA, the GAL, and Spanish Democracy* (New Haven: Yale University Press, 2002), 44–59.
27. Josep Colomer, *Game Theory and the Transition to Democracy: The Spanish Model* (Brookfield, VT: E. Elgar, 1995).
28. Conversi, *The Basques, the Catalans, and Spain,* 141–161.

29. Unzueta Ortiz de Zarate, "Euskadi ta Askatasuna," in Walter Laqueur ed., *Voices of Terror* (New York: Reed, 2004), 499–502.
30. On GAL, see Woodworth, *Dirty War, Clean Hands,* 139–148.
31. Council of Europe, "Report to the Spanish Government on the Visit to Spain Carried Out by the European Committee for the Prevention of Torture and Inhuman or Degrading Treatment or Punishment (CPT)," 1997, www.cpt.coe.int/documents/esp/2000-03-inf-eng.htm#_Toc478979404, accessed May 28, 2006.
32. Josep Colomer, *Game Theory and the Transition to Democracy: The Spanish Model,* (Aldershot, UK: Edward Elgar Publishing, 1995).
33. Rogelio Alonso, "Pathways out of Terrorism in Northern Ireland and the Basque Country: The Misrepresentation of the Irish Model," *Terrorism and Political Violence,* 16, no. 4 (2004): 695–713, and Cynthia L. Irvin, *Militant Nationalism: Between Movement and Party in Ireland and the Basque Country* (Minneapolis: University of Minnesota Press, 1999).
34. Mees, *Nationalism, Violence, and Democracy,* 143–154.
35. For a more detailed chronology see http://news.bbc.co.uk/2/hi/europe/545452.stm.
36. On the prospects for conflict resolution see Jan Mansvelt Beck, *Territory and Terror* (New York: Routledge, 2003), 219–232.
37. R. B. Herath, *Sri Lankan Ethnic Crisis: Towards a Resolution* (Victoria, Canada: Trafford Publishing, 2002), 1–8.
38. *Ibid.*
39. For more on the Donoughmore Constitution see A. Jeyaratnam Wilson, *Sri Lankan Tamil Nationalism* (Vancouver: UBC Press, 2000), 55–63.
40. Sankaran Krishna, *Postcolonial Insecurities: India, Sri Lanka, and the Question of Nationhood* (Minneapolis: University of Minnesota Press, 1999), 103–205, 31–100.
41. Neil DeVotta, *Blowback: Linguistic Nationalism, Institutional Decay, and Ethnic Conflict in Sri Lanka* (Stanford, CA: Stanford University Press, 2004), 1–142.
42. For more on this period, see Wilson, *Sri Lankan Tamil Nationalism,* 101–111.
43. On the ideology and objectives of LTTE, see Pirabakaran, in Walter Laqueur, *Voices of Terror* (New York: Reed, 2004), 454–457.
44. Russell R. Ross and Andrea Motles Savada, "Sri Lanka: A Country Study," in Walter Nubin ed., *Sri Lanka: Current Issues and Historical Background* (New York: Nova Science Publishers, 2002), 90–91.
45. On India's role in Sri Lanka, see Krishna, *Postcolonial Insecurities,* 103–205.
46. On the strategic dilemma facing Rajiv Gandhi see Wilson, *Sri Lankan Tamil Nationalism,* 148–156.
47. Herath, *Sri Lankan Ethnic Crisis,* 62–63.
48. *Ibid.* 113–116.
49. On the question of Tamil autonomy, see DeVotta, *Blowback.*
50. Ganguly and Taras, *Understanding Ethnic Conflict,* 197–200.
51. *Ibid.*
52. For a detailed chronology of key events with regards to LTTE developments see http://news.bbc.co.uk/2/hi/south_asia/1166237.stm, or http://www.c-r.org/our-work/accord/sri-lanka/chronology.php.
53. Tracey C. German, *Russia's Chechen War* (New York: Routledge, 2003), 1–4. Also, for a more detailed chronology see http://news.bbc.co.uk/2/hi/asia-pacific/country_profiles/2357267.stm.
54. Karny Yo'av, *Highlanders: A Journey to the Caucasus in Quest of Memory* (New York: Farrar, Straus and Giroux, 2000).
55. Valery Tishkov, *Chechnya: Life in a War-Torn Society* (Berkeley: University of California Press, 2004), 49–74. See also Ganguly and Taras, *Understanding Ethnic Conflict,* 133–137.

56. Tishkov, *Chechnya*, 75–89.
57. Dzhabrail Gakayev, "Chechnya in Russia and Russia in Chechnya," in Richard Sakawa, ed., *Chechnya: From Past to Future* (London: Anthem Press, 2005), 21–29.
58. German, *Russia's Chechen War*, 129–154, and Olga Oliker, *Russia's Chechen Wars, 1994–2000: Lessons from Urban Combat* (Santa Monica, CA: Rand, 2001), 5–32.
59. Tishkov, *Chechnya*, 168–179.
60. Robert Bruce Ware, "A Multitude of Evils: Mythology and Political Failure in Chechnya," in Richard Sakawa (ed.), *Chechnya: from Past to Future* (London: Anthem Press, 2005), 81–87, 98–101.
61. On the conflicting preferences of Wahhabi Islamists and Chechen nationalists, see Tishkov, *Chechnya*, 176–179, 189–195.
62. BBC, "Chechnya's Black Widow Bombers," July 11, 2003, www.cnn.com/2003/WORLD/europe/07/11/russia.black.widows/, accessed September 2, 2006.
63. Georgie M. Derluguian, *Bourdieu's Secret Admirer in the Caucasus* (Chicago: University of Chicago Press, 2005), 255.
64. For a more detailed chronology see http://news.bbc.co.uk/2/hi/asia-pacific/country_profiles/2357267.stm or www.mipt.org.
65. Sonni Efron, "My Afternoon Tea with a Terrorist," *Los Angeles Times*, 11 July 2006, B13.

Further Reading

Alonso, Rogelio. "Pathways out of Terrorism in Northern Ireland and the Basque Country: The Misrepresentation of the Irish Model." *Terrorism and Political Violence* 16, no. 4 (2004): 695–713.

Bell, J. Bowyer. *The IRA, 1968–2000: Analysis of a Secret Army*. London: Frank Cass, 2000.

Brams, Steve J. and Jeffrey M. Togman. "Cooperation through Threats: the Northern Ireland Case." *PS: Political Science and Politics* 31, no. 1 (1998): 32.

Colomer, Josep. *Game Theory and the Transition to Democracy: The Spanish Model*. Brookfield, VT: E. Elgar, 1995.

Coogan, Tim Pat. *The IRA*. New York: Palgrave MacMillan, 2002.

DeVotta, Neil. *Blowback: Linguistic Nationalism, Institutional Decay, and Ethnic Conflict in Sri Lanka*. Stanford, CA: Stanford University Press, 2004.

English, Richard. *Armed Struggle: The History of the IRA*. New York: Oxford University Press, 2003.

Ghosh, Partha S. *Ethnicity Versus Nationalism: The Devolution Discourse in Sri Lanka*. Thousand Oaks, CA: Sage Publications in association with Indian Council of World Affairs, 2003.

Irvin, Cynthia L. *Militant Nationalism: Between Movement and Party in Ireland and the Basque Country*. Minneapolis: University of Minnesota Press, 1999.

Krishna, Sankaran. *Postcolonial Insecurities: India, Sri Lanka, and the Question of Nationhood*. Minneapolis: University of Minnesota Press, 1999.

Lapidus, Gail W. "Contested Sovereignty: the Tragedy of Chechnya." *International Security* 23, no. 1 (1998): 5–49.

Lieven, Anatol. *Chechnya: Tombstone of Russian Power*. New Haven: Yale University Press, 1998.

Oliker, Olga. *Russia's Chechen Wars, 1994–2000: Lessons from Urban Combat*. Santa Monica, CA: Rand, 2001.

Sullivan, John. *ETA and Basque Nationalism: The Fight for Euskadi, 1890–1986*. London: Routledge, 1988.

Woodworth, Paddy. *Dirty War, Clean Hands: ETA, the GAL, and Spanish Democracy*. New Haven: Yale University Press, 2002.

Religious Militants
versus the State

THE PERIODIC EMERGENCE of religious revivalist movements has been a persistent pattern in the human condition since the dawn of history. Western political theorists have persuasively argued that social turmoil and economic deprivation produce an increase in religious commitment.[1] In a broader sense, there is a causal relationship between situations of societal crisis and religious revivalism. Simply stated—in times of hardship, human beings tend to return to the "old faith" searching for solutions to their existential problems brought on by crises in identity, feelings of alienation and insecurity, and political and social injustice. The return to religious roots provides a deep sense of security and belonging to individuals and societies in times of turmoil. Religious revivalist movements tend to be cyclical in nature. As the crisis conditions besetting the social milieu are resolved, one could expect a gradual decline in religiosity.[2]

The length of the revivalist cycle, and the depth and type of religious resurgence, depend on the gravity of a given crisis milieu. Typically, at the outset, revivalist movements are spiritual in nature, featuring charismatic preachers calling the believers to follow the puritanical origins of their faith, based on literal interpretations of holy texts. All too often, this quest to emulate the pristine fundamentals of a particular religion brings its exponents into conflict with the prevailing values and lifestyles of society. This dynamic becomes more overtly political when the fundamentalist constituency seeks to broaden its appeal in order to change the social order based on its own interpretation of the sacred texts. The ultimate outcome is a confrontation between revivalist religion and the state, where the fundamentalist leaders become eager participants in the political process pushing for societal transformation.

At this point, religion becomes politicized as its leading exponents attempt to utilize the levers of state power to impose their own creed on the rest of society.

The intrusion of religious fundamentalists into the political arena has occurred so often throughout history in many countries belonging to diverse religious traditions that it is not unusual. Yet, in many cases where fundamentalist leaders fail to overcome the resistance to their salvational agenda from their states and societies, a radical fringe of "true believers" emerges to change the "sinful" status quo through violent methods. Typically, these groups are founded or led by charismatic figures, often claiming messianic roles.[3]

Extremist leaders have used the teachings of major religions as well as diverse sects and cults as justifications for political violence throughout history. Usually, the individuals and groups that advocate the use of religious violence to achieve political objectives borrow selectively from scriptural sources to justify their attacks against perceived enemies. Religious violence is potentially more dangerous than ethnic or ideological terrorism, because its perpetrators are firmly convinced of the righteousness of their cause and claim divine sanction for their violent mission. While ethnic nationalists and ideological radicals legitimize their cause in terms of political and social justice, religious militants are more likely to draw upon other-wordly incentives and justifications for violent action. Also, in the case of the major religions, aspiring ideologues can tap into a large existing reservoir of the faithful who may be readily persuaded to support the militant cause. Further, ethnic and ideological preferences are far more likely to be moderated than religious preferences, which claim to originate from God's commandments and are therefore not negotiable. Case studies of groups involved in faith-based violence shall include Aum Shinrikyo of Japan, Hizbullah of Lebanon, Islamists in Kashmir, and Hamas in Palestine. Table 4.1 provides an overview.

Aum Shinrikyo versus Japan

Japan's phenomenal emergence as a leading economic power after its disastrous defeat in World War II took place within a strongly secularist democratic context imposed by the U.S. occupation regime. Yet the demystification of the emperor's divine role and the replacement of imperial Japan's religio-political ideology by Western liberalism left an ideological and spiritual vacuum in Japanese society amid the country's compulsive drive to achieve economic modernization and material success. In the 1970–1980s, this ideological and spiritual vacuum at the heart of Japan's economic miracle was being filled by various foreign and

TABLE 4.1   Religious Militants versus the State: An Overview

Name of Group/ Organization	Target State	Date Founded	Group Membership	Group's First Preference	Leadership Type	Key Leaders	Tactics	Killed/Injured in Interactive Violence
Aum Shinrikyo	Japan	1987	2,000	Ruling Japan or world destruction	Charismatic	Shoko Asahara	Chemical weapons	Around 50 killed, over 6,000 injured
Hizbullah	Israel/ United States	1982	Mass party	Israeli withdrawal from Lebanese territory; protection of Shiite community	Charismatic	Hasan Nasrallah	Trucks bombs, suicide attacks, rocket attacks, snipers, guerrilla tactics	18,000
Kashmiri separatists	India	Mid-1980s	Several thousand	Independence or unity with Pakistan as an Islamist state	Collective	Hafez Muhammad Said, Maulana Masud Azhar	Massacres, car bombs, assassinations, ambushes	80,000
Hamas	Israel	1987	Mass party	Islamic state in all of Palestine	Collective	Shaikh Ahmad Yassin, Abd al-Aziz al-Rantisi, Ismail Haniya, Khalid Mishal	Bombings, suicide attacks, shootings, stabbings, kidnapping	6,870

indigenous cults, sects, and movements, most of which remained at the periphery of the political process. One of the smaller cults was Aum Shinrikyo—a semi-clandestine organization that aspired to play a political, salvational, and even an apocalyptic role within and beyond the confines of the Japanese state.[4] As a case study, the importance of Aum Shinrikyo transcends the Japanese context because of its messianic and millenarian character, reminiscent of similar cults that have grown out of the Jewish, Christian, and Islamic traditions.

On March 20, 1995, Aum Shinrikyo attacked the Tokyo subway system with sarin nerve gas, claiming twelve lives and wounding over 5,000 people. This terrorist act was unprecedented in several aspects:

1. It shocked the Japanese government and society, while serving as a painful reminder of their mass suffering as victims of the atomic attacks on Hiroshima and Nagasaki.
2. It demonstrated the ability of a small messianic cult to develop and deploy sarin gas—a weapon of mass destruction (WMD)—in a terrorist attack in the midst of a highly developed, modern, and secular society.
3. It provided a dangerous example for other terrorist groups in the feasibility of using a WMD device instead of guns and explosives.
4. It revealed the power of a single cult leader, driven by psychosis, in determining the strategic preferences and objectives of a terrorist organization.

Historical Origins

Aum Shinrikyo was the brain child of its founder, Chizuo Matsumoto, who in 1987 bestowed holiness upon himself by adopting the name Shoko Asahara. Born in humble circumstances, Asahara possessed all the attributes of social and physical marginality—partial blindness, poor provincial roots, and difficulties in bettering his lot despite a compulsion to succeed. Sent away to a school for the blind, Asahara was denied the nurturing experience of family life. He grew up unloved, alienated, angry, and determined to compensate for his situation of weakness and marginality by reaching for power and wealth in a life of constant struggle. A good student, Asahara learned judo and sought dominance by using violence to bully classmates and declaring his intention to become Japan's prime minister.[5]

Despite the powerful drive to succeed, Asahara's path was repeatedly blocked. Indeed, he discovered that in Japanese society a marginal man's quest for upward mobility was full of uncertainties and failures. In 1975, he was refused entrance to medical school and instead took up the study of acupuncture, Chinese medicine, and Mao Zedong's revolutionary doctrines. Unbowed by rejection, in 1977 he moved to Tokyo to attend a special school to prepare for the entrance exams to study law at Tokyo University—a prestigious pathway to enter the ranks of the Japanese elite. Once again Asahara faced rejection and disappointment. Having married in 1978, he turned to practicing acupuncture and selling herbal medicines and natural foods until his arrest three years later for fakery. Meanwhile, Asahara had found a new venue to escape the throws of marginality. Beginning in 1981 he joined Agonshu—a cult combining early Buddhism, Tantric Buddhism, Hinduism, and Taoist Yoga. When he left this "New Age" cult in 1984 to establish a yoga training center, Asahara had found a new faith, learned the basics of the guru model of spiritual guidance, and the utility of cultic religion to gain power and influence.[6] Now this deeply conflicted individual had discovered a solution to his identity crisis and a "medium of salvation" to project his personal crisis onto society to acquire disciples, wealth, and power as a charismatic guru.[7]

Psychic Imperatives and Strategic Choices

In the decade leading to the March 1995 Tokyo subway attack, Asahara made successive strategic choices dictated by his developing psychosis: first using cultic religion to gain a following; then founding a political party to acquire power through elections; and after failure with the first two means, unleashing terrorism to trigger a wider apocalyptic conflict. This process of politicizing and radicalizing his movement reflected the progression of his psychosis. In 1985 he had emerged as a full-fledged guru of a growing cult of disciples who swore total allegiance to their leader, an essential requirement to satisfy the needs of Asahara's narcissistic personality and his visions of grandiosity.[8] Meanwhile, the guru's developing creed had eclectically incorporated extremist interpretations of Hinduism, Buddhism, apocalyptic messianism, and the teachings of Nostradamus.[9] After a visit to India and meeting the Dalai Lama in 1987, Asahara synthesized his beliefs by taking Shiva as a primary deity and naming his group Aum Shinrikyo—Aum representing powers of destruction and creation, and Shinrikyo, the teaching of divine truth. Asahara drew many followers by promising liberation from illness and suffering, denouncing materialism, and showing the way to spiritual enlightenment. Soon, it became evident that Asahara saw himself not simply as a guru but a divinely empowered prophet with political and messianic objectives, eventually claiming to be Buddha and Christ reborn. He began to display illusions of grandeur and megalomania as the maximum leader of a totalitarian organization tightly controlled and disciplined. Members of his group, including many young people and university graduates, were indoctrinated, drugged into obedience, and forced to isolate themselves from their families and society to prevent contamination of the "purity" of their faith. Asahara was obsessed with the world's impending destruction in a nuclear war and claimed that only those faithful to his teachings would escape the coming global cataclysm. His emphasis on nuclear annihilation powerfully resonated in Japan, the only country that had suffered atomic destruction. Despite his expectancy of Armageddon, however, in 1989 Asahara made a surprising turn to politics presumably to save Japan and the world.[10]

Asahara versus Japan, 1989–1995

The tipping point in Aum Shinrikyo's strategic preferences occurred in July 1989 when the group sought to register as a religious corporation. At first, the government refused Aum's application because of complaints from its members' families who had been barred from contacting their loved ones. After an aggressive campaign, Aum was eventually granted legal status. Meanwhile, in August 1989 Aum established Shinrito (Truth Party), a political organization, to participate in the electoral process and to expand dissemination of Asahara's message. After a well-financed campaign, the inglorious defeat of all twenty-five Aum candidates in the parliamentary elections of February 1990 dealt a devastating blow to the group and its leader whose expectations of victory were based on serious misperceptions of Japanese political life. Asahara's declared reason for seeking political office—to save society—had been rejected by the electorate. This rejection proved very costly to Aum Shinrikyo because it suffered great losses of followers and funds that had been so essential to Asahara's highly successful religious business enterprise. Indeed, the decline in Aum's fortunes followed the classic pattern of charismatic leadership in messianic and revolutionary movements where failure demonstrates the leader's lack of the "gifts of grace"—divinely given powers. A public revelation of the leader's impotence triggers a cognitive dissonance among believers, who then turn away from what had been their object of veneration and leave his congregation.[11]

The electoral defeat combined with legal problems and widespread public criticism triggered an abrupt shift in Aum's doctrine and strategic goals from saving the world to saving itself in the inevitable nuclear Armageddon. To survive the oncoming disaster, the guru appealed to the people to join Aum and become "superhuman" through tough ascetic practices—the only way to acquire immunity to weapons of mass destruction.[12]

In the early 1990s, Asahara and his followers found themselves in an increasingly hostile environment that was clouded by the leader's own growing sense of paranoia. The Japanese press and police agencies were closely monitoring Aum's activities on the suspicion that Asahara had ordered the murders of several opponents and up to three dozen members. Sensing an existential threat to his cultic enterprise from the Japanese government, Asahara began an urgent search for weapons of mass destruction in order to achieve his dual objectives—to destroy the world along with the hated Japanese regime by triggering an apocalyptic war, and to preside over the rebirth of a new civilization.[13] As the messianic author of the apocalypse, Asahara would ensure the realization of his prophesy of doom for all except his own.

In hopes of acquiring atomic materials and other weapons, Aum's envoys repeatedly visited Russia under the cover of proselytizing among its disadvantaged classes who had been impoverished by the demise of the Soviet Union.[14] After failing to secure weapons in Russia, Asahara in 1993 ordered Aum scientists to manufacture sarin gas and secretly test it in Australia's outback. On June 27, 1994, sarin gas clouds engulfed the city of Matsumoto in central Japan, killing seven and injuring hundreds of people, including three judges who had been scheduled to hear a case against the Aum group. Despite a gas leak from a secret lab in July 1994, the authorities were slow in establishing a connection between Aum and the Matsumoto incident. Only on March 19, 1995, did the police enter Aum offices in Osaka and arrest three members for abducting a dissident member. The next day, anticipating a government crackdown, ten high-ranking Aum operatives launched a gas attack on Tokyo's Kasumigaseki subway station.

This chain of events, from Aum's attempt to enter Japanese politics in 1989 to the subway attack of March 20, 1995, reflected the strange evolution of Asahara's strategic thought process. Clearly, Asahara initially aspired to play a leadership role in Japanese politics by establishing his own political party and running candidates for electoral seats who were defeated despite his unrealistic expectations. This rebuff and the subsequent investigations of Aum enraged Asahara and heightened his sense of paranoia vis-à-vis the government. In summer 1994 he even established an opposition government as his operatives covertly prepared to unleash sarin gas attacks. Asahara's moves were apparently driven by certain miscalculations resulting from his distorted vision of Japanese society. Consumed by hatred of the Japanese regime and fearing its inevitable crackdown of Aum, Asahara struck first, perhaps hoping to destabilize the political system in preparation for an Aum takeover. Falling short of this goal, the attack would wreak mass destruction before Asahara and Aum went down in their self-made cataclysm. In the end, however, Asahara miscalculated the execution of the subway attack and its likely outcome.

Twelve people died and 5,500 were incapacitated from sarin gas bombs released in five Tokyo subway trains on March 20, 1995. Yet the death toll had fallen far short of Asahara's expectations due to technical imperfections of the gas bombs and their delivery systems. Aum's scientists had run out of time to perfect the lethal capacity of their gas weapon in view of Asahara's growing sense of urgency to attack in advance of a police crackdown on his organization.

The Tokyo attacks, followed by similar gassings on Yokohama trains, were a belated wakeup call for the authorities. By May 1995, 200 Aum members were arrested and after weeks of searching, the police discovered Asahara in a secret hideout specially built within his main headquarters in Kamikuishiki.[15] The remaining members of Aum announced their determination to reform its teachings and changed its name to Aleph.[16] Although Asahara was replaced as Aum's leader, the reformed group still viewed him as a "genius mediator" and "spiritual being." Thus ended the strange quest of a self-styled holy man for the contradictory goals of seeking worldly power and/or precipitating the world's end in his messianic mission to build a new one.

The preceding game theoretic analysis of Aum's messianic terrorism has helped highlight the mutual misperceptions of Asahara and the regime, i.e., the guru's misunderstanding of Japanese politics and underestimation of the power of the state, and the government's failure at early detection of Aum's threat potential and indecisive moves to preempt the gas attacks. The analysis further illustrates the utility of modified game theory in revealing the decisive role of leaders like Asahara in the determination of Aum's changing strategic preferences toward Japan and the world. Notably, these preferences arose from the demented soul of a marginal man, whose self-interests were defined by the pursuit of power and wealth. Asahara's case clearly demonstrates the powerful impact of his psychic makeup on the formation and ordering of Aum's policies and preferences.

In the end, the Japanese government achieved its first preference in dismantling the Aum apparatus and forcing it to reform itself and renounce the use of violence. To be sure, even at the height of its power, Aum Shinrikyo lacked the organizational and coercive means to mount a successful challenge to the Japanese state. Clearly, Aum's apocalyptic terrorism—summarized in Table 4.2—was an aberration from the peaceful priorities of post-war Japanese society. Yet, the more fundamental issue for Japan is how a deeply flawed man like Asahara could have organized a violent cult within a homogeneous, modern, and culturally integrated democracy. The social atomization, spiritual alienation, socioeconomic inequities, and highly competitive materialist culture that gave rise to Aum have remained unchanged in Japan's mass society, except for the recent revival of nationalist sentiments and greater activism in world affairs. These nationalist trends, symbolized by Prime Minister Junichiro Koizumi's controversial visits to the shrine of Japan's wartime leaders, could fill the ideological vacuum and reduce

TABLE 4.2   Aum Shinrikyo versus Japan: Strategic Interactions, 1981–1995

Date	Actor and Type (or Event)	Target/Goal	Place	Death Toll/ Damage
1981–1984	Asahara joins Agonshu cult and becomes a guru			
1987	Asahara establishes Aum Shinrikyo, a messianic cult			
1989	Asahara establishes Shinrito (Truth Party) to compete in elections	Strategic shift from religious proselytizing to politics		
Feb. 1990	Asahara and 24 members are defeated in parliamentary elections			
Apr. 1990– May 1994	Attempts to acquire and experiment with chemical, biological, and nuclear weapons	Strategic shift toward increased militancy targeting opponents and government officials	Tokyo, Yokohama, Narita, Russia, Australia	
June 1994	Sarin nerve gas attack	Judges trying Aum Shinrikyo case	Matsumoto neighborhood	7 killed, 270 injured
Sept. 1994– Feb. 1995	Attacks on dissident members, attorneys of victims' families, and rival religious groups	Minimize opposition		1 journalist killed, 20 dissidents killed, and many injured
Mar. 20, 1995	Sarin gas attack in subway	Subway riders	Tokyo	12 killed, 5,500 injured
Apr. 1995– July 1995	Attempted chemical attacks, mostly failed	Subway riders	Yokohama and Tokyo	around 75 injuries and illnesses
Apr. 1995– Oct. 1995	Police crackdown	Aum Shinrikyo leadership		
May 1995	Shoko Asahara arrested			

alienation by providing a strong political identity that could neutralize the cultic creeds that have proliferated since the 1970s. The turn to nationalism, however, could have long-term negative consequences should it evolve into a strident patriotism reminiscent of the extremist mysticism of Imperial Japan.

Hizbullah versus Israel and the United States

Since its emergence in 1982, Hizbullah has been one of the Middle East's most effective and cohesive organizations, both as a potent political force and as a highly motivated perpetrator of violence against adversaries. Although grounded in Lebanon's Shiite minority, the organization defines itself as *Ummat Hizbullah*—Community of God's Partisans—thereby claiming divine sanction for its cause of fighting in defense of oppressed Muslims and their lands.

Hizbullah has been denounced as a terrorist organization by the United States, Britain, and the European Union. Yet, Hizbullah is more than another terrorist group; it is a highly cohesive and well-trained militia and an extensive network of philanthropic organizations, all wrapped into a theocratic party structure led by Shiite clerical cadres. Hizbullah is powerful because it is a mass movement with grassroots support among Lebanon's underprivileged Shiite population and other sectors of society. It adheres to a militant brand of Shiite Islamist ideology which has provided the group with a legitimacy of cause within the Middle East's environment of crisis.[17]

Historical Origins

Hizbullah arose from the crisis conditions that beset Lebanon's Shiites in the early 1970s, within the larger turbulence of Middle Eastern politics. In a region torn apart by the Arab-Israeli struggle and multiple inter-state rivalries, Lebanon's finely balanced consociational polity unraveled in 1975 with the outbreak of a civil war among Christian and Muslim militias and Palestinian fighters, each supported by neighboring governments. These crisis conditions had an especially harsh impact on the Shiite community. Although the Shiites constituted the largest group among Lebanon's seven major sectarian communities, they had been relegated to a political and economic underclass status. The inflow of Palestinian refugees from Israel further destabilized the heavily Shiite populated areas of South Lebanon, where in the 1970s the Shiites bore the brunt of fighting between the PLO and the Israeli army. The incessant bloodshed produced a large outflow of Shiite migrants to Beirut's ghettos. The failure of the Lebanese government and the Shiite feudal leadership (*zuama*) to provide security and economic aid caused many in the Shiite underclass to turn to Islamist ideology and its clerical propagators closely tied to networks of militant Shiite clergy in Iraq and Iran. Thus, the progressive radicalization of the Lebanese Shiites in the 1970s was guided by around a dozen charismatic clerics who had established their own competing organizations dedicated to Islamist activism and armed resistance.

Two dramatic events shaped Lebanese Shiite radicalization—the Iranian Revolution of February 1979 led by Ayatullah Ruhullah Khomeini and the June 1982 Israeli invasion of South Lebanon. To the Lebanese Shiites, the Iranian Revolution symbolized the victory of Shiite Islamism over the Shah's secular pro-American regime; hence, the revolutionary Iranian government led by a charismatic cleric provided an inspiration and a model to emulate. The 1982 Israeli invasion and occupation became the essential trigger—the tipping point—toward the eruption of a Shiite insurgency against the Israeli and American forces in Lebanon.[18]

Ideology and Objectives

Hizbullah's ideology is modeled after Iran's revolutionary creed formulated by the Iranian Ayatullah Khomeini and Iraqi Ayatullah Muhammad Baqir al-Sadr, during their tenure in the 1970s at seminaries in the Iraqi holy city of al-Najaf. In response to the repressive policies of Saddam Hussein in Iraq and the Shah in Iran, these clerics developed a radical ideology of Shiite revivalism committed to the establishment of Islamist theocracies under the guidance of the clerical establishment (*marjiyah*), which would rule by Islamic law (*sharia*). This doctrine, known as the "Guardianship of the Jurisconsult" (*wilayat al-faqih*), endows the ranking Shiite clergy with supreme religious and political power as the successors to the Prophet Muhammad and as expert interpreters of Islamic law.[19] After the 1979 Iranian Revolution, Ayatullah Khomeini became the leading jurisconsult—a model followed by Hizbullah, which has been led by Shiite clerics since its inception.

Hizbullah's political objectives derive from its ideology of clerical supremacy over a Muslim theocratic polity. In practice, the group advocates a liberation theology to replace unjust secular political systems with Islamist polities, to free Lebanon from foreign occupation, liberate the holy city of Jerusalem, and help Hamas in the Palestinians' struggle against Israel. Despite its theocratic bent, Hizbullah can be flexible. It has suspended the goal of establishing an Islamist state in Lebanon, which has a large Christian minority; it has also cooperated with some Sunni Islamist groups such as Hamas and the Muslim Brotherhood despite major doctrinal differences with them. Finally, it has moderated its demands in domestic and international forums periodically, to protect its existential interests.[20]

Dynamics of Interactive Violence, 1982–1984

The Syrian-Iranian Axis. The Lebanese civil war erupted in April 1975, pitting several Maronite Christian militias against a coalition of Arab nationalist, Druze, Shiite, and Palestinian forces. In a bid to prevent the defeat of the Christian militias and contain the fighting, Syrian forces entered Lebanon in mid-1976 and imposed a cease-fire. Meanwhile, Israel had started building military ties to the Maronite militias leading to its 1978 invasion to drive out the PLO from South Lebanon. After Israel's withdrawal under international pressure, PLO forces returned to the region to pose a continuing threat to Israel.

In June 1982, Israel unleashed "Operation Peace for Galilee"—a major invasion of Lebanon aiming to destroy the PLO, reduce Syrian influence, and establish a pro-Israeli government in Beirut under the Maronite Phalangist militia leader Bashir Gemayel, who would sign a peace treaty with Israel. Although Defense Minister Ariel Sharon's military campaign was successful in driving the PLO out of Lebanon, it claimed 14,000 Lebanese and Palestinian lives, and not all of Israel's goals were realized.

In response to Israel's 1982 move into South Lebanon, the Syrian government permitted the deployment of 1,500 Iranian Revolutionary Guards (*Pasdaran*) to train Shiite fighters in Lebanon's Biqa valley, an area under Syrian military control. Deeply worried about its own military inferiority vis-à-vis Israeli forces, Syria also sought Iran's involvement in order to strengthen its own relations with Lebanon's Shiites, among whom Khomeini had become an object of veneration.[21] In a convergence of interests, Syria's secular Arab Baathist regime and Iran's theocracy were determined to deny Israel a foothold in Lebanon under the aegis of a pro-Israeli Phalangist regime in Beirut.

Syrian-Iranian concerns were heightened by the friendly reception given to Israeli soldiers by some Shiites in South Lebanon, who had suffered under PLO's presence. However, in a few months the friendly Shiite attitude was dramatically transformed into anger because of Sharon's unrelenting march to Beirut, in alliance with the Maronite Christian militias, and the oppressive behavior of 120,000 Israeli troops that portended their long-term presence in Lebanon.[22] The resulting milieu of Shiite alienation provided a welcome opportunity for the Iranian revolutionary alternative, a militant revivalist ideology backed by military training, weaponry, and funding. Hence, in 1982–1983 the various radical Shiite and other militias coalesced into an umbrella organization— Ummat Hizbullah.[23]

The American-Israeli Axis. The nascent Syrian-Iranian alliance could not effectively challenge Sharon's juggernaut, as the Israelis established air supremacy by destroying much of the Syrian air force. The PLO forces led by Yasser Arafat retreated to Beirut, squeezed between the advancing Israelis and allied Lebanese Christian militias. In August 1982, it was clear that the Lebanese conflict was jeopardizing U.S. interests in the Arab world, prompting President Ronald Reagan to deploy 800 U.S. Marines as part of a Multinational Peacekeeping Force (MPF) that included an equal number of French and Italian troops, tasked to extricate the besieged Palestinian fighters from Beirut and ship them to other Arab countries. After overseeing the PLO's departure, the MPF withdrew from Lebanon in mid-September 1982, only to be sent back to deal with a more demanding peacekeeping mission. On September 16, 1982, the Israeli command had permitted the entrance of allied Lebanese Phalangist militias into the Sabra and Shatila refugee camps in Beirut, where they raped, maimed, and massacred several thousand Palestinian and Shiite civilians. In order to prevent repetition of such atrocities, President Reagan redeployed the marines in Beirut, while pressing Israel to withdraw from Lebanon. It soon became clear that the marines were sent for a longer stay with a more expansive mission—to create a strong Lebanese army to help implant in Beirut a Maronite Christian regime, allied with Israel and the United States. This change of mission further polarized the Lebanese conflict, solidified the Syrian-Iranian alliance, and inflamed anti-American sentiments across the Arab world. Confronted by powerful U.S. and Israeli conventional forces, Shiite militant factions under Hizbullah's umbrella resorted to terrorist tactics of unprecedented form and lethality.[24]

Hizbullah's primary goal was to provide security for the Lebanon's Shiite population. The strategic objectives that it shared with Iran and Syria were to prevent the implantation of a Maronite-led government in Beirut with U.S. and Israeli support, and to deny Israel and the United States a long-term presence in Lebanon. In order to realize these interrelated objectives, Hizbullah sought to dramatically increase the human costs of a continued U.S./Israeli presence. To this end, Hizbullah mounted a series of devastating attacks that began with the truck bombing of the U.S. Embassy in Beirut on April 18, 1983, killing sixty-three people, including seventeen Americans. Despite the advice of U.S. Defense Secretary Casper Weinberger to withdraw from Lebanon, in mid-September an additional 2,000 marines arrived in Beirut. This action triggered a devastating response. On October 23, 1983, truck bombs destroyed the U.S. Marine barracks and the French encampment in Beirut killing 241 and fifty-eight soldiers respectively. The United States retaliated with air and missile strikes from its naval forces in the Mediterranean—an act which might have provoked the assassination of Dr. Malcolm Kerr, president of the American University of Beirut on March 31, 1984, by Islamic Jihad, a Hizbullah faction.[25] In the same month, President Reagan ordered the total withdrawal of U.S. forces from Lebanon, which was followed by the exit of the French and Italian contingents.

However, the precipitous U.S. departure did not stop Islamic Jihad's campaign of violence. On September 12, 1984, a truck bomb demolished the U.S. Embassy Annex in Beirut, killing twenty-four people, including two Americans. In addition, two U.S. officials, CIA Station Chief William Buckley and Col. William Higgins were kidnapped and slain, and thirty hostages taken, including journalists, professors, and a priest. Consequently, the Reagan administration changed its strategy by initiating secret talks with Iran, offering to sell weapons in exchange for freeing the hostages held in Lebanon. Although the hostages were gradually released, the secret arms deal became public in November 1986, triggering a major political crisis for the White House in the Iran-Contra affair, which also involved funding the anticommunist Contras in Nicaragua with weapons sales to Iran.[26] In sum, the U.S. involvement in the Lebanese civil war proved to be a disaster of the first magnitude both at home and abroad. A superpower had been humbled by being dragged into a quagmire against its interests and being forced to negotiate with Iran, a government that it had refused to recognize, having labeled it a terrorist regime. Meanwhile, the effectiveness of the suicide attacks had laid bare the vulnerability of U.S. conventional forces, a costly lesson about a new modality of violence—suicide bombings, also known as "martyrdom operations"—that would be emulated in the next twenty-five years in different forms in Sri Lanka, Israel/Palestine, Turkey, Russia/Chechnya, Egypt, the United States, Kenya, Tanzania, Yemen, Britain, Jordan, Pakistan, Afghanistan, Kashmir, Saudi Arabia, Algeria, India, and Iraq.[27]

Hizbullah versus Israel, 1984–2000

The campaign to bring about Israel's withdrawal from Lebanon presented Hizbullah with a greater challenge than its struggle against the United States. Israel maintained a strong military presence in Lebanon that could be easily sustained because of its geographic proximity. Yet Israel's determination to remain in Lebanon was undermined by growing domestic opposition, international pressures, and the high costs imposed by Hizbullah's guerrilla attacks. Between November 1983 and June 1985, half-a-dozen major bombings and many other attacks were launched that claimed ninety-six Israeli casualties.[28] The effectiveness of these operations was due to the structural evolution of Hizbullah's insurgency against Israel. The gross asymmetry of power between the Israel Defense Forces (IDF) and the Lebanese insurgents had prompted over a dozen Shiite factions, Sunni militias, and Palestinian guerrillas and fighters from secular and leftist parties to coalesce under Hizbullah's banner. These militants participated in the fighting and even carried out martyrdom operations under Hizbullah's military wing—the Islamic Resistance.[29] In mid-1985, Prime Minister Shimon Peres ordered the redeployment of Israeli forces behind a ten-mile "Security Zone" along the Lebanese-Israeli border. The Security Zone would be policed by the Christian-led South Lebanese Army (SLA) backed by Israeli air and land forces. Meanwhile, Israel had traded over 1,000 Palestinian and Lebanese prisoners for three of its soldiers captured by Hizbullah.

The vacuum created by the Israeli departure was quickly filled by Hizbullah, which began a protracted campaign against SLA/Israeli forces that lasted fifteen years. In the face of Hizbullah's determined attacks, the security zone could not effectively protect northern Israel. Ironically, Israel's ejection of the PLO from South Lebanon in 1982 had brought about a much deadlier foe in Hizbullah. Ethnic nationalist terrorism had been replaced by infinitely more lethal religious terrorism.[30]

The pacification of Lebanon under the 1989 Taif agreement brought Hizbullah under greater Syrian control while permitting it to retain its military capabilities to confront SLA and Israeli forces in the security zone. As the PLO and Israel were engaged in serious negotiations in the early 1990s, Hizbullah operations against the security zone intensified, reflecting Iranian and Syrian displeasure with the U.S. - sponsored peace talks. In February 1992, an Israeli campaign to drive Hizbullah from the border region culminated in the assassination of its leader, Shaikh Abbas al-Musawi, and his family. In response, Musawi's successor, Shaikh Hasan Nasrallah, allegedly ordered the suicide bombing of Israel's embassy in Buenos Aires, Argentina, in March 1992, killing thirty-eight people. This attack represented an ominous expansion of the geographical scope of the conflict. In 1993–1994, massive Israeli artillery attacks and aerial bombings killed dozens of militants and civilians but failed to deter Hizbullah. In May 1994, when Israeli soldiers kidnapped a top Hizbullah official, a bomb destroyed a Buenos Aires Jewish cultural center in July, killing eighty-five people; two similar bombings followed in London.[31] Hizbullah could have been signaling its intention to globalize the carnage beyond Israeli targets to include Jewish organizations and institutions worldwide. In April 1996, Israel's "Operation Grapes of Wrath" failed to crush Hizbullah's forces, while killing over 100 Lebanese civilians who had taken refuge in a UN base in Qana.[32]

By the late 1990s, Israel determined that maintenance of the security zone was too costly, with the loss of over 900 soldiers in an eighteen-year period. In May 2000, Prime Minister Ehud Barak ordered the pullout of Israeli forces from the security zone, which was quickly implemented, leading to the collapse of the South Lebanese Army and takeover of its posts by Hizbullah fighters. The Israeli withdrawal was celebrated as a victory for Hizbullah and boosted its legitimacy as a national resistance movement in Lebanon and the Muslim world.[33]

Despite the Israeli withdrawal, the conflict persisted because of the unresolved status of the Shibaa Farms region and Hizbullah's indirect involvement in the renewed fighting between Israel and the Palestinians. Claiming that the 15-square-kilometer Shibaa Farms was a part of Lebanon, Hizbullah asserted its right to liberate it from Israeli control, while Israel considered the region Syrian territory that Israel had occupied in the 1967 war. Since 2000 there have been periodic clashes between Hizbullah and Israel in and around the Shibaa Farms. In January 2004, through German mediation, Israel and Hizbullah exchanged 436 Palestinian and Lebanese prisoners for an Israeli businessman and the remains of three Israeli soldiers.

After the collapse of the Israel-Palestinian peace process in 2000, Hizbullah actively supported the second Palestinian Intifada by providing training, funds, and weapons. In this context Hizbullah forged close ties with Hamas, representing the confluence of Shiite and Sunni Islamism in pursuit of their shared objective of liberating from Israel the holy lands of Islam, especially Jerusalem. Moreover, Hizbullah has maintained ties with all pro-Iran Shiite groups in Iraq and the Gulf countries, including Shaikh Muqtada al-Sadr's followers, the Dawah party and the Supreme Council of the Islamic Revolution in Iraq (SCIRI)—which have assumed leading roles in Iraq's new government under American tutelage. In Lebanon, Hizbullah's 20,000-strong militia is supplemented by a well-run social service organization that operates schools, hospitals, orphanages, and communications media.[34] In the 2005 elections, Hizbullah won fourteen seats in the 128-member Lebanese Parliament, and held two ministries in the cabinet. With branches in several dozen countries, Hizbullah's global reach is seen as a clear threat to its opponents in the international arena.[35]

Unstable Equilibrium, 2001–2006

As a Shiite Islamist mass party, revolutionary guerrilla outfit, and Lebanese liberation movement, Hizbullah is a unique phenomenon in the Middle East's convoluted landscape. As such, it has faced multiple challenges in terms of its objectives and continued existence as a revolutionary organization. Hizbullah's singular achievement has been the ability to retain its revolutionary zeal and organizational charisma, despite the passage of time and bureaucratization of its structures. However, Hizbullah's expanding role as a Lebanese political party also changed the order of its preferences and objectives. It no longer sought to establish an Islamist state in Lebanon and was content to play a major role in that country's multisectarian democratic political system. Yet, Hizbullah did not dilute its anti-Israeli stance and remained a staunch supporter of the Palestinian Islamist cause, as expressed by Hamas and Islamic Jihad. Although it denounced the September 11, 2001, attacks, Hizbullah still viewed the United States as a prime antagonist in keeping with mainstream opinion in the Muslim world.

The U.S.-led invasion of Iraq in March 2003 presented Hizbullah leaders with a major dilemma and a possible existential challenge. After the overthrow of Saddam Hussein's regime, the United States ushered in a Shiite-dominated government led by the Dawah and SCIRI parties—two of Hizbullah's erstwhile pro-Iranian allies. With a powerful force stationed in Iraq, the United States sought to establish friendly regimes in the Middle East, particularly in Syria and Lebanon; hence, U.S. pressure to destabilize Syria—one of Hizbullah's two main allies—and force the pullout of Syrian forces from Lebanon. The assassination of former Lebanese prime minister Rafiq Hariri in February 2005 was a turning point, which forced Syria to withdraw under accusations of complicity in the murder, leaving Hizbullah in a vulnerable strategic position vis-à-vis Israel and the U.S. military in Iraq. Yet, it was because of its strategic vulnerability that Hizbullah refused to disarm despite calls from the international community as expressed in the September 2004 UN Security Council Resolution 1559. In what appeared to be a significant policy shift in March 2005, the Bush administration stated its willingness to consider Hizbullah a legitimate player in Lebanese politics if it agreed to give up its armaments. As Hizbullah agreed to join Lebanon's national unity government for the first time in July 2005, the organization displayed a strong Arabist posture and Lebanese nationalist identity. Despite its long years of dependence on Iran and Syria, Hizbullah had its own separate identity and interests, and was not an obedient client or proxy for Iran or Syria.[36]

In fall 2005, there had been a cessation of interactive violence between Israel and Hizbullah. It appeared that both sides had reached an uneasy equilibrium signifying their reluctant willingness to coexist. Shaikh Nasrallah may have assumed that Israel would be deterred from major action fearing Hizbullah's missile forces, and Israel believed that its military might would deter Hizbullah from armed provocations.[37] This fragile equilibrium was shattered in July 2006, under the impact of converging events and interests that triggered a full-scale war between Hizbullah and Israel.

An Equilibrium of Terror?

On July 12, 2006, a Hizbullah operation in the western sector of the Lebanese-Israeli border resulted in the kidnapping of two Israeli soldiers, and the death of eight others. This action had taken place outside the contested Shibaa Farms sector where both sides had been carrying out interactive violence against each other's military targets since Israel's 2000 withdrawal. In keeping with previous practice, Hizbullah asked to trade the captured soldiers for Lebanese prisoners long held by Israel. Rejecting these demands, Prime Minister Ehud Olmert launched a massive military campaign by air, naval, and land forces focused on Hizbullah bases as well as strategic and economic targets, destroying Lebanon's infrastructure and creating a huge humanitarian crisis. Hizbullah reacted by unleashing its arsenal of rockets on northern Israel. After thirty-four days of interactive violence over 1,100 Lebanese and 160 Israelis had been killed, thousands were injured, and over a million people displaced on both sides.[38] Given the asymmetry of power between the antagonists, Lebanon had suffered infinitely greater losses, in keeping with Israeli Lt. Gen. Dan Halutz's threat to "turn back the clock in Lebanon by 20 years"—a reflection of his misplaced faith in air power which proved inadequate to uproot Hizbullah after weeks of intensive bombing.[39]

The sudden eruption of the Hizbullah-Israel confrontation raised some key questions regarding the nature and dynamics of political violence in the Middle East and its global implications:

- Why did Hizbullah abduct the two Israeli soldiers on July 12, 2006?
- Why did Israel react with massive military force instead of negotiating with Hizbullah as before?
- Why did President Bush support Israel's month-long invasion of Lebanon instead of pushing for an early cease-fire and negotiations?
- What were the primary and secondary objectives of the two antagonists and the other powers indirectly involved in the conflict?
- To what extent did the antagonists and their supporters achieve their preferences through violence?
- What could be the long-term implications of the conflict?

In order to elucidate the logic of the interactive violence between Israel and Hizbullah, we turn to a game theoretic analysis of the conflict.

Strategic Rationale and Objectives: Hizbullah versus Israel

The capture of two Israeli soldiers represented a continuation of Hizbullah's past operational mode of freeing Lebanese and Palestinian prisoners held by Israel. As in the past, these operations, whenever successful, highlighted the organization's continued role as a "resistance movement" in Lebanon and the larger Arab and Muslim arena. In the Lebanese context, the Hizbullah leadership may have been signaling the government of Fuad Siniora its continued refusal to disarm and its intention to take independent armed action against Israel. Also, the operation may have been intended as a symbolic act of defiance of Israel and a token of solidarity with the Palestinian Hamas regime that was being undermined by a U.S.-led effort to cut off international aid and by IDF killings and mass arrests in Gaza and the West Bank.

Israel's unexpectedly massive response to Hizbullah's micro-level action was intended to change the balance of the game in favor of the Jewish state. The right wing of the Israeli political spectrum led by Likud had long been unhappy with former prime minister Ehud Barak's precipitous withdrawal from South Lebanon in May 2000. The next government, under Prime Minister Ariel Sharon, refrained from major offensives against Hizbullah presumably because it faced the second Palestinian Intifada. When Ehud Olmert became prime minister, however, the correlation of forces appeared to favor Israel. Thus, the strategic rationale for delivering what was planned to be a mortal blow to Hizbullah was based on several regional and domestic political factors.

The Palestinian Factor. The Intifada had been defeated and Palestinian attacks and suicide bombings had been reduced by IDF operations in the Palestinian lands, the building of a concrete barrier, and Israel's withdrawal from Gaza. The Hamas government elected in January 2006 had fallen into disarray amid internecine fighting and economic collapse, and was unable to prevent militants from firing rockets at Israeli border settlements. The weakness of the Hamas government provided a pretext for Israel to degrade Hamas by assassinations and imprisonment of its leading members. It may have seemed logical to the Olmert regime to next target Hizbullah—the only major ally of Hamas.

Signaling Iran, Syria, and other Arab States. The emergence of Iran as a major player in Middle East politics with influence in Lebanon, Syria, Iraq, and the Gulf region, represented a powerful long-term challenge to Israel. Iran's nuclear pretensions, oil wealth, and the confrontational tactics of President Mahmoud Ahmadinejad were seen as necessitating an Israeli response such as the destruction of Hizbullah, Iran's major ally in the Arab context, and the projection of Israel's awesome power in degrading Lebanon's infrastructure. Indeed, the demonstration effect of "shock-and-awe" tactics may have been another of Israel's periodic reminders to its neighbors about its unrivalled position of military superiority.

The American Connection. The diplomatic posture of the Bush administration indicated full U.S. backing for Israel's move against Lebanon. President Bush, more than any of his predecessors, had been an ardent and uncritical supporter of Israel. Clearly, the United States and Israel shared an interest in degrading Hizbullah's power to curb Iran's growing influence not only in Lebanon but also in Iraq, where the U.S. position faced challenges from pro-Iranian militias. Consequently, the United States made every effort to forestall any early attempt to stop the interactive violence, thereby giving the Israeli military a free hand in Lebanon. Both the United States and Israel showed no interest in a prisoner's dilemma situation involving third-party mediation or even indirect negotiations with Hizbullah—a nonstate entity classified by both states as a terrorist organization.

Olmert's Stratagem: Two-Level Game. The dynamic interaction between domestic politics and foreign policy and the leadership factor were essential determinants in Israel's decision to attack Lebanon. A civilian politician, Prime Minister Olmert lacked the charisma and military experience of his predecessor, Ariel Sharon, a factor that also constrained Defense Minister Amir Peretz. As the head of a coalition government, Olmert had to demonstrate toughness early in his tenure in order to upstage hawkish opponents in the Likud party led by Binyamin Netanyahu. Thus, given their lack of military experience and credibility, Olmert and Peretz were forced to cede power to the Israel Defense Forces and its Operations Department, which advocated the use of massive military force instead of negotiations with Hizbullah—a policy that Sharon had opposed during his tenure.[40] Olmert and his generals seem to have forgotten former defense minister Yitzak Rabin's ominous words about the consequences of Israel's 1982–1985 occupation of South Lebanon:

> I believe that among the many surprises, and most of them not for the good, that came out of the war in Lebanon, the most dangerous is that the war let the Shiites out of the bottle. No one predicted it; I couldn't find it in any intelligence report. . . . Lebanon will remain a center of terror. Terror cannot be finished by one war. It's total nonsense; it was an illusion. . . . If as a result of the war in Lebanon, we replace PLO terrorism in southern Lebanon with Shiite terrorism, we have done the worst [thing] in our struggle against terrorism. In twenty years of PLO terrorism, no one PLO terrorist [ever] made himself

[into] a live bomb. . . . In my opinion, the Shiites have the potential for a kind of terrorism that we have not yet experienced.[41]

Order of Preferences

An analysis of the strategic rationale and objectives of the warring sides suggests a ranking of their preferences during the war as follows:

Hizbullah	**Israel**

First Preference

Hizbullah	Israel
• Self-defense and protection of its constituents • Cease-fire and Israeli withdrawal from all Lebanese territory • Demonstration of Israel's military vulnerabilities • Free prisoners held in Israeli jails	• Hizbullah's disarmament and destruction • Demonstration effect of its military might in the region • Free two Israeli soldiers captured by Hizbullah • Sign a treaty with Lebanon, securing Israel's northern border with a UN-backed permanent multinational force • Establishment of a friendly regime in Beirut

Second Preference

Hizbullah	Israel
• Cease-fire and accept a peacekeeping force without giving up armaments or autonomy from the government in Beirut • Free prisoners in Israeli jails	• Degrade Hizbullah's power • Establish a broad security zone in South Lebanon to be policed by a large UN-backed multinational force, but without a peace treaty with Lebanon • Free Israeli soldiers in exchange for a limited number of Lebanese and Palestinian prisoners

Third Preference

Hizbullah	Israel
• Observe a temporary cease-fire • Retreat north to reorganize under UN and government constraints, without total disarmament.	• Accept a face-saving settlement involving multinational forces on both sides of the border backed by a Lebanese promise to restrain Hizbullah attacks on northern Israel • Free Israeli soldiers in exchange for a substantial number of Lebanese and Palestinian prisoners

Fourth Preference

Hizbullah	Israel
• Revert to clandestine guerrilla attacks and martyrdom operations against Israel, foreign troops in Lebanon, and the pro-West Lebanese regime in Beirut • Globalized terrorism versus Israel and United States	• A comprehensive settlement with Syria and Lebanon involving Israeli withdrawal from the Golan Heights, Shibaa Farms, East Jerusalem, and most other Palestinian territories • Agreement to pay reparations for attacks on civilians and infrastructure

Reaching an Equilibrium

In a face-off between a powerful conventional army and a determined popular insurgency, it would have been unlikely for either to
achieve their first preferences. Despite its élan for guerrilla combat and
martyrdom operations, Hizbullah simply lacked the power to defeat the
Israeli invasion or force IDF's retreat from all of Lebanon. Also, it was
unlikely that Israel would achieve its first preference of destroying
Hizbullah altogether. To be sure, in Lebanon, Israel had reverted to its
old strategic doctrine of employing massive force, which ensured a
short-term military victory but repeatedly failed to bring security since
the birth of the Jewish state. In the Middle East, all too often, old antagonists fail to learn from the past—there is not much of a "learning
curve" in updating their beliefs and preferences. Clearly, Hizbullah
chose to remember only its successes against Israel but not its enormous
losses due to Israel's military might. As for Israel, Prime Minister Olmert
sought to neutralize Hizbullah by massive force, which his seven predecessors had failed to do.

Israel's second preference—weakening Hizbullah and establishing
a security zone policed by a peacekeeping force—could be within reach
if a strong multinational force could be organized. However, it would be
difficult for Olmert to settle for his third or fourth preferences due to
opposition from Likud and IDF's doctrinaire hawks, especially after the
human losses suffered by Israel. Hizbullah might have to settle for its
second preference—accepting a cease-fire without giving up its arms or
autonomy. The current standoff could result in a new "equilibrium of
peace" in which neither side would be willing to pay the high costs of
switching their preferences.[42]

Prognosticating Consequences: Short- and Long-term

Prognostications of conflicts are risky because they usually depend
on past patterns of interactive behavior and fail to integrate the role of
unforeseen actors and events. On the basis of the principles of political
physics and game theory, several possible consequences could evolve
from the 2006 Hizbullah-Israel conflict. The first and worst possible outcome would be the renewal of armed conflict that could run the risk of
a larger war involving Syria, Iran, other Arab states, and the United
States. Should Hizbullah suffer defeat in such a war, it is likely to retreat,
go underground, and revert to terrorism both in Lebanon and against
Israeli interests abroad.

A second possible outcome would be an upsurge in Sunni jihadism
seeking to upstage what was perceived as Hizbullah's "victory" against Israel. In this case, Sunni jihadists would use Hizbullah's tactics and strate-

gies as a model for future attacks. After all, Hizbullah's pioneering implementation of the doctrine of Shiite martyrdom in the early 1980s against Israel and the United States acted as a powerful inducement for Sunni Islamists to match the Shiites' zeal and commitment; hence, the adoption of suicide martyrdom in the 1990s by Sunni Islamist groups—Hamas, Palestinian Islamic Jihad, al-Qaida, its affiliates, and others. Consequently, Hizbullah's summer 2006 war with Israel could energize the Sunni jihadi constituency to recruit new members and expand its terrorist reach. Notably, at the war's outset, there was a split between some Sunni Arab regimes (Egypt, Jordan, Saudi Arabia), which blamed Hizbullah for triggering Israel's attack on Lebanon, and their mostly Sunni citizens who tended to support Hizbullah. Should the Lebanese conflict escalate, with U.S. involvement, President Bush and Prime Minister Olmert might well succeed in bringing together Sunnis and Shiites despite deep-rooted animosities dating back to the seventh century. Indeed, there could be a revival of Sunni Islamist militancy against Sunni regimes for their impotence to prevent Lebanon's destruction by standing up to Israel and the United States.

A third possible outcome of the war is short- and long-term blowback. If violent actions have consequences, then leaders who use violence should assess the possible consequences of their actions. In the Arab-Israeli case, as in other conflicts, the decision to use violence is often driven by short-term gains, selfish calculations, and the psychopathologies of leaders on both sides. In such situations, feelings of vengeance, pride, and arrogance could dominate preference formation rather than objective strategic calculations to achieve clear goals. Was Hizbullah's capture of two Israeli soldiers on July 12 the result of Shaikh Nasrallah's sincere desire to exchange prisoners, or was it driven by his egoist compulsion to demonstrate continuing resistance to Israel, or even a persisting vow to take vengeance for his son, who died in 1997 while fighting Israel? Similarly, what was the logic of Israel's systematic degrading of Lebanon's infrastructure? These attacks on civilian targets beyond Hizbullah's strongholds clearly weakened the Lebanese democratic government and infuriated many Lebanese leaders and citizens belonging to the anti-Hizbullah coalition. The magnitude of the attacks could not be easily explained as serving Israel's national interest as they were seen as "war crimes" by human rights organizations.[43] Perhaps Israel sought to create a demonstration effect in Lebanon's ruination for what it saw as a unified front of enemies—Iran, Syria, Hizbullah, and Hamas—forgetting that each had distinct interests. A more probable explanation is that, after a quarter century of suffering casualties and failing to defeat Hizbullah, a vengeful IDF sought to punish all of Lebanon. While such vengeance might be humanly understandable, these acts could follow the law of unintended consequences—General Sharon's

1982 invasion to eject the PLO from South Lebanon gave birth to Hizbullah. Only time will tell what terrible birth could be forthcoming from Lebanon's hot summer of 2006.

Other possible short- and long-term consequences that could emerge from the Hizbullah-Israel 2006 war are:

1. A revival of the Shiite militant networks of the 1980s bringing together Hizbullah-affiliated groups in Iraq, the Arab gulf countries, and Iran, which would constitute a major threat to the U.S. and Western interests and oil supplies.
2. Heightened long-term U.S. vulnerability to terrorist attacks both within and outside the United States.
3. Israel's significant losses in the war could reduce the chances of a two-state solution based on Israeli withdrawal from the Palestinian lands in exchange for peace.
4. Hizbullah's unanticipated strength against a powerful army could encourage other non-state groups and movements in the Muslim world to challenge states, particularly those with low levels of legitimacy.

Kashmiri Separatists and Islamists versus India

The disputed territory of Kashmir has been one of India's most serious problems since its founding in 1947. In the mid-1980s, the Muslim majority of Kashmir began a separatist movement against India—a secular state with a Hindu majority. A decade later, what had started as a nationalist movement began to take an Islamist coloration, similar to transformations in the Chechen and Palestinian conflicts. However, the transition of the Kashmiri cause from a nationalist struggle to an Islamist jihad went further than those of Chechnya and Palestine, partly due to the close proximity of Pakistan and its Islamist grand strategy to counter India's superior power position.

Historical Origins

The Kashmir conflict arose from the partition of the British-ruled Indian subcontinent in 1947 into two independent states—India and Pakistan. Originally, the state of Jammu and Kashmir consisted of five regions—Jammu, Ladakh, Baltistan, Gilgit, and Kashmir Valley—populated by Hindus, Muslims, Sikhs, and Buddhists. In 1846, the area became one of over 560 small autonomous states ruled by maharajas as part of the British Empire. At the time of the partition in August 1947, the Hindu maharaja of Kashmir had opted not to join Muslim Pakistan

TABLE 4.3   Hizbullah versus Israel and the United States: Strategic Interactions, 1982–2006

Date	Actor and Type (or Event)	Target/Goal	Place	Death Toll/Outcome
June 1982	Israel Defense Forces (IDF) attack and invasion	PLO bases in Lebanon	Southern Lebanon and Beirut	800 civilians killed
Sept. 1982	Massacre by Maronite Phalangist militia allied with Israel	Palestinian and Shiite civilians	Sabra and Shatila refugee camps	63 killed
Apr. 1983	Islamic Jihad (Hizbullah) suicide truck bombing	U.S. Embassy	Beirut	63 killed
Oct. 1983	Islamic Jihad (Hizbullah) suicide truck bombing	U.S. Marines and French forces	Beirut	241 U.S. Marines and 58 French soldiers killed
Nov. 1983	Hizbullah car bomb	IDF	Tyre	50 killed
Mar. 1984	President Reagan orders withdrawal of U.S. Marines			
June 1984–June 1985	Series of Hizbullah bomb attacks	IDF posts	South Lebanon	46 killed
Sept. 1984	Islamic Jihad (Hizbullah) suicide truck bombing	U.S. Embassy Annex	Beirut	24 killed
Mid-1985	Israel withdraws its troops except in southern Lebanese "security zone" policed by South Lebanese Army (SLA) and IDF			14,000 killed on both sides since 1982
July 1985–May 2000	Hizbullah versus Israel/SLA; series of interactive attacks, mostly bombings, abductions, and assassinations		Mostly southern Lebanon and northern Israel	200+ killed

TABLE 4.3 Cont.   Hizbullah versus Israel and the United States: Strategic Interactions, 1982–2006

Date	Actor and Type (or Event)	Target/Goal	Place	Death Toll/Outcome
Feb. 1992	Israeli assassination	Shaikh Abbas al-Musawi, Secretary-General of Hizbullah	South Lebanon	8 killed; Hasan Nasrallah chosen as successor
Mar. 1992	Hizbullah suicide bombing	Israeli Embassy	Buenos Aires, Argentina	38 killed
July 1993	"Operation Accountability" launched by Israel	Hizbullah, Palestinian Front for the Liberation of Palestine–General Command (PFLP-GC)	South Lebanon	
July 1994	Hizbullah bombing in retaliation for assassination of Hizbullah operative Mustafa Dirani	Jewish cultural center	Buenos Aires, Argentina	95 killed
Apr. 1996	"Operation Grapes of Wrath" launched by Israel	Hizbullah	Beirut, South Lebanon, Biqaa, Qana	Hundreds dead (mostly civilians)
May 2000	Israel withdraws from South Lebanon/SLA collapses; Hizbullah declares "Liberation Day"			
Feb. 2005	Assassination of former Lebanese PM in car bomb attack	Former prime minister Rafiq Hariri	Beirut	23 killed
Apr. 2005	Syrian forces leave Lebanon			
July–Aug. 2006	Israel invades Lebanon after Hizbullah captures two IDF soldiers	Hizbullah positions in south Lebanon and Biqaa; Lebanese infrastructure		1,100 Lebanese, 160 Israelis killed

despite the two-thirds Muslim majority in his princedom. Facing a Muslim insurgency and a Pakistani invasion, the maharaja requested Indian military assistance in exchange for the accession of Kashmir to India. The ensuing first India-Pakistan war (1947–1949) ended in a UN-arranged cease-fire to be followed by a referendum to determine Kashmir's future, which was never held due to India's refusal. The cease-fire line became the *de facto* border, with India controlling two-thirds and Pakistan one-third of the territory of Kashmir. The Indian portion, known as Jammu and Kashmir, became a constituent state of the Indian union with its own constitution and elected government—an arrangement rejected by Pakistan.[44] In the next half-century the Kashmir issue would be a primary trigger of Indian-Pakistani wars and armed confrontations as well as interactive terrorism between India and Kashmiri separatists and Islamist groups.[45]

India versus Pakistan: Strategic Interaction, 1962–1989

Using a game theoretic analysis, the Kashmir dispute can be depicted as a two-level game where the interaction between the Indian authorities and the Kashmiri militants operates within the larger context of Indian-Pakistani relations. Thus, the dynamics of the Kashmir conflict have both affected and been affected by the correlation of forces between India and Pakistan.

India and Pakistan were born in a common crucible of violence in 1947, amid communal killings, population exchanges, and war over Kashmir. While both sides continued to claim all of Kashmir, India was prepared to accept Kashmir's division along the 1949 cease-fire line, which Pakistan adamantly rejected. Indeed, the seeds of conflict lay in the inherent asymmetry of power between a large, populous, and wealthier India and a smaller and weaker Pakistan. In order to resolve its security dilemma, Pakistan persistently sought to counterbalance its neighbor's power through wars, coalition and alliance formation, acquisition of nuclear weaponry, and sponsorship of insurgency and terrorism in Kashmir and in India itself. India attempted to block Pakistan's moves, seeking to retain its strategic superiority at all cost.

The major moves by the protagonists, as shown in Figure 4.1, are instructive in understanding the logic of their strategic interaction.

FIGURE 4.1   India versus Pakistan: Strategic Interactions, 1947–1989

1947–1949	First India-Pakistan war; Kashmir divided at cease-fire line
1954–1955	Pakistan joins U.S.-led Western coalition against communist bloc; India sponsors establishment of Nonaligned Movement, a coalition of Third World states opposed to taking sides in the Cold War
1962–1963	Pakistan signs border treaty with China; India loses border war with China; Pakistan-China relations and India–Soviet Union ties strengthened
1965	Second India-Pakistan war starts with Pakistan's offensive in Kashmir and Indian counterattack on Lahore (August–September 1965); UN- sponsored cease-fire followed by mutual declaration to solve disputes peacefully
1971	Third India-Pakistan war as the secessionist Awami League wins election in East Pakistan, triggering genocidal massacres by the Pakistani Army that prompts Indian intervention and defeat of Pakistan; East Pakistan declares independence from Pakistan as the state of Bangladesh
1974	India detonates underground nuclear weapons
1975–1989	The separation of East Pakistan and defeat by India in 1971 were cataclysmic losses for Pakistan; Pakistan counteracts India's growing strength by developing nuclear weapons and taking a leadership role in the Islamist coalition to fight the Soviets in Afghanistan

Already beset by internal rebellions and military coups, Pakistan sought to counteract India's growing strength utilizing seven interrelated strategies. Pakistan first aimed to expand and strengthen its alliance with the United States for superpower protection and acquisition of military and economic aid. Second, Pakistan strengthened its ties with China to increase trade and military cooperation. Third, Pakistan sought to obtain nuclear capabilities, with Chinese help. Fourth, Pakistan adopted Islamist ideology and legal precepts to socialize and mobilize its population against India, expand ties with conservative Sunni states, and benefit from their oil wealth and diplomatic clout. Fifth, Pakistan joined a U.S.-led coalition of Western and Muslim states in 1980–1989 and provided a land bridge to mobilize the Afghan Mujahidin against the communist regime and its Soviet allies. This move gave Pakistan access to material and military benefits while allowing it to project power into Afghanistan in a move to acquire "geostrategic depth" and the support of Afghan Pashtun tribes against India. Sixth, Pakistan employed its newly acquired assets from the growing global Islamist coalition to restart the struggle over Kashmir by sponsoring separatist movements backed by jihadist violence. Finally, Pakistan encouraged India's Muslim minority population to engage in Islamist subversion and carry out jihadist attacks in India.

The combination of strategies adopted by Pakistan to deal with its security dilemma were seemingly rational responses of a weaker power seeking to equalize a stronger neighbor. Indeed, after its third defeat and loss of Bengal in 1971, Pakistan viewed itself as facing an existential threat necessitating a series of strategic moves, the most important of which was to become a leading member of the anticommunist grand alliance in Afghanistan. Although this ambitious stratagem brought significant economic and military gains to Pakistan, it also produced some long-term losses—domestic instability and increased risk of armed conflict with India. By pursuing the Islamist option in supporting the jihadist cause in Afghanistan, Pakistan increasingly adopted a semi-theocratic form of internal governance backed by the military. As a result, attempts at democratization were thwarted, as Islamist parties came to dominate the public discourse, the political process, and social relations within the framework of Islamic law.[46] In the late 1980s, flush with the Islamist successes in Afghanistan, the Pakistani leadership returned to its fundamental strategic objective—equalizing the asymmetry of power with India by reopening its Kashmir option.

India versus Pakistan: Order of Preferences on Kashmir

In analyzing six decades of military conflict over Kashmir, interrupted by peace talks, one can set forth an approximate ordering of the preferences of the two sides. These preferences constitute the framework of strategic action in which the Kashmiri struggle against India unfolded.

India	**Pakistan**
First Preference	
• Retain control of Indian part of Kashmir (status quo)	• Annex Indian-controlled Kashmir
Second Preference	
• Division of Indian-held Kashmir — ceding Muslim Northern Areas to Pakistan and retaining Buddhist Ladakh, majority Hindu Jammu, and the Kashmir Valley	• Division of Indian-held Kashmir in favor of Pakistan—to acquire Muslim Northern Areas and the Muslim parts of Jammu and Kashmir Valley
Third Preference	
• Self-governing secular Kashmir state with special ties to India	• Self-governing Islamist Kashmir state with special ties to Pakistan

• Both India and Pakistan are opposed to full independence for a united Kashmir state

Kashmir Separatists versus India, 1986–1989

Although the Indian Constitution granted Kashmir autonomous status, there were growing demands for greater autonomy or independence during the mid-1980s because of turmoil among the local political parties and conflict with the central government in New Delhi. After the United Muslim Front lost the 1987 state legislative election, it accused the government of rigging the contest and resorted to violence. In July 1988, the Jammu and Kashmir Liberation Front (JKLF) bombed two sites in Srinagar, followed by kidnappings in exchange for militants held in Indian jails. Although supported by Pakistan, JKLF was committed to Kashmiri nationalism (Kashmiriyat) and independence from India.[47] Thus, the Kashmiri nationalists' first preference conflicted with Pakistan's first preference of annexing Indian-controlled Kashmir. As a result, the Pakistani military's Inter Services Intelligence (ISI) formed several Islamist militant groups ideologically committed to a Pan-Islamic agenda aiming for the eventual absorption of Kashmir into the Islamic Republic of Pakistan. What began as a secular separatist struggle for independence by Kashmir's Muslim majority was transformed into a religious jihad against India—defined by the Islamists as an "infidel" Hindu state. Among the targets of the insurgents were government buildings, military and police headquarters, Hindu shrines and pilgrims, tourists, election rallies, Kashmiri and Indian political leaders, and the civilian population. The methods of attack included car bombs, land mines, suicide bombings, improvised explosive devices, and coordinated guerrilla raids to massacre large numbers of Hindu civilians and engage in ethnic cleansing operations designed to rid Kashmir of Hindus and other minorities.[48]

Islamist Jihadists versus India, 1989–1999

The Islamization of the Kashmir insurgency to serve Pakistani national interests proved an effective stratagem in harming India and its democratic development. In employing this stratagem, Pakistan's ISI possessed considerable resources in expertise, manpower, and religious fervor. After a decade of stewardship over the Mujahidin insurgency in Afghanistan in the 1980s, ISI leaders simply redeployed their organizational, tactical, and human resources to mobilize Islamist militants in Kashmir and in India proper. As a result, the Kashmiri nationalist elements of JKLF were marginalized and replaced by radical Islamists, while ISI created competing jihadist groups to ensure control over the militants.[49] Meanwhile, an Islamization drive sponsored by ISI aimed to replace the predominantly Sufi culture of Kashmiri Muslims with the strict Sunni Islamism that had been adopted in Pakistan under the military dictatorship of Ziya al-Haq (1977–1989)—the same jihadist Islamism that nurtured the Afghani Mujahidin and ultimately al-Qaida. Because the lethal impact of the Kashmiri militant groups proved inadequate when confronted by India's counterinsurgency measures, ISI deployed non-Kashmiris such as Afghans, Pakistanis, and Middle Eastern jihadists left jobless after the anti-Soviet struggle in Afghanistan. The use of these seasoned Islamist militants by ISI in 1992–1993 represented a major escalation of violence triggering more extensive Indian security measures including police, special forces manned by Kashmiri Muslims, and Indian counterinsurgency units backed by thousands of troops facing the Pakistani-controlled areas of Kashmir. The Indian government's repressive policies were condemned by human rights organizations. These measures included acts of terrorism, which tended to push nationalist Kashmiri youth to join the Islamist groups being trained in Pakistan. Consequently, these attacks progressively intensified, reaching a peak in 1994 with over 6,000 incidents. Meanwhile, the upsurge of Islamist militancy in Kashmir contributed to a growing Hindu fundamentalist fervor in India encouraged by extremist groups within the Bharatiya Janata Party (BJP).[50] The destruction of a mosque in Ayodha in 1992 by Hindu mobs marked the onset of communal rioting between Muslims and Hindus in Mumbai claiming 800 lives, followed by Islamist bombings in the city, killing 250 people and destroying the stock exchange. The Mumbai bombings signaled the opening of a second front of Islamist terrorism directed at India's economic infrastructure and civilian population.

On the Kashmir front, the Indian government responded with a massive security crackdown combined with the reinstatement of democratic governance in 1996 under Chief Minister Dr. Farooq Abdullah and the appropriation of expenditures to spur economic development. These measures, backed by Prime Minister Atal Vajpayee's unilateral cease-fire of November 1997, were welcomed by the secessionist All Party Hurriyat Conference, while facing rejection from the foreign jihadist groups fighting a proxy war for Pakistan such as Hizb-ul-Mujahidin, Jaish-e-Muhammad, Lashkar-e-Taiba, Al-Badr, and Harakat-ul-Mujahidin, all of which operated under the United Jihad Council.[51] Clearly, after two decades of interactive violence, there continued to be a fundamental difference in the objectives of Pakistan (and its jihadist proxies) and the Kashmiri leadership; yet, India could not fully exploit the split because of its heavy-handed policies and the jihadists' assassinations of the moderate Kashmiri Muslim leaders. At the onset of their quest for autonomy and independence in the mid-1980s, the Kashmiri leaders had welcomed Pakistani and Islamist support to achieve their goal. However, they soon discovered that they could not be "free riders" to independence—the price for external support was agreeing to

Kashmir's incorporation into Pakistan.[52] For Pakistan, the continuation of the Kashmir struggle remained a major instrument in its overall long-term strategy to match India's superior power position, which culminated in a violent face-off in 1998–1999 that threatened to transform a low-intensity conflict into a full-scale interstate nuclear war.

Kargil: An Equilibrium of Terror, 1999

In the late 1990s, Pakistan's persistent quest to upgrade its inferior power position vis-à-vis India had succeeded on three fronts. First, the Kashmiri separatist struggle had been transformed into a Pakistan-sponsored Pan-Islamist terrorist movement in Kashmir and India. Second, in Afghanistan the ultra-conservative Taliban regime had been established and could provide both geostrategic depth and jihadist recruits for any future war with India because it was based mostly on Pashtun Afghans and their kinfolk from Pakistan's northern provinces. Finally, Pakistan had acquired nuclear weaponry and delivery systems to balance India's nuclear capabilities.

Emboldened by these new strategic advantages, the Pakistani military chose to escalate the conflict on the Kashmir front in June 1999. The strategic logic of this move was that a "nuclear equilibrium" had been reached when India and Pakistan tested their nuclear weapons in April 1998. This equilibrium would serve as a shield for Pakistan to conduct low-intensity warfare while deterring a major Indian offensive.[53] Some Pakistani military strategists even asserted that the nuclear stand-off would permit the employment of a small military force to alter Kashmir's political and territorial status quo.[54] Furthermore, linking its nuclear capabilities to the Kashmir conflict, Pakistan sought to internationalize it, and attempted to force India to permit outside mediation. These strategic moves formed the background of the summer 1999 conflict as waves of well-equipped Islamist militants and Kashmiri separatists crossed the Line of Control to occupy Indian territory near Kargil. These guerrilla forces included regular Pakistani troops backed by artillery and air strikes that were reciprocated by the Indian side. After two months of fighting, the militants were forced to withdraw as the Clinton administration prevailed upon Pakistan to end the conflict.[55] However, the U.S. involvement did not result in a full-scale prisoner's dilemma situation because of India's opposition to internationalizing the Kashmir conflict.

Conflict Resolution, 2000–2006

Driven by rational calculations of self-interest, in fall 1999 India and Pakistan stepped back from risking nuclear war and began the complex process of reaching a settlement. As a direct result of the Kargil war, Prime Minister Nawaz Sharif's government was replaced in October 1999 by a military regime led by Gen. Pervez Musharraf. In July 2000, Hizb-ul-Mujahidin, one of the main militant groups, declared a cease-fire with Pakistan's approval. India followed suit with a cease-fire in November, but other pro-Pakistan groups continued the armed struggle, demanding that Pakistan be a participant in the negotiations. For its part, India's strategy aimed at dividing the Kashmiri separatist groups from the Islamists allied to the Pakistani regime. In spring 2001, India made a new attempt to start peace talks by inviting General Musharraf to New Delhi, followed by a summit meeting in Agra with Prime Minister Vajpayee. These meetings were inconclusive because India insisted that Pakistan stop supporting "cross-border terrorism," as Pakistan pressed India to recognize Kashmir as the "core issue" between the two countries.[56] However, three ensuing events in 2001 would transform the India-Pakistan confrontation into a trilateral prisoner's dilemma situation.

Nuclear Compellence: Prisoner's Dilemma, September 11, 2001–October 16, 2002

The September 11, 2001, attacks on the United States reconfigured the global strategic landscape and the context of the Indian-Pakistani conflict. As a prime supporter of the Taliban regime, Pakistan was given inducements to join President Bush's "war on terror" against al-Qaida's cadres in Afghanistan. Despite strong Islamist opposition at home, Musharraf succeeded in reorienting Pakistan's strategic posture to assist the U.S. operations against the Taliban and al-Qaida in Afghanistan. However, this reorientation did not apply to Pakistan's relations with India. In the midst of the global revulsion against terrorism after September 11, 2001, a car bomb, detonated by Jaysh-e-Muhammad on October 1 near the Kashmiri state assembly in Srinagar, killed 38 people. An attack on the Indian Parliament in New Delhi followed on December 13, 2001, killing 14 people, while over 200 ministers and members of parliament escaped unhurt. These strikes at the epicenters of India's democratic life provoked a major military buildup on the India-Pakistan border in pursuit of a new Indian strategy of coercive diplomacy—"compellence."[57] The strategy of compellence represents a mix of aggressive diplomacy backed by overwhelming power by state A to compel state B to comply, in a short time-period, with A's demands, under the threat or use of force.[58] To compel Pakistan to stop supporting "cross-border terrorism," India was counting on the superiority of its nuclear and conventional forces over those of Pakistan.

Alarmed by India's massive military buildup, the United States immediately engaged in "trilateral compellence" because of the possibility that a conventional war would turn into a cataclysmic nuclear exchange.[59] A trilateral compellence is a prisoner's dilemma game in which the antagonists attempt to use the "jailer-mediator" as a conduit to force changes in each other's behavior. Thus, India used compellence to threaten Pakistan directly, while applying indirect pressure on Pakistan through the United States. In addition, both India and Pakistan utilized the fear of nuclear war to invite the United States to intervene and force concessions from the other side.[60]

The trilateral compellence strategy yielded inconclusive results. Although nuclear war was avoided and there were temporary reductions in the infiltration of fighters across the Line of Control in Kashmir, India failed to compel Pakistan to stop supporting the jihadists. In January 2002, President Musharraf banned Lashkar-e-Taiba and four other militant groups and made other gestures to placate India. However, there was no let up in violence in Kashmir and other Indian states, including major bombings in Mumbai (2003), New Delhi (2005), Varanasi (2006), and seven commuter trains, again in Mumbai (2006). Despite a four-year peace process from 2002–2006, the losses mounted on both sides. Increasingly, the Kashmir struggle had been transformed from an ethno-nationalist to a religious "holy war" against India by pro-Pakistan Islamist militants, who now included some jihadists belonging to India's Muslim minority. Meanwhile, the growth of militant Islamism in Pakistan had constrained Musharraf's efforts to reach a settlement on Kashmir and to take aggressive action against his domestic jihadist constituency. Several jihadist attempts in 2003 to assassinate Musharraf for his cooperation with U.S. efforts against al-Qaida reflected the vulnerability of the General's regime from home-based militants. In the near term, India and Pakistan are likely to remain at a dangerous nuclear equilibrium with little prospect of a peaceful future.

Hamas versus Israel

The bloody confrontation between Israel and Hamas represents the latest manifestation of the larger conflict between Israelis and Palestinians, itself a subset of the century-long Arab-Israeli struggle. The beginnings of the Arab-Israeli conflict are rooted in the final decades of the collapsing Ottoman Empire at the onset of the twentieth century. The struggle began as a clash of two emerging ethnic nationalisms with a coinciding territorial claim centering on the Holy Land in the Palestinian province of the Ottoman Empire. After six major wars, interspersed with periods of peace and low-intensity violence, the Arab-Israeli conflict remains mostly unresolved. While it has signed peace accords with Egypt and Jordan, Israel remains in a state of belligerency with Syria and Lebanon and retains partial control in the West Bank and Gaza.

Israel's establishment and success in defeating repeated Arab challenges since its founding in 1948 has had powerful repercussions in the Arab world and the greater Islamic orbit, triggering coups d'état and revolutions and contributing to a fundamental ideological reorientation among broad segments of the populace, from secular nationalism to theocratic Islamism. This ideological transformation beginning in the 1960s produced a plethora of extremist groups opposing Arab governments, the United States, and Israel in the name of Islam. What had begun as an ethno-nationalist struggle over territory has assumed a religious coloration evoking deep spiritual commitment and mass mobilization in defense of Islam. At the dawn of the twenty-first century, Islamic revivalism had become a global movement with Islamist groups in every Muslim country and in expatriate communities worldwide, many with political agendas and militant dispositions. One of these Islamist movements is Hamas—representing the partial transformation of secular Palestinian nationalism into an Islamist Palestinian identity as a mobilizing venue to oppose the Israeli state.

Historical Background, 1250 BC–1948

The settlement of Israelites in the land of Canaan dates back to 1250 B.C. The temple in Jerusalem, built during King Solomon's rule (961–922 B.C.) was destroyed by the Babylonians in 586 B.C. and later rebuilt. In 63 B.C. the last Jewish state, Judea, became part of the Roman province of Palestine. An unsuccessful Jewish revolt in 70 A.D. resulted in the sacking of Jerusalem and the destruction of the Second Temple, marking the onset of Jewish dispersion—the Diaspora. In response to another Jewish revolt in 133 A.D. during Emperor Hadrian's rule, the Romans completely destroyed Jerusalem, driving its people into exile and slavery. After the Christianization of the Roman Empire in 312 A.D., Palestine came under Byzantine rule until its conquest in 638 A.D. by Arab Muslim armies. Except for control by the European Crusaders from 1099–1187, various Muslim dynasts ruled the region until the 1918 defeat of the Ottoman Empire in World War I.

Zionism and Arab Nationalism

European antisemitism and pogroms and persecutions in the Russian Empire led to the rise of Jewish nationalism aiming to establish a secure national home for the Jewish people. Inspired by Theodor Herzl's 1896 book, *Der Judenstaat* (*The Jewish State*), the World Zionist Organization was founded expressly to promote the establishment of a Jewish state in Palestine. As a result of Zionist immigration in the late nineteenth and early twentieth centuries, 85,000 Jews were living among 600,000 indigenous Arabs at the outbreak of World War I.[61]

The last decades of the nineteenth century also witnessed the emergence of Arab nationalism as a movement of emancipation from Ottoman Turkish rule. Developments during and after the war set the stage for the clash between the Arab nationalist and Zionist movements that provided the backdrop to the protracted violence in the Middle East until the present time. Driven by the imperative of winning the war against the Ottoman-German alliance, Britain had made three contradictory promises it could not fulfill after the war. Britain promised the Arabs independent statehood as a reward for participating in the 1916 Arab Revolt against the Turks. Britain also promised to view favorably the establishment of a Jewish national home in Palestine, in a 1917 letter by British foreign minister Arthur Balfour, which came to be known as the Balfour Declaration. Finally, Britain promised to give France some land in the Arab provinces of the Ottoman Empire.

Instead of being granted independence, the Arab lands were divided into British and French mandates, with Palestine placed under British control. The next two decades were marked by repeated clashes growing out of Arab opposition to the arrival of thousands of Jews escaping Nazi oppression and genocide. Unable to contain the escalating Jewish-Arab violence, Britain turned to the UN for a solution. In November 1947, the UN General Assembly voted for a plan to partition Palestine, giving 56 percent to a Jewish state and 43 percent to an Arab state, with an international zone around Jerusalem. While the Jewish side accepted the partition plan, the Palestinian Arab leadership rejected it because it failed to recognize the majority status of the Arab community. In the ensuing communal war, Jewish forces succeeded in defeating the Palestinian militias as well as the armies of Jordan, Egypt, Lebanon, Syria, and Iraq that had entered the war after the proclamation of Israeli statehood on May 14, 1948. Thousands of Palestinian Arabs fled the fighting, terrorized by the massacre of Deir Yassin committed by the Jewish extremist groups, Irgun and Lehi. At the end of the fighting, Israel controlled 75 percent of what had been the British Mandate of Palestine, while Jordan annexed the West Bank and East Jerusalem and Egypt kept the Gaza Strip. By early 1949, there were nearly 750,000 Palestinians living in refugee camps in Jordan, Gaza, Lebanon, Syria, and other countries.[62]

Israel versus PLO and Arab Coalitions, 1949–1967

Israel's creation represented a catastrophe to Palestinian Arabs and humiliation to the newly independent Arab states. The defeated Arab armies came home to overthrow civilian governments and establish military regimes that became an enduring feature of the Arab political landscape for the next six decades. The Arabs' strategic responses to counteract Israel's emergence took three dimensions. The first Arab strategic response was the formation of alliances and unity schemes among the Arab states under the banner of Pan-Arabism—an ideological umbrella subsuming the powerful nationalist sentiments sweeping the Arab world. Another strategic response was the quest for external allies to acquire modern weaponry, economic aid and political support, and the final strategic response was the employment of nonconventional warfare, including guerrilla operations by Palestinian fighters.

These strategies were not fully effective due to Arab rivalries, failures in collective action, and the nature of Israeli responses. Despite the grassroots strength of the Pan-Arab movement, symbolized by Egyptian president Gamal Abd al-Nasser, most Arab regimes were unwilling to coalesce against their common foe because of inter-Arab conflicts and divisions brought on by the Cold War. Meanwhile, the growing anti-Western tenor of Arab nationalist sentiments had prompted Nasser to join the nonaligned bloc and break the West's arms embargo by securing weapons from the Soviet Union. These acts of defiance culminated in Nasser's 1956 nationalization of the Suez Canal Company, triggering a tripartite Anglo-French-Israeli invasion of Egypt's Sinai Peninsula in the 1956 Suez War. Egypt's defeat by this powerful coalition of forces turned into a moral victory when joint U.S. and Soviet pressure forced the total withdrawal of the invading armies.[63] Yet the war's outcome also benefited Israel because of Egypt's demilitarization of the Gulf of Aqaba and the establishment of the UN Emergency Force (UNEF) to prevent Palestinian militants from attacking Israel from the Egyptian-controlled Gaza Strip. These gains were outweighed by certain consequences for Israel and the West. The blowback from the Suez War included the following outcomes:

1. radicalization of the Arab nationalist movement
2. overthrow of the pro-Western Hashemite monarchy in Iraq (June 1958)
3. civil war in Lebanon (1958)
4. destabilization of the pro-Western Jordanian monarchy
5. formation of the United Arab Republic with Syria and Egypt (1958)
6. closer economic and political ties between Egypt, Syria, and the Soviet Union
7. emergence of a Palestinian national movement to challenge Israel

The Palestinian Liberation Organization (PLO), created in January 1964 at the Arab Summit in Morocco, was tasked to unite all Palestinian militant groups fighting Israel. In 1966–1967, the resurgence of

Palestinian attacks through Jordan provoked major Israeli counterattacks and mounting tensions that prompted Egypt to demand the removal of UNEF contingents, remilitarize the Sinai, and prohibit Israeli navigation in the Gulf of Aqaba. These provocations led to massive Israeli air strikes beginning on June 5, 1967, that destroyed the air forces of Egypt and the neighboring Arab states, and was followed by rapid advances on land. These advances led to the capture of the Sinai and Gaza from Egypt, the West Bank and Jerusalem from Jordan, and Syria's Golan Heights. While awaiting the start of a mediation effort promised by the Johnson administration, the Arab regimes were caught by complete surprise by the onset of the 1967 Six-Day War, which radically changed the Middle East's geopolitical map and produced a deep ideological shift that would shape Arab beliefs and behavior into the twenty-first century.

Tipping Points toward Radicalism, June 1967–October 1973

Victory in June 1967 transformed Israel into the Middle East's hegemonic power capable of projecting its might to the far reaches of the Arab world. Over a million Palestinian Arabs in the West Bank and Gaza were now brought under Israeli control, and would become the source of opposition and violence, especially as a direct result of confiscations of land and the spread of Jewish settlements. Meanwhile, the defeat delegitimized the Arab governments because of their impotence against Israel, while the PLO factions emerged as heroes—*fidaiyin*—sacrificing themselves in fighting the Israeli occupation. In the ensuing two decades of interactive terrorism (1968–1988), PLO factions attacked Israeli military and civilian targets in Israel and in some European countries, paying a heavy price in Israeli reprisals.[64]

Among the negative outcomes of the Six-Day War for the United States was the significant harm to its interests in the region. Grassroots pressures forced many Arab governments to sever diplomatic relations with Washington and close down U.S. military installations. The reluctance of the Johnson and Nixon administrations to play an effective mediating role and their inaction in pushing for Israeli withdrawal under UN Security Council Resolution 242 confirmed Arab suspicions of U.S. complicity in the 1967 war.[65]

By 1973, all diplomatic efforts to regain the Arab lands lost in 1967 through U.S. mediation had failed, and the Nixon presidency was incapacitated by the Watergate scandal. On October 6, 1973, Egypt and Syria launched major offensives against Israel on Yom Kippur, coinciding with the Muslim observance of Ramadan. Early Arab territorial gains were later partially reversed by Israel at great human cost—the approximate losses of the war were 6,000 Israeli and 8,500 Egyptian and Syrian soldiers.[66] A cease-fire was advanced under UN Security Council Resolution 338, as Saudi Arabia led a five-month oil embargo against states supporting Israel, causing steep increases in prices and major shortages worldwide. The situation called for U.S. diplomatic intervention as Secretary of State Henry Kissinger initiated a protracted prisoner's dilemma process leading to the phased withdrawal of Israeli forces from the Sinai. The Carter administration's attempts to continue Kissinger's work were interrupted by the May 1977 victory of the right-wing Herut (Likud) party led by Menachem Begin. Dedicated to the concept of "Greater Israel," the Begin regime intensified building of Jewish settlements in the occupied lands to foreclose the possibility of any future compromise with the Palestinians. The impasse between Egypt and Israel was broken when President Sadat circumvented Carter's prisoner's dilemma process by flying directly to meet Begin in Jerusalem. After lengthy negotiations requiring Carter's personal involvement, Israel and Egypt signed the Camp David Accords in September 1978, which only promised limited autonomy to the Palestinians and no settlement on Jerusalem.[67] Now Israel had succeeded in isolating Egypt from its Arab allies, which rejected the terms of the settlement and declared a boycott of the most powerful Arab country. The PLO joined the Arab rejectionist states as it continued attacks on Israel, while gaining world recognition as the legitimate representative of Palestinian Arabs. However, hidden behind the drama of diplomatic activity and the ongoing violence between the PLO and Israel, a fundamental shift had occurred in the cultural substructure of Arab societies from secular Arab nationalism to Islamic fundamentalism. Defeated by Israel, humiliated by the West, and deceived by their governments, the Arab masses were turning to Islamism as a medium of spiritual salvation, political mobilization, and violence.[68]

PLO to Hamas: Nationalism to Islamism

Israel's June 1982 invasion of Lebanon effectively degraded the PLO's coercive potential and forced the expulsion of its fighters from Beirut. From his new headquarters in Tunisia, PLO leader Yasser Arafat faced difficulties in controlling the diverse armed factions within the organization, as dissident Palestinian groups challenged the PLO's authority and pursued their own radical agendas in fighting Israel.[69] Meanwhile, despair, hopelessness, and anger were spreading among the Palestinians in the West Bank and Gaza, caught in the throes of a seemingly interminable Israeli occupation. These crisis factors led to the explosion of a rebellion in December 1987—an unplanned, spontaneous popular uprising known as the Intifada. During the next six years, the Intifada was conducted through civil disobedience, strikes, boycotts, protests and stone-throwing against heavily armed Israeli occupation forces.[70] This protracted conflict claimed over 1,000 lives, drawing world attention to the plight of the Palestinians.[71]

Although the Intifada began in a leadership vacuum, the PLO quickly moved in to take the leading role in directing the uprising. However, as the Intifada unfolded, the PLO faced unprecedented challenges to its position as the sole representative of the Palestinian people from Hamas, an acronym for Harakat al-Muqawama al-Islamiya (Islamic Resistance Movement).[72] Hamas presented its ideology as an Islamist alternative to the PLO's secular nationalist creed. In 1988, as the PLO denounced violence in favor of diplomacy to achieve a two-state solution through dialogue with Israel, Hamas pressed for a more militant Islamist strategy that included employment of jihadist terrorism to disrupt the emerging peace process. The failures of successive Israeli governments and Yasser Arafat during the 1990s to reach agreement on a viable Palestinian state, helped to strengthen Hamas and more extremist Islamist groups in the occupied territories. In the midst of protracted crises threatening their very existence, many Palestinians were increasingly turning from PLO's secular nationalism to embrace the Islamist alternative. Indeed, given the harsh circumstances of Israeli occupation, it was ironic that the Palestinians' shift toward Islamism, extending from the first Intifada (1987–1993) to the second Intifada (2000–2005), lagged behind that of other Arab/Muslim countries.[73] Yet, in its Palestinian configuration, the Islamism of Hamas embodied the nationalist aspirations of the Palestinian people while providing a religious framework for their struggle.

Hamas: Origins and Development, 1967–1987

Hamas represents the militant expression of Palestinian Islamism growing out of the Muslim Brotherhood (MB) of Egypt and its affiliates who had fought the Jews and the British authorities in Palestine. After Israel's founding, MB flourished both in the West Bank and Gaza, although in 1954, its activities were banned in Gaza by President Nasser's nationalist regime. Israel's 1967 occupation of these two Palestinian enclaves opened the gates to extensive Islamist proselytizing and activism led by MB clerics. The spread and success of the MB's activities were due in large measure to the permissive policies of the Israeli administration toward Islamic social and cultural endeavors.[74] Israel's leniency toward Hamas sharply contrasted with its repressive measures against PLO's activities, viewed as a direct threat to Israeli control because of PLO's greater popularity in the occupied lands. Israel had chosen to undermine the secular PLO by favoring the MB's Islamists in the 1970s, only to face a greater peril from MB's jihadist progeny—Hamas—in the 1980s–1990s.[75]

In contrast to the West Bank's milder form of Islamism, the MB in Gaza displayed greater dynamism and radicalism because of desperate socioeconomic conditions, Shaikh Ahmad Yassin's charismatic leadership and geographical contiguity with Egypt, which permitted MB's Cairo militants to exercise direct influence over its Gaza branches. A disciple of Sayyid Qutb, Egypt's radical Islamist ideologue, Shaikh Yassin worked diligently between 1967–1976 to establish the MB's institutional and social infrastructure in the Gaza Strip based on *dawah*— the inculcation of Islamist teachings through preaching and education.[76] In 1973, he established the Islamic Center—al-Mujamma al-Islami—to build grassroots structures, centered on mosques, dedicated to combining Islamist ideology and practice through worship, education, and social welfare networks. In the late 1970s and 1980s, the Mujamma expanded its reach into civil society, penetrating the professional associations and taking over mosques and universities, often using coercive methods. Its growing popularity and activities generously funded by wealthy Arab countries and donors, brought the Mujamma into conflict with PLO's al-Fatah and leftist factions, which often ended in violence.

Mujamma to Hamas: Ideological and Strategic Shifts

Mujamma's ideology mirrored that of Egypt's Muslim Brotherhood, which had created and nurtured the group as its Palestinian extension. The MB's basic strategy toward the transformation of the social and political order has been one of gradualism, not revolutionary change.[77] Since its founding by an Egyptian schoolteacher, Hasan al-Banna, in 1928, the MB has been unwaveringly committed to Islamic revivalism by Islamizing society as a prelude to Islamizing the state. Thus, its dominant strategy is to proceed gradually because of the age-old opposition of Sunni Islamist doctrine to creating civil discord—*fitnah*— against Muslim rulers, as well as the risks entailed in using anti-state violence. MB's gradualist strategy guided Mujamma's focus on grassroots preaching and institutional development under the guise of religious education, rather than adopting PLO's tactics of political confrontation with the Israeli military administration. The fact that Mujamma's Islamist message contained potent political symbols pointing to jihadism did not seem to bother the Israeli administration, which was still focused on suppressing PLO's nationalists and leftists and emerging youthful jihadist groups, the largest being Islamic Jihad.[78] However, the continuing radicalization of the Palestinian struggle inexorably pushed Yassin's Mujamma toward armed confrontation with Israel as Table 4.4 shows.

TABLE 4.4   Hamas versus Israel: Strategic Interactions, 1973–2006

Date	Actor and Type (or Event)	Target/Goal	Place	Death Toll/Outcome
1973	Establishment of al-Mujamma al-Islami by Shaikh Yassin as a branch of Muslim Brotherhood	To establish an Islamist order to counter PLO's secularism and Israeli power	Gaza	Build vast network of mosques, schools, and social service agencies
1984–1985	Israel arrests Shaikh Yassin on weapons charges	Israeli policy switch from tolerance to suppression of Mujamma's militancy	Gaza	Released in prisoner exchange
Dec. 1987	Outbreak of First Intifada	Resistance to Israeli occupation	Israel and the occupied territories	1,230 killed through Sept. 1993 on both sides
Dec. 1987	Establishment of Hamas as Mujamma's fighting force	Organized resistance to Israel	Gaza and West Bank	
1988–1991	Demonstrations, rock throwing, and sporadic attacks by Palestinian Islamic Jihad	Civilians and security/military personnel in Israel	Israel and the occupied territories	Massive Israeli crackdown on civilian demonstrators; tight security measures
1992–1993	Increasing number and lethality of attacks by Hamas and Islamic Jihad	Disruption of the Oslo peace process	Israel and the occupied territories	
Sept. 1993	Oslo Accords mediated by Clinton and signed by Rabin and Arafat	Mutual recognition and peaceful coexistence	White House, Washington, D.C.	Increased violence by hardline opposition groups on both sides
1993–1995	Continued intensification of attacks by Hamas and Islamic Jihad, including their first suicide bombings	Prevent implementation of 1993 Oslo agreement	Israel and the occupied territories	282 killed on both sides

Date	Event		Location	Outcome
Nov. 1995	Israeli prime minister Yitzhak Rabin assassinated by Jewish messianic extremist	Disruption of peace process	Tel Aviv	Shimon Peres becomes prime minister
Jan.–June 1996	Series of suicide bombings in reaction to Israeli killing of Hamas bomb maker Yahya Ayyash "the Engineer"	Israeli civilians and soldiers	Throughout Israel	Defeat of dovish Shimon Peres and election of hawkish Netanyahu
1997–1999	Continuing sporadic interactive violence joined by Al-Aqsa Brigades in reaction to Netanyahu's hard-line policies; resurgence of PLO militancy	Palestinian attacks and Israeli counterattacks; efforts by both sides to reduce violence	Israel and the occupied territories	Around 100 people killed
May 1999	Labor leader Ehud Barak wins election and becomes PM	Declares intention to bring peace within one year	Israel	Resumption of peace talks with Arafat; Hamas declares moratorium on suicide attacks
May 2000	Final status talks at Camp David between Clinton, Barak, and Arafat	Final peace settlement	Washington, D.C.	Talks fail to bring about an agreement
Sept. 2000	Likud leader Ariel Sharon visits al-Aqsa/Temple Mount	Defiance of Palestinian claim to Islam's Holy site (Al Quds)	Jerusalem	Massive Palestinian demonstrations marking the start of the second Intifada
Sept. 2000	Second Intifada starts	Resistance to Israeli occupation	Throughout occupied territories	4,012 Palestinians, 1,010 Israelis, and 63 foreigners killed (5,085 total) through Sept. 2006
Dec. 2000	Labor coalition collapses			Barak resigns

TABLE 4.4 Cont.   Hamas versus Israel: Strategic Interactions, 1973–2006

Date	Actor and Type (or Event)	Target/Goal	Place	Death Toll/Outcome
Feb. 2001	Sharon defeats Barak in Israeli elections			
May 2001–Mar. 2004	Second Intifada continues; Hamas/PIJ/al-Aqsa Brigades launch over 50 suicide attacks and other assaults	Israeli civilian and military targets	Throughout Israel and Palestinian lands	Israel responds with an intense campaign including assassinations, air strikes, incursions, and massive military assaults
Mar. 2002	Sharon launches "Operation Defensive Shield"	Reoccupation of the West Bank; undermine Palestinian Authority	West Bank and Gaza Strip	Effective destruction of PA's governing structure
Mar. 2004	Hamas leader Shaikh Ahmad Yassin assassinated by Israeli air strike	Hamas leadership	Outside a Mosque in Gaza	11 killed including Yassin, his bodyguards, and bystanders
Oct. 2004	Israeli Knesset (legislature) votes to withdraw Jewish settlements in Gaza			
Nov. 2004	Arafat dies		France	Mahmoud Abbas is elected head of PLO
Jan. 2005	Mahmoud Abbas elected to succeed Arafat as president of PA; calls for a cease-fire with Israel	To restart peace talks leading to Palestinian statehood	Ramallah, West Bank	Islamist groups halt attacks after Abbas orders a security crackdown
Feb. 2005	Sharon and Abbas agree on a cease-fire after over four years of Intifada			Israel lifts roadblocks but Sharon insists on keeping Jewish settlement blocks in the West Bank

Date	Event	Objective/Target	Location	Outcome
Aug. 2005	Israel removes settlements from Gaza Strip	Concession to Palestinians as part of bargaining for a final peace settlement	Gaza Strip	
July–Dec. 2005	Islamist groups resume attacks with rocket launchings and four suicide bombings, shattering the cease-fire	Israeli civilians and military targets	Throughout Israel	
Jan. 2006	Ariel Sharon suffers massive stroke and goes into a coma			Ehud Olmert takes over as interim PM
Jan. 2006	Hamas wins Palestinian elections by a surprisingly wide margin		Gaza Strip and West Bank	Mahmoud Abbas retains his position as head of PLO/PA
Jan. 2006	Israel and U.S. deny Hamas diplomatic recognition or funding unless it recognizes Israel's "right to exist"; Israel withholds Palestinian tax money			Massive humanitarian crisis
Mar. 2006	Olmert's Kadima party wins Israeli elections; forms government in coalition with Labor Party	Separation from the Palestinians behind West Bank barrier retaining three main settlement blocks and Jerusalem		Olmert's plan rejected by all Palestinian factions
June 2006	Palestinian militants capture Israeli soldier	Prisoner exchange, including all imprisoned Palestinian women and children	Israeli army post near Gaza Strip	2 IDF soldiers killed; 2 Palestinians killed
June 2006– Dec. 2006	Israeli military undertakes massive operations in Gaza including air strikes, tank attacks, and arrest of Hamas leadership	Hamas leadership, Palestinian infrastructure, militants, and civilians	Gaza Strip	60 Hamas ministers and other officials arrested, 300+ Palestinians and 5 Israelis killed

The rise of Palestinian Islamic Jihad (PIJ), committed to violence against Israel, complicated the tripartite game involving Israel, Mujamma, and the PLO factions because it challenged the three actors' dominance of the playing field. Influenced by the Iranian Revolution and the radical offshoots of Egypt's MB, PIJ sought to mobilize the world's Muslims for the liberation of Palestine to be pursued as a first priority.[79] Thus, by seeking to make the Palestinian cause its first preference, Islamic Jihad was infusing Palestinian nationalism with Islamism, while seeking to globalize its Jerusalem-centered agenda to make it the first preference of the worldwide Muslim community. Armed with a potent action program of Palestinian Islamist nationalism, PIJ upstaged both PLO's ineffective secular policies and Mujamma's gradualist Islamist agenda. Clearly, there were sufficient incentives tempting Mujamma to shift strategically from MB's long-term Islamizing agenda to immediate armed action against Israel. Given the power vacuum created by the erosion of PLO's influence and the growing radicalization of Palestinian youth facing an indefinite Israeli occupation, Shaikh Yassin initiated changes in Mujamma's structure and priorities to prepare for armed jihad. In 1984, the IDF cracked down on Mujamma's weapons procurement activities and Yassin was sent to jail, but was soon released in a prisoner exchange. The shaikh's next move was to form a security organization to collect intelligence, impose Islamic rules, and punish collaborators.[80] Prompted by the accelerating drift toward violence during 1986–1987, and pressured from its young militant cadres, the Mujamma decreed the formation of the Movement of Islamic Resistance—Harakat al-Muqawama al-Islamiya—later known by the acronym Hamas, which means "zeal" or "enthusiasm." As the Intifada erupted in December 1987, the Mujamma sought to hide its connection to Hamas in order to protect itself from Israeli reprisals. However, from the onset, Hamas assumed a major role rivaling PLO's leadership position in the Intifada and in May 1988, it became known as the militant arm of the MB, presenting itself as the embodiment of Palestinian Islamist nationalism.[81]

Hamas versus Israel: Zero-Sum Game?

The growing popularity of Hamas as a Palestinian Islamist liberation movement prompted the formation of the United National Command, a coalition of PLO-affiliated secular nationalist groups. As the PLO moved to renounce violence in 1988 in favor of a peace settlement with Israel based on a two-state solution, Hamas emerged as the leading voice of the Palestinian rejectionist front. The Charter of Hamas, promulgated in August 1988, proclaimed the land of Palestine as an Islamic endowment—*waqf*—to remain indivisible until Judgment Day. According to the charter, under Islamic law, no human agency is empowered to give up any part of Palestine, because it is against Islam.[82] Following the ideology of PIJ, Hamas skillfully reframed the Palestine problem as the shared religious responsibility of three groups—the Palestinians, the Arab countries, and the Islamic *ummah.* This fusion of Palestinian nationalism, Pan-Arabism, and Pan-Islamism represents a potentially powerful strategy of building a global coalition of Arabs and Muslims for whom the liberation of Palestine through armed jihad is an individual duty—*fard ayn.* Only then will it be possible for Hamas to establish an Islamic state in all of historic Palestine. This strategy, emphasizing the holiness of Jerusalem—Al-Quds—and heightening the necessity of its liberation in the consciousness of the world's Muslims, has paid dividends in both financial and political support for Hamas. Further, it has made the Israeli occupation one of the primary triggers of Muslim enmity toward the West, particularly the United States. It was no accident that Osama bin Ladin regularly cited the theme of "Zionist-American aggression" in his virulent denunciations to inspire and rally Muslims to the jihadi cause.[83]

By claiming the right to total Islamic control over Palestine, Hamas rejected any form of coexistence with Israel. The only peaceful solution Hamas offers Jews is to live "under the protective shadow of Islam." [84] In the escalating violence in 1989–1990, Hamas had emerged as a leading Palestinian insurgent organization, engaged in a zero-sum game with Israel and a fierce rivalry with the PLO in every aspect of Palestinian life. In the crisis milieu of the Intifada, what had started under Israeli patronage as a religious social service organization had become the implacable foe of Jewish statehood.[85]

As the peace process unfolded in the 1990s, Hamas faced a changed strategic situation that thwarted its objectives and threatened its very existence. Aiming to derail the bilateral peace talks between Israel and the PLO, Hamas and PIJ unleashed a deadly campaign prompting Prime Minister Yitzhak Rabin to deport over 400 Hamas and PIJ leaders to Lebanon in December 1992. Denied entrance into Lebanon, the deportees were stranded at the border, living under tents for almost a year, until readmitted by Israel. Meanwhile, lengthy negotiations under U.S. and Norwegian auspices culminated in the signing of the Oslo Accords in September 1993 by Prime Minister Yitzhak Rabin and Yasser Arafat, president of the Palestinian Authority(PA).[86] In exchange for gradual withdrawal from the specified lands, the PA would end the Intifada and recognize the State of Israel. The prospect of a peaceful settlement and recognition of Israel came as a blow to Hamas, PIJ, and Islamist militants everywhere. In response, Hamas would employ a complex set of strategies in a dynamic prisoner's dilemma context against the PLO and Israel.

Hamas versus PLO versus Israel: Abortive Prisoner's Dilemma, 1993–2000

The depiction of the post-Oslo interactions among Hamas, the PLO, and Israel as a tripartite game helps identify their respective objectives, preferences, incentives, payoffs, and reasons for failure.

Hamas Strategy. The strategy of Hamas consisted of three main components. First, Hamas intensified terrorist attacks against Israeli military and civilian targets, particularly Jewish settlements in Palestinian lands, in an effort to wreck the Oslo peace process. At the same time, Hamas refrained from committing violence against the PLO and the PA, but resisted their attempts to constrain Hamas' freedom of action against Israel. Finally, Hamas signaled the PA and indirectly, Israel, about the possibility of Hamas' participation in future elections and Palestinian governing institutions.

The strategic logic of this three-fold response was to buy Hamas the political space to maneuver flexibly in a constraining environment. Thus, Hamas would employ substantial violence to abort the Oslo process and prevent a two-state solution, while maintaining its own viability as a political force to participate in elections and governance in the event a Palestinian state came into existence. According to this rationale, should Hamas fail to disrupt the Oslo negotiations through terrorism, it would seek to play a strong role in the emerging PLO-controlled PA. Once in power, Hamas would endeavor to establish a Palestinian Islamist theocracy and even recognize Israel, should the latter withdraw to its pre–June 1967 borders.

PLO Strategy. The PLO's strategy was to monopolize power by the PA under President Yasser Arafat's al-Fatah faction, establish maximum PA control over the occupied lands after successive Israeli withdrawals, and press Israel to accelerate turning over land to PA and stop establishing new settlements in the West Bank and Gaza. At the same time, the PLO would work to mobilize international political support from the major European powers and the Arab and Muslim states for the PA's objectives of achieving an early and total Israeli withdrawal and establishment of an independent Palestinian state. The PLO hoped to employ a two-pronged strategy toward Israel by negotiating as a peace partner while keeping alive the threat of force. The force option would be carried out by either not constraining Hamas/PIJ terrorism or by using the PLO's own guerrilla outfit—the al-Aqsa Brigades associated with al-Fatah. The PLO intended to use the growing power of militant Islam as a strategic weapon by signaling to Israel that if it failed to make peace by giving generous concessions to the PA, the alternative would be confronting the more radical Hamas organization.

Israel's Strategy. Israel's strategy was to maximize its security by promoting the establishment of a militarily weak and territorially small Palestinian state, economically dependent on Israel. It would further seek to shape the geographical configuration of the Palestinian state within circumscribed boundaries by land expropriations for military use and strategic placement of Jewish settlements. Finally, Israel would control the logistical ties between Palestinian organizations such as the PA, Hamas, and PIJ, and their external benefactors in order to minimize the threat potential of insurgencies and terrorism.

The pursuit of these strategies and preferences in a tripartite game from 1993 to 2000 ended in failure for all three players. What had promised to be an equilibrium of peace ended up as an equilibrium of terror, due to divisions within each of the parties, unforeseen events, and the absence of strong U.S. presidential leadership until it was too late.

Difficulties befell the Oslo peace process from the outset amid disagreements and escalating violence. In February 1994 an American Jewish settler, Baruch Goldstein, gunned down 29 Palestinians praying at the Mosque of Abraham in Hebron, triggering bloody reprisals from PIJ and Hamas employing drive-by shootings, car bombings, and suicide attacks in emulation of tactics pioneered by Hizbullah of Lebanon.[87] In May 1994, the Cairo agreement between the PLO and Israel provided for IDF's withdrawal from Jericho and parts of Gaza and granted autonomy under the PA, led by Chairman Yasser Arafat. On July 1, 1994, Arafat returned to Gaza in triumph to face the challenges of self-rule with limited resources. In response to continuing Islamist attacks, Israel persisted in its policy of assassinating and imprisoning militants and imposed a blockade on the newly established autonomous areas, while PA security forces were used to detain extremists and establish order. Despite the ongoing mayhem, the Oslo II agreement was concluded in September 1995. This signified Israel's determination to rid itself of the explosive situation in Palestinian urban areas and the PA's interest in demonstrating to the Palestinians its ability to make progress toward their emancipation. Oslo II provided a phased release of Palestinian prisoners held by Israel and established three zones of control in the West Bank:

Zone A—full PA control over all urban centers, except Hebron and Jerusalem (7 percent);
Zone B—joint Israeli-PA control (21 percent);
Zone C—exclusive Israeli control (72 percent).[88]

The concessions under Oslo II infuriated Israel's right-wing and messianist constituencies, culminating in the assassination of Prime Minister Yitzhak Rabin on November 4, 1995, by a Jewish religious zealot. The Oslo peace process had suffered its first near-fatal blow. As Israel mourned the death of the hero of the 1967 War, Shimon Peres became prime minister vowing to continue the peace process. However, in a fateful decision, Peres chose to seek a new electoral mandate from Israelis. Despite a show of toughness in a bloody bombardment of Hizbullah and civilian targets in South Lebanon, Peres' campaign was harmed by deadly Hamas suicide attacks that ensured his narrow defeat by Likud leader Binyamin Netanyahu.[89] Now the Oslo peace process seemed to suffer another near-fatal blow, as Netanyahu infuriated the Arabs by opposing Oslo, lifting the freeze on building settlements in the occupied lands, and permitting archaeological exploration under the al-Aqsa Mosque compound—regarded as one of Islam's most sacred sites. Unable to stop Hamas suicide attacks, Netanyahu was compelled to change course under pressure from the Clinton administration. In January 1997 he ceded 80 percent of Hebron to the PA and in October signed the Wye River Memorandum to effect further withdrawals—which inflamed his right-wing/messianic/settler constituencies. Netanyahu's conciliatory actions led to the collapse of his hard-line Likud government.[90] In May 1999, he was defeated by the Labor party's Ehud Barak, a former general, who promised to achieve Arab-Israeli peace in one year. Meanwhile, increased security measures and a Hamas decision to halt suicide attacks set the stage for a return to negotiations.[91]

Barak, Arafat, and Clinton: Peace at Last?

Ehud Barak assumed power in a milieu of guarded optimism, which soon dissipated given the complexities of making peace in the Middle East. As a first strategic priority, Barak made a brave but unsuccessful attempt to reach a peace settlement with Syria. His next move was to withdraw Israeli forces from southern Lebanon in May 2000, ending eighteen years of occupation. Barak's third venture, both visionary and risky, involved an all-out diplomatic drive for a final settlement on Palestine.

The timing of Barak's Palestinian initiative was problematic because of domestic opposition to further withdrawals, an upsurge in Islamist violence, unrest in the occupied territories, and the impending end of the Clinton presidency. As the aging icon of Palestinian nationhood, Arafat had presided over a corrupt and inefficient regime, facing a growing challenge from Hamas, but unable to deliver independent statehood to his people after five years of negotiations with Israel. Under pressure from Clinton and Barak, Arafat agreed to switch from phased negotiations to final status talks.[92] There were enough incentives for all three leaders to take this risky venture that could leave its indelible mark on their historical legacies.

The two-week negotiations at Camp David represented a prisoner's dilemma situation that was destined to fail because of the constraints and pressures bearing down on all three leaders. In the end, none of the three possessed enough power to act decisively within a short time for reasons implicit in their respective political situations.

The success of a jailer-mediator in a prisoner's dilemma condition is largely dependent on its power, determination, and skills to offer incentives and disincentives to the contending parties. While President Clinton had more than enough determination and skills, he lacked sufficient power and a store of incentives to push Barak and Arafat to conclude a peace accord. As a lame-duck president in the remaining months of his tenure, Clinton could not act as decisively as he had done in bringing together Prime Minister Rabin and Chairman Arafat in September 1993 on the White House lawn. His efforts were further compounded by the tenuous power situations besetting both Barak and Arafat, each facing split domestic constituencies with powerful hawkish foes opposing a peace settlement.

An illustrious former general, Barak lacked the charisma of Rabin and the political experience to prevail in the conflictual milieu of Israeli politics. Despite Barak's idealistic passion to achieve a final peace settlement, his ability to offer sufficient concessions to Arafat was constrained by the unstable coalition he led and the virulent opposition from Ariel Sharon's right-wing Likud party and the settler movement.

As the weakest among the three leaders, Arafat presided over a fractious PLO/PA coalition with declining popular support due to its failures in governance, his inability to gain concessions from Israel, and the growing power of Hamas, driven by jihadist nationalism and rooted in a network of social welfare agencies operating at the mass level. Upstaged by Hamas and undermined by Israeli incursions into Palestinian territory, Arafat was unable to accept Barak's peace offer.

To prevent failure at Camp David, President Clinton made a last attempt by presenting his own plan to break the deadlock. However, Clinton's proposal was too close to Barak's offer and did not provide the minimum concessions acceptable to Arafat regarding territorial contiguity, the status of Jerusalem, and the right of return of Palestinian refugees. The Camp David talks have been a source of great controversy and their failure has been attributed to all sides.[93] Clearly, the incentives to reach a peace equilibrium were not great enough to overcome the obstacles preventing a final settlement.

If Arafat expected to get a better deal by waiting for the next U.S. president or Israeli prime minister, he had grossly miscalculated. On September 28, 2000, in a provocative move, Likud leader Ariel Sharon visited al-Aqsa/Temple Mount (al-Haram al-Sharif), triggering Palestinian demonstrations that culminated in the second Intifada—much bloodier than the first Intifada. In December 2000, Barak's Labor coalition collapsed and the February 2001 elections brought Sharon's Likud coalition into power, soon after George W. Bush's accession to the U.S. presidency.

The Second Intifada and the "Road Map," 2000–2006

The second Intifada was characterized by unprecedented interactive violence between the IDF and the Palestinian militant organizations. Both sides resorted to the progressive escalation of attacks driven by both strategic logic and blind vengeance. Sharon's initial response to the uprising was to continue his predecessor's policies focusing on the capture and assassination of militants, while intensifying air strikes on suspected terrorist sites and tactical incursions into self-rule areas governed by the PA. For its part, Hamas ended its self-imposed 1999–2000 moratorium on major terrorist operations, and unleashed an unrelenting series of suicide attacks in 2001–2002 directed against Israeli cities. Meanwhile, U.S. envoy George Mitchell and CIA director George Tenet had failed to achieve a cease-fire. On March 29, 2002, Sharon launched Operation Defensive Shield to reoccupy the West Bank, and effectively destroyed much of the PA's governing structure.

To be sure, Sharon's announcements and military moves defied strategic logic. As IDF besieged Arafat in his ruined headquarters, Sharon and the United States were pressuring him to rein in the attacks being launched by Hamas and other militant groups—a task far exceeding the chairman's degraded capabilities brought on by IDF's attacks and reoccupation of the West Bank. Clearly, the U.S./Israeli objective was to make Arafat politically irrelevant and instead deal with his newly appointed prime minister, Mahmoud Abbas. In April, the United States introduced its "road map"—a belated plan for a negotiated settlement to be carried out once the violence ended. In June 2002, at a summit meeting with President Bush in Aqaba, Jordan, Abbas called for an end to the Intifada as Sharon expressed his support for a democratic Palestinian state. After a two-month truce, there was a resumption of interactive violence culminating in the resignation of Abbas in September 2003 and Sharon's threat in December to implement a unilateral separation unless Palestinian attacks were stopped. Meanwhile, in order to block attacks inside Israel, Sharon had launched the construction of a massive West Bank barrier, which was denounced by Palestinian and international observers as a ploy to annex land and set permanent boundaries without negotiating with the Palestinians. Although in July 2004 the International Court of Justice in The Hague ruled the barrier as illegal, Israel rejected the ruling as a non-binding judgment.[94]

New Leaders, Old Patterns, 2004–2006

The year 2004 brought major changes of leadership to the bloody evolution of the Israel-Palestinian conflict, yet the basic patterns of interactive violence persisted, along with the equilibrium of terror between the antagonists. Israel continued to pursue its traditional strategy of killing suspected militants and leaders either to deter or crush the Palestinian resistance, all the while building yet more settlements. In March 2004 the aging and blind Hamas leader Shaikh Ahmad Yassin was assassinated in a missile attack, followed by his top aid, Abd al-Aziz al-Rantisi, a month later. In the wake of Palestinian outrage over these killings, Prime Minister Sharon announced his "disengagement plan" to withdraw 8,000 Israeli settlers and soldiers from Gaza. This plan appeared stillborn as the IDF launched a major incursion into the northern Gaza Strip in response to Palestinian rocket attacks and bombings in August–September 2004. Meanwhile, the Palestinian situation had become increasingly chaotic with the PA's authority eroding under incessant Israeli attacks. Internal factionalism among the PA's security forces was compounded by the multiplicity of militant groups fighting Israel that often defied any central control. These included the Izz al-Din al-Qassam Brigades of Hamas, Palestinian Islamic Jihad, and al-Aqsa Brigades associated with PLO's al-Fatah, as well as smaller leftist and other rogue elements operating either independently or together against Israel. Amid the mayhem, Arafat was flown to France for emergency medical treatment and died on November 11, 2004. His burial in Ramallah evoked popular grief as Mahmoud Abbas assumed the PLO's chairmanship and was elected president of PA by a landslide in January 2005. Finally, the symbol of the Palestinian quest for nationhood was gone — the favorite whipping boy incessantly blamed by Israel and the United States for the failures of the peace process had left the scene; yet the conflict persisted.

Despite multiple challenges, in February 2005, President Abbas succeeded in prevailing upon Hamas, PIJ, and other militants to observe a temporary truce that enabled him to join Sharon in Egypt to declare a mutual cease-fire. Against this backdrop, in August, Sharon proceeded to implement his promised withdrawal from Gaza, despite protests from the Jewish settlers. Interactive violence continued as the cease-fire was shattered by new Islamist suicide and rocket attacks followed by Israeli retaliatory responses. In January 2006, as the Palestinians prepared for their elections, Prime Minister Sharon suffered a massive stroke and Ehud Olmert took over as interim prime minister. While Sharon's fate remained unknown, Hamas won a surprise victory over the PLO in the January 25 elections, winning 76 of the 132 seats in the Legislative Council. As President Mahmoud Abbas called upon Hamas to form a national unity government, the United States and Israel declared that they would not have diplomatic relations with a Palestinian government led by the "terrorist" organization unless Hamas agreed to recognize Israel's legitimacy and give up violence. In the following months, Israel, the EU, and the United States withdrew direct funding to the PA. As Ismail Haniya took office as prime minister, the Hamas regime faced a severe financial and humanitarian crisis, internal divisions within its party structure, and difficulties in forming a national unity government with the PLO factions.

The March 2006 Israeli elections brought into office a Kadima / Labor Party coalition government under Prime Minister Olmert. According to Olmert's "convergence" or "realignment" strategy, Israel would move its soldiers and settlers from much of the West Bank behind a unilaterally drawn "eastern border" retaining three settlement blocks and East Jerusalem.[95] With this plan, Olmert hoped to disengage Israel from the Palestinians who would be expected to accept a disjointed statehood in whatever remained of their lands in the West Bank and Gaza. Before Olmert and Abbas could discuss these proposals, violence erupted once again.

In June 2006, Palestinian militants entered Israel through an underground tunnel, ambushing an army outpost and capturing Cpl. Gilad Shalit. In exchange for the return of the captured soldier, they demanded that all imprisoned Palestinian women and children be released by Israel. Instead of negotiating with the Islamist militants, Israel embarked upon a massive military operation in Gaza targeting the Hamas leadership and the Palestinian infrastructure. Over sixty Hamas ministers and government officials were arrested and over two hundred people were killed as Prime Minister Haniya unsuccessfully sought the release of Corporal Shalit. In an attempt to break out of its international isolation and financial crisis, Hamas moderated its rejectionist position on the question of Israel's legitimacy, accepting conditional coexistence with Israel under a long-term renewable cease-fire (*hudna*).[96] These strategic shifts were not given due attention by the United States and Israel as interactive violence persisted in Gaza and the world's attention turned to the war between Israel and Hizbullah in Lebanon beginning in July 2006.

Hamas versus Israel: Changing Preferences and Limited Options

Two important conclusions can be drawn from the evolution of the Israel-Palestine conflict as presented in this case study. First, preferences can change over time depending on the interaction between the antagonists and the impact of external developments. Second, in the case of some protracted conflicts, there could be a decrease in the number of options for one or both sides in the wake of failed attempts at peace and escalations of violence. An analysis of the conflict between Israel and Hamas reveals a reordering of preferences on both sides as listed below.

Israel	**Hamas**

First Preference

Sovereignty over all of Palestine	Sovereignty over all of Palestine

Second Preference

• Expand Israeli state by annexing major West Bank settlement blocks and East Jerusalem • Establish disjointed Palestinian statelets within parts of the West Bank and Gaza (Sharon's preference)	• Independent Palestinian state in pre-1967 West Bank, East Jerusalem, and Gaza • Right of return of Palestinian refugees to Israel and Palestine

Third Preference

• Israeli state with modified boundaries after tradeoffs of land incorporating some settlements but removing others • Palestinian state in Gaza and several contiguous West Bank enclaves with shared control over Muslim/Jewish holy sites in Jerusalem • Acceptance of a small number of Palestinian refugees into Israel (Barak/Clinton preference)	• Independent Palestinian state in West Bank, Gaza, and East Jerusalem with some border modifications in favor of Israel • Limited right of return for refugees and payment of compensation to others

As indicated above, neither Israel nor Hamas has been able to achieve its first preference of having exclusive sovereignty over all of Palestine. Although Israel has the military means to occupy all of the West Bank and Gaza Strip, it would be highly costly both in terms of the international reaction and of maintaining control over an unfriendly and rapidly growing Arab population. Under these circumstances, Israel would have to accept a lower preference and find the means to implement it, through negotiations with the Palestinians or by force. After the failure of the Camp David talks in 2000, Sharon turned to a policy of unilateral implementation of Israel's second preference by starting to build a barrier around major West Bank settlement blocks, which could become a *de facto* border of an expanded Israeli state. Both Hamas and the more moderate PLO clearly opposed the implementation of this preference but were not in a position to negotiate for their preferred solution, which would give them control over Palestine within its pre-1967 borders (West Bank, East Jerusalem, and Gaza). Should there be a return to negotiations, Hamas would likely push for a Palestinian state within those borders as well as the right of return for all Palestinian refugees. It should be remembered that during the Barak-Arafat Camp David talks, Israel was willing to accept its own third preference in exchange for power sharing with the PA over the Muslim holy sites in Jerusalem as well as PA's control over large segments of the West Bank in addition to Gaza. However, Israel was not willing to accept the full right of return for Palestinian refugees.

As the balance of power between Israel and the PA shifted, so did the preferences on each side. Thus, growing Israeli strength as a result of Sharon's projection of power supported by the United States after the September 11, 2001, attacks allowed Israel to upgrade its preference from third to second (see above). In contrast, as the PA's power declined vis-à-vis Israel during the second Intifada because of Sharon's massive use of force, the Palestinian position appeared to soften. In view of the PA's weakened military and diplomatic position and eroding public support, Hamas came in to fill the void by sticking to its first preference, rejecting Israel's legitimacy and projecting strength in resisting the occupation through attacks and suicide bombings. Weakened after five years of the Intifada and facing the challenges of governance after its unexpected victory in the January 2006 elections, Hamas moderated its position by signaling acceptance of its second preference—conditional recognition of Israel in exchange for a Palestinian state within the pre-1967 borders. Given Israel's refusal to accept Hamas conditions, and Hamas refusal to recognize Israel without its promise to make territorial concessions, it appears unlikely that either side will move toward peace in the absence of external pressure or a dramatic increase in the costs of continued violence.

The conflict between Israel and Hamas became increasingly intractable after the summer 2006 Israel-Hizbullah war. Had Prime Minister Olmert succeeded in effectively degrading Hizbullah's threat at little cost, the Israeli public might have been more receptive to his plan for further withdrawals from the West Bank as a prelude to a possible settlement with the Palestinians. Hizbullah's ability to resist the Israeli incursion had a negative impact on Olmert's domestic political standing, substantially reducing popular support for further dismantling of settlements and concessions to the Palestinians. Consequently, Hizbullah's unexpected strength against Israel undercut the negotiating position of Hamas, its major Palestinian ally.

The success of U.S./Israeli efforts to weaken the Hamas regime since it took power created an increasingly chaotic political situation in the Palestinian territories. Coupled with a severe humanitarian crisis, the fractionalization of Palestinian politics led to the breakdown of law and order. With hundreds dead, the democratic election of Hamas had brought increased suffering to the Palestinian people and the erosion of Hamas popular support. The intensification of violence in the Palestinian areas could ultimately harm Israeli and American interests as Islamist elements more radical than Hamas may come to the fore. A catastrophic outcome brought on by U.S./Israeli policies or Palestinian miscalculations could have global consequences, particularly in the Muslim world. Since its inception, Hamas's objectives have focused on the Palestinian cause and its violence has been limited to Israel and the Palestinian territories. Yet, it is likely that the ongoing crisis situation will give birth to globalized Palestinian terrorism as carried out by PLO factions in the 1960–1980s, this time under a pan-Islamist banner. This is a highly unsettling prospect in view of documented evidence that the Israel/Palestine issue has become a principle fault line in contemporary international relations.[97]

Religious Violence: A Comparative Overview

The four case studies on interactive violence between states and religious militants reflect salient commonalities and differences as well as trends presaging future developments in religiously inspired terrorism. Among the case studies, Aum Shinrikyo stands alone as an example of a messianic/millenarian group in contrast to Hizbullah, the Kashmiri separatists, and Hamas, for whom religious militancy provides a mobilizing medium in their pursuit of worldly objectives.

Despite Aum's short lifespan, its millenarian objectives presented a far greater potential threat to peace than those of the other groups because of its "end time" ideology. Indeed, the danger from such millenarian groups springs from their fervent belief that the world's apocalyptic demise is imperative for the birth of a divinely ordained utopia. Although Aum's cultic creed was eclectic, combining apocalyptic notions from different religions, its premise of hastening the world's end is shared by a plethora of fundamentalist groups from the Judaic, Christian, and Islamic traditions. The recent proliferation of apocalyptic groups in these monotheistic faiths and their determination to shape the domestic and foreign policies of states represent a significant threat to world peace and security.[98]

Hizbullah and Hamas are allies sharing a stated commitment to Israel's destruction. While both are Muslim fundamentalist movements, there is a doctrinal divergence between Hizbullah's Shiite ideology and Hamas's Sunnism rooted in Egypt's Muslim Brotherhood. However, these differences are deemphasized by both parties because of their common strategic imperative to confront Israel. Yet, this shared objective should not obscure their differing national identities and self-interests, with Hizbullah fighting to defend Lebanese Shiites and Hamas struggling for the Palestinian cause. Similarly, behind the Kashmiri adoption of Islamist ideology as a mobilization strategy is their nationalist struggle for independence from India. To be sure, the evolution of all these Islamist movements points to two interrelated dialectics that have been emphasized throughout this book: first, that protracted conflicts between states and subnational groups tend to result in radicalization and greater bloodshed; and second, in Islamic contexts, this radicalization often assumes religious coloration and the heightened spiritual zeal of violent jihadism. In the Lebanese Shiite case, the weakness of the more secular and moderate Amal party gave rise to the more radical Hizbullah. In Palestine, the failure of the secular nationalist PLO gave rise to the more radical Hamas. In Kashmir, the ineffectiveness of Kashmiri nationalist separatists paved the way for the ascendance of indigenous and foreign Islamic jihadist organizations like Lashkar-e-Taiba. Therefore, Hizbullah, Hamas, and the Kashmiri jihadists represent the culmination of radicalization processes, which began as nationalist causes and evolved into religious extremism manifesting greater lethal effectiveness and readiness to sacrifice for both worldly and transcendental aims.

Notes

1. Dale W. Wimberly, "Socioeconomic Deprivation and Religious Salience: A Cognitive Behavioral Approach," *The Sociological Quarterly* 25 (1984), 223–224.
2. R. Hrair Dekmejian, *Islam in Revolution,* 2nd ed. (Syracuse: Syracuse University Press, 1995), 4–7.
3. R. Hrair Dekmejian, "Charismatic Leadership in Messianic and Revolutionary Movements," in *Religious Resurgence,* eds. Richard T. Antoun and Mary Hegland (Syracuse: Syracuse University Press, 1987), 78–107.
4. Robert Jay Lifton, *Destroying the World to Save It: Aum Shinrikyo, Apocalyptic Violence, and the New Global Terrorism* (New York: Metropolitan, 1999).
5. D. W. Brackett, *Holy Terror* (New York: Weatherhill, 1996), 61.
6. Lifton, 18–19.
7. On these concepts of Erik Erikson see Dekmejian, "Charismatic Leadership in Messianic and Revolutionary Movements," 85–89.
8. Jerrold M. Post, "Narcissism and the Charismatic Leader-Follower Relationship," *Political Psychology,* 7, no. 4 (1986): 679–687.
9. Daniel A. Metraux, *Aum Shinrikyo and Japanese Youth* (New York: University Press of America, 1999), 20–21; Brackett, 62–63, 94–98.
10. Brackett, 76.
11. Dekmejian, "Charismatic Leadership in Messianic and Revolutionary Movements," 100.
12. Brackett, 96.

13. Metraux, 30–31.
14. Brackett, 99–102.
15. *Ibid.*, 146–166.
16. The organization's website can be found at http://english.aleph.to/.
17. For a comprehensive account see Ahmad Nizar Hamzeh, *In the Path of Hizbullah* (Syracuse: Syracuse University Press, 2004), 1–151.
18. For historical details see Dekmejian, *Islam in Revolution*, 165–168.
19. *Ibid.*, 123–125.
20. Hamzeh, 135–141.
21. Robin Wright, *Sacred Rage* (New York: Simon and Schuster, 1986), 80–90.
22. Judith Palmer Harik, *Hezbollah* (London: I. B. Tauris, 2004), 34–35.
23. Hamzeh, 16–26.
24. Harik, 64–65.
25. Ann Zwicker Kerr, *Come with Me from Lebanon: An American Family Odyssey* (Syracuse: Syracuse University Press, 1994), 3–20.
26. Hala Jabir, *Hezbollah: Born with a Vengeance* (New York: Columbia University Press, 1997), 122–123.
27. Robert A. Pape, "The Strategic Logic of Suicide Terrorism," *American Political Science Review*, 97, no. 3 (2003): 343–361.
28. *Ibid.*, 357.
29. On the composition of the Islamic Resistance see Jabir, *Hezbollah*, 53–54, 114–121, and Dekmejian, *Islam in Revolution*, 166–168.
30. On the transition from ethnic nationalist violence to religious violence see Richard H. Dekmejian. "Fundamentalist Islam: Theories, Typologies, and Trends," *Middle East Review* 17 (1985): 28–33.
31. Aaron Mannes, *Profiles in Terror* (Lanham, MD: Rowman and Littlefield, 2004), 152–153.
32. Harik, 121–122.
33. *Ibid.*, 135–148.
34. *Ibid.*, 81–94.
35. Mannes, 161–168.
36. Lara Deeb, "Hizbullah: A Primer," *Middle East Report Online*, July 31, 2006, http://www.merip.org/mero/mero073106.html.
37. Ephraim Lavie, "The Israel-Hizbullah War: A Zero Sum Game for Everyone?" *Tel Aviv Notes*, no. 182, August 6, 2006, www.tau.ac.il./jcss/.
38. http://news.bbc.co.uk/2/hi/middle_east/5311610.stm.
39. www.guardian.co.uk/comment/story/0,,1833727,00.html.
40. Robert Blecker, "Converging upon War," *MERIP: Middle East Report Online*, July 18, 2006, http://www.merip.org./mero/mero0071806.html.
41. Wright, 233.
42. On Israeli preferences see Lavie, *Tel Aviv Notes*, August 6, 2006.
43. Deeb, *Middle East Reports On Line*.
44. For details see Rob Johnson, *A Region in Turmoil: South Asian Conflicts Since 1947* (London: Reaktion Books, 2005), 91–99.
45. On Kashmir's history see Rai Mridu, *Hindu Rulers, Muslim Subjects* (Princeton: Princeton University Press, 2004), 1–97.
46. Ian Talbot, "Understanding Religious Violence in Contemporary Pakistan: Themes and Theories," in Ravinder Kaur, ed., *Religion, Violence and Political Mobilization in South Asia* (New Delhi: Sage, 2005), 145–163.
47. Bjorn Hettne, "South Asia and the War Against Terrorism," in Kaur, 197–199.
48. Arun R. Swamy, "Déjà vu All Over Again? Why Dialogue Won't Solve the Kashmir Dispute," *Analysis from the East-West Center*, 56 (2001): 5.
49. Johnson, 101–102.

50. Swamy, "Déjà vu?," 5.
51. http://www.fas.org/irp/world/para/mjc.htm.
52. Yoginder Sikand, "Kashmir, from National Liberation to Islamic Jihad," in Walter Laqueur, ed. *Voices of Terror* (New York: Reed, 2004), 467–468.
53. Peter R. Lavoy, "Pakistan's Nuclear Doctrine," in Rafiq Dossani and Henry S. Rowen, eds., *Prospects for Peace in South Asia* (Palo Alto, CA: Stanford University Press, 2005), 288–289.
54. *Ibid.*, 288.
55. Johnson, *A Region in Turmoil*, 109.
56. Rajesh M. Basrur, "Coercive Diplomacy in a Nuclear Environment: The December 13 Crisis," in Dossani and Rowen, *Prospects for Peace in South Asia*, 302–303.
57. *Ibid.*, 305–325.
58. *Ibid.*, 307.
59. *Ibid.*, 310–311.
60. Lavoy, 297, and Basrur, 311. On U.S. foreign policy under President Bush see Samina Yasmeen, "India and Pakistan," in *The Bush Doctrine and the War on Terrorism*, ed. Mary Buckley and Robert Singh (London: Routledge, 2006), 89–103.
61. Don Perotu, *The Middle East Today*, 4th ed. (New York, Praeger, 1903), 270.
62. *Ibid.*, 304.
63. R. H. Dekmejian, *Egypt under Nasir* (Albany: SUNY Press, 1971), 41–47.
64. For a more detailed chronology of attacks and counter-attacks see www.guardian.co.uk/israel/comment/0,,626719,00.html.
65. Anthony Nutting, *Nasser* (New York: E. P. Dutton, 1971), 441–446.
66. http://news.bbc.co.uk/2/shared/spl/hi/middle_east/03/v3_ip_timeline/html/default.stm; for a more detailed chronology see "Quarterly Update on Conflict and Diplomacy," in the *Journal of Palestine Studies.*
67. Charles D. Smith, *Palestine and the Arab-Israeli Conflict* (Boston: Bedford-St. Martin's, 2001), 403–405.
68. Dekmejian, *Islam in Revolution*, 23–32, 75–84.
69. Smith, *Palestine and the Arab-Israeli Conflict*, 408–411.
70. *Ibid.*, 425–436.
71. http://news.bbc.co.uk/2/shared/spl/hi/middle_east/03/v3_ip_timeline/html/default.stm, and Aaron Mannes, *Profiles in Terror: The Guide to Middle East Terrorist Organizations* (Lanham, MD: Rowman and Littlefield, 2004), 274.
72. Shaul Mishal and Avraham Sela, *The Palestinian Hamas* (New York: Columbia University Press, 2000), 40–44, 55–56.
73. Dekmejian, *Islam in Revolution*, 195–196.
74. *Ibid.*, 18.
75. Yossi Melman, "Hamas: When a Former Client Becomes an Implacable Enemy," *Los Angeles Times*, December 20, 1992.
76. Mishal and Sela, 19–20.
77. Dekmejian, *Islam in Revolution*, 57–60, 211–214.
78. Khaled Hroub, *Hamas: Political Thought and Practice* (Washington, DC: Institute of Palestine Studies, 2000), 32–33.
79. *Ibid.*, 196–197; and Mishal and Sela, 32–33.
80. Hroub, *Hamas*, 34–36.
81. Mishal and Sela, 35–37.
82. Yonah Alexander, *Palestinian Religious Terrorism* (Ardsley, NY: Transnational Publishers, 2002), 47–72, and Hroub, 267–291.
83. Bruce Lawrence, ed., *Messages to the World: The Statements of Osama Bin Laden* (London: Verso, 2005), chapters 3, 7, 9, 10, 11, 12, 16, 17, 19, 24.

84. *The Covenant of the Islamic Resistance Movement (Hamas)*, Media Analysis Center, October 1988, 10–11.
85. Melman. "Hamas."
86. Smith, 457–468.
87. *Ibid.*, 466–468.
88. http://news.bbc.co.uk/2/shared/spl/hi/middle_east/03/v3_ip_timeline/html/default.stm.
89. Hroub, 107–109, and Smith, 477–479.
90. Smith, 487–488.
91. Ely Karmon, "Hamas's Terrorism Strategy: Operational Limitations and Political Constraints," *Middle East Review of International Affairs*, 4, no. 1 (2000): 66–79.
92. Shibley Telhami, "Camp David II: Assumptions and Consequences," *Current History*, January 2001, 2.
93. Hussein Agha and Robert Malley, "Camp David: the Tragedy of Errors," *New York Review of Books*, 48, no. 13 (August 9, 2001): 1–16; Aravinda Ananda, "Barak's Visit Fuels Israeli-Palestinian Debate: Look to His Actions, Not His Words," *The Yale Herald* 34, no. 7 (October 18, 2002).
94. International Court of Justice, "Legal Consequences of the Construction of a Wall in the Occupied Palestinian Territory" Press Release, July 9, 2004.
95. Blecker, "Converging upon War."
96. Scott Atran, "Is Hamas Ready to Deal?" *New York Times*, August 17, 2006; Blecker, "Converging upon War."
97. Pew Research Center, "Global Attitudes Project," June 2006.
98. Louis Sahagun, "End Times' Religious Groups Want Apocalypse Soon," *Los Angeles Times*, June 22, 2006.

Further Reading

Antoun, Richard T. *Understanding Fundamentalism: Christian, Islamic, and Jewish Movements*. Walnut Creek, CA: AltaMira, 2001.
Ganguly, Sumit. *The Crisis in Kashmir: Portents of War, Hopes of Peace*. Cambridge, MA: Cambridge University Press, 1997.
Hamzeh, Ahmad Nizar. *In the Path of Hizbullah*. Syracuse: Syracuse University Press, 2004.
Jaber, Hala. *Hezbollah: Born with a Vengeance*. New York: Columbia University Press, 1997.
Kepel, Gilles. *Jihad: The Trail of Political Islam*. Cambridge, Mass: Harvard University Press, 2002.
Levitas, Daniel. *The Terrorist Next Door: The Militia Movement and the Radical Right*. New York: Thomas Dunne/St. Martin's, 2006.
Levitt, Matthew. *Hamas: Politics, Charity, and Terrorism in the Service of Jihad*. New Haven: Yale University Press, 2006.
Lifton, Robert Jay. 1999. *Destroying the World to Save it: Aum Shinrikyo, Apocalyptic Violence, and the New Global Terrorism*. New York: Metropolitan, 1999.
Lustick, Ian. *For the Land and the Lord: Jewish Fundamentalism in Israel*. New York: Council on Foreign Relations, 1988.

Ideological Radicals versus the State

SUBNATIONAL GROUPS MOTIVATED by different ideological beliefs and agendas have persistently challenged the authority of the state since the French Revolution. Although these groups pursue differing ideological objectives, they all share a strongly negative view of the nation-state and its authority structures. These groups may be classified according to their particular political beliefs ranging from the left to the right of the ideological spectrum.

Leftist groups are motivated by class interests and emerge where certain sectors of society suffer economic deprivation vis-à-vis the more privileged classes that dominate the political elite and shape its decisions on who gets what in society. Leftist ideological groups include a variety of communist and socialist revolutionary movements fighting for workers, peasants, and marginalized indigenous communities suffering state repression and economic exploitation.

Leftist violence harks back to the revolutionary movements of the nineteenth century, particularly in Italy, Russia, and France. Secret societies in southern Italy such as the Carbonari flourished in the early 1800s as terrorist organizations fighting the state in the name of the people. Russian leftists such as Sergey Nechaev (1847–1882) advocated systematic terrorism as a part of a strategy to trigger revolutions. Two other Russian thinkers, Mikhail Bakunin (1814–1876) and Prince Pyotr Kropotkin (1842–1921), were instrumental in developing another strain of leftist political thought, anarchism, which was directed at the overthrow of the Tsarist monarchy. Although short-lived, the Narodnaya Volya movement was one of the most deadly anarchist groups. Between 1878 and 1882, this secret society, a quarter of which were women, targeted government functionaries, members of the royal family, police officials, and assassinated Tsar Alexander II.[1] In France, another theater of revolutionary violence, anarchism, socialism, and communism converged. The Paris Commune of 1871 that took power in response to the French defeat in the Franco-Prussian War symbolized this convergence of leftist revolutionary trends. After the suppression of the Paris Commune, the anarchist movement and the larger communist movement experienced a sharp decline. Nevertheless, acts of leftist terrorism persisted until the turn of the century.

The first part of the twentieth century experienced another upsurge in leftist political violence. The ultimate success of leftist revolutionary violence was Vladimir Ilyich Lenin's October Revolution in Russia culminating in the founding of the Soviet Union. The Leninist model of leftist revolution inspired many similar movements across the world with mixed results. The powerful German Communist Party was crushed by Hitler's Nazi regime while French, Greek, Yugoslav, Polish, and Italian communist guerrillas effectively fought the Nazi and Fascist war machines with terrorist tactics. Another upsurge in leftist violence occurred a few decades after World War II in some European and Asian countries. In West Germany, the Red Army Faction (RAF) emerged to terrorize the country's democratic regime in the 1970s and 1980s. The RAF, otherwise known as the Baader-Meinhof gang, bombed department stores, government buildings, and U.S. military installations. Using guerrilla tactics, the RAF operatives also engaged in kidnappings, assassinations, and airplane hijacking in order to disrupt the West German way of life. In particular, its targets included icons of German capitalism, the military-industrial complex, and the U.S. "imperialist" presence as a part of the NATO military forces.[2]

A similar exponent of leftist insurrectionary violence cropped up in Italy in the form of the Red Brigades. The Brigate Rosse (Red Brigades), like Baader-Meinhof, had cross-national links with a variety of European and Middle Eastern groups. Founded in 1970 by three university students, the Red Brigades shared Baader-Meinhof's extreme leftist doctrine directed against Italy's capitalist regime backed by the U.S. military as part of NATO. In the 1970s, the Red Brigades expanded to Italy's major urban centers, attacking police and security forces, *carabinieri* (state police), magistrates, and leading political figures. Two of their major operations included the kidnapping and murder of former prime minister Aldo Moro and the kidnapping of U.S. Brigadier General James Dozier who was later rescued by Italian police. The government's crackdown and mass imprisonment of Red Brigade members virtually eliminated this extremist group from the Italian political scene until their reemergence in the 2000s.[3]

An Asian ideological sibling of the Baader-Meinhof gang and the Red Brigades was the Japanese Red Army (JRA) formed in 1970. Like its German and Italian counterparts, the Japanese Red Army's preeminent aim was to overthrow Japan's democratic regime and monarchy. The JRA was unique in that it was led by a woman, Fusako Shigenobu, and it had close ties with Palestinian guerrilla organizations. Although small in size, the JRA carried out a series of high-profile attacks around the world in the 1970s and 1980s, including the 1972 Lod Airport massacre in Israel, multiple hijackings of Japanese airliners, the takeover of the French Embassy in The Hague in 1974, and attacks on Japanese, Canadian, and American embassies in various countries. Since Shigenobu's arrest in 2000, the JRA has disbanded and disappeared from the terrorist arena.[4] Although leftist political violence has been in decline since the 1980s, it has persisted in Latin America, Asia, and the Middle East.

In contrast to leftists' objective of capturing state power in the name of socioeconomic justice, rightist groups seek to overthrow democratic and leftist governments in order to promote their extremist causes. Inspired by Fascism and Nazi doctrines of racism and supernationalism, the rightists tend to view the state as the instrument of foreign political and economic interests. Right-wing terrorist groups emerged in the first part of the twentieth century. In Russia, the Black Hundred sought to combat left-wing revolutionaries, killing liberal leaders and participating in anti-Jewish pogroms. Germany's defeat in World War I triggered the rise of extreme right-wing groups, culminating in Hitler's Nazi Party takeover. Prior to Hitler's rise, however, the Freikorps emerged as a terrorist group of former soldiers and students seeking vengeance against the enemies of their defeated fatherland. Among the victims of the Freikorps were the communist leaders Rosa Luxemburg and Karl Liebknecht in 1919 and the German Foreign Minister Walther Rathenau in 1922.[5]

Another epicenter of right-wing terrorism was the Balkans. The Croatian Ustashe fought for independence using terrorist tactics such as the dual assassinations of King Alexander of Yugoslavia and Prime Minister Barthou of France in April 1934. In Romania, the Iron Guard engaged in terrorism as the militant arm of a right-wing political party. Rightist violence also made its appearance in the Middle East. In Egypt, government-sponsored assassins killed the Muslim Brotherhood's founder, Hasan al-Banna (1949), and in Palestine Revisionist Zionist groups such as the Stern Gang and the Irgun targeted Palestinian Arabs and British forces.[6] In addition, right-wing paramilitaries have fought as pro-government vigilantes against insurgent leftist movements in some Latin American countries. These rightist militias include the Contras in Nicaragua, the United Self Defense Forces in Colombia, and various government-sponsored paramilitary groups in Mexico. Finally, the United States has seen waves of rightist violence since the nineteenth century based on racial hatred and doctrines of white supremacy directed against blacks, Jews, Catholics, and other minorities. Two cases of ideological violence will be investigated in this chapter—right wing extremists in the United States and Sendero Luminoso of Peru. Table 5.1 provides a profile of these groups.

Right-Wing Extremists versus the United States

Despite America's long experience with democratic pluralism, right-wing extremism has persisted in disrupting the social peace with periodic acts of violence. Historically, right-wing extremism has been associated with groups preaching doctrines of intolerance toward racial and ethnic minorities and advocating strategic reorientations of U.S. foreign policy. Among the latter were sympathizers of Nazi Germany who opposed U.S. participation in World War II against the Axis powers. Since the 1950s, American rightists have vehemently condemned U.S. involvement in the United Nations and other multinational organizations that they consider as threats to U.S. sovereignty.

Of greater concern are the various white supremacist groups because of their propensity to use violence against citizens and government agencies. The earliest and best known of these racist organizations, the Ku Klux Klan (KKK), was responsible for hundreds of terrorist acts including lynchings, violent demonstrations, destruction of property, and murders aimed primarily at African Americans. This organization was greatly weakened by government crackdowns, legislation, shifts in public opinion, and more recently by the legal actions of the Southern Poverty Law Center, which resulted in the confiscation of the Klan's properties for crimes committed against African Americans. Yet, the Klan's White Power ideology is shared by several hundred "hate groups" that have proliferated in recent decades. The plethora of right-wing groups that emerged in the 1970s and 1980s came to be known as the "Patriot" movement.[7]

Terrorists of the Right: A Profile

The individuals and groups responsible for acts of right-wing political violence in the United States are difficult to categorize under a single label because of their diversity, small size, and autonomous nature. The KKK is one of the oldest rightist perpetrators of violence in the United States. Confederate Army veterans first established the KKK after the American Civil War to resist the Reconstruction and the ending of slavery. After its suppression by President Ulysses S. Grant in the early 1870s, the KKK reemerged in 1915 and by the 1920s had over two

TABLE 5.1   Ideological Violence versus the State: An Overview

Name of Group	Target	Date Founded	Size	First Preference	Leadership Type	Key Leaders	Tactics	Killed in Interactive Violence
Patriot/Militia Movement	U.S. federal government/minority groups	1970s–1980s	50,000	Establish white power regime in U.S.	Decentralized	William L. Pierce, Rev. Richard Butler	Shooting, bombing, robbery	200
Sendero Luminoso	Peruvian government	1979	1,000	Take state power	Charismatic	Abimael Guzmán	Bombing, assassinations, murder	27,000

million members, mostly from the working class.[8] Klan groups participated in lynchings, castrations, assassinations of socialists and communists, cross burnings, and propaganda against Jews, Catholics, and immigrants. The Klan declined during the Great Depression and World
War II because of internal corruption among its leaders and popular revulsion against the brutality of its actions and its Nazi sympathies.[9]

Klan groups returned forcefully in the early 1950s to resist the Civil
Rights movement, particularly the Supreme Court's decision in *Brown v.
Board of Education* (1954). Most Klan attacks were directed against African American individuals and families in the southern states, particularly those who resisted white supremacists' attempts to degrade African
Americans. Among major instances of violence perpetrated by Klan
groups in the 1960s were the murders of NAACP leaders Medgar Evers
(1963) and Vernon Dahmer Sr. (1966) in Mississippi; the bombing of
the 16th Street Baptist Church in Alabama (1963); and the murders of
civil-rights workers James Cheney, Andrew Goodman, and Michael
Schwerner (1964). In the 1970s, Klansmen continued to operate, opposing affirmative action, immigration, and integration, and carrying
out a series of bomb attacks on school busses. Klan membership saw a
steep decline in the 1980s and 1990s. However, despite the government's efforts to crackdown on the Klan, the number of Klan groups increased from 162 to 179 between 2004 and 2005.[10]

In the last two decades, the Klan's ideology has inspired a variety of
racist offshoots such as the skinheads, neo-Nazis, and other far-right
groups associated with the Christian Identity movement such as the
Phineas Priesthood, Posse Comitatus and the Aryan Nations. These
groups preach an eclectic ideology of Biblical vengeance, white racism,
and hatred of Blacks, Jews, Catholics, and other people of color. The targets of the Phineas Priests are government officials, banks, abortion
clinics, blacks, homosexuals, and advocates of world government. James
Earl Ray, the killer of Rev. Martin Luther King Jr., belonged to the
Phineas Priesthood, a movement without a structured organization and
leadership, whose members could operate independently as "lone
wolves" acting on their own initiative.[11]

Another white supremacist group, Posse Comitatus, was formed in
Wisconsin in the mid-1970s as a loosely organized radical movement
based in the countryside. Founded by William Potter Gale, the Posse
Comitatus was virulently racist and antisemitic and opposed to the U.S.
federal government and its authority to tax and impose laws at the local
level. Its ideology and spirit of vigilantism gave rise to new extremist
groups such as the Militia and Patriot movements.[12]

While sharing the Christian Identity ideology of the Phineas Priesthood and the Posse Comitatus, Rev. Richard Butler's Aryan Nations was
a tightly organized congregation with an armed militia.[13] In the mid-

1970s, Butler established his Aryan Nations headquarters at Hayden Lake in the Idaho panhandle, a remote area that soon became a point of ingathering for rightist extremists. An outspoken neo-Nazi, Butler declared war against the "Zionist Occupational Government" (ZOG), denied the occurrence of the Holocaust and preached a fiery doctrine of white purity ordained by God.[14] The organization faced an existential challenge in 2001 when its Idaho compound was dismantled after being sold in order to pay a legal judgment associated with one of its members' conviction of murder in California. In his last years, Butler's control of the Aryan Nations was challenged by several rivals. The organization was split into competing groups even before the passing of Reverend Butler in September 2004.

The Militia Movement

In the early 1990s, the militant segments of the Patriot movement emerged as self-styled "militias"—armed bands of super-patriots claiming to defend the traditional values and interests of white Protestant Americans. The rise of the militia movement was polycentric, with grassroots support mostly from white males in small cities and rural counties. By 1995, dozens of militia groups had been formed throughout the country.

The emergence of the Militia movement was spurned by the FBI's bloody confrontation in 1992 with white supremacist Randy Weaver at Ruby Ridge, Idaho, the federal government's 1993 accidental torching of the Branch Davidian compound in Waco, Texas, and the passage of gun-control legislation prompted by the assassination attempt on President Reagan.[15] Because of the Soviet demise in 1991, there was a major switch in the targets of right-wing ideologues from the "communist conspiracy" to the U.S. federal government, the United Nations, and foreign organizations ostensibly threatening to impose a "New World Order."[16]

The proliferation of rightist radical groups culminated in the bombing of the Murrah Federal Building in Oklahoma City on April 19, 1995, killing 168 FBI and other civilian employees. The principle culprit was Timothy J. McVeigh, a former serviceman discharged after the 1991 Persian Gulf War, who shared the antigovernment anger of the radical right, prompting him to target a federal building. Although McVeigh had circulated among various Patriot groups, he operated as a "lone wolf" with only two associates, in blowing up the Murrah building. The mass slaughter at Oklahoma City was a wake-up call to federal and state agencies about the growing threat of the radical right to domestic tranquility.[17]

In many ways McVeigh personified the core constituency of the radical right, its social and economic roots, and its emotional impulse to embrace anti-state terrorism. This constituency consisted of a nebulous class of disinherited Americans, predominantly white Protestant Christians with roots in the small towns and rural counties of the hinterland. America's headlong drive toward globalization, combined with the massive increase of the immigrant population had a destabilizing impact on what had been a white middle- and lower-middle-class population. As their class position eroded through unemployment and low wages, this growing underclass of whites suffered an identity crisis as Americans who felt economically dispossessed, culturally alienated, and politically marginalized. As patriotic Americans, they had fought or sent their children to fight and die in countless wars and some of their progeny had reached the heights of power in Washington, only to forget their roots in the countryside. Thus, the political elite in Washington were looked upon as the prime enemy— "class traitors" who had betrayed their kinfolk. Simply stated, the militiamen/patriots were "angry white guys," culturally alienated from the American mainstream, whose real grievances were overshadowed by racist and xenophobic outbursts against a changing society and world they could neither comprehend nor accept.[18]

While McVeigh's act of bloody revenge against the federal government seemed to have energized the radical right, it also brought the full force of the authorities upon the militia/patriot movement. The ideological connection between the Oklahoma City carnage and the radical right was *The Turner Diaries,* a book found among McVeigh's possessions after his arrest. A popular bestseller among rightist circles, *The Turner Diaries* contained a fictional blueprint for revolution depicting an attack strikingly similar to that of Oklahoma City. Authored by William L. Pierce, leader of the neo-Nazi National Alliance, the book targets government officials, blacks, Jews, immigrants, liberals, and gun-control advocates.[19] Pierce, a former assistant professor of physics at Oregon State University, produced numerous racist and antisemitic books, cassettes, and videotapes in addition to *The Turner Diaries,* which had sold 200,000 copies by the time of the Oklahoma City bombing.[20]

In October 1996, the Militia movement's Third Continental Congress met in Kansas City to marshal its growing following numbering over 850 patriot groups.[21] Yet despite the movement's apparent strength, 1996 proved to be the tipping point as its membership quickly declined because of the powerful blowback from the Oklahoma City bombing. That attack evoked widespread public anger, along with a clampdown by the FBI and local police agencies. In 2000, the Southern Poverty Law Center could identify only 194 patriot groups—a four-fold drop in four years.[22] This precipitous decline, however, did not signify the neutralization of the radical right. While many of its adherents and their grievances may have been silenced, small cadres of extremists continued to plan and carry out attacks against government and civilian buildings and personnel. In the ten years after the Oklahoma City bombing, these extremists hatched sixty plots, including seventeen attacks, thirty-eight aborted conspiracies and other violent acts.[23] However, there has been a sharp increase in the number of hate groups, mostly right-wing, in the United States in the last five years—a rise of 33 percent. These include neo-Nazis, particularly the growing Nationalist Socialist Movement, skinheads, and other groups angered by Hispanic immigration and U.S. difficulties in the Iraq War.[24]

Right-Wing Extremism in the Military

Since the early days of the American Republic, there have been frequent instances of illicit ties between right-wing extremists and the U.S. military, which constitute an ongoing danger to the democratic system. During the Cold War years, some top military commanders as well as servicemen periodically promoted right-wing and antisemitic causes during and after their military service. In addition, KKK chapters were discovered in the Marine Corps in 1976, and the U.S. Army and Navy in 1979. In 1986, it was again revealed that military personnel were providing guerrilla training and weapons to a Klan paramilitary group, which prompted the Department of Defense to crack down on such practices. Yet this policy did not prevent continued illegal relationships between military personnel and extremist groups, which persisted through the April 1995 Oklahoma City bombing carried out by an Army veteran. Furthermore, in 1995, three white paratroopers were convicted in the murder of a black couple at Fort Bragg, North Carolina, and another nineteen paratroopers were discharged for participation in neo-Nazi activities. During the 1996 Atlanta Summer Olympics, former paratrooper Eric Rudolph detonated a bomb, killing one and wounding 111 people. This antigovernment extremist went on to bomb a lesbian nightclub and two abortion clinics, killing a police officer and eluding capture until 2003. These events prompted Defense Secretary William Perry in 1996 to strengthen the rules against the involvement of military personnel in white supremacist and neo-Nazi groups.[25]

Since the beginning of the Iraq War, the application of the Pentagon's zero-tolerance policy for participation in racial hate groups has been found wanting in a report issued by the Southern Poverty Law Center. According to its investigation, neo-Nazi groups have systematically infiltrated the military and the National Alliance magazine has urged skinheads to join the army's light infantry units in order to train for the coming "race war."[26] The application of the Pentagon's anti-hate group policies has been further impeded by pressure on recruiters to meet quotas given the growing difficulty of enlisting new soldiers to fight in Iraq and Afghanistan. It is estimated that there are thousands of soldiers involved in right-wing extremist groups and activities in the army alone and that many of these have served in Iraq.[27] Clearly the connection between the U.S. military and right-wing extremists will represent a significant threat to American democracy for the foreseeable future.

To be sure, the focus of U.S. security agencies on Islamist militants since September 11, 2001, has left the radical right "terrorists-in-waiting" unattended. However, given the socioeconomic marginalization of a growing number of white Americans and the psychosocial consequences of the Iraq War, the radical right is likely to pose a growing domestic threat. In its present form, the U.S. political and economic system is unprepared to deal with the problems of the radical rightist constituency, except by force.

In the short run, however, the right-wing extremist groups appear to pose a diminishing challenge to the authorities because of recent successes by the FBI and local law enforcement agencies in detecting plots and conspiracies before their execution (see Table 5.2). This reality raises the larger question as to the rationale motivating right-wing extremist individuals and groups to engage in violent challenges to the immense power of the United States in the face of repeated failures. There are several factors that go into the extremists' strategic decision to carry out attacks against the United States despite the gross imbalance of forces. As discussed in Chapter 1, from a game theoretic perspective, the strategic decision to commit violence depends on a variety of social, psychological, and cultural factors, in addition to considerations of material self-interest. First, these perpetrators may be acting out of blind vengeance for specific perceived wrongs committed by the government against themselves or their ideological coterie. Second, victory may be calculated by them not only in terms of bloodshed or overthrow of the government, but in their capacity to terrorize targeted opponents. Finally, by engaging in attacks, they may be less concerned with prevailing than with signaling to their in-group and expanding support for their cause among potential sympathizers. Clearly, the ordered preferences and strategic behavior of right-wing individuals and groups are shaped by their peculiar ideological worldview. As such, long-term solutions to their grievances would have to combine policies addressing the declining economic and political fortunes of the white underclass along with grassroots educational reforms to socialize them into the mainstream of American society.

TABLE 5.2 Right-Wing Extremists versus the State: Strategic Interactions, 1995–2004

Date	Group (type)	Event	Damage/Outcome
Apr. 1995	Timothy McVeigh (lone wolf)	Bombing of the Murrah Federal Building in Oklahoma City	168 killed
July 1995	Charles Ray Polk (lone wolf)	Plot to bomb IRS building in Austin, Texas, foiled when Polk is arrested purchasing weapons from undercover police	Sentenced to 21 years in jail
Oct. 1995	Sons of Gestapo (neo-Nazi)	Derailing of Amtrak passenger train in Hyder, Arizona; perpetrators escape	1 killed, many injured
Nov. 1995	Oklahoma Constitutional Militia	Plot to bomb Southern Poverty Law Center, gay bars, and abortion clinics foiled	3 militia members arrested
Dec. 1995	Joseph Bailey (lone wolf)	Failed bombing attempt at IRS building in Reno, Nevada	Sentenced to 36 years in prison
Jan. 1996	Aryan Republican Army (neo-Nazi)	String of bank robberies ends in shootout with FBI in Ohio	6 members arrested
Apr. 1996	Larry Wayne Shoemaker (lone wolf)	Racist murder based on *Turner Diaries* in Jackson, Mississippi	1 black man killed, 7 others injured
July 1996	Viper Team Arizona Militia	Conspiracy to attack government buildings foiled	12 members imprisoned on various charges
July 1996	Eric Rudolph (lone wolf)	Bombing of Atlanta Summer Olympics	1 killed, over 100 injured
July 1996	Washington State Militia	Plot to attack government foiled	5 convicted of weapons charges, including leader
Oct. 1996	Phineas Priesthood (Christian Identity)	Two bank robberies, four bombings	3 sentenced to life terms
Oct. 1996	Mountaineer Militia	Plot to bomb FBI office in Virginia foiled	4 imprisoned

TABLE 5.2 Cont.   Right-Wing Extremists versus the State: Strategic Interactions, 1995–2004

Date	Group (type)	Event	Damage/Outcome
Jan. 1997	Eric Rudolph (lone wolf)	Bomb attack on an abortion clinic in Sandy Springs, Georgia	7 people injured
Jan. 1997	KKK/Black Dawn (military group)	Raid on private home/arsenal of former Marine and KKK member Ricky Salyers	Salyers sentenced to 3 years
Mar. 1997	Brandon Blasz (militia member)	Plot to bomb federal building, IRS, and TV station foiled in Kalamazoo, Michigan	Sentenced to 3 years on weapons charges
Apr. 1997	Ku Klux Klan (white supremacist)	Plot to bomb gas refinery foiled when one member informs police	4 members imprisoned
Apr. 1997	National Alliance (neo-Nazi)	Member Todd Van Biber accidentally explodes pipe bomb; arrested for plot to bomb and rob banks	Released after 2 years imprisonment
Apr. 1997	Montana Freemen (militia)	Explosion of weapons cache leads to capture of massive arsenal in Yuba City, California	7 convicted on weapons charges
May 1997	Sons of Liberty (militia)	Arson attack on IRS building in Colorado Springs, Colorado	5 imprisoned
July 1997	Third Continental Congress (militia)	Plot to attack U.S. military base in Ft. Hood, Texas	7 arrested
Jan. 1998	Eric Rudolph (lone wolf)	Bombing of abortion clinic near Birmingham, Alabama	1 killed, 1 injured; Rudolph sentenced to life in prison
Feb. 1998	The New Order (KKK, white supremacist)	Plot to kill a federal judge and Morris Dees of SPLC foiled in East St. Louis, Illinois	6 imprisoned on weapons charges and conspiracy
July 1998	Paul T. Chastain (lone wolf)	Member of South Carolina militia with mass arsenal arrested after threats to kill Attorney General and FBI director	Sentenced to 15 years in prison
Oct. 1998	James C. Koppe (lone wolf)	Dr. Barnette Slepian, gynecologist, assassinated by sniper in Amherst, New York	4 imprisoned

Date	Group	Event	Outcome
July 1999	World Church of the Creator (neo-Nazi)	Member Benjamin Smith goes on killing spree in Illinois and Indiana targeting minorities and ultimately killing himself	3 killed (including Smith), 9 injured
Aug. 1999	Aryan Nations (white supremacist)	Buford Furrow kills a Filipino mailman and opens fire at a Jewish community center in San Fernando Valley, California	1 killed, 5 injured; Furrow sentenced to two life terms
Dec. 1999	San Joaquin Militia	Plot to blow up propane tanks and other infrastructure to provoke insurrection foiled	2 members arrested
Dec. 1999	Southeastern States Alliance (militia coalition)	Leader Donald Beauregard arrested on conspiracy and terrorism charges; plot to bomb energy facilities in Florida and Georgia foiled	Imprisoned
Apr. 2000	Richard Baumhammers (lone wolf)	Racist murder	5 killed; Baumhammers sentenced to death
Dec. 2001	Jewish Defense League (right-wing Jewish group)	Chair Irving Rueben and Earl Krugel arrested for conspiracy to bomb office of Representative Darrell Issa and King Fahd mosque	Rueben commits suicide in prison; Krugel sentenced to 10 yrs in prison
July 2002	Ku Klux Klan (white supremacist)	Leader, Charles Robert Barefoot, Jr., plots to blow up sheriff's office in North Carolina; arrested on weapons charges	Sentenced to two years in prison
Feb. 2003	White Knights of the KKK (Christian Identity)	Imperial Wizard David Wayne Hull arrested on weapons charges and plot to bomb abortion clinics	Sentenced to 12 years in prison
Apr. 2003	William Krar (lone wolf)	Arrested on weapons charges after discovery of massive arsenal in Noonday, Texas	Sentenced to 11 years in prison
Apr. 2004	Aryan Nations (white supremacist)	Sean Gillespie firebombs Oklahoma City synagogue; makes film to inspire others	Sentenced to 35 years in prison

Sendero Luminoso versus Peru

The Shining Path (Sendero Luminoso) was among the most powerful in a series of Latin American leftist movements over the last forty years, which included the FARC (Revolutionary Armed Forces of Colombia), the MST (Landless Workers Movement) in Brazil, the EZLN (Zapatista National Liberation Army) in Mexico, the FMLN (Farabundo Martí National Liberation Front) in El Salvador, and the FSLN in Nicaragua (Sandinista National Liberation Front). Sendero is a Marxist organization that sought to overthrow the Peruvian government in the 1980s and 1990s. At the height of its power in 1989–1992, Sendero was Latin America's most dynamic insurgency, posing a major threat to the survival of the Peruvian regime and its transition from an autocracy to a nascent democracy.

Historical Catalysts of Violence

The political system of Peru was no exception to the *caudillo*-style of rulership that has characterized most Latin American countries. The *caudillo*, usually a military or civilian autocrat, ruled with the support of the armed forces that constituted the most organized and effective player in the political process. After the civilian administration of President Fernando Belaúnde (1963–1968), Peru returned to the *caudillo* pattern as the military took power under Generals Juan Velasco (1968–1975) and Francisco Bermudez (1975–1980). After Bermudez ousted Velasco in 1975, he implemented a severe austerity program that triggered massive protests and a sharp decline in economic conditions, especially among the lower classes, mostly consisting of indigenous people. In 1980, the discredited military elite was forced to step aside and permit a transition back to democracy. Hence, on May 18, Belaúnde was elected president for the second time in a landslide victory, facing a milieu of rising popular expectations of socioeconomic betterment.[28] Indeed, ambitious land reforms implemented by General Velasco's regime had not dampened revolutionary activity because of corruption, decreasing levels of production, and the unevenness of its impact on the peasants. These problems were particularly acute in Ayacucho, the epicenter of Sendero's power, where the benefits of agrarian redistribution were minimal compared to the rest of the country.[29] In the midst of declining incomes, increased unemployment, poverty, and severe food shortages, the Ayacucho region provided fertile soil for the growth of Sendero Luminoso.[30] In addition, the Ayacucho area was destabilized by conflicts among the hundreds of indigenous communities that had been displaced centuries earlier.[31]

Leadership and Ideology

Sendero Luminoso was the creation of Dr. Abimael Guzmán Reynoso, a professor of philosophy at the National University of San Cristobal in Ayacucho (UNSCH). An illegitimate child born in 1934, Guzmán suffered social and psychological crises in his formative years, which would shape his revolutionary life. After the death of his mother, the five-year-old child was forced to live with uncles because his father refused to give him shelter. Although Guzmán rejoined his father at the age of twelve, he had already developed deep feelings of resentment toward the man who had illegitimately fathered him but refused ownership of his child. The cumulative impact of social and psychological marginality along with feelings of insecurity and worthlessness led to Guzmán's progressive alienation from society despite his success in Jesuit school and the university. A socially awkward young man, Guzmán had few friends but showed a strict dedication to his studies and a knack for organizing.[32] Initially attracted to Kantian philosophy, Guzmán soon shifted to Marxist political thought and its practice in the Soviet Union and China.[33]

As an aspiring philosopher, Guzmán's encounter with the pervasive poverty in Peruvian society contributed to his growing alienation and anger at the ruling order. In 1960, Guzmán joined the Peruvian Communist Party, which he would reshape as Sendero Luminoso—the violent embodiment of his personality and the venue for his quest to compensate for his childhood deprivations by assuming supreme power in the name of the exploited masses. In this process, Guzmán's resentment of his uncaring father translated into a rejection of all political authority, particularly the ruling elite in Lima that Sendero's revolutionaries would seek to fight and overthrow.

In preparation for his revolutionary mission, Guzmán thrice visited China to study the "people's war" doctrine and the practice of Maoist insurgency—a peasant-based movement that would begin in the countryside and move toward the urban centers, eventually toppling the regime.[34] He also met Ché Guevara, the icon of Cuban revolutionism in Latin America and Africa. These visits were decisive in Guzmán's recreation of the Peruvian Communist Party into Sendero Luminoso—a rigidly hierarchical organization led by a Political Bureau. The party's military wing—the Popular Guerrilla Army—consisted of highly mobile detachments operating in both urban and rural areas. Micro-level operations—assassinations, logistics, and small-scale attacks—were conducted by local militias. The behavior of all party members and combatants was tightly regulated under Sendero law consisting of puritanical injunctions—obey orders, do not steal, share everything you capture, do not mistreat prisoners, pay for what you buy, and do not take liberties with men or women.[35] Yet, these disciplinary practices of good conduct were not meant to restrain the Sendero guerrillas from utilizing various terrorist tactics against the regime—e.g., beheadings, castrations, arson, donkey bombs, car bombs, assassinations, sabotaging electrical grids, and disrupting delivery of goods to urban centers.[36] Despite its often brutal use of violence, Sendero did not see itself as a terrorist organization. Indeed, its members saw violence as the only legitimate way of fighting the terror imposed on them by the state. This rationale of legitimizing violence was proclaimed in a poem by Luis Placencia and printed in the Sendero newspaper, *El Diario,* in June 1988:

> Onward guerrilla, ignore them
> If they call you "terrorist" or "criminal" . . .
> Terrorism . . . this is terrorism?
> What peace and calm existed? . . .
> You are terrorists
> who make a man a slave. . . .
> Terrorism is terror,
> and I feel that daily
> when hunger and pain
> take children to the grave. . . .
> Terrorism! you will shout
> you will kill . . . you will accuse
> but history will sing
> of glory, of freedom
> of another land
> of another sea.[37]

The Sendero structure and leadership closely approximated the Leninist "vanguard" party cadre of mostly middle class intellectuals whose alienation from the state had led them to become full-time professional revolutionaries dedicated to lead the struggle for the emancipation of the exploited masses. To be sure, virtually none of the Sendero leadership was from Peru's toiling masses. Indeed, Guzmán and his circle of colleagues (*socios*) were mostly white professors and intellectuals from wealthy families; yet in contrast to Lenin's and Mao's communist party politburos, up to half of Guzmán's top cadre were women.[38]

Guzmán's leadership style was profoundly affected by his domineering personality and his need to have absolute control over the party. A voracious reader since his youth, he regarded the writings of Marx, Lenin, and Mao Zedong as the scriptural foundations of his movement. He was more likely to have a book under his arm than a gun over his shoulder. In leadership style, Guzmán possessed Stalinist and Maoist attributes tending toward a cult of personality. Sendero's propagandists praised him as the "Fourth Sword of World Revolution," the "Red Sun" or "Puka Inti," and "el Maestro." [39] He saw himself as the rightful heir of the ideological legacies of Marx, Lenin, and Mao—an eclectic mix of communist revolutionary thought that Guzmán sought to put into practice in Peru.

Strategic Thought and Bases of Support

Sendero's ideology was often referred to as "Gonzalo Thought," after one of Guzmán's favorite pseudonyms as a revolutionary leader. Gonzalo Thought emphasized the centrality of class struggle against U.S. imperialism and its "puppet," the Peruvian government. In this struggle, the vanguard party—Sendero Luminoso—would lead the masses in unleashing revolutionary violence to achieve victory. This strategy would move in three stages. The first "defensive" stage would build support through indoctrination and secure territory until the movement could reach the second stage—"strategic equilibrium." Sendero Luminoso garnered vast support and gained control of territory in many localities by punishing corrupt local officials and business owners (generally through murder) and by redistributing resources. By May 1991, Sendero claimed to have reached the second stage of "strategic equilibrium"—the point at which, from their perspective, they were on an even footing with the Peruvian government. Thus, at the height of its power, Sendero Luminoso was poised to begin the final "offensive" phase in which the party would take the reins of government.[40]

Such strategic leverage could not have been achieved without the dedication of local level party members. The core support base for the party consisted of teachers and university professors who were able to disseminate Gonzalo Thought in the classroom and develop networks of committed senderistas to carry out party operations in their local settings. As a professor at UNSCH, Guzmán developed this network of teachers and intellectuals who were also joined by women, peasants, and the urban poor.[41] Claiming to lead a "people's war," Guzmán used Inca and Christian symbols to mobilize the indigenous peasants, without any deep commitment to ethnic values. Despite the relatively high level of participation of women in the party's leadership and ranks, Sendero did not have a strong feminist bent. In its ideology, organization and goals, Sendero was a Latin American variant of the Leninist/Stalinist/Maoist totalitarian party determined to topple the Peruvian regime.[42] Guzmán's failure to give greater consideration to the cultural milieu of his indigenous constituencies may have contributed to the government's ability to recruit many of them to participate in counter-Sendero peasant organizations (*rondas*). This strategic misstep resulted from a blind spot in Guzmán's Marxist revolutionary worldview in which class struggle became the catch-all under which ethnicity, gender, and other elements of identity were subsumed.[43]

Sendero's Emergence: Initiation and Deployment

In 1970, Guzmán was expelled from the Peruvian Communist Party and went on to establish the Communist Party of Peru-Shining Path (PCP-SL). Throughout the 1970s, Sendero continued to organize its growing network of teachers, professors, and students. Sendero's intensive preparatory work for armed action, carried out in training sessions between September 1979 and March 1980, culminated in its first attack on May 17 on a voter registration office in Chuschi the night before the presidential election. Despite this attack, however, Belaúnde was elected with broad-based popular support, which was seen as a threat to the discredited and ineffective military bureaucracy of outgoing President Bermudez. Afraid that the new government would discover the inefficiency of its intelligence programs, the outgoing military regime "evacuated" all of the files it had gathered on Sendero's activities. As a result of this cover-up, Belaúnde underestimated the gravity of Sendero's threat and was slow in responding to its "Initiation Plan" during which Sendero was reported to have carried out over 1,300 operations. Most of these actions involved small-scale violence and arson, as well as attacks on electrical grids. In this period, the Belaúnde administration's first preference was regime maintenance and not emerging provincial threats. Reluctant to alienate the military, Belaúnde decided not to pursue the crucial missing files.[44] This strategic decision, based on the government's desire to consolidate its power internally and its underestimation of Sendero's threat, emboldened Guzmán to ratchet up the frequency and intensity of attacks. Guzmán had successfully exploited the delicate political circumstances of Peru's democratic transition in planning the timing of his attacks. For a chronology of the interactions between Sendero and the government see Table 5.3.

In January 1981, Sendero began its "Deployment Plan"—two years of heightened guerrilla activity that reportedly exceeded 5,300 attacks.[45] This dramatic increase in violence forced Belaúnde to acknowledge the significance of Sendero's threat potential, which led to a hardening of state policies toward the group. The situation signified the onset of severe interactive violence, where the interests of the two sides could not be reconciled because they had asymmetrical preferences and lacked a forum for communication or compromise acceptable to both parties. Sendero's first and only preference was the regime's overthrow, and the regime's first and only preference became Sendero's total defeat. The outcome was a zero-sum game—a fight to the finish!

TABLE 5.3   Sendero Luminoso versus Peru: Strategic Interactions, 1970–1992

Date	Actor and Type (or Event)	Death Toll/Outcome
1970	Guzmán expelled from Peruvian Communist Party	Establishes Communist Party of Peru-Sendero Luminoso (PCP-SL)
1979–1980	Intensive indoctrination and military training	
May 1980 – Dec. 1980	"Initiation Plan"	1,342 operations; Belaúnde caught off guard
May 1980	Sendero's first attack; arson on voter registration office in Chuschi aiming to disrupt elections	Minimal impact
July 1980	Attacks on electrical grids in Lima; bombings in Cangallo and Huancapi	Signal to Belaúnde on his first day in office; disruption of electrical power
Jan. 1981 – Jan. 1983	"Deployment Plan"	5,350 armed actions
May 1983 – Sept. 1986	"Plan to Conquer Bases"	28,621 actions; government unleashes dirty war; 13,405 killed on both sides
Summer 1983	Sendero moves into Upper Huallaga Valley, a coca-growing area	Government declares "state of emergency" in late 1984
July 1985	Pres. Alan García takes office	
June 1986	Military massacre in Frontón Prison	250 Sendero prisoners killed
1986	Shift from state terror to economic development in Ayacucho by García	Weakening of support for Sendero among peasantry
Dec. 1986 – July 1989	"Plan to Develop Bases"	63,052 actions
Aug. 1989– Aug. 1992	"Great Plan to Develop Bases and Serve the Conquest of Power"	23,000+ actions
July 1990	Fujimori assumes presidency; program of state terror undertaken by Vladimiro Montesinos, head of National Intelligence Service	Severe austerity program, strengthening of *rondas*, and establishment of GEIN
May 1991	"Strategic Equilibrium" apex of Sendero power	Sendero control of 40 percent of Peruvian territory
Apr. 1992	Fujimori carries out *autogolpe*	Major attacks by Sendero on infrastructure and armed strikes; 63 killed, hundreds injured
Sept. 1992	Guzmán captured by GEIN in Lima	Rapid unraveling of Sendero Luminoso

Dirty War, 1983–1986

In the next phase of Guzmán's strategy, "Plan to Conquer Bases," Sendero units spread throughout the country resulting in a quantum increase in attacks—over 28,000 in a three-year period.[46] In a belated response to this growing challenge, Belaúnde reluctantly turned to the military establishment—a major shift, given the longstanding tension between the civilian and military sectors of government. The deployment of the Second Infantry division in late 1982 in the Sendero-held areas around Ayacucho represented a classic example of state terrorism. The military's scorched earth campaign in 1983–1984, cut a path of destruction through villages and farmlands, amid the torture and massacre of the peasantry.[47]

The regime's brutal offensives were matched by Sendero's ill-conceived responses, targeting suspected collaborators among the Andean peasantry—the key segment of the population that Guzmán's Maoist movement ostensibly sought to mobilize. Sendero's "people's trials" and mass executions of villagers deeply alienated the peasantry, caught in an intolerable vise between the terrorism of Sendero's guerrillas and the military's state-sponsored terrorism.

In an attempt to match the military's aggressive campaign, in summer 1983, Sendero moved into the Upper Huallaga Valley, a major coca-growing region. This move may have cut off the flow of funds from the coca trade to the regime's allies, although its benefits to Sendero remained unclear. In late 1984, Sendero's increasing attacks prompted the regime to declare a state of emergency as its hold on the Upper Huallaga region began to crumble. Sendero's numerous bombings of police stations and other government targets were matched by the Peruvian military's massacres of hundreds of Sendero adherents and suspected members.[48]

Policy Shifts, 1986–1990

After the inauguration of President Alan García Perez in July 1985, the tempo of interactive terrorism continued its upward trend with no end in sight. On June 19, 1986, the military slaughtered 250 suspected Sendero members at El Frontón prison—thereafter commemorated as "Heroism Day" on the Sendero calendar. Sendero struck back with over 63,000 operations between 1986 and 1989 as a part of its "Plan to Develop Bases." As the conflict trudged forward, President García made two important policy changes in the context of his regime's overall strategy toward Sendero. First, he initiated a shift away from the military's wholesale use of state terror, to investing in the economic development of Ayacucho and the southern highlands. This effort aimed at the reduction of Sendero's grassroots support by providing large-scale employment to thousands of people. Included in this outreach was a plan to strengthen the *rondas,* community self-defense patrols made up of groups of peasants armed by the government. Second, García established the National Anti-Terrorism Directorate (DINCOTE)—an organization specifically charged with the campaign against Sendero. While the results were not immediately seen, these initiatives, more than any of the policies concocted by either Belaúnde or Alberto Fujimori, García's successor, were decisive in the ultimate defeat of Sendero, which by the late 1980s fielded over 20,000 guerrillas and controlled nearly half of Peru's territory.[49]

Personalismo and Strategic Failure, 1990–1992

As Alberto Fujimori assumed the presidency in July 1990, Sendero continued to expand its power with the establishment of "Raucana"—a "liberated area" on the outskirts of Lima, the capital city. Fujimori's presidency marked a return to autocratic rule based on the newly formed National Intelligence Service under Vladimiro Montesinos, which targeted dissident groups and individuals, especially in the universities, through imprisonment, murders, and disappearances. To confront Sendero, Fujimori continued to strengthen the *rondas* and established GEIN (Special Intelligence Group) within DINCOTE, drawing on technical support from the U.S. Central Intelligence Agency. In November 1991, a system of "faceless" military courts was empowered to convict thousands of suspected "terrorists" for "treason against the mother country." Fujimori's dictatorial quest culminated in April 1992 when he carried out an *autogolpe* (self-coup), by shutting down the legislature and scrapping the constitution.[50] In a sense, Fujimori's response to Guzmán's *personalismo* was to establish a personality cult of his own. This reversion to large-scale state terrorism was met by Sendero's spectacular acts of violence, as, in May 1991, it claimed to have achieved "a strategic equilibrium" in fighting the regime. In July 1992, a series of bombings in Lima brought the city to a standstill. Fujimori's reversion to full-scale state terrorism apparently could not contain Sendero's continuing prowess. Then, on September 12, 1992, while Fujimori was fishing, Guzmán was unexpectedly captured by GEIN units at a safehouse in Lima with several other Sendero leaders.[51] Table 5.4 outlines the impact of thirteen years of Sendero violence against the Peruvian state.

TABLE 5.4   Sendero Luminoso: A Profile

Former size	20,000+
Present size	<1,000
Imprisoned	2,600
Total killed by both sides	27,000
Economic damage	$23 billion
Political assassinations	593

Source: Victor Manuel Quechua, *Peru ... 13 Años de Oprobio,* 3d ed. (Lima: Tetis Graf).

Collapse and Rebirth? 1992–2006

Guzmán's capture in the heart of Lima was the ultimate blow to the Sendero movement for several strategic reasons. It provided the Fujimori regime with an unexpected opportunity to achieve its first preference—the destruction of the Sendero insurgency. Given Guzmán's centrality to his totalitarian organization as supreme strategist, ideologue, and icon, there could be little doubt that Sendero's viability as a revolutionary movement was seriously degraded by his capture. The circumstances of Guzmán's arrest in the company of three female leaders, followed by Fujimori's display of Sendero's proud leader in an iron cage, had a devastating impact on the rank and file, while laying bare his failures in leadership and strategic judgment. What was Guzmán doing in enemy territory, having taken up the urban bourgeois lifestyle that had characterized his family background? Was Guzmán's strategic decision to move his Mao-style rural-based insurgency into the urban sphere too premature? Did he misjudge Sendero's strength relative to the regime's growing capabilities by deciding to take up residence in Lima? And finally, why didn't he develop stronger leadership cadres that would be capable of taking over the helm after his departure?

In retrospect, it was clear that Guzmán had made a series of strategic mistakes prompted by his authoritarian personality, Maoist ideology, and personal arrogance. As an urban bourgeois Maoist intellectual, he could not understand and exploit the deep roots of Peru's indigenous culture. Guzmán in Peru, like Guevara in Bolivia, had failed to recognize the cultural difficulties of revolutionizing the Andean peasantry. Despite its early successes in mobilizing the indigenous people, Sendero's violent methods and cultural insensitivity drove some of the peasantry into an alliance with the regime, which organized them into self-defense units and armed them to fight Gonzalo's guerrillas.

In September 1993, a humbled Guzmán made a call for peace talks from his prison cell that was promptly rejected by both the Fujimori regime and Sendero's remnants. Basking in the glow of victory, Fujimori had no interest in Guzmán's offer to seek a "political solution." Although Guzmán did not reject violence in making his peace offer, he had been forced to make a strategic change from his first preference of regime takeover, to a reluctant acceptance of the regime's authority in exchange for the freedom of several thousand imprisoned Senderistas. Guzmán's proposal split the Sendero cadres, already weakened by the regime's mass arrests and killings. A faction led by Feliciano Oskar Durand continued the insurgency until his capture in 1999.[52]

In an ironic twist of fate, Fujimori was driven from power in 2000 after a popular outburst against his corrupt authoritarian rule and allegations of electoral malfeasance. There was a return to democracy after the election of President Alejandro Toledo, a man of indigenous origins. The Toledo regime was unable to cope with Peru's multifaceted economic problems, including the growing ranks of the poor, which exceed fifteen million. Yet, despite the many failures of the Fujimori and Toledo governments, Sendero has registered only a modest revival as a serious insurgency. In March 2002, a car bomb, attributed to Sendero, killed nine people outside the U.S. Embassy before the visit of President George W. Bush to Lima, and was followed by occasional acts of terrorism against the security forces. Estimates place Sendero strength at around 1,000, consisting of radical peasants and teachers, mostly centered in the Huallaga, Ene, and Apurimac valleys. The geographic location of its strength raises the possibility of Sendero's evolution from left-wing terrorism to narco-terrorism. Although the Toledo regime viewed Sendero as a low-level threat, there were periodic indications of its continued existence. In April 2004, Sendero commander Camarada Artemio issued an ultimatum to the government to find a political solution to the "internal war" or face a resumption of terrorism. In June 2004, an aging Guzmán went on a hunger strike demanding amnesty, while bombs were detonated at a police station. In October 2005, the government granted Guzmán a retrial resulting in a second conviction.

Future Scenarios

While the likelihood of a major Sendero revival remains low, the ever-growing maldistribution of wealth and misrule could trigger new threats to Peru's stability. Three possible scenarios are:

1. The revival of the Tupac Amaru Revolutionary Movement (MRTA), an urban guerrilla group that was crushed by Fujimori after MRTA's December 1996 takeover of the Japanese Embassy during a diplomatic reception celebrating Japanese independence.
2. The revival of Sendero or a new leftist insurgent group with roots in

both the cities and the countryside, particularly among indigenous people who are now more conscious of their identity and better educated than Sendero's peasant recruits of the 1980s.

3. An unorganized and unplanned mass uprising of poor urbanites and peasants, should President Alan García, re-elected in June 2006, fail to improve grassroots economic conditions.

Ideological Violence: A Comparative Analysis

The investigation of violence by ideologically motivated groups against state authority reveals several significant patterns. The progressive decline of leftist revolutionary violence in Europe, Japan, the Middle East, and Latin American since the late 1980s paralleled the weakening and collapse of the Soviet Union. The strong democratic cultures of Italy, Japan, and West Germany combined with energetic counterterrorism efforts facilitated the neutralization of leftist ideological terrorism in these countries. Future ideological terrorism in the European states is more likely to come from the right, given strong anti-immigrant sentiments throughout Europe exacerbated by the effects of globalization. In contrast, in some Latin American countries such as Mexico, Ecuador, Venezuela, and Bolivia, leftist organizations have been replaced by identity-based movements using primarily electoral means to gain power without resorting to violence. In the Middle East, leftist ideologies have given way to Islamist radicalism as discussed in Chapters 4 and 6. A similar ideological shift toward religious fundamentalism has been under way in the United States in the form of politicized Christianity often mixed with white racism and xenophobia. Should the democratic experiments in Latin America, Africa, Eastern Europe, and Asia fail, there is a high likelihood that both right- and left-wing violence will rise to challenge state authority once again.

Notes

1. Pamala L. Griset and Sue Mahan, *Terrorism in Perspective* (Thousand Oaks, CA: Sage Publications, 2003), 7–8; and Walter Laqueur, ed., *Voices of Terror,* (New York: Reed, 2004), 50–51.
2. Stefan Aust, *The Baader-Meinhof Group: The Inside Story of a Phenomenon* (London: Bodley Head, 1987).
3. For a more detailed account see Robert C. Meade, *Red Brigades: The Story of Italian Terrorism* (London: Macmillan, 1990).
4. William Farrell, *Blood and Rage: The Story of the Japanese Red Army* (Lexington, MA: Lexington Books, 1990).
5. Walter Laqueur, *The New Terrorism* (New York: Oxford University Press, 1999).

6. *Ibid.*, 22–23.
7. For an overview of these groups see Jeffrey Kaplan, ed., *Encyclopedia of White Power: A Sourcebook on the Radical Racist Right* (Walnut Creek, CA: Altamira Press, 2000); also see www.splcenter.org.
8. James W. Vander Zanden, "The Klan Revival," *The American Journal of Sociology* 65, no. 5 (1960): 456–462.
9. Richard T. Schaefer, "The Ku Klux Klan: Continuity and Change," *Phylon* 32 no. 2 (1971): 143–157.
10. Mark Potok, "The Year in Hate, 2005," *Southern Poverty Law Center Intelligence Report*, Spring 2006.
11. Jonathan R. White, "Political Eschatology: A Theology of Antigovernment Extremism," *American Behavioral Scientist* 44, no. 6 (2001): 937–956.
12. Daniel Levitas, *The Terrorist Next Door: The Militia Movement and the Radical Right* (New York: St. Martin's, 2002), 153–164, 201–203, 383–391.
13. See Robert Kline and Richard H. Dekmejian, *Terrorism: A World in Shadows, Part IV* (a documentary film shown on the Discovery Channel, 1990).
14. Brian Levin, "Cyberhate," *The American Behavioral Scientist* 45, no. 6 (2002): 958–988.
15. Daniel Junas, "Angry White Guys with Guns: The Rise of the Militias," *Covert Action Quarterly*, Spring 1995, 20–25.
16. Griset and Mahan, *Terrorism in Perspective*, 102–104.
17. Lou Michel and Dan Herbeck, *American Terrorist: Timothy McVeigh and the Oklahoma City Bombing* (New York: Regan Books, 2001).
18. Junas, "Angry White Guys."
19. Levitas, *The Terrorist Next Door*, 326–327, 336–338.
20. Jack Nelson, "Book Called 'Blueprint for Revolution,'" *Los Angeles Times*, April 23, 1995.
21. Jo Thomas, "Militias Hold a Congress, and Not a Gun is Seen," *New York Times*, November 1, 1996.
22. Robert L. Jackson, "Militia Movement: A 'Shadow' of Its Past, Study Finds," *Los Angeles Times*, May 9, 2001.
23. Andrew Blejwas, Anthony Griggs, and Mark Potok, "Terror from the Right," *Southern Poverty Law Center Intelligence Report*, Summer 2005.
24. Potok, "The Year in Hate, 2005."
25. David Holthouse, "A Few Bad Men," *Southern Poverty Law Center Intelligence Report*, Summer 2006.
26. John Kifner, "Hate Groups Infiltrating the Military, Group Asserts," *The New York Times*, July 7, 2006.
27. www.splcenter.org.
28. Gustavo Gorriti, *The Shining Path: A History of the Millenarian War in Peru* (Chapel Hill: University of North Carolina Press, 1999), 7–8.
29. James F. Rochlin, *Vanguard Revolutionaries in Latin America: Peru, Colombia, Mexico*, (Boulder, CO: Lynne Rienner, 2003), 30–32.
30. Cynthia McClintock, *Revolutionary Movements in Latin America* (Washington, DC: United States Institute of Peace, 1998), 157–200.
31. Ton de Wit and Vera Gianotten, "The Center's Multiple Failures," in *The Shining Path of Peru*, ed. David Scott Palmer (New York: St. Martin's, 1992), 47–50.
32. Simon Strong, *Shining Path: Terror and Revolution in Peru* (New York: Times Books, 1993), 3–7.
33. Gustavo Gorriti, "Shining Path's Stalin and Trotsky," in *The Shining Path of Peru*, ed. David Scott Palmer (New York: St. Martin's, 1992), 152–153.
34. Strong, *Shining Path*, 66–74.

35. Victor Manuel Quechua, *Peru . . . 13 Años de Oprobio,* 3d ed. (Lima: Tetis Graf, 1995), 135–137; and Strong, *Shining Path,* 82.
36. McClintock, *Revolutionary Movements in Latin America,* 68–69.
37. Strong, *Shining Path,* 79
38. *Ibid.,* 71.
39. Strong, *Shining Path,* 23–27.
40. Rochlin, *Vanguard Revolutionaries,* 60–64.
41. McClintock, *Revolutionary Movements in Latin America,* 271–272.
42. Orin Starn, "Maoism in the Andes: the Communist Party of Peru—Shining Path and the Refusal of History," *Journal of Latin American Studies* 27, no. 2 (1995).
43. Rochlin, *Vanguard Revolutionaries,* 33–35.
44. Gorriti, *The Shining Path,* 43–54.
45. *Ibid.*
46. *Ibid.,* 61.
47. On the government's genocidal killings see Strong, *Shining Path,* 92–95.
48. For more detailed statistics see Rochlin, *Vanguard Revolutionaries,* 65–66.
49. *Ibid.,* 70.
50. McClintock, *Revolutionary Movements in Latin America,* 147–149 and Rochlin, *Vanguard Revolutionaries,* 67–69
51. Gorriti, *The Shining Path,* xvi.
52. Rochlin, *Vanguard Revolutionaries,* 71.

Further Reading

Aust, Stefan. *The Baader-Meinhof Group: The Inside Story of a Phenomenon.* London: Bodley Head, 1987.
Dinnerstein, Leonard. *Anti-Semitism in America.* New York: Oxford University Press, 1994,
Farrell, William. *Blood and Rage: The Story of the Japanese Red Army.* Lexington, MA: Lexington Books, 1990.
Gorriti, Gustavo. *The Shining Path: A History of the Millenarian War in Peru.* Chapel Hill: University of North Carolina Press, 1999.
Kaplan, Jeffrey, ed. *Encyclopedia of White Power: A Sourcebook on the Radical Racist Right.* Walnut Creek, CA: Altamira Press, 2000.
Levitas, Daniel. *The Terrorist Next Door: The Militia Movement and the Radical Right.* New York: St. Martin's, 2002.
McClintock, Cynthia. *Revolutionary Movements in Latin America: El Salvador's FMLN & Peru's Shining Path.* Washington, DC: United States Institute of Peace, 1998.
Michel, Lou, and Dan Herbeck. *American Terrorist: Timothy McVeigh and the Oklahoma City Bombing.* New York: Regan Books, 2001.
Rochlin, James F. *Vanguard Revolutionaries in Latin America.* Boulder, CO: Lynne Rienner, 2003.
Ryan, Nick. *Into a World of Hate: A Journey among the Extreme Right.* New York: Routledge, 2004.
Strong, Simon. *Shining Path: Terror and Revolution in Peru.* New York: Times Books, 1993.

Transnational Terrorism: Al-Qaida versus the United States and Allied Regimes

IN THE ANNALS OF POLITICAL VIOLENCE, al-Qaida is *sui generis*; in terms of ideology, organization, and lethal potential, it is one of a kind. As such, it represents an unprecedented challenge to state authority and to the larger international system. Although it shares the rationale of religious extremism with radical Islamist groups based in various countries, al-Qaida's strategic logic of violence transcends national boundaries to assume a global reach in targeting its perceived enemies within and outside the Muslim world.

Al-Qaida's Arab Origins

Al-Qaida represents the culmination of a radicalization process within the Islamic world resulting from centuries of decline in its geostrategic position. At the zenith of Arab imperial power under the Umayyad and Abbasid caliphates, the Muslim civilization had become the epicenter of great intellectual, scientific, and cultural achievements, unrivalled in its day. A series of dynastic, ethnic, and sectarian conflicts led to the progressive demise of the Abbasid caliphate in Baghdad in the tenth and eleventh centuries as power was usurped by various Persian, Turkic, and Kurdish dynasties and military leaders (sultans) who divided and ruled parts of the empire. Although the Kurdish general, Saladin, saved the Abbasid Empire by defeating the Crusaders in 1187, the Mongols under Hulagu sacked and destroyed Baghdad in 1258.[1] This ended the declining primacy of the Arabs, as various newly Islamized

Turkic tribal dynasties took up the cause of Islam as a means to legitimize their rule and mobilize the Muslims to confront external foes. The most successful of these Turkic tribal rulers were the Ottomans (1299–1922) who captured Constantinople in 1453 and ruled the Balkans and most of the Arab lands for over 400 years. The Ottoman sultan Selim I proclaimed himself caliph, as successor to the Prophet Muhammad, after his conquest of Egypt in 1517. This marked the transfer of caliphal power from the Arabs to the Ottoman Turks, who became the champions of the majority Sunni sect of Islam. Meanwhile, the Persian part of the Abbasid caliphate was ruled by several Shiite dynasties of Turkic origin, in keeping with the dominance of the Shiite sect in the region.[2]

Beginning in the eighteenth century, both the Ottoman and Persian empires were in sharp decline because of internal struggles, dysfunctional political systems, and inability to modernize their societies quickly to confront the challenges of European ascendance. Indeed, the Islamic ummah   the global community of Muslims—was in retreat everywhere from the Ottoman Empire, to Persia, to the Indian subcontinent. Islam was being challenged by Western ideologies of nationalism, secularism, capitalism, and socialism as European cultural penetration posed a growing threat to the religious traditions of Muslim societies. Meanwhile, Muslim power was in retreat on the political and military fronts with the declining fortunes of the Ottoman and Persian empires, while millions of Muslims lived under Russian, Dutch, British, and French imperial rule. The archaic dynasties ruling the Ottoman Empire, Persia, and Egypt were beset by widespread crises of legitimacy because of their despotic and corrupt practices at home and military impotence vis-à-vis the West.[3]

Crisis and Response: Islamic Resurgence

The crisis milieu of the Muslim ummah evoked diverse responses from ruling elites and thinkers, ranging from emulating European models of nation-building and modernization, to searching for indigenous Islamic solutions by modernizing and reforming traditional practices. The first option would involve acceptance of the existing division of the ummah into nation-states based on ethno-linguistic boundaries, where indigenous nationalisms held sway. The second option centered on maintaining and strengthening the spiritual and ideological unity of the ummah by reviving and reforming Islam as a prelude to establishing a politically united Pan-Islamic state. The chief exponent of Islamic reformist revival and unity was Shaikh Jamal al-Din al-Afghani (1838–1897), who unsuccessfully sought to rally the world's Muslims to unite under the Ottoman sultan. However, his ideas of reforming Islam as a means of revitalizing the faith and society found expression in the Salafiya movement of Egypt at the turn of the twentieth century.[4]

While the Salafiya represented a rationalist approach to Islamic revivalism and reform, three other movements had preceded it as militant expressions of Muslim resurgence—the Sanusiya resisted European imperialism in North Africa; the Mahdiya battled Ottoman/British control of the Sudan; and the Wahhabiya fought the Ottomans to consolidate Saudi rule over Arabia. These revivalist movements sought to emulate the puritanical tenets of early Islam to confront their present-day problems. This fundamentalist trend gained momentum throughout the twentieth century in response to the rise of Western hegemony and a succession of events that progressively exacerbated the crisis conditions besetting the Islamic world.[5] As a direct result of the century-long intensification of crisis conditions, three successive manifestations of Islamic resurgence inexorably led to the violent face-off between extremist Islam and the Western powers and allied Muslim states at the dawn of the twenty-first century:

1. Religious Islamism—Islam's revivalist or fundamentalist expression, which became pervasive throughout the ummah as a cultural and spiritual mass movement (1890–   ).
2. Political Islamism—Islam's politicized expression as represented by groups of activists seeking to transform religious revivalism into a political force to replace the ruling regimes of Muslim countries with theocratic Islamist governments based on Islamic law (shariah) (1940–   ).
3. Radical Islamism—Islam's extremist expression as represented by the militant fringe of the political Islamist movement, which advocates use of violence to achieve the twin objectives of establishing Islamist regimes in Muslim countries and freeing the ummah from the West's political, military, economic, and cultural dominance (1970–   ).

The phases and dialectics of the expansion and radicalization of Islamism in response to specific crisis events during the twentieth century are outlined below.

Imperialism versus Nationalism, 1914–1948

The Ottoman-German alliance in World War I presented Britain with a powerful challenge in the heart of the Middle East. In 1916, Britain helped the restive Arab subjects of Ottoman Turkey to rebel against the sultans by promising to establish an independent Arab caliphate stretching from the Arabian Peninsula to northern Syria.[6] Although the Arab Revolt led by Sharif Hussein ibn Ali of Mecca and Lawrence of Arabia was eminently successful, Britain reneged on its bargain by dividing the region into "mandates" of imperial control—Britain in Iraq and Palestine, and France in Syria and Lebanon. Britain also retained its dominant position in Egypt, Iran, and the Gulf region, while the Saudis took control of Arabia after defeating Sharif Hussein, whose sons, Abdullah and Faisal, were given the newly created kingdoms of Transjordan and Iraq respectively, as consolation prizes by Colonial Secretary Winston Churchill. This settlement was a heavy blow to the aspirations of the nascent Arab nationalist movement and led to several unsuccessful rebellions in Syria, Palestine, and Iraq.

The suppression of the Arab nationalist cause in the eastern Arab lands and Egypt gave rise to an alternative venue of resistance to social decay and foreign rule—Islamism. In 1929, Hasan al-Banna founded the Muslim Brotherhood in Egypt, dedicated to reviving Islam as a puritanical religion shaping all aspects of life from spirituality to social and political conduct, regardless of ethnic, national, racial, or linguistic differences.[7] Despite opposition from the British and secular nationalist parties, the Muslim Brotherhood rapidly expanded in Egypt and in other Arab countries.

A key theater of Arab resistance to British control was Palestine, where growing Jewish immigration fleeing Nazi-occupied Europe and Zionist aspirations of independent statehood fueled popular anger. Britain suppressed repeated Arab revolts in Palestine, while vainly seeking to befriend the Arabs throughout the region with new promises of independence before the outbreak of World War II. As several Arab countries gained independence during the Cold War period, British and French influences continued to wane, only to be replaced by American power.

Zionism versus Arab Nationalism, 1948–1967

Caught in the vortex of growing Jewish and Arab interactive violence, Britain withdrew from Palestine on May 15, 1948, as Israel declared its independence. In the ensuing war, Israel's victory over the Arabs produced a massive outpouring of Palestinian refugees and a series of political earthquakes in the Arab countries. The blowback from the Arab defeat triggered a new wave of Arab nationalism that focused on Arab unity as the means to defeat Israel and resist the growing influence of its Western allies. A series of revolutions and coups d'état brought the military to power in Syria, Egypt, Iraq, and Yemen as popular Arab sentiments turned away from joining Western alliances against the Soviet Union and toward nonalignment in world affairs. At the epicenter of Pan-Arabism—the Arab unity movement—was Egyptian president Lt. Col. Gamal Abd al-Nasser, whose policies of nonalignment, rapprochement with the Soviets, and nationalization of the Suez Canal made his regime a natural target of the Western powers; hence, the October 1956 Anglo-French-Israeli invasion of Egypt which was only reversed through the joint efforts of the United States and the Soviet Union.[8]

Nasser's defiant stance brought him a mass following as the charismatic embodiment of Arab hopes and aspirations. However, his efforts to unite the Arab countries failed because of resistance from the ruling elites, the West, and even the Soviet Union. Both the West and Soviets saw a united Arab entity stretching from Morocco to the Persian Gulf and backed by great oil wealth as an undesirable outcome. To Israel, any Arab unity scheme represented an existential threat because of the danger posed by the combined Arab armies. An additional danger to Israel was pan-Arab support for the Palestinian resistance movement which mounted repeated attacks from bases in Jordan and Syria. In response to massive Israeli retaliation for these Palestinian attacks, Egypt militarized the Sinai, requested the withdrawal of the United Nations Emergency Forces (UNEF), and closed the Gulf of Aqaba to Israeli shipping in May 1967. Considering this closure an act of war, on June 5, Israel launched a surprise air attack that destroyed the air forces of Egypt, Syria, Jordan, and Iraq. In a six-day campaign Israel occupied the Sinai Peninsula, the Gaza Strip, Jordan's West Bank, and Syria's Golan Heights.[9] In one blow Nasser's Pan-Arabist march had been broken at a terrible cost to the Arabs and with severe ramifications for the Unites States and the West.

Tipping Point I: Secular Nationalism to Islamism, 1967–1970

The Pan-Arabist movement led by Egypt's Nasser and the Baath parties of Syria and Iraq had a strongly secular and leftist orientation that sought to appeal to all Arabs, both Muslim and Christian. Thus, the secular nationalist foundations of Pan-Arabism made it anathema to the Islamist movement. In Egypt, the Muslim Brotherhood's challenges to Nasser were brutally suppressed in the 1950s and 1960s, which radicalized the Islamist dissidents, many of whom fled to neighboring countries where they spread the call to reject Pan-Arabism in favor of establishing Islamist states. The calamitous Arab defeat in 1967 was greeted by the long-suppressed Islamists as "just punishment" for the Arab nationalist leaders because they had "sinned" against Islam, while Israel had won because it had remained true to its Jewish faith.[10] This transcendental strategic logic found resonance among the Arab grassroots, shocked by the 1967 defeat, as Pan-Arabist leaders were put on the defensive in the face of public criticism and mass protests. Consequently, the defeat of June 1967 became a "tipping point"—representing the delegitimation of Pan-Arabism and its progressive substitution by the Islamist creed. In the crisis environment engendered by the war's outcome, there was a growing movement back to Islamic roots as an alternative source of identity, spiritual solace, and political mobilization. The Muslim Brotherhood's preachers were only too ready to reinforce the strategic implications of this ideological transformation—Pan-Arabism could not defeat Israel and confront the West, therefore Islam is the solution.[11] The practical logic of the Islamist approach is that true believers will fight with greater vigor and readiness for self-sacrifice to defend Islam, and transforming a Pan-Arab struggle into a Pan-Islamic jihad will greatly expand the scope of conflict and bring a quantum increase in the number of combatants to confront Israel and its supporters. In other words, an ethnic nationlist conflict between Israel and the Arabs would be transformed into a religious conflict between Israel and the whole Muslim world.

Strategic Cooptation and Radicalization, 1971–1981

Strategic opportunism has been a time-tested hallmark of political leadership. The Islamist upsurge after the 1967 war was a clear signal to political leaders to change their ideological positions and embrace Islam as a medium of self-legitimation and as an instrument to achieve political objectives. The 1970s witnessed a slew of secular nationalist leaders moving toward Islamism in different degrees by adopting its rhetoric and coopting Islamist opposition groups. Contrary to the leaders' objectives, these measures did not weaken the Islamist movement, but increased its legitimacy and grassroots support. The use of revivalist Islam as a tool by political opportunists would prove a perilous stratagem to its practitioners.

Among the leaders seeking to ride the Islamist wave was Anwar al-Sadat, who assumed Egypt's presidency after the death of President Nasser in September 1970. In an effort to gain support and legitimacy, Sadat gradually jettisoned Pan-Arabism in favor of a tilt toward Islamism that included freeing the Muslim Brethren from prison and permitting them to preach and proselytize in public.[12] These policies helped Sadat to consolidate power and unite the people during the Yom Kippur/Ramadan War of October 1973, where the partial success of Egyptian arms against Israel was ascribed to the pervasive Islamist fervor among the troops.[13] In the postwar years, however, Sadat's rapprochement with the Muslim Brethren would be tested and turn into antagonism as Islamism quickly dominated the public space and radical Islamist groups began a violent campaign against the Egyptian state. Between 1974 and 1981, three radical groups were engaged in interactive violence with Sadat's regime: the Islamic Liberation Party (Hizb al-Tahrir al-Islami), the

Society of Muslims (Gamaa al-Islamiya/Takfir wal-Hijra) and the Jihad Organization (Tanzim al-Jihad). These three militant organizations and a plethora of smaller clandestine groups were the Muslim Brotherhood's younger offshoots, whose members were radicalized in Nasser's prisons and dedicated to the regime's violent displacement by an Islamist order.[14] In ideology, these militants rejected the Brotherhood's strategic choice of achieving a gradual evolution toward establishing an Islamist state through preaching and political participation.

The great teacher of the new radical generation was Sayyid Qutb who presided over the ideological "tipping point" from the Brotherhood's Islamist gradualism to jihadist violence. Qutb's brief visit to the United States had alienated him from the "decadent" culture of the West, and his suffering in Nasser's prisons had driven him to advocate revolution, which led to his death by hanging. Qutb saw the world as a terrible place of injustice, suffering, and ignorance of Islam's divine guidance. The duty of good Muslims was to transform the world through preaching and armed jihad to be led by a dedicated "vanguard" of believers in order to establish Allah's sovereignty on earth to end all sin, suffering, and repression.[15] By providing scriptural justification for a puritanical vanguard of revolutionaries to overthrow the "sinful" ruling elites and establish a global Islamist theocracy, Qutb was to become the single most important ideological godfather of al-Qaida.

Qutb's radical disciples in Egypt were mainly focused on Sadat's postwar tilt toward seeking an accommodation with Israel under American aegis. To be sure, the Islamists, as well as some secular Egyptians, were profoundly angered by Sadat's decision to stop the fighting in the 1973 war and embrace U.S. secretary of state Henry Kissinger's peacemaking mission. Yet, the Islamist militant groups could not agree on strategy and tactics, and their jihadist enthusiasm disposed them to miscalculate the government's coercive potential and the popular reaction. The battle was joined prematurely with the Islamic Liberation Party's abortive attack on the Technical Military Academy in April 1974. This misadventure triggered a massive crackdown on all the radical groups and the execution of their leading figures. Meanwhile, Sadat's growing ties with the West, his surprise 1977 visit to Israel, and signing of the 1978 Camp David Accords had unraveled his alliance with the Muslim Brotherhood. After returning from a visit to President Ronald Reagan in September 1981, Sadat decreed mass arrests of Islamists and other critics in a preemptive move that led to a tragic outcome. On October 6, 1981, Sadat was assassinated during a parade by a small military contingent belonging to Tanzim al-Jihad. The assassins were led by Lt. Khalid al-Islambuli, who cited three reasons for the killing during his trial: (1) the regime's rejection of Islamic law that had brought suffering upon the Muslims; (2) Sadat's decision to make peace with Israel; and (3) the arrest, persecution, and humiliation of Islamists in September 1981. These motivations were derived from Tanzim al-Jihad's ideological framework found in a clandestine treatise—Abd al-Salam Faraj's *Al-Jihad: The Forgotten Pillar*.[16] This book opened up a new phase in Islamist radicalization building upon Qutb's doctrines—an important element in the evolution toward al-Qaida's worldview of globalized terror. The doctrinal essence of Faraj's book is as follows:

1. Muslim rulers who reject the laws of Islam are apostates and infidels, to be punished by death.
2. The duty of true Muslims ordained by Allah is to declare jihad against Muslim countries governed by the laws of unbelievers and Muslim leaders trained in the West by Christians, Communists, and Zionists.
3. Abstaining from armed jihad is the main reason for the sorry situation of the world's Muslims—humiliated, degraded, defeated, and divided.
4. Armed struggle is the only acceptable form of jihad, and perpetual jihad against an infidel state is the highest obligation for every Muslim and the only solution for all true Muslims who desire to overthrow tyranny and establish peace under Islam.
5. Islam can succeed only through the force of arms, as in the past when small groups of earnest believers could spread the message through conquest.
6. In managing armed jihad, first fight the internal infidel—infidel regimes—and then the external infidel—the non-Muslim countries.[17]

The progressive radicalization of Islamist doctrine in the 1970s by Faraj and others led to a new synthesis that was tested in jihadist struggles beyond the confines of Egypt and other Arab and Muslim countries. The Afghan war (1980–1989) presented an auspicious opportunity where younger members of Tanzim al-Jihad and other extremists came to use their jihadi skills in cooperation with fellow fighters from other countries, among them a young man from Saudi Arabia—Osama bin Ladin.

Tipping Point II: Afghanistan from Polycentrism to Transnationalism, 1980–1989

Until the Afghan war the Islamist movement was polycentric, as the emerging radical groups were struggling mainly against their own governments and lacked strong cross-national ties in ideology and organization. The 1979 Soviet invasion of Afghanistan to support the Afghan communist regime was countered by an insurrectionary movement supported by the United States, Pakistan, and the Arab monarchies of the

Persian Gulf. This decade-long Afghan conflict had a formative impact on the Islamist movement by providing an opportunity (1) to operate freely on neutral ground, away from the harsh controls of Arab and Muslim regimes; (2) to achieve doctrinal synthesis, organizational integration, and unity of objectives; (3) to acquire fighting experience and to test their skills against powerful antagonists; and (4) to transform the jihadists from an Arab to a multinational Islamist confraternity. Thus, the Afghan war constituted a second tipping point that transformed Islamist militancy from a polycentric to a cohesive transnational movement.

When Arab jihadist groups trekked to Afghanistan in the early 1980s, their attempts to rebel had already been systematically defeated in their countries of origin. In Saudi Arabia, the government had effectively ended the November 1979 takeover of the Grand Mosque of Mecca by the Ikhwan group. In Egypt, the jihadist upsurge was decimated by President Husni Mubarak's regime after Sadat's assassination. In Syria, the Muslim Brotherhood's 1979–1982 uprising was brutally suppressed in Hama. Moreover, the Islamist threat had been effectively neutralized in Jordan, Iraq, and the Sudan. Thus, the jihadists' migration to Afghanistan brought about an ingathering of the defeated, representing the remnants of Arab Islamist radicals looking for a safe haven and an opportunity to redirect their anger toward the Afghan communist regime in Kabul and its Soviet supporters. The only instances of Islamist success had been the 1979 Iranian Revolution and the emergence of its Hizbullah allies in Lebanon, both authored by Shiite Islamists who were regarded as doctrinal deviants by the Sunni jihadists congregating in Afghanistan. To be sure, the Shiite success in Iran and Lebanon had left the Sunni Islamists with a sense of psychological inferiority, because these victories challenged the historic Sunni position of superiority over the Shiites. Thus, the Iranian Revolution and Hizbullah's emergence spurred Sunni jihadists to match the Shiites' unprecedented jihadi prowess and to emulate Shiite strategy and tactics.

The jihadist cause in Afghanistan brought together different Islamist leaders and groups, representing various strains of radical Sunni Islamist ideology. These included Egyptian Islamist groups Gamaa and Dr. Ayman al-Zawahiri's Tanzim al-Jihad, radical Palestinian Islamist scholar Shaikh Abdallah Azzam, Saudi millionaire Osama bin Ladin, and Deobandi Islamist leaders representing South Asian variants of Muslim radicalism. Out of the interaction of these individuals and their strategic doctrines, an ideological synthesis was achieved which would guide their anti-Soviet struggle and subsequent global jihadi campaign.[18]

The foremost ideologue of the Arab jihadists was Shaikh Azzam, founder of the Office of Services (Maktab al-Khadamat) in Peshawar,

Pakistan, in 1984, for the recruitment and training of a Muslim army to fight in Afghanistan.[19] Millionaire bin Laden, who had been mentored by Azzam in radical Islamist thought, funded this organization. In 1986, bin Ladin also established al-Masadah (The Lion's Den), as he came under the influence of Egyptian militants who advocated a global jihad in sharp disagreement with Azzam's first preference for establishing an Islamic state in Afghanistan. After a car bomb killed Azzam in November 1989, the struggle to control his organization was won by an extremist faction associated with bin Ladin and Zawahiri, whose first preference was to globalize the Islamist armed struggle beyond its Afghan epicenter. The shift in the strategic focus from Afghanistan to global Islamism was energized by the Soviet withdrawal in February 1989, for which the Arab mujahidin claimed sole credit. Now the Sunni jihadist confraternity felt that it had more than matched the victory of the Shiite Islamists in Iran and Lebanon. Having defeated "ungodly" communist materialism, the Sunni jihadists confidently turned to plan a global struggle against the "ungodly" capitalist materialists of the West led by the United States, the erstwhile patron of the Mujahidin campaign against the Soviets in Afghanistan.

Unholy Alliance and Blowback, 1989–1991

The creation of a multinational confraternity of jihadists in Afghanistan represented an "unholy alliance" between the United States, its Muslim client states, and hard-core Islamists—an alliance of convenience that would entail a very costly long-term blowback against all participants. The short-term aim of the Afghan adventure for the United States was the containment of Soviet expansionism without direct military involvement, as in Vietnam. While this geostrategic objective was shared by all members of the U.S.-led coalition, the allied Muslim states' support for the Afghan jihad flowed from narrow calculations of self-interest, i.e., domestic stability and regime survival. Indeed, it made good strategic sense for the Arab/Muslim states to encourage and even fund the dispatch of their home-grown jihadists to join the Afghan resistance because this would reinforce their Islamic legitimacy while getting rid of troublemakers at home. In a classic case of the "law of unintended consequences," the U.S.-sponsored anti-Soviet Muslim coalition had used political Islamism in its most radical modality as an instrument to achieve its immediate objectives, oblivious to the long-term perils of its collective stratagem. The Afghan misadventure set the stage for the next phase in the Islamic radicalization process, which would become a globalized conspiracy against Arab/Muslim regimes, the West, and especially the United States.

After the 1989 Soviet withdrawal, U.S. attention quickly shifted away from Afghanistan, which became mired in a protracted civil war among the Afghan mujahidin factions, supported by Pakistan, Iran, and Russia. Meanwhile, the Arab and other non-Afghan jihadists expelled by Pakistan returned home as unwelcome heroes full of revolutionary fervor aimed at toppling their own governments. The ensuing struggle opened a new phase of Islamist radicalization that was further catalyzed by two new factors—the 1991 Gulf War and the Palestinian intifada against Israel.

Al-Qaida: Vanguard of Global Islamist Jihad

The progressive emergence of al-Qaida from its Arab roots to a violent organization with a global reach represented the culmination of a century-long radicalizing process, accentuated by a succession of crises impacting the Muslim countries. The final phase of this cycle came in the early 1990s, amid the confluence of new crisis factors from within and outside the Muslim countries that collectively fuelled al-Qaida's ascendance as the radical vanguard of the Islamist movement.

Among the factors exacerbating the Arab/Muslim crisis milieu were the unresolved issues of Palestinian statehood and Muslim rights in Jerusalem, which had functioned as persistent triggers of Islamic radicalization over the preceding half-century. In late 1987, the Palestinian question came to the fore with the outbreak of the intifada against Israel in the occupied territories. After several unsuccessful attempts by the Clinton administration to resolve the Palestinian-Israeli conflict, a second intifada broke out in 2000, lasting for five years. Given the Palestinians' situation of continued deprivation and suffering, they have provided an endless source of terrorists for al-Qaida and other jihadist groups.

Another factor contributing to Islamic radicalization in the 1990s was the persecution of Muslims in over a dozen countries—e.g., Chechens in Russia; Kashmir separatists by India; Bosnian Muslims and Albanians by Serbia—and the suppression of Islamist opposition groups in the Arab countries and the newly independent states of Central Asia. In the Arab context, the major jihadi challenges were centered in Algeria, Egypt, and Saudi Arabia. In Algeria, the military regime's decision to nullify the 1992 electoral victory of the Islamic Salvation Front (FIS) triggered a decade-long insurrection claiming over 100,000 victims.[20] In Egypt, militants led by Gamaa al-Islamiya targeted government officials, Coptic Christians, and foreign tourists. President Mubarak unleashed a massive campaign that ended in a 1997 agreement with the Islamists to stop the interactive violence. Meanwhile,

Tanzim al-Jihad, Egypt's other major jihadi group, along with Gamaa militants, went on to join bin Ladin's al-Qaida.

The Afghan blowback proved particularly destabilizing for Saudi Arabia because of the kingdom's crucial role in the 1991 Gulf War. Saddam Hussein's sudden march into Kuwait in August 1990 posed a major threat to Saudi Arabia and its oil fields. The Iraqi move polarized Saudi society as King Fahd opted for a U.S.-led coalition of forces, instead of taking an offer by Osama bin Ladin to mobilize a broad-based mujahidin army of Afghan war veterans to confront Saddam's secularist Baath regime.[21] The king's decision also evoked an immediate challenge from his home-grown Salafi movement which shared bin Ladin's doctrinal opposition to the stationing of non-Muslim forces in the kingdom, because it constituted desecration of Islam's "holy soil."[22] Table 6.1 outlines the chronology of al-Qaida's violent actions.

After Kuwait's liberation in January 1991, the coalition forces were withdrawn, except for a contingent of U.S. troops stationed at bases in the Saudi desert. In their opposition to the U.S. military presence, the kingdom's radical Salafi Islamists made common cause with bin Ladin's followers, inviting the suppression of both groups by the regime. The expansion and use of these bases to project U.S. power throughout the region later created an immense backlash by provoking attacks against U.S. targets in Saudi Arabia and becoming a rallying symbol for bin Ladin's global jihadist constituency.

Transnational Terrorism versus United States and Allies: Phase I, 1992–1995

In 1991, Osama bin Ladin left Saudi Arabia for Afghanistan, and in 1992, was given refuge in Sudan by the Islamist military government of General Umar Hasan al-Bashir. The regime's Islamist affinities with al-Qaida and bin Ladin's enormous wealth provided a welcome environment to establish several training encampments. Bin Ladin's five-year stay in Sudan was a period of preparation and expansion of al-Qaida's umbrella to include jihadist groups from over fifty countries. Having lost his Saudi citizenship, bin Ladin was a stateless man, preferring to operate "under the radar" as a businessman, to minimize retaliation from his enemies. Therefore, al-Qaida's role in Islamist terrorism in 1992–1995 appears to have involved mostly funding and training. Early terrorist episodes that al-Qaida may have funded include the bombing of the World Trade Center by a group under Ramzi Yusif (February 1993); the downing of a Black Hawk helicopter, killing eighteen U.S. soldiers in Somalia (October 1993); and, an explosion aboard a Philippine plane killing a Japanese businessman (December 1994). The latter was a test run by

TABLE 6.1   Osama bin Ladin/Al-Qaida versus the United States and Allies: Strategic Interactions, 1973–2005

Date	Actor and Type (or Event)	Target/Goal	Place	Death Toll/Outcome
Oct. 1973	Yom Kippur/Ramadan War—Egypt and Syria	Israel	Sinai/Golan Heights	Bin Ladin's political radicalization
1980	Bin Ladin travels to Peshawar, Pakistan	To organize Arab mujahidin fighting Soviet forces in Afghanistan	Peshawar, Pakistan and Afghanistan	Soviet withdrawal from Afghanistan
1988	Al-Qaida founded	Western and allied Muslim regimes	Afghanistan	
1989–1990	Civil war in Afghanistan		Afghanistan	Bin Ladin returns to Saudi Arabia
Aug. 1990	Iraq invades Kuwait; Bin Ladin proposal rejected by King Fahd		Kuwait, Iraq, Saudi Arabia	Bin Ladin angry at presence of American-led troops on holy soil
1991–1995	Bin Ladin in exile in Sudan protected by Hasan al-Turabi and General al-Bashir	Safe haven to organize future fighters	Khartoum, Sudan	Bin Ladin running businesses and training jihadists
Oct. 1993	Rocket attacks and ground fighting	U.S. Marines	Somalia	18 U.S. soldiers killed; U.S. withdraws troops
May 1996	Sudanese regime expels bin Ladin and he takes refuge in Afghanistan		Afghanistan	Establishes training camps
1998	World Islamic Front brings together four jihadist groups under al-Qaida's umbrella	United States/Western and Muslim allies	Afghanistan	Issues fatwa calling for the killing of Americans

TABLE 6.1 Cont. Osama bin Ladin/Al-Qaida versus the United States and Allies: Strategic Interactions, 1973–2005

Date	Actor and Type (or Event)	Target/Goal	Place	Death Toll/Outcome
Aug. 1998	Truck bombings	U.S. embassies	Kenya and Tanzania	224 killed; over 4,500 injured; US air strikes in Sudan and Afghanistan
Oct. 2000	Suicide boat bombing	USS *Cole*	Aden, Yemen	17 U.S. sailors killed
Sept. 2001	Suicide plane bombings	World Trade Center and Pentagon	New York, Washington, D.C., Pennsylvania	Over 3,000 killed; thousands injured
Oct. 2001	U.S. attack on Afghanistan	Destroy al-Qaida bases and oust Taliban regime	Afghanistan	Taliban defeated and Al-Qaida remnants flee to Tora Bora
Apr. 2002	Suicide bombing	Synagogue	Djerba, Tunisia	19 killed
Oct. 2002	Suicide bombings by Jamaa Islamiya (al-Qaida affiliate)	Nightclubs	Bali, Indonesia	202 killed
May 2003	Ground attack and bombings	Riyadh foreign nationals' compound and U.S. office	Riyadh, Saudi Arabia	34 killed
May 2003	Suicide bombings by Salafiya Jihadiya (al-Qaida affiliate)	Spanish restaurant, hotel, Jewish center, and Belgian consulate	Casablanca, Morocco	45 killed; including 12 attackers
Aug. 2003	Suicide bombing	Hotel	Jakarta, Indonesia	12 killed; 150 injured
Dec. 2003	Suicide bombings	Synagogues	Istanbul, Turkey	23 killed; 300 injured
Dec. 2003	Bomb attacks (al-Qaida affiliates)	British consulate and bank	Istanbul, Turkey	27 killed; 450 wounded

Date	Type	Target	Location	Casualties
2004–present	Suicide attacks	U.S. forces, Iraqi government, and Shiite opponents	Iraq	Several thousand killed
Mar. 2004	Ten bombs (al-Qaida affiliate in Morocco)	Four trains	Madrid	191 killed; 1,800 injured
Apr. 2004	Bin Ladin offers conditional truce to Europe	Attempt to split Europe from United States		
May 2004	Shootings	Foreigners	Al Khobar, Saudi Arabia	22 killed
July 2005	Train and bus bombing (al-Qaida affiliates)	Three trains and one bus	London	52 killed; 700 injured
July 2005	Suicide bombings (al-Qa'idah affiliate)	Hotels	Sinai, Egypt	64 killed; 200 injured
Oct. 2005	Suicide bombings	Tourist areas	Bali, Indonesia	22 killed
Nov. 2005	Suicide bombings (Zarqawi/al-Qaida of Mesopotamia)	Hotels	Amman, Jordan	57 killed
Jan. 2006	Bin Ladin offers United States conditional long-term truce			Rejected by United States

Ramzi Yusif for the Bojinka Plot to blow up twelve airplanes bound for the United States, which was uncovered in January 1995 by the Philippine police.[23]

The year 1995 was a turning point for al-Qaida as its paramount leader came under growing pressure from the Sudanese authorities and two prominent foes—Saudi Arabia and the United States. In May 1996, the Sudanese regime was forced to expel bin Ladin and his entourage who were welcomed in Afghanistan by the newly ascendant Taliban theocracy. Consisting mostly of Pashtun tribesmen and supported by Pakistan's military intelligence, the Taliban emerged as a powerful Islamist army in the mid-1990s to dominate most of Afghanistan. In Taliban leader Shaikh Umar, bin Ladin found a true soul mate in Islamist extremism, which produced a firm alliance and a relatively safe haven for al-Qaida's expanding operations.[24] Under Taliban protection, up to 10,000 jihadists were trained in bin Ladin's camps learning insurgency and terrorist tactics while undergoing indoctrination in al-Qaida's ideological tenets. In its most radical form, this ideology is based on the following precepts:

1. The true Islam is struggle (*sira*) plus confrontation (*tasadum*) and forcible conversion to Islam (*ikrah*). These are God's commandments that cannot be changed.
2. There can be no peace, coexistence, or dialogue between Islam and the United States and other non-Muslims in the West. While non-Muslim minorities belonging to *ahl al-kitab* (Christians and Jews) are accepted to live in the Islamic countries and subject to pay a poll tax (*jizya*), the people of the United States and the Western countries are considered *ahl al-kitab* living in the Abode of War (*dar al-harb*); hence, they have the choice to face fighting as *muharibin* (enemy fighters), or convert to Islam. There will be eternal conflict between Islam and the non-Muslims because Islam represents the truth, while non-Islam is falsehood.
3. True Muslims should follow the twin laws of *al-wala wal-bara*. *Wal-bara* dictates the detachment and separation of the Muslims from the non-Muslim infidels (*kuffar*). *Al-wala* commands fellowship and brotherhood among Muslims, including mutual help and loyalty. If a Muslim makes a wrong judgment, he can be excused, unless he cooperates with the West/United States or preaches coexistence with them, in which case he will be subject to *takfir*—denouncement and expulsion from the Muslim community as an infidel (*kafir*.)
4. Jihad is a *rahma*—an act of mercy by Allah for all people to practice. Therefore, by fighting the non-Muslims you help them to become Muslims and save them from hellfire.
5. Jihad is a constant process of war. There are two modalities of jihad: offensive jihad (*jihad al-talab*) and defensive jihad (*jihad al-dafi*). If one is

unable to wage offensive jihad as a state because of weakness, then one resorts to defensive jihad as practiced by al-Qaida on September 11, 2001, to resist U.S. oppression. Such defensive jihad can be done without the permission of the leaders of the Muslim states; it can be undertaken by any true Muslim.

6. All Arab-Muslim regimes and individuals who help socialists, secularists, communists, and the United States are *kharij al-milla*—those who have left the Islamic nation, and therefore are targets of denouncement (*takfir*). Instead, Muslims should manifest hatred (*muadat*) toward their enemies in the West, because the threat facing Islam from the West is both ideational and civilizational, which makes for *jihad hatmiyya* (the imperative of jihad) in the inevitable struggle of *jihad al-shamil* (total war).[25]

The foregoing ideological tenets provide doctrinal justification for al-Qaida's global strategy where fighting jihad is both an individual and collective duty. This strategy is seen by al-Qaida as "defensive jihad" because its attacks are merely responses to attacks against the Muslims by the United States and its network of allied Islamic and non-Muslim governments. Based on this logic, al-Qaida chooses its targets and the rationales for attacking them. First, the United States is targeted because it is seen as a direct threat to Islam due to its military presence and attacks on Muslims on the holy soil of Saudi Arabia and other Muslim territories, and its support for states that occupy Muslim lands and persecute Muslims such as Israel, India, Russia, the Philippines, and some European countries. Second, Muslim countries are targeted because they are led by "apostate" rulers who suppress their Muslim subjects, e.g., Egypt, Saudi Arabia, Algeria, Turkey, Indonesia, Tunisia, and Jordan.

It is important to understand the fundamental logic of al-Qaida's position of defensive jihad. In the perceptions of bin Ladin and the broad sweep of the Islamist spectrum, Islam has been and is being aggressed upon by a U.S.-led coalition of Western and Muslim countries. Thus, al-Qaida's attacks are simply "defensive" responses to these aggressive actions. Consequently, al-Qaida's terrorism would cease as soon as U.S. power and influence is withdrawn from the lands of Islam, particularly from Islam's holy soil of Saudi Arabia and the city of Jerusalem.

There is plenty of evidence that a sense of humiliation and victimhood has pervaded the Muslim communities around the world which is directly blamed on the United States and allied countries. However, broad segments of the Muslim faithful continue to disagree with the strategic wisdom and religious justification of al-Qaida's use of violence. Many Muslims before and after the September 11, 2001, attacks opposed anti-Western terrorism because they considered it harmful to their interests and saw it as an aberration of the Islamic religion and its innate peaceful nature. Between al-Qaida's jihadist confraternity and the Muslims opposing terrorism is the broad "mainstream" of the transnational Islamic community that is being pulled in two opposing directions in the context of the U.S.–al-Qaida confrontation. In game theoretic terms, the loyalty of the nebulous Muslim "mainstream" becomes the key factor in determining the outcome of the decade-long interactive violence between al-Qaida and the U.S.-led group of states. Thus, the interactive behavior of both sides in terms of policies, rhetoric, and violence is likely to determine the direction of the evolution of the "mainstream" toward or away from jihadism. In a decade of interactive violence (1996–2006), the competition between al-Qaida and the West for the political and ideological sympathy of Islam's "mainstream" took different forms and outcomes, with neither side clearly ascendant in winning its preferences.

Transnational Terrorism versus the United States and Allies: Phase II, 1996–2001

A stateless itinerant in the Sudan, rejected by the leaders of his homeland, bin Ladin sent an open letter to King Fahd in August 1995 calling for the removal of U.S. forces from Saudi Arabia.[26] What did the emerging leader of the global jihadist movement expect to achieve by addressing one of his prime enemies? Was he playing power politics in an attempt to legitimize his leadership role in the international arena? Beyond this simple realist explanation, the strategic rationale of bin Ladin's move should also be understood within the context of Islamist doctrine, where it is incumbent for Muslims to advise the ruler about the Islamist illegitimacy of his policies and invite him to rectify them. Should the ruler refuse to heed the warning and fail to change his "unIslamic" ways, he will be cast out of the ummah (*takfir*) and, as an apostate, will become a legitimate target of killing. According to this Islamist logic, bin Ladin was simply doing his duty under Islamic law to give King Fahd one last chance to reverse his pro-U.S. policies before being judged an apostate and an appropriate target of attack.[27]

Also, it is possible that in 1995–1996 bin Ladin still nurtured hopes of reconciliation with some pro-Islamist members of the Saudi royal family. In this vein, he denied complicity in the attacks against U.S./Saudi targets in Riyadh (November 1995) and Dammam (June 1996), the latter claiming the lives of nineteen U.S. military personnel.[28] Indeed, the authorship of these attacks, possibly by Saudi Salafi dissidents or pro-Iranian Hizbullah Shiites, has remained inconclusive. The key factor, however, was the impact of the two acts of terrorism on al-Qaida's strategic learning process. After these episodes, it became clear that there was a low level of U.S. expectancy of the terrorists' ability to attack, an increase of support for such attacks from mainstream Muslims, and a lack of forceful response from the American authorities. Once settled in Afghanistan, bin Ladin issued a personal "Declaration of Jihad" in August 1996 that cited a list of wrongs committed by the U.S.-led "Judeo-Crusader" alliance against the Muslims in Palestine, Iraq, Chechnya, and Bosnia. He also attacked the Saudi regime for its "treacherous behavior" in allowing the American military presence and misruling the people, and called for King Fahd's abdication, perhaps in reaction to Saudi attempts to assassinate him in Afghanistan.[29]

On the terrorist front, 1997 was a quiet year, as al-Qaida focused on strengthening its home base in Afghanistan in preparation for the struggle ahead. Meanwhile, bin Ladin continued to rally his followers across the Muslim world to rise up against their "apostate" rulers and their American patron. In March 1997, bin Ladin readily agreed to an interview with CNN's Peter Arnett, as a means to project his jihadist message upon a global audience. In this interview, bin Ladin denounced the Saudi government for being "a branch or an agent" of the United States, and, while specifying American troops as the primary target of jihad, confirmed that U.S. civilians were also at risk for supporting their government.[30]

In 1998, al-Qaida issued two messages, the gravity of which were unappreciated by the U.S. government. The first was "The Declaration of Jihad Against Jews and Crusaders" issued in February 1998 by the newly formed "World Islamic Front" representing four radical groups united under al-Qaida's umbrella: Tanzim al-Jihad (Egypt), Gamaa al-Islamiya (Egypt), Jamiat al-Ulama (Pakistan), and Harakat al-Jihad (Bangladesh). This legal opinion (*fatwa*) by Islamist leaders, excerpted in Box 6.1, declared the imperative obligation of each Muslim to wage jihad against the Americans, both military and civilian, until they leave the Muslim lands.[31] Significantly, this *fatwa* warned of American eagerness to destroy Iraq—a chilling prediction of the March 2003 U.S. invasion six years later that would provoke a new wave of jihadist violence.[32]

In game theoretic terms, between 1995 and 1998 bin Ladin appeared to have shifted his objectives from the limited goal of expelling the U.S. from the "holy soil" of Saudi Arabia, to fighting U.S. "aggression" throughout the Muslim world. How realistic and rational were bin Ladin's demands and change of preferences? Did he really expect his American, Saudi Arabian, and other foes to accommodate his demands? As a hunted fugitive, bin Ladin could have been reacting with fury against his enemies; or perhaps he saw the ongoing radicalization of the Muslim masses as a prelude to large-scale Islamist rebellions against pro-U.S. regimes in the Muslim world. In either case, the die was cast in his pursuit of the global jihadist cause to the end.

Box 6.1
World Islamic Front Fatwa

From World Islamic Front, *"Jihad Against Jews and Crusaders,"*
February 23, 1998.

. . . On that basis, and in compliance with Allah's order, we issue the following fatwa to all Muslims:

The ruling to kill the Americans and their allies—civilians and military—is an individual duty for every Muslim who can do it in any country in which it is possible to do it, in order to liberate the al-Aqsa Mosque and the holy mosque [Mecca] from their grip, and in order for their armies to move out of all the lands of Islam, defeated and unable to threaten any Muslim. This is in accordance with the words of Almighty Allah, "and fight the pagans all together as they fight you all together," and "fight them until there is no more tumult or oppression, and there prevail justice and faith in Allah."

This is in addition to the words of Almighty Allah: "And why should ye not fight in the cause of Allah and of those who, being weak, are ill-treated (and oppressed)?—women and children—whose cry is: 'Our Lord, rescue us from this town, whose people are oppressors; and raise for us from thee one who will help!'"

We—with Allah's help—call on every Muslim who believes in Allah and wishes to be rewarded to comply with Allah's order to kill the Americans and plunder their money wherever and whenever they find it. We also call on Muslim ulema, leaders, youths, and soldiers to launch the raid on Satan's U.S. troops and the devil's supporters allying with them, and to displace those who are behind them so that they may learn a lesson.

Source: Excerpted from the Federation of American Scientists, http://www.fas.org/irp/world/para/docs/980223-fatwa.htm. Accessed December 1, 2006.

On August 6, 1998, al-Qaida's second in command, Dr. Ayman al-Zawahiri, issued an ominous "message" to Americans, "We are interested in briefly telling the Americans that their message has been received and that the response, which we hope they will read carefully, is being [prepared], because we—with God's help—will write it in the language that they understand." [33] On the next day, the U.S. embassies in Nairobi, Kenya, and Dar es-Salaam, Tanzania were bombed simultaneously. The Kenya bombing killed 213 people and injured over 4,500, while the Tanzania bombing claimed 11 lives and injured 85 people. [34] Al-Qaida's strategic rationale in launching these attacks was to impose high costs on the United States by signaling that U.S. interests worldwide were legitimate targets.

To a lethargic America, the embassy attacks were a wakeup call, prompting President Clinton to launch Tomahawk missiles at al-Qaida camps in Afghanistan and a pharmaceutical plant in Sudan suspected of producing chemical weapons. Although these attacks were ineffective, the United States had adopted a new offensive posture and special security measures that could abort further al-Qaida attacks and lead to the arrest of its operatives. In November 1998, the U.S. government announced its indictment of bin Ladin and other top al-Qaida leaders. In mid-December, Clinton ordered round-the-clock bombing of Iraq to undermine Saddam Hussein's regime. In response, bin Ladin gave a lengthy interview on Al Jazeera television decrying the suffering of the Iraqi people and asserting the right and the duty of Muslim countries such as Pakistan to acquire nuclear weapons to match Israel's nuclear arsenal. [35]

With the approaching end of the millennium, there were clear signs of intensive al-Qaida activity in Malaysia, Jordan, Germany, Canada, and Indonesia. In November 1999, Jordanian security discovered a "millennium plot" to blow up the Radisson Hotel and other sites in Amman. A second millennium plot was aborted by chance when a vigilant U.S. police officer stopped Ahmad Rassam at Port Angeles, Washington, with a carload of explosives from Canada. The intended target of the Algerian jihadist was the Los Angeles International Airport. The new U.S. posture of vigilance failed to prevent the October 12, 2000, attack on the USS *Cole,* during a refueling stop in Aden, Yemen. Two suicide jihadists had rammed a skiff full of explosives into the destroyer's side killing seventeen sailors and incapacitating the modern warship that had to be brought back to the United States aboard a salvage vessel.

The Cataclysm: September 11, 2001

On September 11, 2001, nineteen al-Qaida operatives took control of four U.S. airliners; two were crashed into the Twin Towers of the New York World Trade Center, one into the Pentagon, and the fourth plane, diverted from an undetermined Washington, D.C., target by a melee between the hijackers and passengers, crashed into the Pennsylvania countryside. This unprecedented attack on the United States targeted the preeminent symbols of American economic and military might, claiming around 3,000 lives and billions of dollars in economic losses.

In the ten months leading to September 11, 2001, there were over a dozen indications of mounting threats to the United States from al-Qaida, which went unheeded by ranking officials in the Bush administration.[36] It has been amply documented that the strategic priorities of the incoming administration were focused on Iraq, Iran, and other global issues and not on the Islamic world's growing anti-Americanism fuelling al-Qaida's looming lethal potential. Thus, the September 11, 2001, attacks represented a high point in the progressive winning set for al-Qaida. Its decision to bring violence to American shores was the result of a number of developments since 1995–1996:

1. Expansion of al-Qaida's power base in human, material, and lethal resources, as well as development of organizational and technical skills;
2. Self-confidence drawn from previous successes and increased support among mainstream Muslims;
3. Ability to conduct terrorist operations at relatively low cost to al-Qaida;
4. Perception of American political weakness and unwillingness to aggressively confront al-Qaida on a global scale;
5. Failure of the United States to modify its policies in the Muslim world and the resulting intensification of anti-American sentiments among mainstream Muslims.

Nevertheless the September 11, 2001, attacks transformed the game, because the United States not only had failed to defend its overseas interests, but also its own territory. Hence, the United States reacted intensely to the September 11, 2001, attacks by securing its territory and launching a global offensive against its perceived enemies. Among its first moves were implementing the USA PATRIOT Act to increase domestic surveillance, attacking al-Qaida's home base in Afghanistan, destroying the Taliban theocracy, and strengthening military and intelligence cooperation with allied regimes to hunt down al-Qaida's operatives and disrupt its funding and communication networks. Thus, the United States's first priority was the prevention of attacks on its own territory, and its second priority was securing its overseas interests. In regard to the first priority, the United States succeeded in the period after

September 11, 2001, in preventing new attacks within its own territory. However, regarding its second objective—securing its overseas interests—the United States had mixed results because al-Qaida and its ideological offshoots remain a lethal challenge. Indeed, securing these interests would require the United States to win over Islam's mainstream constituency by supplementing military efforts with economic incentives and diplomatic and propaganda campaigns.

In the competition between the United States and al-Qaida for the support of the Islamic mainstream, the United States faces a difficult dilemma. On the one hand, the United States has strengthened the Muslim world's authoritarian regimes to secure their cooperation against al-Qaida—a policy that would cause the mainstream to move away from the United States. On the other hand, the United States has offered some incentives to the mainstream in the form of promises of economic development funds and a push for political reform, which could destabilize the Muslim regimes and hinder their ability to fight al-Qaida.

Although the United States was successful in securing the cooperation of indigenous regimes in fighting al-Qaida, it failed to fully protect U.S. interests abroad as well as the interests of its allies. The situation after September 11, 2001, indicated that al-Qaida and its affiliates were still capable of terrorizing U.S. allies and U.S. overseas interests as demonstrated by attacks in Kuwait, Yemen, Tunisia, Pakistan, Morocco, Egypt, Indonesia, Jordan, the Philippines, Turkey, Kenya, Spain, Britain, Saudi Arabia, Afghanistan, and Iraq.

The heightened cycle of violence since September 11, 2001, in over a dozen countries, has imposed immense costs on all involved. Al-Qaida has borne the dual costs of attacking and being attacked in terms of the death or capture of leaders and cadres, disruption of its financial and organizational networks, and loss of secure bases. At the same time, the United States has paid the dual costs of the September 11, 2001, and other al-Qaida attacks, as well as the expenses of securing its territory and fighting al-Qaida abroad; similar costs have been born by U.S. allies attacked by al-Qaida, its allies, and offshoots. Table 6.2 summarizes some of these costs.

In prognosticating the probability of continued violence, a high value is placed on the sentiments and support of the Islamic mainstream in the evolving competition between the United States and al-Qaida to win over the nebulous constituency of mainstream Muslims. The winning set for each player is a function of:

1. the offers tended to the mainstream by each player;
2. the support given by the mainstream to either player;
3. the required threshold of costs to cause a shift in the mainstream's position toward one or the other player.

TABLE 6.2   September 11, 2001—Human and Financial Costs

Number killed in the World Trade Center towers and the aircraft that crashed into them	2,823
Number of companies housed in the World Trade Center	430
Number of people working in the World Trade Center on an average day prior to September 11, 2001	50,000
Number of people killed in the Pentagon and the plane that struck it	189
Number of people killed in rural Pennsylvania crash	45
Number of orphans created by the September 11, 2001 attacks	1,300
Value of property losses and insurance costs	$21 billion
Estimated number of jobs lost in lower Manhattan area after September 11, 2001	100,000
Days after September 11, 2001, that the United States began bombing Afghanistan	26
Number of U.S. bombs dropped in Afghanistan in the following six months	22,000
Estimated proportion that didn't explode, leaving land mines	10 percent
Estimated civilian death toll from U.S. bombing campaign in Afghanistan (six months after bombing began)	3,500

Source: Tom Templeton and Tom Lumley, "9/11 in Numbers," *The Observer,* August 18, 2002.

The ebb-and-flow of developments since September 11, 2001, suggests that the United States has not offered sufficient incentives to the Islamic mainstream to effect a positive shift favoring its position. To win over the mainstream is a complex and difficult task requiring policy incentives that go well beyond military means and calculations based on myopic and ethnocentric views of material self-interest. When people are willing to die for a "holy" cause, the cultural imperative of Islamist identity brings about the redefinition of interests to encompass the collective self-interests of the community as a whole and recalculation of payoffs to include heavenly rewards for earthly behavior.

The logic of the ongoing U.S.–al-Qaida strategic violence suggests that in order to move the mainstream toward the United States and minimize al-Qaida support, the United States needs to invest heavily in the mainstream. Hence, the strategic necessity of offering a set of incentives that addresses the basic interests of the Islamic mainstream:

1. provide financial and technical aid to promote comprehensive economic development;

2. support implementation of gradual political reforms and liberalization in the Arab-Muslim countries within their present authoritarian structures—any U.S. attempts to topple these regimes could either result in the chaos of Iraq or a takeover by Islamists, such as Egypt's Muslim Brotherhood, neither outcome being consistent with U.S. interests;
3. move decisively toward a resolution of the Arab-Israeli conflict by pushing for a final settlement of the Palestinian-Israeli standoff and the future of the Muslim holy sites in Jerusalem;
4. effect a gradual reduction and eventual elimination of the U.S. military presence in the Muslim countries.

Prospects and Trends

The strategic struggle between the U.S.-led coalition and al-Qaida promises to be long and costly to both sides. Even if strategic wisdom and cohesion prevail in the U.S.-led coalition, with decisive moves to tilt the mainstream's balance away from al-Qaida, it will take some time to reorient Islamic popular attitudes and achieve peaceful coexistence. It could be that continuing attacks by al-Qaida-affiliated groups in Europe and in Arab and Muslim countries, would create a blowback harming al-Qaida, because such terrorism has caused suffering to broad segments of the Islamic mainstream in terms of increased discrimination, arbitrary arrests, and repression. Although suicide bombings against Israel still retain considerable support among Muslims, similar attacks in Tunisia (April 11, 2002), Indonesia (October 12, 2002 and October 1, 2005), Saudi Arabia (May 12, 2003 and May 29, 2004); Morocco (May 16, 2003), Turkey (December 15 and 20, 2003), Spain (March 11, 2004), Britain (July 7, 2005), Egypt (July 23, 2005), and Jordan (November 9, 2005) have brought great misery and death to countless Muslims. While these attacks are bound to reduce al-Qaida's support base, the Iraqi imbroglio has been a boon to bin Ladin's cause in terms of the intensification of anti-U.S. and anti-Shiite attitudes among the Sunni mainstream, which is likely to have long-term consequences. As to bin Ladin, his violent jihadism is likely to persist in the foreseeable future as a broad-based movement, but with weakened organizational ties. Should bin Ladin suffer death at the hands of his enemies, he will become a holy martyr to his followers who would seek vengeance for years to come.[37]

A retrospective assessment of al-Qaida's stratagems and activities since September 11, 2001, reveals several important patterns and developments:

1. The systematic U.S. destruction of al-Qaida's leadership cadres and bases has weakened the centrality of its role in planning and implementing global operations.

2. Bin Ladin's theory and practice of jihadism symbolized by September 11, 2001, have become a model emulated by aspiring jihadist groups in many Muslim and non-Muslim countries around the world.

3. The Iraqi war has provided the jihadist movement an unexpected venue for strategic and tactical experimentation against a powerful and technically advanced military force.

4. To the global jihadist constituency, the U.S.-led invasion of Iraq represented a powerful validation of bin Ladin's ideological assertion of American hegemonic intentions and, as such, it has served as a powerful tool for recruitment throughout the Muslim world.

5. It is likely that the low cost and easy availability of opportunities to harm the United States in Iraq may have diverted attacks from other parts of the world, particularly the United States, where the cost of mounting attacks is much higher and the likelihood of success is much lower due to increased security measures.

6. Given Europe's proximity to the Arab world and its large Muslim minority, after the March 2004 Madrid train bombings, bin Ladin sought to use the threat of terrorist violence to exploit the differences between American and European policy preferences by offering the Europeans a peace plan to stop attacks in exchange for withdrawal of European soldiers from Muslim lands. This offer is excerpted in Box 6.2.

7. On al-Qaida's list of the West's transgressions, Israel's control of Jerusalem and Palestine constitutes a persistent source of Muslim anger against the West, and without a satisfactory solution, will continue to be used as a mobilizing tool for global jihadism.

8. As the stronger player, the United States continues to insist on its first preference—al-Qaida's destruction, victory over global jihadism, and maintenance of the U.S. hegemonic presence in the Muslim world. This maximal preference corresponds to the extremist position of jihadists committed to their first preference of perpetual war between Islam and the West until Islamist victory. However, bin Ladin's recent statements suggest conditional acceptance of a second preference—to cease attacks against the West if U.S. hegemony is withdrawn.

Box 6.2
Bin Laden, "To the Peoples of Europe"

From Osama bin Laden, "To the Peoples of Europe,"
April 15, 2004.

. . . Evil kills its perpetrators and oppression's pastures are fatal.

There is a lesson in what is happening in occupied Palestine, and what happened on September 11 and March 11 are your goods returned to you. It is well known that security is a vital necessity for every human being. We will not let you monopolize it for yourselves, just as sensible people would not let their leaders compromise their security. On this basis, we warn you:

Since we have reacted in kind, your description of us as terrorists and of our actions as terrorism necessarily means that you are and your actions must be defined likewise. Our actions are but a reaction to yours—your destruction and murder of our people, whether in Afghanistan, Iraq, or Palestine. Look, for example, at the event that terrorized the world, the murder of the wheelchair-bound Shaikh Ahmed Yassin, God have mercy on his soul. We give God our pledge that we will take revenge on America for his death, with God's will. . . .

We are determined, with God's will, to continue our struggle and to build on what we have already done in order to stop the merchants of war. In response to the positive initiatives that have been reflected in recent events and opinions polls showing that most people in Europe want peace, I call upon just men, especially scholars, media, and businessmen, to form a permanent commission to raise awareness among Europeans of the justice of our causes, primarily Palestine, making use of the enormous potential of the media.

So I present to them this peace proposal, which is essentially a commitment to cease operations against any state that pledges not to attack Muslims or intervene in their affairs, including the American conspiracy against the great Islamic world. This peace can be renewed at the end of a government's terms and the beginning of a new

Box 6.2 continued

one, with the consent of both sides. It will come into effect on the departure of its last soldier from our lands, and it is available for a period of three months from the day this statement is broadcast.

Whoever chooses war over peace will find us ready for the fight. Whoever chooses peace can see that we have responded positively Therefore, stop spilling our blood in order to save your own.

Source: Bruce Lawrence, ed., *Messages to the World: The Statements of Osama bin Laden* (London: Verso, 2005), 234–235.

Notes

1. Philip K. Hitti, *History of the Arabs from the Earliest Times to the Present,* 10th ed. (New York: St. Martin's, 1970).
2. Marshall Hodgson, *Venture of Islam,* vol. 2. (Chicago: University of Chicago Press, 1974), 16–58, 99–133.
3. Efraim Karsh and Inari Karsh, *Empires of the Sand: The Struggle for Mastery in the Middle East, 1789–1923* (Cambridge, MA: Harvard University Press, 1999).
4. Nikki Keddie, *Sayyid Jamal ad-Din "al-Afghani": A Political Biography* (Berkeley: University of California Press, 1972), 81–129.
5. R. Hrair Dekmejian, *Islam in Revolution,* 2d ed. (Syracuse, NY: Syracuse University Press, 1995), 23–32, 173–176.
6. Charles D. Smith, *Palestine and the Arab-Israeli Conflict,* 4th ed. (New York: St. Martin's, 2001), 62–67.
7. Ishak Musa Husaini, *The Moslem Brethren* (Beirut: Khayat's, 1956), 25–38.
8. Anthony Nutting, *Nasser* (New York: E.P. Dutton, 1972), 74–195.
9. *Ibid.,* 397–416.
10. Dekmejian, *Islam in Revolution,* 79.
11. *Ibid.,* 213.
12. Nazih Ayubi, *Political Islam* (New York: Routledge, 1993), 75–76.
13. *Ibid.,* 80.
14. Ayubi, *Political Islam,* 72–87.
15. Dekmejian, *Islam in Revolution,* 84–87.
16. Ayubi, *Political Islam,* 143–144.
17. Dekmejian, *Islam in Revolution,* 94–95.
18. Gilles Kepel, *Jihad: The Trail of Political Islam* (Cambridge, MA: Harvard University Press, 2002), 136–150, 217–236.
19. *Ibid.,* 144–147.
20. Monte Palmer and Princess Palmer, *At the Heart of Terror* (New York: Rowman and Littlefield, 2004), 107–109.
21. *Ibid.,* 100.
22. R. Hrair Dekmejian, "The Rise of Political Islamism in Saudi Arabia," *Middle East Journal* 48, no. 4 (1994): 627–643.

23. David Martin Jones, Michael L. R. Smith, and Mark Weeding, "Looking for the Pattern: al Qaeda in Southeast Asia—the Genealogy of a Terror Network," *Studies in Conflict and Terrorism* 26(2003): 443–457.
24. Palmer and Palmer, *At the Heart of Terror*, 118–120.
25. These precepts represent the most extreme configuration of al-Qaida's Islamist ideology as propounded by a "New Generation" of Saudi ulama from Najd province who called for a "new Islamic awakening" in support of al-Qaida after September 11, 2001. See unpublished paper, R. H. Dekmejian, 2003, Saudi Arabia and Radical Islamism: History and Prospects.
26. www.pbs.org/frontline.
27. For doctrinal justification of this claim see Dekmejian, *Islam in Revolution*, 94–95.
28. Bruce Lawrence, ed., *Messages to the World: The Statements of Osama bin Laden* (London: Verso, 2005), 40–41.
29. *Ibid.*, 23–30.
30. *Ibid.*, 44–57.
31. Walter Laqueur, ed., *Voices of Terror: Manifestos, Writings, and Manuals of Al-Qaeda, Hamas and Other Terrorists from around the World and throughout the Ages* (New York: Reed, 2004), 411–412.
32. Lawrence, *Messages to the World*, 58–62.
33. "Islamic Jihad Vows Revenge," *BBC* August 7, 1998, http://news.bbc.co.uk/2/hi/world/monitoring/147484.stm.
34. Kepel, *Jihad*, 320.
35. Lawrence, *Messages to the World*, 58–94.
36. The 9/11 Commission, *The 9/11 Commission Report*, (2004): 254–277.
37. R. Hrair Dekmejian, "Bin Laden's Endgame Will be Shrouded in Martyrdom," *Los Angeles Times*, November 19, 2001.

Further Reading

Bergen, Peter. *Holy War, Inc.: Inside the Secret World of Osama bin Laden.* New York: Simon and Schuster, 2001.

Dekmejian, R. Hrair. *Islam in Revolution*, 2d ed. Syracuse, NY: Syracuse University Press, 1995.

Esposito, John L. *Unholy War: Terror in the Name of Islam.* New York: Oxford University Press, 2002.

Greenberg, Karen J., ed. *Al-Qaeda Now.* New York: Cambridge University Press, 2005.

Kepel, Gilles. *Jihad: The Trail of Political Islam.* Cambridge, MA: Harvard University Press, 2002.

Laqueur, Walter ed. *Voices of Terror: Manifestos, Writings, and Manuals of Al-Qaeda, Hamas, and other Terrorists from around the World and throughout the Ages.* New York: Reed, 2004.

Lawrence, Bruce, ed. *Messages to the World: The Statements of Osama bin Laden.* London: Verso, 2005.

McDermott, Terry. *Perfect Soldiers.* New York: Harper, 2006.

National Commission on Terrorist Attacks upon the United States. *The 9/11 Commission Report.* http://www.9-11commission.gov/.

Palmer, Monte, and Princess Palmer. *At the Heart of Terror: Islam, Jihadists, and America's War on Terrorism.* New York: Rowman and Littlefield, 2004.

Vidino, Lorenzo. *Al-Qaeda in Europe: The New Battleground of International Jihad.* Amherst, NY: Prometheus Books, 2006.

State Terrorism, Politicide, and Genocide

THE STATE, WITH ITS MONOPOLY of power and authority, has been the primary agent of violence against humankind since recorded history. Yet the millions killed in history's march over three millennia were exceeded many times during the twentieth century's wholesale human cataclysms brought on by global wars, revolutions, and genocides. According to the estimates of Professor R. J. Rummel, the first eighty-eight years of the twentieth century claimed over 169 million lives—a democide of unprecedented proportions. This was made possible by the rise of the centralized modern nation-state and its use of technological advances in communication, transportation, and mass killing; hence, Rummel's law of democide—"power kills, absolute power kills absolutely."[1]

States use different types and amounts of violence depending on their intended targets. Beyond the use of violence in conventional wars between states, governments employ various forms of violence, overtly or covertly, against two types of targets: external targets such as individuals, states or non-governmental groups based outside the country; and internal targets which individually or collectively are perceived as threats to the ruling order.

Thus, state terrorism may be used both to influence the politics of another state and to suppress threats at home. Because these forms of violence are generally illegal under international law, governments often attempt to operate secretly. Tactics will differ depending on the objectives sought. Likewise, a state will take into account the risk involved in fighting an opponent before allocating resources to achieve its objectives through violent means. Examples of the different types of state terrorism are discussed below.

State-Sponsored Terrorism: Transnational Targets

The most direct method of employing force against external enemies is by using the state's special forces and clandestine services. In the
Cold War era the superpowers and lesser states routinely used their intelligence services to destabilize and overthrow enemy regimes, sometimes in alliance with dissident groups in the target country. This is how
the United States effected regime changes in Iran (1953), Nicaragua
(1954), Congo (1968), and Chile (1973). A more ambitious agenda of
state-sponsored violence was that pursued by the Soviet Union. The Soviets and their communist allies not only sought regime changes
through violence, but also backed Middle Eastern and West European
terrorist groups to serve their strategic interests.[2] Also, different forms
of transnational violence were part of the British and French repertoire
during and after the heyday of imperialism. In recent decades, Israel's
clandestine services have frequently engaged in transnational counterterrorism operations targeting violent organizations and their leaders
and employing terrorist tactics against enemy regimes.

These lessons of state sponsorship were not lost on lesser powers
particularly with the proliferation of terrorist organizations after the
1970s. According to Daniel Byman, twenty of the thirty-six terrorist
groups listed by the State Department in 2002 had received state support at some point in their history and eight still enjoyed such support—
Hamas, Harakat al-Mujahidin, Hizbullah, Jaysh-e-Muhammad,
Lashkar-e-Taiba, Palestinian Islamic Jihad, Popular Front for the Liberation of Palestine (PFLP), and the Popular Front for the Liberation of
Palestine General Command (PFLP-GC).[3] The most notable state sponsors of terrorist groups were Iran (Hizbullah, Hamas), Syria (PFLP,
PFLP-GC, Hamas), Pakistan (Islamist groups in Kashmir), Afghanistan
(al-Qaida), Cuba (FARC, ELN, ETA), Libya (Abu Sayyaf, IRA), North
Korea (Red Army Faction), and Sudan (al-Qaida, Hamas).[4]

There is a symbiotic relationship between a state sponsor and its allied terrorist organization, a situation of mutual dependence which
functions to achieve their respective strategic interests vis-à-vis an enemy regime. Thus, in exchange for the state's support, a terrorist group
will act as a proxy force to destabilize an unfriendly neighbor or undermine the influence of an external enemy. Iran's long-term sponsorship
of Hizbullah, with Syrian support, has had a decisive role in preventing
the establishment of a pro-U.S. regime in Lebanon, which would have
friendly relations with Israel. Similarly, Iranian support for Hamas and
Palestinian Islamic Jihad has helped disrupt the peace process between
Israel and the PLO, and Pakistan's sponsorship of various Islamist
groups has effectively challenged Indian control over Kashmir.[5]

The relationship between a sponsoring state and a terrorist group may provide short-term benefits to both parties. However, a long-term connection could prove perilous to one or both sides. For example, the patron state may be unable to control the actions of its terrorist client or the latter may find its interests compromised by its state sponsor. Sometimes support for a strong terrorist group by a weak state might backfire. A case-in-point was the symbiotic relationship between the Taliban and al-Qaida, brought together by their shared jihadist ideology and revolutionary aims against their common enemies. The nascent Taliban theocracy was a relatively weak entity in 1996 when it welcomed bin Ladin to Afghanistan. Yet despite their obvious commonalities, there were significant differences in the interests and priorities of each party. The Taliban's first preference was to defeat the Northern Alliance of Tajiks, Uzbeks, and Hazaras. Although bin Ladin did provide strong support to the Taliban's war effort in the north, al-Qaida's first and ultimate preference was to launch a Pan-Islamist jihadist movement dedicated to the use of terrorism to achieve its global objectives. In contrast, the Taliban's self-interest required international recognition as the legitimate government of Afghanistan and security from external threats. In 1997–2000 the Taliban faced growing pressures from the United States and the international community to expel al-Qaida for its growing terrorist reach against U.S. targets.[6] Significantly, Mullah Umar, the Taliban leader, rebuffed all requests to deport bin Ladin, even after September 11, 2001, when the Saudi itinerant had become a global icon to the resurgent Islamist confraternity. The Taliban apparently lacked the military resources to expel al-Qaida, even if Mullah Umar had dared to double-cross his ideological soul mate and the latter's growing Islamist constituency in Pakistan and among the tribal peoples of the borderlands. As a result, the U.S.-led invasion in November 2001 overthrew the Taliban regime and destroyed al-Qaida's cadres and encampments. Although greatly weakened, Mullah Umar, bin Ladin, and their alliance survived the war, and remain a threat to President Hamid Karzai's regime and the U.S.-led NATO forces in Afghanistan. The symbiotic relationship between them had gone beyond mutual dependence to a situation of osmosis—an interpenetration of interests, ideology, and marriage ties, which remained unbroken even after defeat.

State-Sponsored Terrorism: Domestic Targets

Aside from the export of terrorism beyond their borders, governments frequently use violence and coercion against internal groups and individuals which are seen as threats to the ruling elite or to regime stability. In fact, the strategic use of state coercion to subdue or eliminate internal challengers has been a persistent feature in the behavior of ruling elites since time immemorial. All too often, governments have claimed a "sovereign right" to use violence within their borders, and rejected diplomatic or humanitarian intervention by other states, the UN, or other nongovernmental organizations.[7]

The spectrum of internal violence ranges from the suppression of minority groups and opposition leaders to fighting dissident groups and insurgencies. Given their command of significant coercive capabilities and resources, and their indifference to legal constraints, governing elites often use violence— assassinations, extra-judicial killings, torture, imprisonment, rape, slavery, disappearances, destruction or dispossession of property, and mass killings of dissidents and opposition groups—to secure their hold on power.[8] Although such domestic terrorism is the hallmark of totalitarian dictatorships, military oligarchies, and other autocracies, many democratic or democratizing states also practice these methods on a periodic basis.

At the core of the coercive behavior of governments toward their citizenry is the fundamental problem of the violation of human rights. According to Amnesty International, a large majority of the states represented at the United Nations have been in violation of the human rights of their people in various degrees.[9] Yet, what is needed in the present context is to identify the states that routinely use domestic violence for explicitly political purposes.

At one end of the spectrum are a small number of totalitarian and autocratic states which rule through a culture of repression that they engender in their subjects by word or deed, where any individual or collective act of disobedience or dissidence is immediately crushed. The totalitarian regime of present-day North Korea represents the most extreme case of such state terror, followed by several milder forms of repressive behavior in many states including Myanmar, China, Zimbabwe, Cuba, Colombia, Algeria, Sudan, Congo, Vietnam, and Libya. In these and a plethora of other states, the strategic aim of the threat or actual use of violence is to discourage any popular movement toward reform or democratization that would threaten the political elite and the political system itself. In these states, the routinized use of violence has become a part of the political culture affecting broad segments of the population.

Beyond the use of violence as a general strategy to dampen grassroots activism or resistance, some states target specific groups or individuals seen as a threat to the regime. For example, in China the Falung Gong, pro-Vatican Catholic Christians, Tibetans, and Uigur separatists have been targeted along with advocates of liberalization because they all are regarded as dangerous dissidents that could destabilize or harm

Chinese state interests.[10] Iran, a Shiite Islamist theocracy, has used various forms of violence against student demonstrations and populist movements seeking liberalization, while targeting specific ethnic and religious minorities suspected of separatism or subversive activities such as Kurds, Arabs, Jews, Bahais, and evangelical Christians. In Syria and Algeria, the liberalization process has been incremental, as these military-backed regimes have had to rely on the protracted use of state power to defeat Islamist insurgencies. Because these insurgencies are a serious threat to the secular order, there has been broad use of indiscriminate violence against Islamist extremists as well as the larger Islamist communities that may have supported them. In addition, periodic acts of Islamist terrorism have been countered with the full use of the state's coercive apparatus in places such as Egypt, Saudi Arabia, Morocco, Jordan, Libya, Tunisia, India, and Turkey. Similar uses of state violence have occurred in the Russian Federation in confronting the growing ethno-Islamist challenges in Chechnya and the neighboring, mostly Muslim republics. In four former Soviet Republics—Azerbaijan, Uzbekistan, Belarus, and Turkmenistan—the authorities have repeatedly suppressed opposition elements seeking liberalization through rigged elections and the naked use of force against dissident leaders and political parties.

State repression is particularly severe in countries experiencing insurgencies, civil wars, or conflicts with neighboring states. The counterinsurgency measures of President Alvaro Uribe's government in Colombia resulted in hundreds of deaths and the displacement of thousands of people. In Iraq, the raging civil war has claimed thousands of lives every month, while the Israeli-Palestinian conflict continues its lethal march through history. The cumulative effect of intertribal civil wars in the Congo has claimed millions of lives. In the Darfur region, the use of genocidal terror by the Sudanese military regime, combined with a border war with Chad has made the province one of the most deadly places on earth.[11]

The strategic interaction between state power and real or perceived domestic dissidents or opposition groups presents some conceptual and strategic problems. Autocratic states and leaders, ever sensitive to challenges to their power stakes, will often view domestic opponents as existential threats to be fought by any means and defeated at all costs. This situation could represent a zero-sum game even when some of their opponents are uninterested in taking power or are prepared to accept the gradual implementation of liberalizing reforms by an autocratic regime. Should such regimes stick to their first preferences and respond with violence even to peaceful demands for reform, the most likely result will be the radicalization of the opposition and the upgrading of its preferences, which could begin with anti-state terrorism and possibly escalate into a full-scale insurgency. The outcome could be either the overthrow of the regime or winning important concessions from it after some bloodshed. Another likely outcome is for the regime to win by using its superior forces to defeat the opposition at the cost of great human suffering and mass casualties. All too frequently, what begins as micro-level state repression against ethnic, religious, or ideological groups escalates into mass atrocities aimed at the total elimination of the victim population. The question then becomes—at what point does violence by the state against real or perceived opposition groups become politicide/genocide? What are the attributes of the crucial transition from state repression to politicide or genocide by the state? These critical issues will be elucidated in the next chapters.

Politicide/Genocide

Despite the overwhelming frequency of mass killings, systematic studies of genocides were late in coming. Only in the early 1980s did social scientists begin to tackle the critical subject of comparative genocide, in an attempt to identify the preconditions and explain the dynamics of mass murder. The recurrence of genocide in Cambodia, Iraq, the Balkans, Rwanda, Congo, East Pakistan, and Sudan evoked wider scholarly attention after the end of the Cold War. These instances of genocide clearly demonstrated that the solemn pledges of the international community framed in the 1948 UN Genocide Convention lacked practical force, and that humanity's cry—"never again"—after the Holocaust, would go unheeded by world leaders and perpetrators of genocide.

The practice of mass extermination of peoples and social collectives—national, racial, ethnic, linguistic, religious, tribal, sexual, political, and socioeconomic—has been a universal phenomenon throughout history, with a cyclical dialectic that seems to follow certain inexorable "laws" of political dynamics. While it may be difficult to identify these "laws," it is possible to discern, through comparative analysis, the determinants of genocide or the preconditions for genocides to occur. The first task, however, is to explore the origins of the word genocide.

Genocide: Definition and Determinants

The author of the term "genocide" was Rafael Lemkin (1900–1959), a Polish Jew, who had escaped the Holocaust and taken refuge in the United States. An international lawyer with a powerful moral force, Lemkin dedicated his short life to the study, documentation, and recognition of genocide as a crime under international law. In 1943, Lemkin derived the word "genocide" from the Greek *genos*, meaning tribe, race, or group, and the Latin *caedare*, to kill. One of the first to investigate the extermination of the Armenian subjects of the Ottoman Empire in 1915–1923, Lemkin helplessly watched the systematic destruction of European Jewry during World War II, including members of his family. Bearing witness to the twin human cataclysms besetting the Armenians and Jews, Lemkin became the indefatigable backer and promoter of the Genocide Convention that was adopted by the United Nations on December 9, 1948.[12]

Under Article 2 of the convention, genocide is defined as:

... any of the following acts committed with the intent to destroy, in whole or in part, a national, ethnical, racial, or religious group, as such:

a) Killing members of the group;
b) Causing serious bodily or mental harm to members of the group;
c) Deliberately inflicting on the group conditions of life calculated to bring about its physical destruction in whole or in part;
d) Imposing measures intended to prevent births within the group;
e) Forcibly transferring children of the group to another group.[13]

Article 3 specifies the acts that are punishable under the convention:

a) Genocide;
b) Conspiring to commit genocide;
c) Direct and public incitement to commit genocide;
d) Attempt to commit genocide;
e) Complicity in genocide.[14]

Furthermore, Article 4 incorporates the principle of individual accountability from the Charter of the 1945 Nuremberg Tribunal, whereby persons committing genocide "shall be punished, whether they are constitutionally responsible rulers, public officials or private individuals."[15]

Critics in the human rights community have sought to widen the social categories covered under the 1948 Genocide Convention. In particular, the convention in its present form does not specify the mass murder of groups defined by political beliefs, socioeconomic status, disability, slavery, gender, or sexual orientation.[16] However, in common usage, genocide is used to include these groups and other categories of people that have been subjected to targeted mass killing. Other critics, mostly traditional American conservative groups, opposed the ratification of the convention because they believed it violated U.S. sovereignty, particularly its provision for an international tribunal that could try American citizens. These considerations delayed U.S. ratification for thirty-seven years. After a nineteen-year campaign by Senator William Proxmire, (D-Wisc.), and with support from Senator Robert Dole, (R-Kan.), and President Ronald Reagan, the Senate finally passed the Genocide Convention on February 11, 1986.[17]

What causes a regime to commit genocide—to murder the members of a particular segment of society? On the surface, genocide appears to be a supremely irrational act, an act of savagery driven by hatred, intolerance, vengeance, or madness. Scholars from different disciplines have advanced various explanations of genocide ranging from the human instinct for destruction to social structural causes such as the impact of colonialism and capitalism and the dynamics of the political milieu.[18] To be sure, it is a conceptual challenge to generalize across the genocides of the twentieth century because of the uniqueness of each episode. What is possible is to identify some common determinants or preconditions that have led to genocidal outcomes. An overview of twentieth century genocides points to nine preconditions as follows:

1. *Historical Antecedents:* Evidence of conflictual intergroup relations, intolerance, or violent acts by the politically dominant group against a subordinate group.
2. *Crisis Milieu:* A society beset by crises—war, shifting identities, ideological conflict, economic decline, and social disintegration or political turmoil.
3. *Pathological Leadership:* Totalitarian political elites with marginal social backgrounds and a pathological obsession that defines their negative view of the subordinate group whose destruction is seen as an absolute necessity for the survival of the political system and the hegemony of the dominant group.
4. *Ideological Imperative:* A chiliastic official ideology that defines the negative attributes of the subordinate group, dehumanizes it, and justifies its extermination in order to remove a perceived existential threat to the dominant group and the state itself.
5. *Central Control and Technological Capability:* Elite control over a centralized party that possesses modern technological capabilities for effective organization, communication, transport, and mass killing necessary to maximize the efficiency of the genocidal outcome.
6. *Bureaucratic Apparatus:* A centralized bureaucratic organization, consisting of specialized cadres, expressly charged with implementing the ruling elite's ultimate preference—the destruction of the target population.

7. *Planning and Programming:* The preoccupation of the regime and its specialized bureaucratic organs with extensive secret planning, programming, and monitoring that is necessary to implement its ideological prescription to exterminate the targeted group.

8. *Public Support or Acquiescence:* The use of propaganda and incentives by the ruling elite to garner the support or acquiescence of the citizenry belonging to the dominant group in order to legitimize and facilitate the mass extermination of the subordinate group.

9. *The Genocidal Outcome:* The cathartic effect of the genocidal act as the ultimate "solution" to the multiple crises besetting the elite and society. Thus, the collective act of genocide becomes a gateway to a promised utopia—in Erik Erikson's words, a "medium of salvation" that would resolve a society's crisis of identity and overcome its existential problems.

The list of nine preconditions of genocide provides a framework for the comparative analysis of genocides in different times and cultural settings in terms of their similarities and differences.[19] For example, the framework helps distinguish the "modernity" and "efficiency" of twentieth-century genocides from the relative "inefficiency" of those of earlier periods. The succession of politicides, genocides, and democides before the twentieth century claimed an estimated 133 million lives, stretching over three millennia.[20] Yet despite the enormity of these human losses, these were "low-tech" affairs, where the perpetrators employed relatively inefficient methods to kill en masse. The situation changed dramatically after the Industrial Revolution and the progressive modernization of the instruments of killing, which greatly increased their lethal effectiveness and contributed to the strengthening of the state's coercive power. The technological revolution of the nineteenth and twentieth centuries further reinforced the coercive power of the state with quantum advances in the means of communication, transportation, and social control. These developments set the stage for twentieth century genocides—a form of mass extermination that could be considered *sui generis* in certain of its characteristics. In contrast to the massacres of earlier epochs, the ever-expanding coercive, penetrative, and control capabilities of ruling elites enabled them to kill on an unprecedented scale and speed—169 million lives in the first eighty-eight years of the twentieth century.[21] The confluence and concentration of these technological, coercive, and political factors in the hands of newly empowered political elites who rose to power from marginal roots contributed directly to maximal increases in the scale, speed, and efficiency of the genocidal process. This dynamic regarding the lethal consequences of unlimited elite power underlines Professor R. J. Rummel's "Power Principle": "The more power a government has, the more it can act arbitrarily according to the whims and desires of the elite." [22]

TABLE 7.1   Major Genocides, 1900–2006

Genocide	Dates	Number Killed
Armenians in the Ottoman Empire	1915–1923	1.5 million
Holocaust in the Third Reich	1939–1945	6 million
Tibetans in China	1959–1960	1.2 million
Bengalis in East Pakistan/Bangladesh	1971	1.5 million
Cambodians under the Khmer Rouge	1975–1979	2 million
Kurds in Iraq	1987–1988	100,000
Tutsis in Rwanda	1994	900,000
Bosnian Muslims in Yugoslavia	1992–1995	200,000
Darfur tribes in Sudan	2003–current	150,000

The nine point framework of determinants of genocide also reveals the similarities between twentieth and pre-twentieth-century mass killings. One overarching similarity is the rationality of the act of mass killing—the intentional targeting of a subject people for mass extermination in order to achieve a political objective.

Twentieth-Century Genocides: A Rational Choice Analysis

Using the modified rational choice/game theoretic framework of this book, five major twentieth-century genocides are selected as case studies. Viewing genocides from a rational choice perspective provides a novel way to seek answers to the quintessential questions of all time about the rationale, motivations, and dynamics of mass murder.

This type of analysis proceeds from the fundamental assumption that genocides are driven by a certain rationality shared by political elites in control of the state apparatus. As Helen Fein states: "Genocide . . . is usually a rational act: that is, the perpetrators calculate the likelihood of success, given their values and objectives."[23] Thus, the rationality of genocide involves the elite's intention to target certain groups—a strategic choice that requires special planning, programming, and implementation to achieve specific objectives. The rationality of the decision to commit genocide as a first strategic preference springs from the political elite's own vision of its self-interests, which it readily equates with the interests of the state itself.

Several stages mark the nascence, development, and implementation of a genocidal policy:

1. A sense of hatred and distrust toward the targeted group by high-ranking elites possibly driven by past inter-group conflicts, social marginality, personal enmities, or cultural antagonisms formed early in life;

2. The calculation of costs and benefits in planning and organizing the genocidal policy, while scanning the political environment for the opportune moment to implement it through stratagems of secrecy, deception, and surprise to minimize the chance of external intervention and reduce the likelihood of resistance by the victims.
3. The diffusion of the elite's negative values and attitudes toward the targeted group among large cohorts of middle and lower ranking members of the party or regime;
4. The formal incorporation of these negative values and attitudes into the regime's official ideology to include a justification for violence against the targeted group, now viewed as an existential threat;
5. The propagation of the official ideology to strengthen the regime's legitimacy and gain general acceptance for its genocidal policies among the dominant segment of the population, by appealing to primordial identities and fears, and emphasizing the potential economic and psychological benefits of participation in mass killing;
6. The transformation of ideology into policy through a series of strategic decisions framed by the crisis environment.

Thus, the pathological compulsion to dehumanize and target a population often arises out of the formative experiences of the political elite under crisis conditions. To achieve such pathologically generated objectives, leaders choose rational strategies that involve mobilizing support among mass sectors of the population and creating the organizational capacities necessary for implementation of the genocide. Consequently, the rationality of the genocidal act is bounded by the psychological, historical, ideological, and political determinants shaping the elite's self-view, world view, and ultimate mission.

Politicide: The Cambodian Genocide

The rationality of targeted mass killing becomes more pronounced in the case of politicide in which governments use genocidal violence against a target group because of its political beliefs, real or imputed, and the perceived or actual threat it poses to state power.[24] While genocide is always political, what distinguishes politicide is that the victims are primarily differentiated on the basis of their perceived or actual political ideology and their collective potential to confront the regime in power. This case study of the Cambodian genocide demonstrates how the strategic interaction between a state and a politically defined subnational group can evolve into politicide. Table 7.2 lists key events in Cambodia.

TABLE 7.2   Cambodian Genocide: Strategic Interactions, 1953–1998

Date	Event	Target/Goal	Death Toll/Outcome
Nov. 1953	French defeated by Vietnamese communists	Independence from colonial rule	North and South Vietnam, Laos, and Cambodia gain independence
1954–1970	Kingdom of Cambodia under Prince Sihanouk	Nonalignment in foreign affairs and neutrality in U.S.-Vietnamese War	
1965	Sihanouk breaks relations with United States; United States escalates Vietnam War		Repression of Cambodian communists by Sihanouk
1967	Khmer Rouge insurgency	Overthrow the regime	Defeated by Sihanouk
1969	U.S. B-52 bombardment of Vietnamese sanctuaries in Cambodia	To destroy Vietnamese communist forces and allies in Cambodia	Massive destruction of civilian areas; failure to defeat Vietnamese; peasant migration to cities
1970	Sihanouk overthrown by Gen. Lon Nol with U.S. support	Installation of pro-U.S. regime in Cambodia	Lon Nol takes power; Sihanouk joins Khmer Rouge and Vietnamese communists
1973	U.S. B-52 bombardment of Cambodian countryside	Support for Lon Nol regime's fight against Khmer Rouge	50,000–150,000 civilians killed (1969–1973)
Apr. 1975	Khmer Rouge overthrows Lon Nol regime	Establish a communist state	Evacuation of cities; purge of Lon Nol functionaries, moderate communists, and ethnic minorities
1976	Deportation of 100,000s to northwest		Mass famine
1977	Purges of moderate communists and dissidents; Khmer Rouge massacres in Thailand, Vietnam, and Laos	To sustain Pol Pot's eroding power	Growing opposition to Pol Pot
1978	Massive purges spark Vietnam-backed uprising		Brutally defeated

Year	Event	Objective	Outcome
1979	Vietnamese/Khmer Rouge dissidents defeat Pol Pot by invading Cambodia	Destruction of Khmer Rouge	Continued fighting between new government and Khmer Rouge remnants
1989	Vietnamese troops withdraw from Cambodia		
1990	U.S. withdraws support for Khmer Rouge	Realignment of U.S. policy to conform to international norms	
1991	Paris Agreement	Unite Cambodian factions under Sihanouk's Supreme National Council	Rejected by Khmer Rouge
1993	General elections	Establish a united, viable government	Boycotted by Khmer Rouge; continued Khmer Rouge attacks
1996–1997	Khmer Rouge splits		Internal fighting
1998	Pol Pot dies		Remaining Khmer Rouge surrender to Hun Sen regime

The tragic history of the Cambodian people in the twentieth century is intimately tied to a confluence of imperial interests, regional rivalries, and superpower conflicts. Since 1863, Cambodia, or Kampuchea, was a protectorate of the far-flung French empire that included the neighboring countries of Vietnam and Laos. As a consequence of France's defeat by the North Vietnamese communists in 1953, Cambodia was granted independence in 1954 under Prince Norodom Sihanouk. Despite his great popularity and tactical skills, Sihanouk proved to be a tragic figure, vainly trying to save his country from the unfolding cataclysm that soon enveloped the Vietnamese peninsula.

Sihanouk ruled over an autocratic monarchy from 1954 to 1970. From the outset, he antagonized the Americans by pursuing a policy of nonalignment in the Cold War and neutrality in the Vietnam War. Beginning in 1958, the CIA funded right-wing opposition groups to undermine the Sihanouk regime, and in 1965, the communist Khmer Rouge led by Pol Pot began to organize in the countryside. The dual challenges facing Sihanouk from the right and the left destabilized the monarchy and later led to its demise.[25]

Crisis Milieu: The Vietnam War, 1965–1975

The preconditions for the occurrence of genocide in Cambodia could be found in the complex interaction of conflictual events and developments that were triggered by the escalating U.S. involvement in the war between North and South Vietnam. By 1968, with over half a million troops committed to the Vietnamese imbroglio and 4,000 soldiers killed in the Tet Offensive alone, the United States had little hope for success.[26] Domestic opposition to the war grew to the extent that President Lyndon Johnson declined to seek reelection. In November 1968, Richard Nixon won the presidency promising to end the Vietnam War with a "secret formula." Instead, his policies ended up intensifying and expanding the conflict beyond Vietnam's borders, into Laos and the Cambodian countryside.

The Nixon administration's strategic logic targeted the Vietnamese communist forces in Cambodia as a means to defeat the North Vietnamese and Viet Cong in South Vietnam. To achieve this objective, in March 1969, Nixon secretly authorized the mass bombing of Cambodian territories bordering Vietnam that were thought to harbor North Vietnamese bases and sanctuaries. As part of its Cambodian strategy, in March 1970 the United States instigated a coup d'état against Prince Sihanouk by Prime Minister Lon Nol, an incompetent and corrupt pro-American general. Clearly, Sihanouk was considered an impediment by the United States, because of his ties to communist China and commitment to Cambodia's neutrality in the Vietnam War. A month after Sihanouk's ouster, over 74,000 American and South Vietnamese troops invaded Cambodia.[27] At the same time, Nixon ordered an expansion of the bombing campaign that had failed to destroy the communist bases in Cambodia. The unleashing of this massive air and ground attack reflected Nixon's fury at the inability of the U.S. military to turn back the communist successes on the Vietnamese peninsula (see Box 7.1). The ensuing five-year civil war pitted the Lon Nol regime, supported by the

---

Box 7.1
Nixon and Kissinger Discuss Cambodia

Excerpts from a telephone conversation between President Richard Nixon and Secretary of State Henry Kissinger, December 9, 1970, 8:45 p.m.

President Nixon: I want them to hit everything they can. I want them to use the big planes, the small planes, everything that will help out here and let's start giving them a little shock. There must be something we can do. Let L. Abrams, he's to take personal charge and dismiss the Air Force commander if necessary over there. And I want Haig to look into this when he is over there.
Henry Kissinger: Absolutely.
President Nixon: We have got to do a better job because we are just coming to the crunch. Right now there is a chance to win this goddamn war and that's probably what we are going to have to do because we are not going to do anything at the conference table. But we aren't going to win it with the people—the kind of assholes come in here like today saying well now there is a crisis in Cambodia. Hell, I have been asking about it for the last two weeks you know and you said no there isn't one. . . .
President Nixon: That's right. Just say there is or there isn't. And no fooling around. But let me tell you on this business on Cambodia—I want something done tonight. I don't want any screwing around and I want that Air Force to make its study immediately of anything in conventional World War II type craft that can be used over there. I am disappointed in what they have been doing. I want a new plan. I want it fast and let's get going. Also, the program for the South Vietnamese to make the ground attack is laid on, it's approved as of today. Have it go the first time it gets dry enough to go. Now get going on these things and don't let them delay so long. . . .

Source: Yale University, Cambodian Genocide Project. http://www.yale.edu/cgp/us.html.

United States and South Vietnam, against a coalition of pro-Sihanouk forces which were backed by China, led by the Vietnamese communists, and included the Cambodian Communist Party—the Khmer Rouge.

Khmer Rouge Ascendant, 1970–1975

President Nixon's Cambodian strategy proved a massive failure and a prelude to a genocidal outcome. After dropping 2,757,107 tons of explosives on Cambodia, the United States had not achieved any of its objectives.[28] The United States/South Vietnamese invasion of Cambodia neither weakened the communists nor helped Lon Nol's political survival. On the contrary, the invasion generated deep anti-Americanism and greatly strengthened support for the Khmer Rouge. Growing U.S. domestic opposition to the Vietnam War hastened the withdrawal of American forces from the region and the fall of Saigon to the Vietnamese communists. The Lon Nol regime collapsed and on April 17, 1975, the Khmer Rouge made a triumphant entry into Phnom Penh, Cambodia's capital city.

In 1950, the Khmer Rouge, which was the Cambodian Communist Party, had joined forces with the Vietnamese communists to fight French colonial rule. The leadership of Khmer Rouge including its preeminent leader, Pol Pot, was heavily influenced by French communist ideology. Pol Pot was the pseudonym of Saloth Sar, who had become an earnest convert to communism while a student in Paris in 1949–1952. These were the heady years of the communist upsurge in France when many young colonial expatriates came under the ideological influence of the French Communist Party.[29] The exposure in France of Pol Pot and other Khmer Rouge leaders to Soviet-style communism was supplemented by the Maoist ideology of peasant revolutionism after Mao Zedong's 1949 communist victory in China. To be sure, the Chinese communist model of revolutionary success based on the peasantry was better suited to the Cambodian situation than the Marxist-Leninist model of urban-based revolution.

Sihanouk's oppressive rule strengthened the ideological commitment of the Khmer Rouge leadership to Maoism. Soon after Pol Pot became the party's secretary-general in 1960, the Khmer Rouge fled into the countryside to escape Sihanouk's repression. This migration fostered a Maoist-style rural revolution that soon received strong support from the communist Chinese government, and led to the 1967 peasant uprising in Samlaut. Lon Nol's overthrow of Sihanouk in 1970 brought about a strategic realignment as the Khmer Rouge fought the ensuing civil war on the prince's side, benefiting from his charisma but later treating him as a mere figurehead.

Politicide, 1975–1979

The Khmer Rouge capture of Phnom Penh in April 1975 caught the world by surprise. Beyond its top leaders—Pol Pot, Khieu Samphan, and Ieng Sary—there was little known about the Khmer Rouge. True to their revolutionary nurturing, these men had organized a totalitarian movement over which they exercised complete ideological and operational control. In terms of behavioral code, Khmer Rouge cadres were extremely secretive, highly disciplined, brutally puritanical, and most efficient in implementing the leadership's orders.[30] Driven by a mixture of heightened xenophobia and determination to implement his utopian vision of a classless agrarian communist society, Pol Pot began the systematic reengineering of Cambodian society through genocide (see Box 7.2).

Box 7.2
Cambodia under Pol Pot

Excerpts from the United Nations Commission on Human Rights Report.

(i) . . . forcible and precipitate evacuation of the population of Phnom Penh and other cities and towns ordered by the Kampuchean authorities. . . .

(ii) . . . a large number of former military officers, senior officials, policemen, intelligence agents, country officials, and military police were executed in various parts of the country as part of a systematic campaign of extermination, and . . . in a very large number of cases the wives and children of such categories of persons were also executed. . . .

(v) . . . so-called intellectuals such as doctors, engineers, professors, teachers, and students, have also been summarily executed. . . .

(vi) . . . many ordinary persons have died as a result of being forced to perform exhausting manual labor, under a strict regime, without being provided with sufficient food, rest, or medical care. . . .

Source: United Nations Commission on Human Rights Report ECN./4/1335 (30 January 1979), reprinted in Leo Kuper, *Genocide* (New Haven, CT: Yale University Press, 1981), 155–156.

Ominous signs of Khmer Rouge's genocidal practices had appeared in the countryside prior to the fall of Phnom Penh, but few foreign observers took notice. At the macro level, the regime was bent on committing "autogenocide"—the destruction of broad segments of Cambodian society—killing an estimated total of two million people.[31] This general category of victims, constituting one quarter of the country's population, subsumed certain "undesirable" groups that were targeted for extermination. The urban population constituted the most general category of undesirables, and one of the Khmer Rouge's first acts after assuming power was the violent eviction of the inhabitants of Phnom Penh. But why would Pol Pot, the reclusive leader of Khmer Rouge, decree such a heinous first preference? The answer could be found in the regimes' Maoist ideology and Pol Pot's psychological predisposition against specific political groups in Cambodia's population.

In driving the city dwellers into the countryside, Pol Pot was moving against a set of "class enemies," particularly the "bourgeoisie" that included the intelligentsia, Buddhist monks, professionals, landowners, bureaucrats, skilled workers, and even those who wore glasses or had a modicum of education.[32] Other groups condemned to liquidation included members of the old regime, the Cham Muslims, Vietnamese, Chinese, and Thais. In ideological terms, the regime considered these categories not only as threats to its hold on power but as impediments to its grand design of building an agrarian communist polity which would require unsocialized individuals with a blank mind—*tabula rasa*—who could be easily indoctrinated to become the docile automatons of the new order. This prescription to "cleanse" society reflected Pol Pot's personal preferences driven by his paranoia and hatred of the bourgeoisie—the class to which he and many educated Cambodians belonged. In a sense, Pol Pot's alienation from the Cambodian bourgeoisie made him a "class traitor" bent on the extermination of his own class cohorts. The targeting of a class of people, mostly educated city dwellers regarded as possessing political beliefs and agendas detrimental to the regime, constituted a classic case of politicide.

Pol Pot's ultimate model for the creation of his new order was Mao's 1966 Cultural Revolution. The mass mobilization and reeducation campaigns initiated by Mao deeply impressed Pol Pot during his several visits to China. Once in power, Pol Pot sought to emulate Mao's "Great Leap Forward" with the passion of a true believer, exceeding the ferocity of the Chinese experience.[33] The history and culture of Cambodia, rooted in Theravada Buddhism, were systematically targeted and destroyed.[34] All previous means of social intercourse were abolished, including money, markets, private property, schools, and other venues of organized life. Pol Pot, the former schoolteacher, instituted a mass reeducation campaign focusing on children, who were separated from their parents for indoctrination and training as child soldiers and instruments of social control.[35] All social relations were tightly regulated and even sexual contact required special authorization.

After the curtain of totalitarian control was clamped down, Cambodia was hermetically sealed from its neighbors. As in other genocidal situations, the regime operated in utmost secrecy by unleashing its black-uniformed soldiers on the populace. Recruited from the poor peasantry and indoctrinated during the civil war, Khmer Rouge cadres displayed a high degree of bureaucratic efficiency in implementing the regime's strategic objectives with a vengeance toward the richer, educated urbanites. Herded into prisons and communal gulags in the countryside, up to two million perished during a three-year period from starvation, executions, exhaustion from overwork, and deportation. The meticulous record keeping of the Khmer Rouge, including photographs of the victims, left a damning record of the atrocities. Among the centers of systematic carnage were Tuol Sleng prison and the Choeung Ek area, later memorialized in the 1984 film *The Killing Fields*.[36]

Defeat, Denial and Redress, 1979–2000

The demise of the Khmer Rouge regime, like its birth, came through defeat in war. In late December 1978, a powerful Vietnamese force, backed by dissident Khmer Rouge factions, invaded Cambodia in retaliation for Khmer Rouge incursions into Vietnam. Phnom Penh fell to these combined forces on January 7, 1979. As the Khmer Rouge leaders took refuge in the northern jungles near Thailand, a new pro-Vietnamese regime took power, led by former Khmer Rouge leaders Heng Samrin and Hun Sen. Because of deep-seated U.S. enmity toward communist Vietnam and the exigencies of the Cold War, the international community refused to recognize the new regime in Phnom Penh. With support from China, Thailand, Britain, and the United States, the remnants of Pol Pot's army continued to fight the Heng Samrin–Hun Sen government for another fifteen years. Only in 1990 did the United States cease supporting the Khmer Rouge, although it continued to oppose the use of the word genocide to describe the atrocities committed by the Pol Pot regime.[37] Meanwhile, the Khmer Rouge was permitted to continue holding Cambodia's UN seat, while orchestrating repeated campaigns to deny the genocide. Ultimately, however, its attempts to cover up its authorship of the genocide were in vain.

In 1989, Vietnamese forces withdrew from Cambodia under international pressure, and in October 1991 the UN took control under the Paris Agreement that empowered Prince Sihanouk's Supreme National Council to represent the country's diverse factions.[38] While the world belatedly recognized Khmer Rouge's mass killings as genocide in the

1990s, repeated defections weakened Pol Pot's base of power on the Thai border. The group's final breakup came in 1996–1997 amid factional fighting leading to Pol Pot's capture in June 1997 by his former colleagues.

Ironically, the Khmer Rouge's precipitous collapse did not result in the prompt persecution and punishment of its leading cadres for authorship of genocide and other crimes against humanity. The exigencies of Cambodia's internal politics and lack of strong pressure from the international community continued to delay and prevent the administration of justice. Soon after the United States offered to assist in efforts to bring Pol Pot to justice, he was reported to have died in his sleep in April 1998. In 1999, Prime Minister Hun Sen finally agreed to a UN plan to try Khmer Rouge leaders, although he opposed the presence of foreign magistrates on the tribunal. The resistance of the Hun Sen government to a genuinely international tribunal was based on the fear that it would destabilize the regime and expose the complicity of its leading members in Khmer Rouge's genocidal acts prior to their defection.[39] A satisfactory accounting and punishment for these crimes and giving restitution to the families of the victims would have to await the advent of a new regime, untainted by Khmer Rouge's bloody legacy.

Rationality of Politicide

The Cambodian genocidal process unfolded in two broad phases. The first involved the Khmer Rouge insurrection against the U.S.-supported Lon Nol regime and the second was the implementation of Pol Pot's revolutionary vision through politicide. The first phase was eminently successful, as the Khmer Rouge was able to mobilize opposition to Lon Nol's dictatorial policies and to his U.S. backers who had killed thousands and destroyed wide swaths of Cambodian agricultural land. In this winning enterprise, Pol Pot had been able to gain Chinese backing as well as the national legitimacy derived from Prince Sihanouk's popularity after his overthrow by the Lon Nol regime. Thus, with the power it had amassed in the countryside, the Khmer Rouge was able to achieve its first preference by overthrowing Lon Nol and assuming control of the Cambodian state.

In the second phase, the Khmer Rouge faced the classic dilemma of successful revolutionaries who are then obligated to rule a state. After defeating the powerful U.S.-backed Lon Nol, Pol Pot's revolutionary cadres confronted the tasks of governance. Pol Pot's first preference was to become a worthy successor to the icons of communism—Lenin, Stalin, and Mao—by forging a truly revolutionary communist utopia based on the peasantry. The implementation of this vision required the establishment of a totalitarian order through substantial social engineering, which Pol Pot began to carry out immediately after assuming power. As a result, the Khmer Rouge targeted the mostly urban social classes, which were considered incompatible with Pol Pot's vision of an ideal society. Hence, all perceived opponents were subjected to politicide. Ultimately, Pol Pot's pathological pursuit of his utopia resulted in a number of strategic miscalculations. The enormity of the killings destroyed Cambodia's productive capacity, skilled workers, educational system, and infrastructure, devastating the economy and bringing about mass famine. The irrationality of Pol Pot's vision clouded his calculations of self-interest and led to the fractionalization of the Khmer Rouge, growing opposition to his regime, and eventual defeat at the hands of a coalition of Khmer Rouge dissidents and Vietnamese forces.

Finally, the Cambodian politicide is instructive because it follows the well-established pattern of other genocides. First, the genocide was preconditioned by the presence of pathological leadership with a genocidal ideology, ruling over a totalitarian party that had absolute control over the population. Second, the Cambodian genocide occurred in wartime when the perpetrating state had full control over the victims and the chances of outside intervention on behalf of the victims were minimal. Third, the dynamics of the Cambodian genocide followed the law of unintended consequences: first, the American priority to defeat the Vietnamese communists led to the decision to destabilize and overthrow the Sihanouk regime, resulting in the emergence of the Khmer Rouge, an ally of communist China; second, communist Chinese support for the Khmer Rouge resulted in the establishment of a radical Maoist regime, far more extremist than the Chinese had intended; and finally, the destructive violence employed by the pro-Chinese Khmer Rouge led to a Vietnamese-led invasion of Cambodia and the formation of a pro-Vietnamese government in Phnom Penh antithetical to Chinese interests.

Notes

1. R. J. Rummel, *Death by Government* (New Brunswick, NJ: Transaction Publishers, 1994), 1–27.
2. For details see Walter Laqueur, *The New Terrorism* (New York: Oxford University Press, 1999), 158–168.
3. Daniel Byman, *Deadly Connections* (New York: Cambridge University Press, 2005), 3.
4. "Overview of State-Sponsored Terrorism," in Thomas J. Badey ed., *Violence and Terrorism 05/06*, 8th ed. (Dubuque, IA: McGraw-Hill, 2004), 44–48.
5. For details see Byman, *Deadly Connections*, 79–115, 155–185.

6. On the relationship between the Taliban and al-Qaida see Gilles Kepel, *Jihad: The Trail of Political Islam* (Cambridge, MA: Harvard University Press, 2002), 205–236.

7. Debra L. DeLaet, *The Global Struggle for Human Rights* (Belmont, CA: Thomson Gale, 2006), 3–4. See also Leo Kuper, *Genocide* (New Haven, CT: Yale University Press, 1981), 161–185.

8. Darren J. O'Byrne, *Human Rights* (New York: Longman, 2003), 164–298.

9. For a description of these violations see Amnesty International, *Annual Report* (Washington, DC: Amnesty International, 2006), http://web.amnesty.org/report2006/index-eng.

10. *Ibid.*, "Global Overview."

11. *Ibid.*

12. Samantha Power, *A Problem from Hell: America and the Age of Genocide* (New York: Basic Books, 2003), 17–60.

13. Office of the High Commissioner for Human Rights, "Convention on the Prevention and Punishment of the Crime of Genocide," http://www.unhchr.ch/html/menu3/b/p_genoci.htm.

14. *Ibid.*

15. *Ibid.*

16. Scott Strauss, "Contested Meanings and Conflicting Imperatives: A Conceptual Analysis of Genocide," in William L. Hewitt, ed., *Defining the Horrific* (Upper Saddle River, NJ: Pearson Prentice Hall, 2004), 7–10.

17. Power, *A Problem from Hell*, 65–85.

18. For a summary of these positions see O'Byrne, *Human Rights*, 311–323.

19. R. Hrair Dekmejian, "Determinants of Genocide: Armenians and Jews as Case Studies," in *The Armenian Genocide in Perspective*, ed. Richard G. Hovannisian (New Brunswick, NJ: Transaction Books, 1986), 86–92.

20. For summary of these killings see Rummel, *Death by Government*, 45–75.

21. *Ibid.*

22. *Ibid.*, 1.

23. Helen Fein, "The Prevention of Genocide: Rwanda and Yugoslavia Reconsidered," Working Paper of the Institute for the Study of Genocide (New York, 1994), 5.

24. For other definitions of politicide see Rummel, *Death by Government*, 31; O'Byrne, *Human Rights*, 301, 321–323; and Manus Midlarsky, *The Killing Trap: Genocide in the Twentieth Century* (New York: Cambridge University Press, 2005), 24–25.

25. Patricia Marchak, *Reigns of Terror* (Montreal: McGill-Queens University Press, 2003), 22–23.

26. On the Tet Offensive see Don Oberdorfer, *Tet!* (New York: Doubleday, 1971).

27. Power, *A Problem from Hell*, 92.

28. Yale Cambodian Genocide Program, http://www.yale.edu/cgp/maplicity.html.

29. Power, *A Problem from Hell*, 109–110.

30. Marchak, *Reigns of Terror*, 235–236.

31. Rummel, *Death by Government*, 159.

32. Michael Vickery, *Cambodia, 1975–1982* (Boston: South End Press, 1984), 26.

33. David P. Chandler, *Brother Number One: A Political Biography of Pol Pot* (Boulder, CO: Westview, 1999), 71–73.

34. Sydney Schamberg, "Cambodia," in Roy Gutman and David Rieff (eds.), *Crimes of War: What the Public Should Know* (New York: Norton, 1999), 58–65.

35. Kuper, *Genocide*, 156–158.

36. Doug Bandow, "Genocide at the Cambodian Killing Fields," in William Dudley, ed., *Genocide* (San Diego: Greenhaven Press, 2001), 35–38.

37. Power, *A Problem from Hell,* 146–154.
38. On the difficulties of interfactional peacemaking see Michael W. Doyle, "War and Peace in Cambodia," in Barbara F. Walter and Jack Snyder eds., *Civil Wars, Insecurity, and Intervention* (New York: Columbia University Press, 1999), 181–217.
39. Power, *A Problem from Hell,* 486–490.

Further Reading

Becker, Elizabeth. *When the War is Over: The Voices of Cambodia's Revolution and its People.* New York: Simon and Schuster, 1986.
Chandler, David. *Voices from S-21: Terror and History in Pol Pot's Secret Prison.* Berkeley: University of California Press, 1999.
DeLaet, Debra. *The Global Struggle for Human Rights: Universal Principles in World Politics.* Belmont, CA: Thomson Wadsworth, 2006.
Gellately, Robert, and Ben Kiernan. *The Specter of Genocide: Mass Murder in Historical Perspective.* New York: Cambridge University Press, 2003.
Hinton, Alex. *Why Did They Kill?: Cambodia in the Shadow of Genocide.* Berkeley: University of California Press, 2005.
Horowitz, Irving Louis. *Taking Lives: Genocide and State Power.* New Brunswick, NJ: Transaction Publishers, 1980.
Kiernan, Ben. *The Pol Pot Regime: Race, Power, and Genocide in Cambodia under the Khmer Rouge, 1975–79.* 2d ed. New Haven, CT: Yale Nota Bene, 2002.
Kuper, Leo. *Genocide: Its Political Use in the Twentieth Century.* New Haven, CT: Yale University Press, 1982.
Menjívar, Cecilia, and Néstor Rodríguez, eds. *When States Kill: Latin America, the U.S., and Technologies of Terror.* Austin: University of Texas Press, 2005.
Midlarsky, Manus. *The Killing Trap: Genocide in the Twentieth Century.* New York: Cambridge University Press, 2005.
O'Leary, Brendan, John McGarry, and Khaled Smith, eds. *The Future of Kurdistan in Iraq.* Philadelphia: University of Pennsylvania Press, 2005.
Power, Samantha. *A Problem from Hell: America and the Age of Genocide.* New York: Basic Books, 2003.
Ron, James. *Frontiers and Ghettos: State Violence in Serbia and Israel.* Berkeley: University of California Press, 2003.
Rummel, R. J. *Death by Government.* New Brunswick, NJ: Transaction Publishers, 1994.
Selden, Mark and Alvin Y. So, eds. *War and State Terrorism: The United States, Japan, and the Asia-Pacific in the Long Twentieth Century.* Lanham, MD: Rowman and Littlefield, 2004.
Shaw, Martin. *War and Genocide: Organized Killing in Modern Society.* Cambridge: Polity Press, 2003.

The Armenian Genocide and the Jewish Holocaust

IN THE ANNALS OF GENOCIDE, the mass victimization of Armenians and Jews established painful precedents that would be emulated in the subsequent decades of the twentieth century. The two episodes of mass murder were separated by about twenty years. Both were executed with great secrecy as the rest of the world was preoccupied by the tumult of two major wars. Given the overwhelming power of the Ottoman and Nazi states, and total control over their societies, the Armenians and Jews were left at the mercy of the perpetrators of genocide. While these genocides happened in different times and places, there were lessons to be learned and unlearned from the unique circumstances of each and the common characteristics shared by the two tragedies.

The Armenian Genocide

The systematic destruction of an estimated 1.5 million Armenians of the Ottoman Empire in 1915–1923 has often been described as the "the forgotten genocide."[1] While it received wide coverage in the world's major newspapers during World War I, the Armenian tragedy was soon forgotten amid the exigencies of the inter-war years. No less an "authority" than Adolf Hitler ruefully observed just before his invasion of Poland in 1939, "Who today, after all, speaks of the annihilation of the Armenians?"[2]

One person who did not forget was Rafael Lemkin, a Jewish lawyer from Poland, who, since the 1920s had been carefully researching and documenting the mass victimization of the Armenians. Lemkin's pioneering investigative work, combined with his role in the authorship and passage of the UN Genocide Convention in 1948, sparked a wave of scholarship on genocides. The voluminous literary output that followed has been a fitting testament to Lemkin's passionate devotion and sacrifice for a noble cause. The cumulative result of the new scholarship has brought a better understanding of the anatomy of genocides. Also, these studies have greatly contributed to the growing international recognition of the Armenian genocide as a genocide under international law, as Lemkin defined it over half a century ago.[3]

Comparative studies of contemporary mass murder have acknowledged the precedent-setting role of the Armenian genocide. As the first genocide of the twentieth century, the Armenian case has served as a prototype and precursor to the human cataclysms that were to follow—the Holocaust, the Kurdish massacres, Cambodia, Tibet, Bangladesh, Bosnia, Rwanda, Darfur, and others. Clearly, the Armenian case served as a prototype for Hitler's execution of the Holocaust and was emulated by mass killers in subsequent decades.[4] Viewed from an analytic perspective, the Armenian case represents a prototype because it features virtually all of the causal and instrumental attributes that have characterized subsequent twentieth-century genocides. These prototypic characteristics range from historical antecedents and crisis milieu to the strategic and ideological predisposition of leaders bent on using modern means to organize mass killings by a centralized apparatus with public support or acquiescence.[5]

Historical Antecedents

Armenian statehood emerged in the second millennium B.C., and lasted until 1375 A.D. with interruptions brought on by foreign domination. The Armenian plateau stretching westward from the plain of Mount Ararat, situated at the strategic crossroads between Asia and Europe, was a geopolitical epicenter of persistent conflict among rival empires and civilizations. In 301 A.D., Armenia adopted Christianity as the state religion, which became a primary pillar of Armenian national identity and survival under successive conquests by the Byzantines, Persians, and rival Muslim dynasties. Under Muslim rule, the Armenians were given the legal status of a *millet*— an ethno-religious minority to be protected under Islamic law. The Armenian Church hierarchy was charged with governing the *millet*, the payment of taxes, and ensuring the loyalty of the community to the ruler. By the fifteenth century, Armenians lived in two adjacent Muslim imperial jurisdictions—the Sunni Ottoman empire and the Shiite Persian empire. The Russian conquest of the northern Persian lands in the nineteenth century brought large numbers of Armenians under Christian Orthodox rule.[6]

Crisis Milieu, 1774–1894

Despite their second-class status as a Christian minority, the Armenians endured under the discriminatory practices of Ottoman rule as obedient subjects. The situation of Armenians and other minorities began to change with the decline of Ottoman power in the eighteenth and nineteenth centuries. The non-Muslim minorities were caught in a vicious cycle—the empire's failures at modernization and inability to confront the European encroachments led to conflicts within the Ottoman elite and growing intolerance toward the minority peoples who were increasingly turning to Europe for protection. The result was the rise of ethnic nationalist movements often supported by competing European powers each seeking to dominate a slice of the Ottoman realm. Driven by imperial lust, the conflicting stratagems of the European powers centered on the sponsorship of one or another of the restive minorities in order to dismantle the empire known as "The Sick Man of Europe." The nineteenth century witnessed the loss of Ottoman territories including Greece, the Balkan provinces, Egypt, and the Sudan. Confronted with a collapsing empire, a group known as the Ottoman Liberals sought to implement basic reforms that promised to extend a modicum of security and civil rights to the minority peoples through a constitution and parliamentary representation. The reformist era, known as the *Tanzimat,* began in 1839 but came to an abrupt end with the 1878 accession of Sultan Abdul-Hamid II, who cancelled the Ottoman constitution and closed down the new parliament. For the next four decades, Abdul-Hamid ruled with unprecedented savagery for which he came to be known as "The Red Sultan."[7]

While some of the minority peoples of the empire pressed for independence with European support, the Armenians merely sought protection for their lives and property from corrupt officials and marauding bands. The secular and ecclesiastical leadership of the community expressed full loyalty to the Ottoman sultan, while petitioning for decent treatment, especially for the Armenians living in the provinces left helpless in the hands of predatory officials. To be sure, the Armenians' rejection of separatism and persistent quest for security and basic human rights as a first preference was a sound move in view of their demographic and geopolitical situation. Unlike the Kurds, Arabs, or the Balkan Christians, the Armenians were dispersed throughout the Ottoman realm and lacked the means to challenge the authorities.[8] Despite this reality, however, Sultan Abdul-Hamid feared that Armenian demands for reform would eventually lead to separatism. The sultan's repression and rejection of reforms and the threat of European intervention, gave rise to "the Armenian Question"—what to do with what had been the empire's most obedient minority.[9] The answer to this ominous question evoked a series of strategic responses from Sultan Abdul-Hamid and his successors. The sultan used periodic pogroms, culminating in the massacres of 1894–1896, which claimed between 100,000 and 200,000 Armenian lives.[10] The aim of the "Hamidean massacres" was to scare the Armenians into total submission and to silence their pleas for reform that could be used as a pretext for European intervention and breakup of the empire. Two decades later the sultan's successful micro-genocidal policies were used as a model by the Young Turk (CUP) regime to develop a grand strategy to resolve the Armenian Question with finality through genocide. Table 8.1 sets out a chronology of the Armenian genocide.

Hamidean Massacres, 1894–1896

As the nine-step model in Chapter 7 shows, genocides are usually preceded by the interaction of domestic and international forces that exacerbate the crisis conditions in society and shape the strategic behavior of ruling elites toward their subjects. As a prelude to the "great event" of genocide, the leadership may "signal" its genocidal intentions by targeted acts of oppression, pogroms, restrictive laws, and destruction of property. All these signs of trouble became clearly discernable after 1878—destined to become the "tipping point" toward the pursuit of genocidal objectives. The two events that made 1878 a disastrous juncture for the Armenians were the Treaty of San Stefano (February 1878) and the Congress of Berlin (June 1878). As a result of Russian victories over Ottoman Turkey, the Treaty of San Stefano granted independence to Serbia, Montenegro, and Romania, and autonomy to Bulgaria. In the East, Russia annexed some border districts, while agreeing to withdraw from the Armenian-populated Ottoman provinces after the implementation of reforms to protect the Armenians.

Alarmed at Russia's successes, British diplomacy quickly marshaled a coalition of European powers to meet in Berlin to revise the San Stefano treaty in favor of Ottoman Turkey. This revision weakened the Armenian cause by relegating to the sultan the implementation of reforms in keeping with the old adage of "placing the wolf in charge of the sheep." Soon the great powers returned to their global imperial games and the Armenians were left defenseless at the sultan's mercy. The cumulative effect of the San Stefano and Berlin treaties was the internationalization of the Armenian question that immensely increased the physical vulnerability of the Ottoman Armenians as a primary target of the sultan's ire, without providing protective mechanisms in case the sultan proceeded to massacre his subjects.[11] The "no-win" situation of the Armenians vis-à-vis the sultan could be viewed as a prisoner's dilemma, in which the European jailer/mediators—Britain, Russia, Germany,

TABLE 8.1   The Armenian Genocide, 1878–1923

Date	Event	Target/Goal	Death Toll/Outcome
1878	Sultan Abdul-Hamid II cancels Ottoman constitution and parliament	To establish a Pan-Islamic state as a means to prevent the collapse of the Ottoman Empire	Repression of minorities; Armenian demands for reform with European support
1894–1896	Hamidean massacres	Suppress demands for reform and eliminate European pretext for intervention	Up to 200,000 Armenians killed
July 1908	Committee of Union and Progress (CUP) a.k.a. Young Turk Party military rebellion	Establish a constitutional regime	Sultan Abdul-Hamid II accepts constitutional rule
Apr. 1909	Failed countercoup by sultan	Retake power	30,000 Armenians massacred at Adana; sultan exiled
1908–1912	Ottoman defeats in Libya and the Balkans; European pressures for reform		
Jan. 1913	Coup d'état by CUP extremist Turkish nationalists; triumvirate of Talat, Enver, and Jemal takes power	Establish Pan-Turanist regime	Pan-Turanism becomes official ideology of the state; Turkification of minorities
Feb. 1914	CUP regime signs Armenian Reform Act under Russian/British pressure	Security and autonomy in the Armenian areas	Government repression of Armenians
July 1914	Outbreak of World War I; CUP regime joins Germany and Austro-Hungary	To defeat Russia	Up to 100,000 Armenian soldiers join the Ottoman military
Jan. 1915	Enver Pasha's Pan-Turanist March defeated by Russia		
Feb. 1915	Enver praises Armenian soldiers; gives the order to carry out genocide in a secret top level meeting	Strategic deception of the Armenians	CUP finalizes its genocidal plans

TABLE 8.1 Cont. The Armenian Genocide, 1878–1923

Date	Event	Target/Goal	Death Toll/Outcome
Apr. 1915	Armenian leaders and intellectuals arrested in Constantinople; mass deportations and massacres begin	Eliminate the Armenian leadership prior to genocide	Up to 1.5 million Armenians killed
May 1915	Britain, France, and Russia issue a joint warning to CUP regime threatening to hold individual leaders responsible for crimes against "humanity and civilization"	Halt the massacre of Armenians	Ignored by CUP
Jan. 1918	President Wilson's Declaration of Fourteen Points; twelfth point promises security and autonomy for the Armenians	Recognition of genocide and restitution of Armenian rights	Not implemented
May 1918	Founding of the Armenian Republic		
Oct. 1918	World War I ends		Ottoman Turkey defeated
Apr. 1919– Jan. 1920	Turkish military tribunal finds CUP leaders guilty of Armenian massacres		Several CUP leaders found guilty; many released after negotiations with Britain
May 1920	Proposal for an American mandate over Armenia rejected by Congress		Armenian Republic invaded by Soviet and Turkish armies
Aug. 1920	Treaty of Sévres signed by Turkey, the Western Allies, and the Armenian Republic		Turkey accepts responsibility for massacres
May 1921	Republic of Armenia incorporated into the Soviet Union	Protection from Turkish military threats	
1920–1922	Ataturk's nationalist forces continue to massacre Armenians, Greeks, and others		
July 1923	Treaty of Lausanne recognizes the Turkish Republic and eliminates Turkish obligations under the Treaty of Sévres		Turkey adopts a policy to deny the Armenian massacres

and Austro-Hungary—did not operate as a unitary actor, but worked independently at cross-purposes based on their mutually conflicting interests. In this case, the unwillingness of the "jailers" to assert their combined power over the "prisoners" had deadly results.

In the fifteen years after the Congress of Berlin, the leadership of the Armenian community sought to placate the sultan with expressions of loyalty and support for the territorial integrity of the Ottoman empire.[12] However, the deep sense of betrayal by Europe and the sultan's continued oppression drove some Armenians in the 1880s to form self-defense units in a few provincial locations, which in the 1890s evolved into political groupings. Yet, even among the more militant elements, the overwhelming preference was for cultural freedom and regional autonomy, not separation and independence. After 1890, the sultan's government intensified its oppression by prohibiting all Armenian cultural events and publications, the use of the word "Armenia," and the teaching of the Armenian language.

The first phase of mass killings began in August 1894, and only by May 1895 had the European powers managed to pressure the sultan to carry out the promised reforms. In September 1895, a peaceful demonstration by Armenians in the capital city resulted in 2,000 casualties, prompting another protest by the Great Powers. By early October, however, the regime had unleashed the second phase of mass slaughter. The killings persisted until December 1896 despite the sultan's solemn promises to protect the Armenian population. The 26-month long carnage was a learning process for the sultan. Despite their diplomatic protestations, the Great Powers were unprepared to use military force, which gave the sultan a free hand to kill an estimated 100,000–200,000 Armenians, forcing 100,000 to convert to Islam and a similar number to escape the country. The ability of a genocidal regime to get away with mass murder had been amply demonstrated. As for the Armenians, who paid a terrible price in lives and property, the lessons of the Hamidean massacres should have been instructive in the formation of their future strategic preferences. These lessons, springing from the Armenians' geostrategic demographic position and the predatory nature of the Ottoman regime were as follows:

1. The futility of appealing to the Ottoman regime to institute reforms to protect the civil rights of its non-Muslim *millets,* such as the Armenians, because such reforms were totally alien to the culture of a predatory empire based on absolute imperial rule over its subject peoples, particularly the non-Muslims.

2. The futility and danger of appealing to the so-called "Christian" European powers to intercede with the Ottoman regime to implement reforms or intervene to stop the mass killings.

3. The futility of engaging in limited acts of self-defense or demonstrations against a powerful regime and the danger that such acts would trigger further atrocities.

The Armenian leadership should have clearly understood that the foregoing actions had placed the Armenian population in an existential danger of the first magnitude in the hands of the Ottoman military, marauding Turkish and Circassian bands, and the Hamidiye Cavalry, a Kurdish force named after the sultan, all expressly tasked to target the Armenians in the provinces. In these circumstances, the sole rational option for the Armenians would have been to accept their position of subservience leaving them at the mercy of the ruling order. For the Turkish perpetrators, however, the Hamidean massacres of 1894–1896 constituted a learning experience—a bloody model to emulate on a larger scale in an attempt to exterminate the empire's Armenian population in 1915.

Constitutional Autocracy, 1908–1913

Beyond the victimization of the Armenians, Sultan Abdul-Hamid's tyrannical rule had deeply affected his Turkish subjects, including the intelligentsia and the younger military officers. Many of these disaffected Turks had fled to Europe where they joined expatriates from other oppressed minorities to organize a broad coalition aiming to replace sultanic rule with a constitutional monarchy. The most prominent of these reformist groups was the Committee of Union and Progress (CUP, or *Ittihad ve Terakki Teshkilati*) that came to be known in Europe as the "Young Turks." Founded by Ahmed Reza, a liberal intellectual, the CUP advocated an ambitious reform program of Ottomanism, which would preserve the empire under a constitutional regime with the participation of the elected members of all the minorities who would enjoy equal rights with the Muslims, in peace and security. The CUP's Ottomanist agenda attracted strong support from the empire's minorities including Jews, Albanians, Armenians, and Arabs, all working to end the sultan's oppressive rule.[13]

The outbreak of a rebellion in July 1908 by CUP officers in Salonika prompted the sultan to feign acceptance of constitutional rule, until his supporters attempted a countercoup in April 1909, which ended in his final overthrow and exile. In the midst of these struggles, between April 15–25, 30,000 Armenians were slaughtered in the Adana province by the sultan's allies in the military.[14] Even after the CUP's inaction during this ominous event, the Armenian leadership continued to support the CUP government, while awaiting its promises of providing security to the Armenians living in the provinces. These hopes were never realized because of the convergence of critical external events and the radicalization of the CUP government.

Soon after taking power in 1908, the CUP regime was confronted with external and internal challenges that completely transformed its ideology, strategic objectives, and leadership cadres. This transformation radicalized the ruling elite with disastrous consequences for the Armenian minority and the empire itself.

Among the external calamities that befell the regime were the annexation of Bosnia and Herzegovina by Austro-Hungary, Bulgaria's declaration of independence (1908), the loss of Macedonia and Thrace in the Balkan war (1912), and the Italian takeover of Libya (1912). These successive defeats, combined with growing European pressures to institute constitutional reforms, triggered a military coup d'état in January 1913 that brought to power an extremist faction of the CUP with a radical agenda to save the collapsing empire. The new oligarchy was led by a triumvirate—Minister of War, Enver, Interior Minister and Grand Vizier Talat and Marine Minister Jemal—representing a group of ambitious and angry men hailing from the margins of Ottoman Turkish society who had captured the reigns of power at a critical moment.[15] They did not share the goals of the liberal Ottomanists who had founded the CUP based on constitutionalism and reformism for the empire's polyglot peoples. The triumvirate's vision of empire, based on exclusivist Turkish nationalism and an expansive geostrategic rationale, was even more extreme than that of Sultan Abdul-Hamid.

The Geopolitics of Pan-Turanism

All Ottoman governments since the empire's decline shared the common goals of preserving its might and territorial integrity under a predominantly Turkish ruling elite. Sultan Abdul-Hamid had relied on oppressive rule combined with Pan-Islamist calls for unity of all Muslims against Europe and the empire's non-Muslim minorities. On the other hand, in its early years (1908–1912), the CUP advanced the Ottomanist solution to preserve the empire through constitutional reforms embracing its diverse peoples. In sharp contrast, the CUP triumvirate rejected both the constitutionalist and Pan-Islamist solutions in favor of Pan-Turanism—a secular ideology of Turkish supernationalism, combined with totalitarian rule and an irredentist geopolitical doctrine. A crucial strategic element in this imperial design was the forging of a strong alliance with Germany. The logic of the German connection flowed from the CUP's urgent need for a powerful partner that could provide the military, technological, and economic means to strengthen the empire, while protecting it from the other European powers. This rapprochement and the pervasive German presence in the empire, had a formative influence on the ideology and policies of the CUP leadership. In the imperial German Reich, the CUP elite saw a most worthy model of emulation for building a militarily strong and internally united Turkish state. Indeed, the Prussian example of success in building an all-powerful German state in the six decades after the Napoleonic invasion was a compelling path for the Turkish leaders who were desperately searching for ways to sustain the Ottoman realm. Therefore, it was no accident that the CUP triumvirate adopted the ideology of Pan-Turanism also known as Pan-Turkism—a replica of Pan-Germanic supernationalism mixed with European authoritarian and racialist political thought.[16] In searching for a "Teutonic" mythology of the German variety, the Pan-Turanists sought to revive and recreate a pre-Ottoman and pre-Islamic Turkish past in a mythical land they called "Turan"—a reference to the original Central Asian homeland of Turkic tribes such as the Ottomans who had progressively conquered the Persian, Arab, and Byzantine territories beginning with the eighth century.[17]

The proponents of Pan-Turanism envisaged the creation of an exclusively Turkish superstate based on the Ottoman empire, which would unify all Turkic-speaking peoples of Russia, the Caucasus, and Central Asia. The first advocates of Pan-Turanism were several expatriate intellectuals from the Turkic Muslim regions of the Russian empire who had found refuge in Ottoman Turkey escaping Tsarist oppression. These men sought to strengthen the Ottoman empire to liberate their homelands from Russian rule. Another exponent of Pan-Turanism was Zia Gökalp—an ethnic Kurd—who advocated the mass adoption of a Pan-Turkish identity and unity in the utopian quest to recreate "Turan."[18] These were men from socially and politically marginal backgrounds whose theoretical writings became mainstream once Pan-Turanism was adopted as the official ideology of the militant wing of the CUP which captured power in January 1913.[19]

The geostrategic imperatives of the Pan-Turanist creed were the unification and liberation of Turkic peoples and the social homogenization of the empire's non-Turkic inhabitants through Turkification—the forced imposition of a Turkish identity on Arabs, Kurds, Armenians, Jews, Greeks, Assyrians, and other ethnic groups.

Was there an alternative to Turkification? The answer would depend on the regime's strategic response toward the empire's three largest minorities—the Arabs, Kurds, and Armenians. The Arabs, mostly Muslim and minority Christian, were subjected to brutal oppression and killings that led them to rebel in 1916—a successful effort because of their remote geographical location and British assistance.[20] The Kurds, mostly subservient to their tribal shaikhs, were coopted by the regime to massacre the Armenians, only to suffer the ravages of forceful Turkification and politicide in later decades. The CUP's Pan-

Turanist policies were especially threatening to the Armenians who were left in an acutely vulnerable position given their Christian identity, demographic location, and continuing quest for security under Ottoman rule. The CUP triumvirate came to view the Armenians as a fundamental ethno-religious impediment to Turkification as well as a geostrategic obstacle in the land corridor to Asia that would inhibit the grand scheme of a Pan-Turanist empire.[21] Thus, the strategic utility of resolving the Armenian Question with finality seemed compelling to the CUP leadership in 1913 as it began a meticulous planning process to convert Pan-Turanist ideology into practice.

A Prisoner's Dilemma unto Death, 1913–1915

The strategic interaction between the CUP regime and the Armenian minority can be viewed as a prisoner's dilemma situation with the European powers in the role of "jailer-mediator"—a replication of what had occurred in 1876–1895. The relationship between the CUP triumvirate and the Armenian leadership was one of complete asymmetry in terms of coercive power and political might. The countervailing power that might have been used against the CUP by a strong third party—in this case the Europeans—was made ineffective by its variegated character and inability to behave as a unitary actor. Without the coercive pressure of this external force, the asymmetric power relationship present at the outset of the game could not reach a state of equilibrium that would ensure the survival of the weaker party. Instead, it reproduced itself in a grossly unequal payoff structure—the Armenian genocide.

The fractured Armenian leadership consisted of the Armenian Orthodox patriarch and a handful of representatives in the Ottoman parliament belonging to several political parties. Except for some primitive firearms, the Armenian population lacked the means to mount any serious challenge to the regime. Their helpless situation had been amply demonstrated during the Hamidean (1894–1896) and Adana (1909) massacres. In the perilous circumstances of the 1910s, the Armenian leadership pursued three seemingly contradictory strategies: expressions of complete loyalty to the CUP government; appeals to the CUP to institute reforms in the Armenian-populated Eastern provinces based on autonomy; and appeals to the European powers to press the CUP regime to begin the long-promised implementation of these reforms. Although some Armenian leaders were weary of relying on European support, most believed that decisive European diplomatic intervention was the only way to bring the Turkish leadership to implement a reform program. However, since its inception, the CUP regime strongly opposed reformist schemes based on autonomy through European mediation, fearing that these would inevitably lead to separatism and independence. Ranking CUP leaders such as Talat repeatedly warned the Armenian leadership to desist from dependence on the Europeans because they were the common enemy of the Turks and the Armenians.[22] However, the Armenians deeply distrusted the CUP regime, fearing that without European intercession their collective security would be grievously endangered. This belief was based on the progressive deterioration of the Armenians' situation in the provinces in 1912–1913 despite their manifestations of loyalty to the Ottoman empire, such as volunteering to fight in the 1912 Balkan war.[23]

Armenian hopes for European mediation were kept alive by the ongoing negotiations among the six major powers, culminating in the Reform Act of February 8, 1914, that the Turkish government signed under duress. This document represented a Russo-German compromise that would create two Armenian provinces to be administered by European inspectors-general. Although this reform plan fell far short of Armenian expectations, it created a false sense of optimism, which abruptly ended with the outbreak of the Great War in July 1914.[24]

The Armenian Genocide: Rationale and Planning

The CUP party that controlled the Ottoman regime had two faces. Its public face represented a commitment to reform, civility, and equality among all the citizens of the empire. In sharp contrast, the party's leaders functioned in utmost secrecy in planning and organizing the systematic destruction of the Christian minorities, particularly the Armenian population. The first signs of such strategic planning appeared in Talat's speech of August 6, 1910, to a secret conclave of CUP leaders. His recommendations on how to deal with the non-Muslim population were secretly approved in November 1910 by the party's Central Committee at its Tenth Congress in Salonika. These decisions, leaked to European diplomatic personnel by dissident CUP members, involved first, rejection of the constitutional reforms of equality between Muslims and non-Muslims considered *giawur* or infidels because such reforms do not conform to Islamic law (*shariah*); second, the forcible homogenization of these minorities through Turkification, resettlement of Muslims, and the deportation and massacre of the non-Muslims; and third, the need to ensure control of the military in order to implement the foregoing objectives.[25]

Meanwhile, the geopolitical imperative to neutralize the Armenian presence in Turkey's Eastern provinces was implicitly formalized in the secret Turkish-German pact of August 2, 1914, where Germany pledged to assume responsibility to rectify the empire's eastern frontiers in order to provide a "link" with the Muslim peoples of Russia.[26] Both sides must have understood that such a "link" would require the forceful removal or destruction of the Armenian population—a central strategic objective of the Pan-Turanist project.

The implementation of these genocidal schemes required detailed planning and organization, which became the responsibility of two European-educated Turkish physicians—Dr. Mehmet Nazim and Dr. Behaeddin Shakir.[27] These two leading members of CUP's central committee were dedicated Pan-Turanists who had advocated a genocidal solution for the Armenian question as early as 1906–1907, prior to the party's takeover of power in 1908. The guiding strategy of these men, working directly under Interior Minister Talat, was the neutralization of the "internal enemy"—the Armenian minority.[28] Their plan of action had been framed in the secret party conclave of December 1914 and was later leaked to the British High Commissioner in Constantinople by Ahmet Essad, a high Turkish intelligence official. This revealing ten-point document—dubbed by the British as "The Ten Commandments"—is partially reproduced below:

1. . . . close all Armenian societies, and arrest all who worked against [the] Government at any time among them and send them into the provinces such as Bagdad or Mosul, and wipe them out either on the road or there.
2. Collect arms.
3. Excite Moslem opinion by suitable and special means, in places as Van, Erzeroum, Adana, where as a point of fact the Armenians have already won the hatred of the Moslems; provoke organized massacres as the Russians did at Baku.
4. Leave all executive to the people in provinces such as Erzeroum, Van, Mamuret al Aziz, and Bitlis, and use military disciplinary forces (i.e., Gendarmerie) ostensibly to stop massacres, while on the contrary in places as Adana, Sivas, Broussa, Ismidt, and Smyrna actively help the Moslems with military force.
5. Apply measures to exterminate all males under 50, priests and teachers; leave girls and children to be Islamized.
6. Carry away the families of all who succeed in escaping and apply measures to cut them off from all connection with their native place.
7. On the ground that Armenian officials may be spies, expel and drive them out absolutely from every government department or post.
8. Kill off in an appropriate manner all Armenians in the army—this to be left to the military to do.
9. All action to begin everywhere simultaneously, and thus leave no time for preparation of defensive measures.
10. Pay attention to the strictly confidential nature of these instructions, which may not go beyond two or three persons.[29]

These "Ten Commandments" and many similar documents clearly set forth the strategic logic of the CUP party and government—the Armenian population constituted an existential threat to the Ottoman empire and a demographic impediment to its grand design to establish a Pan-Turanist state uniting the Turkic peoples from the Balkans to the far reaches of Central Asia. According to this rationale, the elimination of the Armenian presence had to become a priority objective second only to waging war against the empire's two main enemies, Russia and Britain.

The Killing Machine

The decision and plans of the CUP to destroy the Armenian population required an efficient bureaucratic apparatus that was organized and coordinated by Talat's Interior Ministry. As its primary instrument of mass murder, the regime established *Teshkilati Mahsuse*—the Special Organization—under Dr. Behaeddin Shakir. This paramilitary force of over 30,000 was staffed by active and reserve military officers who were placed in charge of thousands of criminals expressly released from prison to join the *Teshkilati Mahsuse* (TM).[30] These ex-convicts, called *chete*, were organized into roving Butcher Battalions (*Kassab Taburu*) to systematically carry out the deportation and massacre of the Armenians. The killing apparatus was supplemented by the provincial gendarmes and the Ottoman army that was charged with the forced removal of the Armenians under the Temporary Law of Deportation of May 27, 1915. In essence, the *Teshkilati Mahsuse* represented a fusion of the CUP elite under Talat and the military elite under Enver, with Dr. Shakir as chief executioner coordinating a centralized hierarchy of cadres and *chete* squads consisting of former convicts, Kurds, Circassians, and other Muslim minority groups. These elements were driven to kill en masse by several ideological and material incentives. The party-military leadership was chiefly driven by Pan-Turanist geopolitical and racial objectives while the lower ranks were energized by the regime's declaration of jihad against the "infidel" Armenians. Aside from ideology, all ranks of the *Teshkilati Mahsuse* were driven by the powerful incentives of plundering the Armenians' wealth and property and forcing the surviving women and children into involuntary servitude.[31]

Implementation of Genocide, 1914–1919

The regime's genocidal stratagems were secrecy, deception, and surprise, combined with a sense of urgency and efficiency. The plot to destroy the Armenians had been hatched in utmost secrecy by a small cohort of CUP leaders, who used various techniques of deception to mislead the European observers and the leaders of the Armenian community, to minimize the risk of external intervention, and to catch their victims by surprise before they could organize any resistance. Given their possession of overwhelming coercive power and the total vulnerability of the Armenians, Talat and Enver were so confident of their success that they did not even consider a second preference to their genocidal objective.[32] Once the regime formally launched the mass killings in spring 1915, they were implemented with a heightened sense of urgency and efficiency to ensure that the job was done quickly and comprehensively before the vicissitudes of war or intervention would abort the completion of the ghastly enterprise. Specially selected party functionaries were dispatched to oversee the mass deportations and killings. Turkish governors, mayors, or military officials who showed reluctance to carry out the massacres because of religious or moral reasons were summarily dismissed, replaced, or killed by the CUP's field officers. Similarly, the regime punished Turkish religious and community leaders who had sought to protect or hide their Armenian neighbors from the killing squads.[33]

The chronology of the Armenian genocide may be divided into four phases. The first phase, July 1914 through April 1915, was a "prelude" that began with the outbreak of World War I as Armenians loyally participated in the war effort both on the Eastern and Western fronts. In December 1914, Enver Pasha, Minister of War, led the Pan-Turanist March toward the Caucasus to implement his grand design to liberate the Turkic peoples of Russia. Enver's offensive turned into a disastrous defeat by the Russian Army at Sarikamish in January 1915, which drove the Germanophile general to look for a scapegoat. In a ploy to trick his Armenian soldiers, Enver thanked them in early February for fighting loyally at Sarikamish, while decreeing their extermination at a secret party conclave two weeks later.[34] Now the Armenians had been officially targeted as the scapegoats for Enver's defeat on the pretext that a small number of Armenian expatriates from Turkey had fought on the Russian side. As Enver's victims, an estimated 100,000 Armenian soldiers of the Ottoman army were disarmed and thrown into labor battalions and eventually massacred by the Turkish military.[35] Meanwhile, all remaining Armenian citizens were ordered to surrender their arms amid house-to-house searches. Between March and April 1915, all the signs of a final reckoning were apparent as the regime moved quickly to carry out wholesale deportations and massacres throughout the country. Although in a few instances such as Zeitun (April 8) and Van (April 17), the Armenians refused to disarm and fought to the death, most of the victims were deceived by official pronouncements that spoke of "deportations" and "temporary wartime relocation."[36] The Armenians were totally helpless in the face of a tightly organized killing machine, centrally

coordinated via telegraph, armed with modern weaponry, and ideologically energized by a fusion of Pan-Turanist racism and Islamist jihadism,
supplemented by the material incentives of pillage.

The second phase of the genocide began in mid-April 1915 with
the dispatch of secret orders from Talat and Enver to all provincial officials. These mass killings were far more systematic and comprehensive
than the earlier atrocities. The first step was the decapitation of the Armenian community's cultural leadership as 600 notables, writers, intellectuals, and public figures were arrested in Constantinople and murdered—a cohort that ironically included Armenian members of the
Ottoman parliament who had loyally served the CUP regime.[37] Despite
its efforts at secrecy and denial, the massacres were widely reported in
the world's newspapers, triggering large-scale protests and calls for intervention. In May 1915, the British, French, and Russian governments
warned that the Armenian massacres were "crimes against humanity
and civilization," for which all members of the Ottoman government
would be held individually responsible.[38] In July 1915, U.S. Ambassador
Henry Morgenthau in Constantinople was reporting that, "a campaign
of race extermination is in progress" as he valiantly but vainly confronted Talat to stop the mass slaughter. Morgenthau's repeated en-
treaties infuriated Talat: "Why are you so interested in the Armenians?
You are a Jew, these people are Christians. . . . Why can't you let us do
with these Christians as we please?" On another occasion Talat asserted:
"We have already disposed of three quarters of the Armenians. . . . The
hatred between the Turks and the Armenians is now so intense that we
have got to finish with them. If we don't they will plan their revenge." Talat went on to confirm his personal role as supreme executioner: "I have
accomplished more toward solving the Armenian problem in three
months than Abdul Hamid accomplished in thirty years!"[39]

At the start of the third phase of the massacres in spring 1916, an
estimated 800,000 Armenians were reported to have perished.[40] The
new effort was a mopping-up operation to ensure the destruction of the
remaining refugee population huddled in camps or roaming the deso-
late deserts of Syria, Iraq, and Arabia. In October 1918, the Ottoman regime accepted defeat and its top leaders fled the country to escape punishment by the victorious allies. The CUP had failed to save the empire,
but had mostly succeeded in the final solution of the Armenian question
in what became known as the "First Genocide of the Twentieth Century."
Yet, a fourth phase of killing awaited the Armenians during Mustafa Kemal's nationalist uprising (1920–1923). Several thousand Armenians
were killed by Turkish irregulars and Kemalist forces in such places as
Izmir, Cilicia and the eastern provinces.

Reckoning, Restitution, and Denial, 1920–2006

According to the estimates of a large number of scholars and governments, up to 1.5 million Armenians had perished and another 300,000 mostly women and children were Turkified by forceful conversion to Islam.[41] Despite the CUP's best efforts, many Armenians survived through the acts of righteous Turkish officials, officers, and civilians who refused to carry out the regime's orders because of humanitarian and religious motives.[42] In some instances, local Muslim clerics and preachers (*muftis* and *imams*) and heads of the religious brotherhoods (*sufis*) protected the Armenians at great risk to themselves, because they deeply believed in Islam's strict prohibitions on killing innocent people.[43] These men of faith knew that the regime's declaration of jihad against the Armenians was racially motivated because the CUP leaders were unbelievers with no fealty to Islam but to the Pan-Turanist project of Turkic racial supremacy. Yet another category of righteous Muslims were the Arabs who gave refuge to the Armenians driven to the Syrian desert, thereby rejecting the regime's call to jihad. Later, in 1916, the Arabs rose up in rebellion against the CUP and its policies of Turkification. Also, a large number of survivors owed their lives to foreign missionaries, military officers, and consular officials—Americans, Germans, Norwegians, Swedes, Austrians, Danes— who saved and cared for countless Armenian refugees and orphans both during and after the atrocities. The total number of survivors represented less than twenty percent of the Armenian population of the Ottoman empire.[44]

The Allied powers had promised to punish the CUP leadership and provide restitution to the remnants of the Armenian people by granting them independent statehood. In response to the atrocities against the Armenians, the governments of France, Britain, and Russia warned that because of "these new crimes of Turkey against humanity and civilization, the allied Governments publicly inform the Sublime Porte that they will hold personally responsible for the said crimes all members of the Ottoman Government as well as those of its agents who are found to be involved in such massacres."[45] In the context of international law, this marked the beginning of asserting individual responsibility of government officials for what came to be known as "crimes against humanity" and later, genocide. After the fall of the CUP regime in October 1918, the new Turkish government instituted a series of military tribunals that tried, convicted, and sentenced a large number of CUP leaders and officials for crimes against the Armenian people.[46] However, most of these sentences were not carried out because of British duplicity and the weakness of the new Turkish regime that faced a growing challenge from nationalist insurgents led by General Mustafa Kemal.

Eventually, leading members of the CUP who had escaped Turkey were assassinated by a small contingent of Armenian young men whose families had been killed during the genocide—Grand Vizier Said Halim (Rome 1921), Dr. Behaeddin Shakir (Berlin 1922), General Jemal Pasha (Tiflis 1922), Minister of War Enver Pasha (Bukhara 1922). The chief architect of the genocide, Talat Pasha, was assassinated in March 1921, but his 24-year old killer was acquitted by a Berlin court.[47] Meanwhile, a fledgling Armenian Republic had been established on May 28, 1918, that soon came under attack by the resurgent armies of Mustafa Kemal, who would later be known as Ataturk. To protect the new state, President Woodrow Wilson proposed a U.S. mandate over Armenia that faced defeat in the Senate by a combination of isolationists and oil and business interests who sought to befriend Turkey.[48] As Turkish armies reoccupied the Western portions of the nascent Armenian Republic, its remaining territories were overrun by communist forces in December 1920. Armenia then became a part of the Soviet Union until its independence after the USSR's demise in 1991. Meanwhile, in the 1920s, the Turkish Republic had passed laws authorizing confiscation of all "abandoned" property by the Armenians and prohibited their return to Turkey.[49]

A fundamental policy priority since the early days of the Turkish Republic has been the denial of the Armenian genocide. The systematic campaign to deny one of the most comprehensively documented genocides in history has involved detailed planning, generous funding, worldwide lobbying, cooptation of "experts" to rewrite history and threats against governments, organizations, and scholars which have officially recognized the Armenian massacres as genocide.[50]

Although Mustafa Kemal Ataturk, the founding president of the Republic of Turkey, denounced the CUP leaders for the atrocities they committed against "Christians" in wartime, his successors made denial a central tenet of their policy both at home and abroad.[51] Any mention of the Armenian genocide has been prohibited in Turkish textbooks and historiography and Turkish writers and scholars who have dared to write about the events of 1915 have been denounced and severely punished. Among the most prominent Turkish writers to be persecuted by the Turkish government for writing on the Armenian genocide are the 2006 Nobel Prize winner Orhan Pamuk and Professor Elif Shafak of the University of Arizona. Confronted with growing calls from the international community to recognize the Armenian genocide, the Turkish government has improvised several denialist strategies that fly in the face of the compelling historical record of eyewitness accounts by foreign and Turkish officials, the testimony of survivors, and the massive documentary evidence found in German, British, American, French, and other archives that have been scrutinized and analyzed by dozens of internationally renown scholars.[52] The persistent Turkish denialist position is prompted by: the perceived dishonor that recognition would bring to the Turkish nation; the immense costs of compensation and reparations that Turkey might have to pay to the Armenians for the mass killings and expropriation of the victims' properties; and the possibility that recognition of the crime would open up sensitive territorial issues regarding lands forcibly taken by Turkey from the short-lived Armenian Republic (1918–1920).

Since the Armenian Republic became independent from the Soviet Union in 1991, Turkey has refused to establish diplomatic relations with it because of Armenia's ongoing conflict with Azerbaijan. Nevertheless, Turkey and Armenia remain engaged in an interactive relationship where the historic concerns of security, territory, and genocide still play a decisive role. In the complex geopolitics of the Caucasus region, dominated by the confluence of interests involving Iran, Iraq, Russia, the United States, and the Kurds, the burden of painful memories will continue to shape the Armenian-Turkish relationship for years to come.

The Jewish Holocaust

Europe emerging from the ravages of World War I became the crucible of conflicting national interests, clashing ideologies, and social forces. At the center of this tumultuous milieu stood a defeated Germany, whose aspirations for continental empire lay in ruins. Born in the wake of the Napoleonic invasions and bred on a strident nationalist creed for a century, the German imperial Reich was dismantled by the post-war settlement and humbled by territorial losses, financial reparations, and the psychological burdens of defeat. The nascent democratic culture of the Weimar Republic proved unable to heal Germany's many wounds and fell victim to the resurgent forces of revanchism. Yet, beyond the demise of Germany's brief democratic experiment, the ultimate victim of the revanchist vengeance would be European Jewry. In an unpredictable confluence of crisis factors—psychological, economic, ideological, and political—Germany, Europe's foremost icon of high culture and education became the perpetrator of the greatest genocide of all time.

Rational choice theory, in modified form, brings a fresh perspective to the analysis of the factors leading to the Holocaust. Such an approach focuses on strategic interactions while capturing the psychological, sociological, and economic factors that produced the genocidal outcome. At the basic level, the immense power of Hitler's Third Reich was pitted against the German Jewish community numbering 565,000.[53] Thus, the strategic interaction between the Nazi state and the Jewish minority in the pre-genocidal phase represented a power differential of vast proportions. German Jews were the most culturally assimilated of the Jewish communities in Europe. After the fall of the Weimar Republic, they had no political influence and absolutely no coercive means to challenge the state. In contrast, Jews had a notable presence in the economic, cultural, and scientific spheres, which however was hardly sufficient as an instrument to undermine the Nazi regime.[54]

Beyond the great power differential between the Nazis and German Jews, there was an asymmetry in their mutual perceptions and preferences. Given the regime's secrecy, there was great uncertainty among Jews about Nazi intentions and policies toward them. As fully assimilated citizens who had fought loyally in the German armies in World War I, many Jews regarded the regime's predatory behavior as a temporary aberration; only a few foresaw the possibility of genocide.[55] In sharp contrast, those in the top ranks of the Nazi elite possessed considerable certainty about what they intended to do to the Jews.

Crisis and Response: Hitler as Savior

The rise of Nazism as an ideology and movement was a response to the crisis conditions in Weimar Germany. These crisis factors were at once ideological, political, military, economic, and psychological. Political instability was fueled by ongoing communist-Nazi clashes, an economy burdened by reparations and the worldwide depression, and the discordant influences of military leaders and business interests. Below the clashing ideologies and interests was pervasive anger and alienation, particularly among the middle and lower classes caught in the throws of economic deprivation and psychological insecurity. These were average Germans for whom the cumulative impact of the crisis factors was disproportionately greater than for the more privileged classes.[56] In this sense, the loss of honor of a defeated nation had a damaging influence on the German masses, producing a profound psychological crisis—in Erik Erikson's terms, a crisis of identity.[57]

It has been observed that in times of psychological and existential crises, society is beset by a mass psychosis and a pervasive expectancy for a savior with a salvational promise of a bright future. Such messianic saviors emerge as charismatic leaders who have a powerful impact on their societies in crisis, which could lead to beneficial or disastrous outcomes depending on the leader's belief system and psychological attributes.[58] In Germany's case, Adolf Hitler marched into the void of power and identity to project a chiliastic message and totalitarian agenda that were fated to leave a cataclysmic imprint on and beyond the European continent.

Nazism: Leadership, Party, and the Ideological Imperative

The German National Socialist Party represented an extension of Hitler's persona in terms of its members' backgrounds, ideology, and aspirations. As a centrally controlled hierarchical apparatus, the party was Hitler's personal instrument to impose his will on society. Although Hitler stood unchallenged as the charismatic embodiment of the Third Reich, he shared certain background characteristics with both the Nazi elite and the rank and file. In social background, a large number of Nazi elites were "marginal men" who had come from outside Germany's political, socioeconomic, and cultural mainstream. Notably, many Nazi leaders were *Volksdeutsch,* born in peripheral areas in and outside Germany, e.g., Hitler, Alfred Rosenberg, Rudolf Hess, Hermann Göring, Ernst Röhm and Ernst Kaltenbrunner.[59] Their geographical marginality was reinforced by their lowly socioeconomic and occupational status and erratic life histories. Hitler personified many of the salient attributes of marginality in German society of that time—genealogical anomaly, Austrian birth, lower class status, and psychological infirmity. In general, many of these men were failures who found success only after joining the Nazi party. The party apparatus composed mostly of marginal men, angrily seeking to compensate for their past deprivations, ruled over Germany with totalitarian brutality. The Jewish minority was its primary scapegoat. But why target the Jews?

National Socialism as the ideology of the Nazi party and government was derived from the salvational message that Hitler successfully projected upon a crisis-torn Germany awaiting deliverance. While rooted in the German past, Hitlerite ideology possessed a strongly revivalist tenor, mixed with German exceptionalism and racism. By recalling Germany's glorious past as Europe's preeminent power in the nineteenth century, Hitler summoned the Germans to answer the call of destiny to create the "Thousand-Year Reich." Here was a deeply conflicted man hailing from Austria with a utopian vision of an all-powerful conquering Reich that most Germans came to share as they internalized their führer's values, beliefs, and action program. Hitler's emphasis on German unity and greatness provided a cure to a people beset by a sense of shame and dishonor, reaffirming their individual and collective identity as Germans, and propelling them toward war and genocide.[60] The ultimate target of Hitler's personal struggle was world Jewry, which he perceived as controlling the Soviet Union, sowing unrest, and striving to dominate the world.[61]

The racist component of Nazi ideology was rooted in nineteenth-century theories of human differences based on "race" which flourished in the age of rampant imperialism and Social Darwinism. In the Nazi ideological framework, these theories of race became mixed with traditional European antisemitism to produce a rabid doctrine that viewed the elimination of the Jewish people as the ultimate good. Thus, Jews were classified as *Untermenschen* (subhuman people), along with other "impure" elements—Gypsies, homosexuals, indigents, and communists—whose extermination was imperative for Germany's survival and victory. Among these groups, the Jews were seen as the most dangerous existential threat because they were blamed for Germany's defeat in World War I and for the rise of communism in Europe and Russia. As such, the Jews were the ultimate political scapegoat for Germany's misfortunes. Futhermore, as *Untermenschen,* the Jews were considered racially inferior, a threat to the purity of the German master race and culture.[62] Reichsführer Heinrich Himmler described the Jews as "bacterium" and "scum" who had to be eliminated to secure the German future.[63] Thus, the Nazi plan for Jewish extermination was driven by a mix of political and racial motives that converged into a categorical imperative—a first preference to be implemented in a most effective manner even if it would hurt the war effort.

The stated determination of Hitler and the Nazi leadership in the 1920s to "solve" the Jewish question remained unshakable as a first preference after they took power in 1933. However, in 1938–1940, there were at least three preferences on the modalities to bring about the "Final Solution." The first was to create a Jewish "reservation" in the Lublin region of eastern Poland, a marshy area that would serve as an enormous prison, presumably a holding place until final decimation.[64] Second, leading Nazis like Göring and Himmler seriously considered "the Madagascar Plan"—the deportation of European Jewry to the French colonial island off East Africa. This solution, first advanced in 1885 by Paul de Lagarde, had Hitler's approval presumably because it was expected to benefit Germany economically; in Himmler's words, it was "the mildest and best" way, "if one rejects the Bolshevik method of physical extermination of a people."[65] With the onset of what proved to be a protracted war, the Lublin and Madagascar plans were abandoned as the leadership adopted an alternative modality of solving the Jewish question—the mass murder of European Jewry in ghettos and concentration camps in German-occupied territories. As he was planning to attack the Soviet Union in early 1941, Hitler decided to kill all the Jews of Europe.[66]

The Shoah: Organization and Implementation

While the Nazi leadership debated the modalities to "solve" the Jewish question, it had already imposed upon Germany a totalitarian system and established the legal and organizational means to victimize the Jews. Soon after Hitler's assumption of dictatorial power, the first phase of Jewish deprivation and dehumanization started March 24, 1933 with a series of laws and decrees.[67] Table 8.2 lists a chronology of the Final Solution. Between April 1933 and January 1936, Jews were defined as "non-Aryan" and prohibited from owning land, editing newspapers, and participating in military service, labor unions, and cultural organizations. In September 1935, the Nuremberg race laws were decreed, followed by a temporary decrease in anti-Jewish measures in 1936 prompted by the Nazi desire to impress foreign visitors coming to the August 1936 Olympic Games in Berlin.[68]

Phase two began with Hitler's Anschluss of Austria in March 1938 as the elite *Schutzstaffel* (SS) was assigned to oversee Jewish affairs and Adolf Eichmann was put in charge of the Office of Jewish Emigration. For the next eighteen months the regime unleashed the "Aryanization" campaign by the takeover of Jewish wealth, property, and businesses, aiming at the pauperization of the whole minority. The high point of the gathering storm was *Kristallnacht*—"The Night of Broken Glass"—a pogrom resulting in the destruction of Jewish businesses and property throughout Germany and Austria on November 9–10, 1938, ostensibly triggered by the killing of a German diplomat in France by a Jewish emigré from Poland. On that night German and Austrian Jewry were dealt a heavy blow—30,000 arrested, 7,500 stores looted, and 191 synagogues destroyed.[69]

The third phase of the Nazi "war" against the Jews opened with Hitler's Reichstag speech of January 30, 1939, threatening the destruction of European Jewry.

> Today I want to be a prophet once more: If international finance Jewry inside and outside of Europe should succeed once more in plunging nations into another world war, the consequence will not be the Bolshevization of the earth and thereby the victory of Jewry, but the annihilation of the Jewish race in Europe.[70]

These threats were then systematically carried out after the German invasion of Poland on September 1, 1939, and the outbreak of World War II. After Germany's precipitous conquest of France, Northern and Eastern Europe, the Balkans, and Western Soviet territories from 1939 to 1942, the fate of European Jewry was practically sealed. Meanwhile, the Nazi killing machine was made ready for *Aktionen* against the Jews under SS leader Reinhard Heydrich, who reported directly to Göring and Himmler. Indeed, a modern bureaucratic machine was imperative for making the German Reich *Judenrein*—clean of Jews.[71]

The complex task of *Aktionen*—the coordination and implementation of genocide—was entrusted to Heydrich's *Schutzstaffel* (Defense Echelons) and its ancillary elements. These consisted of the

TABLE 8.2   The Holocaust, 1933–1945

Date	Event
Jan. 1933	Hitler becomes chancellor of Germany
Mar. 1933	First concentration camp established at Dachau
Apr. 1933	Nazi boycott of Jewish businesses; Nazi decree defining Jews as non-Aryan
Sept. 1993	Jews prohibited from owning land
Jan. 1934	Jews banned from German Labor Front
May 1934	Jews denied national health insurance
Aug. 1934	Hitler gets 90 percent "yes" vote from Germans approving his dictatorial power as Führer
May 1935	Jews banned from military service
Sept. 1935	Nuremberg race laws define who is considered a "Jew"
June 1936	Himmler appointed chief of German police
Aug. 1936	Nazis temporarily refrain from anti-Jewish actions as Olympic Games are held in Berlin
Jan. 1937	Jews banned from professional occupations and denied tax reductions
Mar. 1938	Hitler declares Anschluss with Austria
Apr. 1938	Jews forced to register wealth, property, and businesses
July 1938	Jews forced to apply for identity cards
Aug. 1938	Jewish passports stamped with a large "J" as Jews are forced to add the name Sarah or Israel to their passports to prevent them from seeking asylum in other countries
Nov. 1938	*Kristallnacht,* "the Night of Broken Glass" pogrom
Dec. 1938	Law for Aryanization of all Jewish businesses
Jan. 1939	Göring orders Heydrich to speed up emigration of Jews as Hitler threatens Jews during Reichstag speech
Mar. 1939	Decree Regarding Employment of Jews allows regime to take Jews for forced labor
Sept. 1939	Germany invades Poland on Sept. 1; two days later England and France declare war on Germany; Heydrich issues instructions to *Einsatzgrüppen* in Poland to start ghettoization; Poland divided between Soviet Union and Germany
Oct. 1939	Decree allows forced labor for Polish Jews
Jan. 1940	Auschwitz concentration camp established in Poland
July 1940	Eichmann's Madagascar Plan to deport European Jews
June 1941	Germany invades Soviet Union
July 1941	Mobile killing squads (*Einsatzgrüppen*) begin mass killing of Jews behind the advancing German army
Dec. 1941	Nazis begin mass gassing of Jews at Chelmno in Poland

Jan. 1942	Wannsee Conference to coordinate logistics of the Final Solution
Sept. 1942	Hitler's "prophecy" speech about the future of the Jews
Feb. 1943	Germans defeated at Stalingrad
Apr. 1943	Warsaw Ghetto Uprising crushed
June 1943	Himmler orders liquidation of all Jewish ghettoes in Poland
Oct. 1943	Denmark transports 7,220 Danish Jews safely to Sweden; Himmler openly discusses Final Solution
Mar. 1944	President Roosevelt issues condemnation of German and Japanese "crimes against humanity"
Jan. 1945	Liberation of Auschwitz by Soviet Red Army
Apr. 1945	Berlin taken by Soviet troops; Hitler commits suicide in bunker

Einsatzgrüppen (Mobile Killing Squads) and the *Totenkopfverbände* (Death Head Units). While these organizations were expressly tasked to kill en masse, the German military, the Gestapo (Secret Police), and the Order Police (*Ordnungspolizei*) also participated in achieving the Final Solution. Heydrich's strategy consisted of three steps: ghettoization—using deception in gathering the Jews in city ghettos run by Jewish administrative councils (*Judenräte*) under Nazi control; transportation of the Jews from the ghettos by railroad to concentration camps for slave labor and eventual death, usually by Zyklon B gas or carbon monoxide; and killing the remaining Jews by more conventional means—shooting, starvation, forced labor, and death marches.[72]

As the massive structure of ghettoes and concentration camps was put in place, Eichmann was still peddling the Madagascar Plan in mid-1940, which was followed by attempts to expatriate a limited number of Jews in exchange for equipment and large payments from Jewish or Allied sources outside the Third Reich. Such deals seemed attractive as a "humanitarian" cover for Germany's real intentions as well as a potential source of funds, commodities, and equipment that were desperately needed by the Reich. These schemes were soon forgotten amid the victorious march of the German army across Europe and the Nazi elite's passionate impulse to carry out the genocide:

> The time is near when a machine will go into motion which is going to prepare a grave for the world's criminal—Judah—from which there will be no resurrection.

> —Julius Streicher, *Der Stürmer,* January 1940

Now judgment has begun and it will reach its conclusion only when knowledge of the Jews has been erased from the earth.

—*Der Stürmer,* January 1941

I ask nothing of the Jews except that they should disappear.

—Hans Frank, Gauleiter of Poland, 1941

Gentlemen, I must ask you to rid yourselves of all feelings of pity. We must annihilate the Jews wherever we find them and wherever it is possible in order to maintain there the structure of the Reich as a whole.

—Hans Frank, Gauleiter of Poland, 1941

In 1939–1942, the process of ghettoizing Jews in cities and concentration camps was expanded to the conquered territories. Meanwhile, *Einsatzgrüppen,* operating behind the advancing German Army, were killing thousands of Jews in Poland, Ukraine, Latvia, Russia—a practice emulated by the pro-Nazi governments of Hungary, Romania, Lithuania, Slovakia, and Vichy France. The Bulgarians showed some resistance to Nazi orders, but Denmark alone among the Nazi-occupied states secretly evacuated most of its 8,000 Jewish citizens to Sweden, despite the high risk of defying Hitler's will.[73]

The Final Solution, 1942–1945

The pogroms and mass killings of 1941 in Ukraine (Babi Yar and Odessa), Poland, Romania, Yugoslavia, Lithuania, and Latvia were a prelude to the fourth and final phase of the Jewish genocide. These early pilot projects had successfully tested the Third Reich's human, organizational, and technical capabilities for mass murder. The end game was set to go in December 1941 when America entered the war against Germany after the Japanese bombing of Pearl Harbor, with President Roosevelt's declaration that "Never before has there been a greater challenge to life, liberty and civilization."[74]

The seminal enabling event of the Final Solution was the Wannsee Conference of January 20, 1942.[75] Convened by Heydrich at a mansion near Berlin, the aim of this gathering of top Nazi functionaries was the administration and coordination of killing millions of people on a scale unprecedented in history in its immensity of scope and geographical reach. Heydrich, in the role of chief executioner, had tight control over millions of Jews forced into over a dozen strategically placed city ghettos and fifteen major concentration camps. As the gas chambers carried out the programmatic agenda of the Nazi bureaucracy, Hitler reiterated his "prophecy" about the fate of the Jews in a September 1942 speech:

> At one time, the Jews of Germany laughed about my prophecies. I do not know whether they are still laughing or whether they have already lost all desire to laugh. But right now I can only repeat: they will stop laughing everywhere and I shall be right also in that prophecy.[76]

Meanwhile, in December 1941, the Chelmno extermination camp had already begun "processing" Jews and Gypsies using carbon monoxide and later Zyklon B gas, a derivative of prussic acid. Similar operations ensued in Auschwitz-Birkenau, Belzec, Sobibor, Trenblinka, Majdanek, and other camps using crematoria and gas vans. Faced with crowding and backlog in the concentration camps, in June 1943, Himmler ordered the liquidation of all ghettos including—Bialystok, Mizocz, Krakow, Warsaw, Vilna, Minsk, Riga, and Lodz.

The progressive defeat of Hitler's armies by the Soviet Union and the 1944 Allied landings in France created panic among the Nazi leaders, prompting them to quicken the pace of Jewish extermination.[77] In an ironic twist, at a time of shortages in manpower and resources, the compulsion to complete the genocidal plan remained an obsession—a first preference equal to or even exceeding the war against external foes. As Germany's collapse became manifest, there was a concerted attempt to hide the mass murders by unearthing dead bodies and burning them in huge pits and later destroying the crematoria.[78] Meanwhile, Theresienstadt (Terezín) was maintained as a model camp, complete with an orchestra, cafe, and children's opera, near Prague to deceive the Red Cross and other international visitors about the fair treatment of Jewish prisoners.

The gassings ceased in late 1944, after the Soviet liberation of Poland, Hungary, and East Germany, as U.S.-British forces advanced in the West, capturing Buchenwald, Bergen-Belsen, Dachau, and Mauthausen in the spring of 1945. Meanwhile, the remaining prisoners of many of the camps were marched around Germany (January–April 1945) in exhausting "Death Marches," where many died from starvation, exposure, and shootings. On April 30, 1945, Hitler committed suicide in his bunker and a week later, Germany surrendered. In the course of its twelve-year lifespan, the Third Reich had waged a protracted campaign to degrade, impoverish, dehumanize, and then destroy an estimated six million Jews—three-fourths of European Jewry. Table 8.3 lists the lives lost by country.[79]

TABLE 8.3   Estimated Jewish Deaths during the Holocaust

Country	Minimum Loss	Maximum Loss
Austria	50,000	50,000
Belgium	28,900	28,900
Bohemia and Moravia (the Czech lands)	78,150	78,150
Denmark	60	60
Estonia	1,500	2,000
Finland	7	7
France	77,320	77,320
Germany	134,500	141,500
Greece	60,000	67,000
Hungary	550,000	569,000
Italy	7,680	7,680
Latvia	70,000	71,500
Lithuania	140,000	143,000
Luxembourg	1,950	1,950
Netherlands	100,000	100,000
Norway	762	762
Poland	2,900,000	3,000,000
Romania	271,000	287,000
Slovakia	68,000	71,000
Soviet Union	1,000,000	1,100,000
Yugoslavia	56,200	63,300
Total	5,596,029	5,860,129

Source: Yehuda Bauer and Robert Rozett, "Estimated Jewish Losses in the Holocaust," in *Encyclopedia of the Holocaust* (New York: Macmillan, 1990), 1799.

What was the response of the targeted people? Did they offer any resistance to the victimizers? A combination of factors rendered resistance extremely difficult. The totalitarian controls of the Nazi state, imposed with tight bureaucratic discipline, were simply irresistible. Even high-ranking dissident German officials and generals had failed to challenge the Hitlerite regime. Thus, the different categories of *Untermenschen*—Jews, Gypsies, homosexuals, Poles, the disabled, and communist prisoners—were totally helpless before the Nazi killing apparatus. The strategic use of secrecy, cunning, and deception blinded the victims until they were at the gates of hell when it was too late to resist.

Yet, surprisingly there were instances when the victims rebelled in the face of the inevitable prospect of dying at the hands of Nazis. Jewish revolts in the concentration camps of Treblinka, Sobibor, Sachsenhausen, and Auschwitz, and in the Warsaw Ghetto were all brutally suppressed.[80] Some inmates escaped to tell the world about the mechanized routine of human destruction. Another source of Jewish resistance was escapees hiding in woods and forests across Europe. These desperate groups became the seeds of resistance, fighting as partisans against great odds. Several dozen such Jewish guerrilla groups were active during World War II.

Retribution, Restitution, and Denial

There was no external power willing to save the Jews, only the well-intentioned statements by Allied leaders accusing the Nazis of "crimes against humanity." While the Allies' strategic options were limited, tactical bombing might have saved some prisoners by disrupting the German supply lines. Far more serious was the Allies' failure to provide a haven for Jews escaping the Nazi killing trap. Strict U.S. immigration policies, combined with Britain's wartime troubles in Palestine and the Allied preoccupation with quickening the German and Japanese defeat, were the factors that worked against saving Jewish lives as a priority in a crowded war agenda. Yet, the victorious Allies did provide a measure of retribution by the capture and punishment of the Nazi perpetrators.

The occupation of Germany by the Allies—United States, Britain, France, and the Soviet Union—was followed by mass arrests of top Nazi leaders and functionaries who bore direct responsibility for the wartime ravages committed by the Third Reich. The Allied governments sought to punish the Nazi elite for authorship of "an unjust or illegal war" and the immense human and material losses suffered by their armies and the peoples under German rule. Thus, the genocide of European Jewry and other groups constituted a subset of the "crimes against humanity" perpetrated by the Nazi leaders during the war itself—not those preceding September 1, 1939. Thus, the International Military Tribunal, sitting at Nuremberg in 1945 and 1946, convicted nineteen Nazi defendants for crimes against peace, war crimes, and crimes against humanity—a concept that had been used by the Allies to condemn Ottoman Turkey for the Armenian massacres during World War I. The Nuremberg judgments were flawed because they punished crimes in wartime and not those committed by a government against its own citizens in peacetime. This stance infuriated Rafael Lemkin, who had come to search for his relatives and to follow the tribunal's proceedings. To his chagrin, he discovered at Nuremberg that forty-nine members of his family, including his parents, had perished under Nazi rule. Under the heavy burden of personal loss, Lemkin valiantly lobbied for the inclusion of "genocide" in the tribunal's proceedings. His efforts ended in failure because the Allied governments sitting on the tribunal were unwilling to tolerate any diminution of state sovereignty by the criminalization of atrocities committed by a state internally in peacetime.[81] The Allies feared that such a broad definition of crimes against humanity could apply to the mistreatment of their own citizens and subjects. Yet, despite its shortcomings, the Nuremberg judgment set an important precedent in recognizing individual responsibility under international law whereby not only states but also individuals would be held responsible for crimes against humanity. Henceforth, functionaries working in a government hierarchy could not escape culpability by hiding behind national sovereignty or by simply asserting that they were carrying out orders from higher officials.

The Nuremberg tribunal convicted nineteen Nazi leaders to death and imprisonment. Hitler, Göring, Himmler, and Goebbels committed suicide while some, like Adolf Eichmann, escaped to live in hiding in Latin America. In addition, several thousand second-echelon Nazi leaders and lower ranking officials were tried by Allied tribunals and punished for war crimes or for crimes against humanity. However, given the immensity of the genocidal enterprise, many more Germans had been participants in the murder of the Jews and other targeted victims. As Daniel Goldhagen demonstrates, large segments of German society actively or passively contributed to the Holocaust, but went unpunished.[82] Notably, the Soviet jurists serving on the Allied tribunals were more adamant in punishing the Nazi perpetrators because the German invasion of the Russian heartland had inflicted far greater human and material losses relative to the combined losses suffered by France, Britain, and the United States.[83]

The onset of the Cold War dampened the hunt for Nazi culprits. Now the priority of the United States was to build a viable democracy in West Germany, firmly situated in NATO in order to confront East Germany and the Soviet bloc. This strategic objective prompted the Western Allies to "whitewash" some repentant former Nazis in order to secure their services in certain key military, political, and scientific positions. Since the 1950s, the task of hunting Nazi culprits has been taken up by the government of Israel and the Simon Wiesenthal Center in Vienna. In 1960, Israeli agents secretly captured Adolf Eichmann in Argentina, who was tried in a Jerusalem court, convicted, and charged for his key role in implementing the Final Solution.[84] Many lower ranking Nazis were uncovered by Simon Wiesenthal and punished by courts in their countries of residence.

Given the enormity of the crime, no amount of retribution or restitution could compensate for the losses and heal the wounds and memories of genocide. In some ways, restitution was easier to accomplish than retribution. As a budding democracy and member of the Western Alliance, West Germany was eager to provide restitution for the Holocaust in the form of economic, political, and military support for Israel.

Yet restitution for genocide required a moral dimension that transcended its material aspects. The West German leadership—Chancellors Adenaur, Erhard, and Brandt—owned up to the crime committed by the Hitler regime by inculcating the German citizenry with a sense of genuine remorse and fostering redemptive socialization to counter the vestiges of Nazi ideology in the new German polity. This task was accomplished by enacting new laws, implementing educational reforms, and establishing institutions and monuments commemorating the Holocaust. Germany's forthright acknowledgment of the Jewish genocide and willingness to make amends and provide restitution to the survivors was in sharp contrast to Turkey's denialist position toward the Armenian genocide and Japan's reluctance to apologize for atrocities committed against the Chinese and Koreans during World War II.

It has been widely demonstrated that the culmination of the genocidal process is denial, and the Holocaust is no exception. Despite thousands of eyewitness accounts from survivors, government archives, systematic documentation, and scholarship, the Holocaust has not been spared the scourge of denial. At the forefront are a plethora of white supremacists and neo-Nazi groups in the United States and Europe for whom antisemitism is an article of faith. Other denialists include some revisionist historians like David Irving of Britain and the Iranian president Mahmoud Ahmadinejad. As is the case with other genocides, the necessity of countering Holocaust denialists remains an ongoing task.[85] One salutary effort to address this issue is Steven Spielberg's Survivors of the Shoah Visual History Foundation Archives at the University of Southern California, which contain over 52,000 video-recorded eyewitness accounts and testimonies from Holocaust survivors.[86] Holocaust denialists have used most of the twelve tactics identified by Israel Charny in his "Templates for Gross Denial of a Known Genocide: A Manual."[87] Gregory Stanton summarizes these tactics as follows:

1. Question and minimize the statistics.
2. Attack the motivations of the truth-tellers.
3. Claim that the deaths were inadvertent, as a result of famine, migration, or disease, not because of willful murder.
4. Emphasize the strangeness of the victims.
5. Rationalize the deaths as the result of tribal conflict.
6. Blame "out of control" forces for committing the killings.

7. Avoid antagonizing the genocidists, who might walk out of the "peace process."
8. Justify denial in favor of current economic interests.
9. Claim that the victims are receiving good treatment, while baldly denying the charges of genocide outright.
10. Claim that what is going on doesn't fit the definition of genocide.
11. Blame the victims.
12. Say that peace and reconciliation are more important than blaming people for genocide, especially if the genocide happened in the past.[88]

The Holocaust: A Retrospective Analysis

A retrospective look at the Third Reich and its "war" against the Jews shows a tragic balance sheet of winners and losers that had consequences beyond Europe. Although Nazi Germany lost the war, it was eminently successful in the destruction of three-fourths of European Jewry—an enterprise driven by hatred and the imperative to find living space (*Lebensraum*) considered necessary for expansion and survival of the racially superior Germans in the European heartland. In the Nazi perception, the Jews represented an existential threat to the Third Reich by virtue of their presence in Europe's heartland, their racial impurity, control over the Soviet Union and world communism, and economic influence in the Western countries. From 1939 to 1943, winning the war seemed to be the Nazi's first preference, followed by Jewish extermination. There appeared to be a reversal of priorities in 1944–1945. At the prospect of imminent defeat, the genocidal imperative seemed to assume first priority—the obsessive first preference of the Third Reich. Thus, from the Nazi perspective, they were both losers in war and winners for killing Jews. From the Jewish perspective, the Holocaust represented an unprecedented collective cataclysm (Shoah) since the Roman massacres and expulsion of Jews from Jerusalem. Arguably, the only consolation for the Jews was the founding of Israel, to the extent that the Holocaust generated Western support and mobilized Jewish efforts to seek independent statehood in Palestine.

After the passage of a half-century, scholars still debate the causal factors responsible for the Holocaust. How did what was supposed to be a modern and rational culture produce such an irrational outcome? At the confluence of multiple destabilizing forces—military defeat, economic depression, and street fighting—Weimar Germany had become a cauldron of social psychopathologies—a condition that fit Jung's definition of "mass psychosis" and "psychic epidemics."[89] Thus, Hitler's emergence as charismatic leader became possible by the "fit" between his personal pathology and that of the German masses experiencing mass psychosis. Charismatic relationships between leaders and followers are intensely spiritual and emotional, and the Germans who were looking for solutions to their existential problems made a rational choice in supporting Hitler. The führer's message, that many Germans came to share, became the ideology of the Third Reich known as Nazism, which transformed their belief system and gave them a new identity and a medium of salvation through genocide.[90] Thus, Hitler's charisma and message had become "routinized" in building a new polity based on new identities and new aspirations, fundamentally altering German perceptions of rational ends. Given these aims, seemingly irrational policies such as the invasion of Poland, the attack on Russia, or the extermination of Jews can be understood as rational efforts to achieve the goals of the regime. While these policies may have appeared irrational to those outside the charismatic's cultural milieu, they were eminently rational to the "true believers" in the Nazi ideological sphere. Thus, from the perspective of the Nazi milieu, the Holocaust appeared to be a supremely rational act.

Was the Holocaust Unique?

The uniqueness of the Holocaust among other genocides has evoked considerable debate among both scholars and laymen. On a broad scale, every genocide is an inherently unique event because of its historical specificity. Moreover, to the victims and survivors of a genocidal incident, their personal victimhood is unparalleled in its enormity. The uniqueness of the Holocaust has been asserted on a number of grounds:

1. the enormous number of victims;
2. the massive scale of the bureaucratic apparatus and its use of modern technology and means of organization to carry out the killings;
3. the huge territorial expanse encompassing German-occupied Europe over which genocide was implemented;
4. the pathological Nazi ideology that included a "biomedical vision" necessitating the elimination of all Jews throughout the world without exception; and
5. the epicentric role of Hitler as the embodiment of the Nazi determination to destroy the Jews.[91]

Despite these unique characteristics, there are a number of similarities between the Holocaust and other genocides. Indeed, a comparative analysis of the Armenian and Jewish experiences reveals a number of important similarities. Both genocides occurred in times of crisis marked by revolutions, followed by wars. Both were the violent outcome of a series of strategic decisions taken by a regime against its perceived enemies and according to its ordered preferences. The preponderance of power of the Turkish CUP regime and the Nazi Reich vis-à-vis the Armenians and Jews left the two peoples totally helpless and unable to offer effective armed resistance, especially in the absence of external aid or intervention. Moreover, the Turkish and Nazi elites consisted mostly of marginal men hailing from the déclassé elements of their societies who had succeeded in taking absolute power and were bent on compensating for their marginal origins by reengineering their societies according to their pathological ideologies. Although in an objective sense neither the Ottoman Armenians nor European Jewry constituted a real threat to their respective governments, both were perceived and defined as existential threats necessitating total annihilation. In the ideological rhetoric of Pan-Turanism and Nazism, both groups were dehumanized, degraded, and devalued as unwanted social elements deserving extermination. Also, in both cases, major military defeats catalyzed the genocidal process. In Turkey, Enver's defeat by Russia (1915) led the CUP to hasten the implementation of the massacres, while in the Nazi case, Hitler's defeat at Stalingrad (1943), made the Final Solution the regime's first preference to be pursued with utmost urgency. Finally, both genocidal ideologies shared the promise of achieving mythical utopias at the culmination of the genocidal process—the Pan-Turkist land of "Turan" and Hitler's "Thousand-Year Reich."

Notes

1. C. L. Sulzberger, "The People God Forgot," *New York Times,* November 29, 1970; William L. Hewitt, "The Almost Forgotten Genocide: Armenia," in William L. Hewitt, ed., *Defining the Horrific* (Upper Saddle River, NJ: Pearson, 2004), 95–96; and Marjorie Housepian, "The Unremembered Genocide," *Commentary* 42, no. 3 (1966).
2. Louis P. Lockner, *What About Germany?* (New York: Dodd, Mead & Co., 1942), 2; and Kevork Bardakjian, *Hitler and the Armenian Genocide* (Cambridge, MA: Zoryan Institute, 1985).
3. Samantha Power, *"A Problem from Hell": America and the Age of Genocide* (New York: Harper Perennial, 2002), 40–43.
4. Irving Louis Horowitz, *Taking Lives: Genocide and State Power,* 4th ed. (New Brunswick, NJ: Transaction, 1997), 156.
5. R. Hrair Dekmejian, "Determinants of Genocide: Armenians and Jews as Case Studies," in Richard G. Hovannisian, ed., *The Armenian Genocide in Perspective* (New Brunswick, NJ: Transaction, 1986).
6. For historical details see Richard G. Hovannisian (ed.), *The Armenian People from Ancient to Modern Times,* vols. 1 and 2 (New York: St. Martin's, 1997).
7. Donald Bloxham, *The Great Game of Genocide* (New York: Oxford University Press, 2005), 31–49.
8. Richard G. Hovannisian, "The Armenian Question in the Ottoman Empire, 1876–1914," in Richard G. Hovanissian, ed., *The Armenian People from Ancient to Modern Times,* vol. 2 (New York: St. Martin's Press, 1997), 204–206.

9. Arman J. Kirakossian, *British Diplomacy and the Armenian Question from the 1830s to 1914* (Princeton, NJ: Gomidas Institute Books, 2003), 1–343.
10. For different estimates see Bloxham, *The Great Game of Genocide*, 51–57; and Vahakan N. Dadrian, *The History of the Armenian Genocide* (Providence, RI: Berghahn, 1995), 152–157.
11. Bloxham, *The Great Game*, 44–46; and Kirakossian, *British Diplomacy*, 72–82.
12. Hovannisian, "The Armenian Question in the Ottoman Empire," 211–212.
13. For details see Ernest E. Ramsaur, Jr., *The Young Turks: Prelude to the Revolutions of 1908* (Princeton, NJ: Princeton University Press, 1957).
14. Patrick B. Kindross, *The Ottoman Centuries: The Rise and Fall of the Turkish Empire* (New York: Morrow, 1977), 559–560; and Bloxham, *The Great Game of Genocide*, 60,–62.
15. Christopher J. Walker, *Armenia: The Survival of a Nation* (London: Croom Helm, 1980), 189–195.
16. Christopher J. Walker, "World War I and the Armenian Genocide," in Richard G. Hovannisian, ed., *The Armenian People from Ancient to Modern Times*, vol. 2 (New York: St. Martin's, 1997), 239–242.
17. On Pan-Turanism, also known as Pan-Turkism, see Charles Warren Hostler, *Turkism and the Soviets* (London: G. Allen & Unwin, 1957); Jacob M. Landau, *Pan-Turkism in Turkey: A Study of Irredentism* (Hamden, CT: Archon, 1981), Zarevand, *United and Independent Turania: Aims and Designs of the Turks* (Leiden: E. J. Brill, 1971).
18. Zia Gökalp, *Turkish Nationalism and Western Civilization* (New York: Columbia University Press, 1959).
19. On the marginality of the Young Turk (CUP) elite see Dekmejian, "Determinants of Genocide," 92–93; for a comparison of Pan-Turkism and Nazism, see Walker, *Armenia*, 191–192.
20. Marshall G. S. Hodgson, *The Venture of Islam*, vol. 3 (Chicago: University of Chicago Press, 1958), 277.
21. Peter Balakian, *The Burning Tigris: the Armenian Genocide and America's Response* (New York: Harper Collins, 2003), 165–166.
22. *Ibid.*, 172–173.
23. Walker, "World War I and the Armenian Genocide," 244.
24. Walker, *Armenia*, 194–195.
25. *British Documents on the Origins of the War 1898–1914*, Part I (London, 1926). See also Vahakn N. Dadrian, *Warrant for Genocide* (New Brunswick: Transaction Publishers, 2000), 96–99.
26. Ulrich Trumpener, *Germany and the Ottoman Empire, 1914–1918* (Princeton, NJ: Princeton University Press, 1968), 28.
27. On these two physicians see Walker, "World War I and the Armenian Genocide," 254–258.
28. Dadrian, *History of the Armenian Genocide*, 209.
29. Quoted in Balakian, *The Burning Tigris*, 189–190.
30. Bloxham, *The Great Game*, 70.
31. On *Teshkilati Mahsuse*, see Vahakn N. Dadrian, "The Role of the Special Organisation in the Armenian Genocide during the First World War," in Panikos Panayi, ed., *Minorities in Wartime* (Providence, RI: Berg Publishers, 1993).
32. Henry Morgenthau, *Ambassador Morgenthau's Story* (New York: Doubleday, 1918), 337–338, 351–352.
33. Balakian, *The Burning Tigris*, 335.
34. Walker, *Armenia*, 198–200.

35. Robert F. Melson, *Revolution and Genocide: On the Origins of the Armenian Genocide and the Holocaust* (Chicago: University of Chicago Press, 1996), 143–144; and Walker, "World War I and the Armenian Genocide," 246–247.

36. Bloxham, *The Great Game*, 76–78, 80–83.

37. Walker, "World War I and the Armenian Genocide," 252.

38. Leo Kuper, *Genocide: Its Political Use in the Twentieth Century* (New Haven, CT: Yale University Press, 1981), 20.

39. Excerpts of this conversation are quoted from Power, *"A Problem from Hell,"* 7–9.

40. "800,000 Armenians Counted Destroyed," *New York Times*, October 7, 1915.

41. On these estimates see Walker, *Armenia*, p. 230; Walker, "World War I and the Armenian Genocide"; R. J. Rummel, *Death by Government* (New Brunswick, NJ: Transaction, 1994), 222–236; and, Kuper, *Genocide*, 105.

42. Walker, "World War I and the Armenian Genocide," 267–268.

43. *Ibid.*, 272.

44. This estimate is based on Kuper, *Genocide*, 113–115; and Walker, *Armenia*, 349–350.

45. Quoted in William A. Schabas, *Genocide in International Law* (New York: Cambridge University Press, 2000), 16–17.

46. Dadrian, *History of the Armenian Genocide*, 317–343.

47. Balakian, *The Burning Tigris*, 344–346.

48. *Ibid.*, 349–376.

49. Walker, *Armenia*, 347–348.

50. For details see Bloxham, *The Great Game*, 5–9, 223–229; Kuper, *Genocide*, 113–114; Richard G. Hovannisian, ed., *Remembrance and Denial: The Case of the Armenian Genocide* (Detroit: Wayne State University Press; 1998); Roger W. Smith, Eric Markusen, and Robert Jay Lifton, "Professional Ethics and the Denial of Armenian Genocide," *Holocaust and Genocide Studies* 9, no. 1 (1995): 1–22.

51. On Ataturk's condemnation of the CUP see Harut Sassounian, *The Armenian Genocide: Documents and Declarations* (Glendale, CA: 90th Anniversary of the Armenian Genocide Commemorative Committee of California, 2005), 13.

52. For example, see Manus Midlarsky, *The Killing Trap* (New York: Cambridge University Press, 2003); Patricia Marchak, *Reigns of Terror* (Montreal: McGill-Queen's University Press, 2003); Melson, *Revolution and Genocide*; Yair Auron, *The Banality of Indifference: Zionism and the Armenian Genocide* (New Brunswick, NJ: Transaction, 2000); Facing History and Ourselves, *Crimes against Humanity and Civilization: The Genocide of the Armenians* (Brookline, MA.: Facing History and Ourselves National Foundation, 2004); Donald E. Miller and Lorna Touryan Miller, *Survivors: An Oral History of the Armenian Genocide* (Berkeley, CA: University of California Press, 1993); Israel W. Charny, ed., *Encyclopedia of Genocide* (Santa Barbara, CA: ABC-Clio, 1999); Ervin Staub, *The Roots of Evil: The Origins of Genocide and Other Group Violence* (New York: Cambridge University Press, 1989); and Yves Ternon, *The Armenians: History of a Genocide* (Delmar, NY: Caravan Books, 1981). See also the signed declarations by these and other scholars in Sassounian, *The Armenian Genocide*, 61–65.

53. Midlarsky, *The Killing Trap*, 139.

54. *Ibid.*

55. Staub, *The Roots of Evil*, 158–159.

56. On the crisis conditions besetting Weimar Germany see Melson, *Revolution and Genocide*, 173–203.

57. Erik Erikson, *Young Man Luther* (New York: Norton, 1958), 14–15.

58. R. Hrair Dekmejian, "Charismatic Leadership in Messianic and Revolutionary Movements," in *Religious Resurgence*, eds. by R. Antoun and M. Hegland (Syracuse, NY: Syracuse University Press, 1987), 78–107.

59. See statistical analysis of biographical data from *The Fuehrer Lexicon* (1934) by Daniel Lerner, Ithiel de Sola Poole, and George K. Schueller, in Harold Lasswell and Daniel Lerner, ed., *World Revolutionary Elites* (Cambridge, Mass.: MIT Press, 1965).
60. Staub, *The Roots of Evil*, 98–99.
61. Yehuda Bauer, *The Holocaust in Historical Perspective* (Seattle: University of Washington Press, 1978), 42.
62. *Ibid.*, 97–98.
63. Midlarsky, *The Killing Trap*, 170.
64. Daniel Johan Goldhagen, *Hitler's Willing Executioners: Ordinary Germans and the Holocaust* (New York: Alfred A. Knopf, 1996), 146.
65. For more on the Madagascar Plan see Christopher Browning, "Madagascar Plan," *Encyclopedia of the Holocaust*, ed. Israel Gutman (New York: MacMillan, 1990); and Yehuda Bauer, "Genocide: Was it the Nazi's Original Plan?" *Annals of the American Academy of Political and Social Science* 450 (1980): 35–45.
66. Goldhagen, *Hitler's Willing Executioners*, 147–149.
67. For a timeline of these events see www.historyplace.com/worldwar2/holocaust/timeline.html#warsaw.
68. Melson, *Revolution and Genocide*, 216–224.
69. Goldhagen, *Hitler's Willing Executioners*, 99–106; Melson, *Revolution and Genocide*, 226–227; and Yehuda Bauer, *A History of the Holocaust* (New York: F. Watts, 1982), 108.
70. Raul Hilberg, *The Destruction of European Jews* (New York: Holms and Meir, 1985), 257
71. Zygmunt Bauman, *Modernity and the Holocaust* (Ithaca: Cornell University Press, 1989), 104–105.
72. For details see Goldhagen, *Hitler's Willing Executioners*, 144–158; Melson, *Revolution and Genocide*, 236–240.
73. Staub, *The Roots of Evil*, 152.
74. The Avalon Project at Yale Law School, www.yale.edu/lawweb/avalon/wwii/dec/dec04.htm.
75. Melson, *Revolution and Genocide*, 237–240.
76. Hilberg, *The Destruction of European Jews*, 266.
77. Staub, *The Roots of Evil*, 149–150.
78. Horowitz, *Taking Lives*, 220, 292.
79. For estimates of the number of Jews killed in the Holocaust see Kuper, *Genocide*, 134–135; Goldhagen, *Hitler's Willing Executioners*, 413–414; Rummel, *Death by Government*, 111–122.
80. On the strategic calculation of rebellion see Midlarsky, *The Killing Trap*, 287–206.
81. Power, *A Problem from Hell*, 48–51.
82. For details see Goldhagen, *Hitler's Willing Executioners*.
83. See Rummel, *Death by Government*, 112.
84. Hannah Arendt, *Eichmann in Jerusalem: A Report on the Banality of Evil* (New York: Viking Press, 1963).
85. For more on denial see Deborah Lipstadt, *Denying the Holocaust: The Growing Assault on Truth and Memory* (New York: Free Press, 1993).
86. Survivors of the Shoah Visual History Archives, University of Southern California. www.usc.edu/libraries/archives/arc/libraries/sfa/.
87. Israel Charny, *The Encyclopedia of Genocide*, Vol.1 (Santa Barbara, CA: ABC-Clio, 1999), 168
88. Genocide Watch, www.genocidewatch.org/SudanTwelveWaysToDenyAGenocidebyGregStanton.htm.

89. Walter Langer, "The Next Assignment," in Bruce Mazlish, ed., *Psychoanalysis and History* (New York: Grosset and Dunlap, 1963), 93.
90. Dekmejian, "Determinants of Genocide," 91–92.
91. On the unique aspects of the Holocaust see Melson, *Revolution and Genocide*, 248–257; Goldhagen, *Hitler's Willing Executioners*, 412–415; Robert J. Lifton, *The Nazi Doctors* (New York: Basic Books, 1986); Bauer, *The Holocaust in Historical Perspective*, 30–38; and Horowitz, *Taking Lives*, 239–259.

Further Reading

Arendt, Hannah. *Eichmann in Jerusalem: A Report on the Banality of Evil*. New York: Viking Press, 1963.

Auron, Yair. *The Banality of Indifference: Zionism and the Armenian Genocide*. New Brunswick, NJ: Transaction, 2000.

Balakian, Peter. *The Burning Tigris: The Armenian Genocide and America's Response*. New York: Harper Collins, 2003.

Bauer, Yehuda. *Rethinking the Holocaust*. New Haven: Yale University Press, 2001.

Bauman, Zygmunt. *Modernity and the Holocaust*. Ithaca: Cornell University Press, 1989.

Bloxham, Donald. *The Great Game of Genocide: Imperialism, Nationalism and the Destruction of the Ottoman Armenians*. New York: Oxford University Press, 2005.

Bryce, James. *The Treatment of the Armenians in the Ottoman Empire, 1915–16*. Princeton, NJ: Gomidas Institute Books, 2000.

Charny, Israel W., ed. *Encyclopedia of Genocide*. Santa Barbara, CA: ABC-Clio, 1999.

Dadrian, Vahakn N. *The History of the Armenian Genocide*. Providence, RI: Berghahn, 1997.

Friedlander, Saul. *Nazi Germany and the Jews*. London: Weidenfeld and Nicolson, 1997.

Goldhagen, Daniel J. *Hitler's Willing Executioners*. New York: Alfred A. Knopf, 1996.

Hilberg, Raul. *The Destruction of the European Jews*. New York: Holms and Meir, 1985.

Hoffer, Eric. *The True Believer: Thoughts on the Nature of Mass Movements*. Alexandria, VA: Time-Life, 1951.

Horowitz, Irving Louis. *Taking Lives: Genocide and State Power*. New Brunswick, NJ: Transaction, 1997.

Hovannisian, Richard, ed. *The Armenian Genocide in Perspective*. New Brunswick, NJ: Transaction, 1986.

Lanzmann, Claude. *Shoah: An Oral History of the Holocaust*. New York: Pantheon Books, 1985.

Lipstadt, Deborah L. *Denying the Holocaust: The Growing Assault on Truth and Memory*. New York: Free Press, 1993.

Melson, Robert F. *Revolution and Genocide: On the Origins of the Armenian Genocide and the Holocaust*. Chicago: University of Chicago Press, 1996.

Miller, Donald E. and Lorna Touryan Miller. *Survivors: An Oral History of the Armenian Genocide*. Berkeley, CA: University of California Press, 1993.

Power, Samantha. *"A Problem from Hell": America and the Age of Genocide*. New York: Harper Perennial, 2002.

Reich, Wilhelm. *The Mass Psychology of Fascism*. New York: Farrar, Straus, and Giroux, 1970.

Rosenbaum, Ron. *Explaining Hitler*. New York: Random House, 1998.

Rubenstein, Richard L. *The Cunning of History*. New York: Harper and Row, 1975.

Walter, Langer. *The Mind of Adolf Hitler*. New York: Basic Books, 1972.

The Kurdish and Rwandan Genocides

THE KURDISH AND THE RWANDAN GENOCIDES represent the tragic culmination of a string of mass killings that marked the twentieth century. One might have expected that the cycle of exterminations that began with the Armenian genocide and the Holocaust would have been instructive to the international community in devising modalities to prevent further atrocities. Amid the guarded optimism at the Cold War's end, the Kurdish and Rwandan genocides reminded the world that the cyclical propensity of mass murder was driven by an inexorable dialectic of violent human behavior.

The Kurdish Genocide

The Kurds, one of the ancient peoples of the Middle East, trace their origins to the Medes of the seventh century B.C. Kurdish is an Indo-European language akin to Persian and spoken in several dialects. The dominant form of social organization of the Kurds is tribalism, in which shaikhs still play a leading social and political role in community life. Except for brief interludes in Persia, the Kurdish people have been stateless since the Medean Kingdom.[1] Although Kurdish leaders like Saladin (1137/8–1193) played key roles in the wars and governance of the Islamic realm, the Kurdish people remained subjects of Arab, Persian, and Turkish imperial dynasts. The Kurds' tribal structure, dispersed population, and rural habitat militated against their assumption of primacy in the Muslim lands.

Despite their relative isolation in the interior regions of the Ottoman and Persian empires, the Kurds could not escape the impact of competing ethnic nationalisms among the polyglot peoples of the Middle East. As an officially Sunni Muslim state, the Ottoman Empire had coopted the mostly Sunni Kurds by encouraging their predatory raids against Armenian, Assyrian, and other Christian communities for economic benefit. Meanwhile, nationalist trends emerged in the early 1840s led by the Kurdish emir Bedr Khan and were suppressed by the Ottoman army supported by German military advisors.[2]

This Kurdish national movement, however, remained in its infancy at the outbreak of World War I as it lacked strong leadership and broad appeal among the Kurdish population. As a result, the Kurds missed an opportunity they have come to regret. Instead of rebelling against the Ottoman Young Turk regime (CUP) during World War I to secure independence, Kurdish irregulars became a key instrument of genocide against the Armenians and other Christian subjects of the empire.[3] The Ottoman defeat in World War I by the Allied powers resulted in the signing of the Treaty of Sèvres (1920) that provided for the creation of independent Kurdish and Armenian states in the eastern provinces of the Ottoman territories. The new republican regime of Turkey led by Mustafa Kemal Atatürk (1881–1938) rejected this treaty and effectively suppressed Kurdish pretensions of independence. The Turkish campaign against the Kurds culminated in the 1937–1938 Dersim Massacres.[4] Meanwhile, the Kurdish-populated territories had been divided between Turkey, Iran, British-ruled Iraq, and French-ruled Syria. Successive Kurdish revolts in these four countries would destabilize the Middle East region well into the twenty-first century. Table 9.1 provides a chronology of key events in the Kurdish genocide.

Kurdish Genocide in Iraq

Iraq was a British creation—an artificial state expressly designed to maximize imperial geopolitical and economic interests. In drawing Iraq's boundaries, the British split the Arab heartland by giving Syria to France, retaining Palestine, and leaving the rest of Arabia to be ruled by the Saudis and the Hashemites. As a British mandate under the League of Nations, Iraq brought together a mosaic of incongruent communities—Kurds, Sunni and Shiite Arabs, Turkomans, Persians, Chaldeans, Assyrians, and other sects. Despite King Faisal's benevolent reign, the British faced successive rebellions by the Sunnis, Shiites, Kurds, and Assyrians which were crushed at great cost. After World War II, the British vainly sought to make Iraq the cornerstone of the Western alliance system against the Soviets by forming the Baghdad Pact. After the violent overthrow of the royal family by the Iraqi Army in June 1958, the British were forced to leave the country. This pattern of coup d'état politics per-

TABLE 9.1   Kurdish Genocide in Iraq and Turkey, 1920–2006

Date	Event	Death Toll/Outcome
1920	Treaty of Sèvres promises an independent Kurdish state	Rejected by Atatürk in 1923
1923–1943	Repeated Kurdish uprisings crushed by British forces in Iraq	Thousands killed
1937–1938	Dersim Massacres	Thousands killed
1958	Overthrow of the Hashemite monarchy	Kurdish nationalists begin to organize freely
1961–1970	Kurdish rebellion in Northern Iraq	
1970	Baathist regime offers Kurds limited autonomy	
1971	Mullah Mustafa al-Barzani rejects government's offer	Barzani continues revolt with support of U.S., Iran, and Israel
1974	Vice president Saddam Hussein imposes a Kurdish autonomy agreement	Rejected by Barzani because Kirkuk oilfields not included
1975	Iran-Iraq Algiers Agreement ends the shah's support for the Kurdish rebellion	Rebellion collapses and KDP splits with the establishment of PUK
1979	Barzani dies in Washington, D.C.	Barzani's son Massoud takes control of KDP
1980	Outbreak of Iran-Iraq war	1 million casualties on both sides
1980–1990	Reemergence of Kurdish resistance in Turkey led by PKK under Abdullah Ocalan	Massive counterattacks by Turkish military; 3,000 Kurdish villages destroyed, 378,335 displaced
1987	KDP and PUK join forces to create a united front to resist Saddam	
1987–1989	Anfal campaigns by Chemical Ali	200,000 killed
Aug. 1990	Saddam's invasion of Kuwait	
Jan. 1991	American-led coalition liberates Kuwait	Thousands of Iraqi troops killed

TABLE 9.1 Cont.   Kurdish Genocide in Iraq and Turkey, 1920–2006

Date	Event	Death Toll/Outcome
Apr. 1991	Kurdish rebellion	1,000s killed; 400,000 refugees flee to Turkey
Apr. 1991	UN establishes no-fly zone in Northern Iraq	Safe haven for the Kurds
1991–1994	Kurdish politicians arrested and political parties dissolved in Turkey	Reemergence of Kurdish resistance against Turkish regime
May 1992	Elections in autonomous region establish Kurdish power-sharing government in Northern Iraq	
1999	PKK leader Ocalan captured and announces cease-fire with Turkish regime	Decline in interactive violence in Turkey
Aug. 2002– May 2005	Turkish regime initiates reforms under EU pressure	Grants some cultural rights to the Kurds
May 2005–present	PKK ends cease-fire; Turkish military resumes repression	
2005–2006	Kurdish autonomous region incorporated into Iraqi state under new U.S.-sponsored constitution	PUK leader Jalal Talabani elected president of new Iraqi Republic

sisted until the July 1968 takeover by the Baath Party led by Gen. Ahmad Hasan al-Bakr.[5]

As an avowedly Arab nationalist party, the Baath used totalitarian practices to entrench itself as the undisputed ruler over Iraq's diverse population. Although all of Iraq's societal elements were included in the Baath's governing apparatus, the party was controlled by the Sunni Arab minority (20 percent)—in keeping with the political predominance of Sunni Arabs since Ottoman times. The Sunni hegemony, coupled with Baath's secular ideology, alienated the Shiite majority (60 percent), while the regime's Arabization policies were resisted by the Kurds.

The Prelude to Genocide, 1958–1979. The bloody overthrow of the Hashemite monarchy in June 1958 detached Iraq from the Western alliance system leading to a succession of Arab nationalist military regimes. These developments laid the groundwork for a series of Kurdish rebellions in Iraq's northern provinces from 1961 to 1975, supported by Iran, Israel, and the United States. All three powers sought to weaken the Arab nationalist Baathist government in Baghdad for their respective strategic reasons; hence their readiness to help the restive Kurds of Iraq to rebel under the leadership of Mullah Mustafa al-Barzani.[6] To complicate matters, the Kurds failed to present a united front toward the government in Baghdad due to traditional factionalism, particularly between Barzani's Kurdish Democratic Party (KDP) and Jalal Talabani's Patriotic Union of Kurdistan (PUK). This split weakened the Kurdish ranks in their future faceoffs with the Baathist regime in Baghdad.[7]

In 1970, two years after its takeover of power, the Iraqi regime offered the Kurds self-rule within a proposed Kurdistan Autonomous Region, an area half the size of the territory that the Kurds claimed as their own. The Kurds rejected the Baathi offer, which left out the crucial oil-rich Kirkuk province, thus opening the way for the renewal of interactive violence amid changing geopolitical circumstances that increasingly favored the Baghdad regime.[8] With its massive oil wealth, Iraq was emerging as a major player in the Organization of Petroleum Exporting Countries (OPEC), a role which had opened up new strategic venues and opportunities to be exploited. The person symbolizing the new face of Iraq was Saddam Hussein, the powerful vice president, who had emerged as the Baath party's chief strategist on the Kurdish issue.[9] In March 1974, Saddam Hussein ordered the unilateral imposition of the Kurdish autonomy plan, triggering an upsurge of resistance led by Barzani who had been assured of U.S. support.[10] In response, Saddam began the "Arabization" of the Kurdish lands—the onset of a fifteen-year period of violent strategic interaction between the Kurdish groups and Saddam, for whom the Kurdish issue had become a personal obsession.

In order to isolate the Kurds, Saddam sought a rapprochement with the United States and its ally, the shah of Iran, within the OPEC framework. In a classic prisoner's dilemma situation, an OPEC member, Algeria, became the mediator between the shah and Saddam, with the backing of U.S. Secretary of State Henry Kissinger. This U.S.-sponsored process resulted in the March 1975 Algiers Agreement—a *quid pro quo* with payoffs to Iran and Iraq to the detriment of the Kurds. The strategic bargain involved Iraqi recognition of Iranian demands to gain access to the Shatt al-Arab waterway in exchange for the withdrawal of Iranian, Israeli, and American support for the Kurdish forces.[11] Without Iranian support, the Kurds were totally exposed and the Iraqi military immediately took advantage of this vulnerability. The final outcome was the collapse of the Kurdish resistance in the face of the murderous advance of Iraqi troops. This led to massive ethnic cleansing and the deportation of over 200,000 Kurds between 1975 and 1980.[12] Kurdish villages were bulldozed as thousands were deported to the deserts of southern Iraq or took refuge in Iranian territory. After the collapse of the Barzani uprising in 1975, he came to Washington to plead the Kurdish case without success and died there three years later. The role of the United States in this conflict had profound consequences for the future of the region. By providing limited support to the Kurds through Iran, the United States had used them as a threat to force Saddam to make peace with Iran while weakening his ties to the Soviet Union. This represented a prelude to a new U.S.-Iraqi strategic relationship in the 1980s that would prove perilous to the Kurds.

War and Genocide, 1980–1989. The Islamist clerical theocracy established after the 1979 Iranian Revolution constituted an immediate threat to both Iraqi and American interests. In September 1980, Saddam ordered a massive invasion of Iran, expecting Ayatullah Khomeini's revolutionary regime to collapse under the blows of an Iraqi blitzkrieg. This was a gross miscalculation and the war dragged on until 1988 with over one million casualties.[13] As Saddam's forces marched victoriously into Iranian territory during the war's early phase, he restarted the Arabization campaign by repopulating the Kurdish regions with Arabs while accusing Kurds of pro-Iranian sympathies.

The tide of war turned in Iran's favor in the mid-1980s, as Iraq was forced onto the defensive, holding off the Iranian onslaught with massive military and financial support from America's Arab allies, the European powers, and the Soviet Union—all of whom united to deny Iran a victory over Iraq. Yet, despite the precarious situation of his army on the Iranian front, Saddam committed significant military resources to the continuing extermination of the Kurdish population, which had become his regime's second priority after the war itself. Saddam knew that he could get away with mass murder in the thickening fog of war while still continuing to receive the support of the United States and allied governments because he was fighting their common Iranian enemy. In March 1987, he appointed his relative, Ali Hasan al-Majid, as secretary general of the Northern Bureau to plan the "Anfal" campaign designed to plunder and destroy the Kurds on mass.[14] Box 9.1 sets out a directive planning the genocide sent from the secretary general to his subordinates.

Between February and October 1988, Majid unleashed eight Anfals—"scourges"—using all types of conventional weapons, and even gas bombs in order to maximize the killing. According to Human Rights Watch, each Anfal began with chemical bomb attacks from the air, followed by military offensives, killing without distinguishing between Kurdish civilians and *Pesh Merga* fighters. On March 16, 1988, true to his reputation as "Chemical Ali," Majid launched an air attack dropping gas bombs on the Kurdish town of Halabja near the Iranian border, killing over 5,000 and injuring 7,000 of the inhabitants.[15] Having used chemical bombs to stop Iranian battlefield advances, the Iraqi leadership had no compunction in punishing the Kurds by unleashing on them a variety of deadly agents—mustard gas, sarin gas, VX gas, tabun, and aflatoxin. The final Anfal, from August to September 1988, culminated in the escape of 65,000 Kurds to Turkey—from one enemy territory to another. The Anfal claimed up to 200,000 lives, with the killings continuing well into 1989.[16] By late August 1988, Saddam had emerged as a regional hegemon basking in the halo of his twin victories against Iran and the Kurds. Two more wars would be fought before Iraq's Kurds were freed from the specter of Saddam's genocidal designs.

The United States and the Kurds, 1991–2006. Strategic interactions between contending parties are based on the decisions of the two sides that reflect each other's perceptions and preferences. All too often the two parties miscalculate because of their uncertainty and incomplete information about each other's intentions. On the basis of the moves made by each side in a strategic interaction, there is a mutual learning process that could lead to the modification of their preferences. Clearly, the Kurds were fated to be at the epicenter of a complex and dynamic geostrategic game that involved Iraq, Iran, Turkey, Israel, and the United States. To their misfortune, there was a lag in the Kurds' learning process vis-à-vis Saddam and the other participants in the "Great Game" being played in the 1970s and 1980s.

After the Kurds' repeated miscalculations regarding Saddam and their erstwhile Iranian, American, and Israeli allies, the Anfal massacres and deportations left no doubt among the Kurdish leadership about the intractability of Saddam's genocidal policies. By rejecting the 1970 offer of an "autonomous" region in Northern Iraq and resisting Saddam's efforts to implement it by force, the Kurds had enraged the Iraqi

Box 9.1
Call to Genocide

Below is the full text of directive SF/4008 sent by Hassan al-Majid to his subordinates calling for genocide in the Kurdish "prohibited" regions:

June 20, 1987

From: Northern Bureau Command
To: First Corps Command, Second Corps Command, Fifth Corps Command
Subject: *Procedure to deal with the villages that are prohibited for security reasons*

In view of the fact that the officially announced deadline for the amalgamation of these villages expires on June 21, 1987, we have decided that the following action should be taken with effect from June 22, 1987:

1. All the villages in which subversives, agents of Iran and similar traitors to Iraq are still to be found shall be regarded as out of bounds for security reasons;
2. They shall be regarded as operational zones that are strictly out of bounds to all persons and animals and in which the troops can open fire at will, without any restrictions, unless otherwise instructed by our Bureau;
3. Travel to and from these zones, as well as all agricultural, animal husbandry, and industrial activities shall be prohibited and carefully monitored by all the competent agencies within their respective fields of jurisdiction;
4. The corps commanders shall carry out random bombardments using artillery, helicopters and aircraft, at all times of the day or night *in order to kill the largest number of persons present in those prohibited zones,* keeping us informed of the results; [emphasis added]
5. All persons captured in those villages shall be detained and interrogated by the security services and *those between the ages of 15 and 70 shall be executed after any useful information has been obtained from them,* of which we should be duly notified; [emphasis added]
6. Those who surrender to the governmental or Party authorities shall be interrogated by the competent agencies for a maximum period of three days, which may be extended to ten days if necessary, provided that we are notified of such cases. If the interrogation requires a longer period of time, approval must be obtained from us by telephone or telegraph or through comrade Taher [Tawfiq] al-Ani;
7. *Everything seized by the advisers [mustashars] and troops of the National Defense Battalions shall be retained by them, with the exception of heavy, mounted and medium weapons. They can keep the light weapons, notifying us only of the number of these weapons. The Corps commanders shall promptly bring this to the attention of all the advisers, company commanders and platoon leaders and shall provide us with detailed information concerning their activities in the National Defense Battalions.* [emphasis added]

For information and action within your respective fields of jurisdiction. Keep us informed.

[Signed]
Comrade
Ali Hassan al-Majid
Member of the Regional Command
Secretary General of the Northern Bureau

cc: Chairman of the Legislative Council; Chairman of the Executive Council

Source: Human Rights Watch. *Genocide in Iraq: The Anfal Campaign against the Kurds.* New York: Human Rights Watch, 1993.

strongman, a rage that inevitably led to mass atrocities given the Iraqi leader's psychological predispositions. Indeed, there was an eerie consistency in Saddam's behavior toward his foes, ranging from perceived Baathi rivals to unfriendly neighboring regimes or outside powers. This behavioral pattern is traceable to Saddam's deprived childhood and social marginality, and consisted of two successive phases: an initial attempt at flexibility to achieve a temporary accommodation with an antagonist; and an all-out campaign to destroy or neutralize his opponent, should the latter persist in its rejectionist stance.[17] The transition from stage one to stage two was marked by an immense rage that shaped all his calculations and inevitably pointed to a zero-sum solution; hence, Saddam's order to Chemical Ali to implement the Anfal program. In Saddam's mind the Kurds had come to represent more than an existential threat to Iraq; they were an impediment to Saddam's ultimate dream of building a powerful and expansive state as the nucleus of a future Pan-Arab emporium. Because Saddam equated his own self-view of greatness with the quest for an Iraqi-led Arab superstate, any opponent of his cause was defined as a mortal enemy meriting extermination.

Once Saddam had pulverized the Kurds and pushed back the Iranian military threat, he turned to settling accounts with the Arab regimes of the Persian Gulf, which had given Iraq massive support during the war with Iran. In order to prevent an Iranian victory over Iraq, Saudi Arabia, Kuwait, and the United Arab Emirates had given billions of dollars to Saddam. At the war's end Saddam demanded that his rich neighbors continue transferring large sums to pay for Iraq's reconstruction in gratitude for the immense sacrifices Iraqis had made in fighting Iran. Saddam's demands were rejected, particularly by Kuwait, which even dared to ask for repayment of Iraq's wartime debts and refused to discuss their border conflict involving the Rumaila oilfield.[18] The Kuwaiti stance infuriated Saddam who viewed the small shaikhdom as an integral part of Iraqi territory that had been "stolen" by the British imperial authorities. In his rage at Kuwait's defiance, Saddam quickly occupied the country on August 2, 1990, proclaiming it as Iraq's nineteenth province. In one blow, he had turned his beneficiaries, led by the United States, into enemies. Saddam's gross miscalculation and his refusal to heed UN Security Council Resolution 660 for full withdrawal led to the 1991 Gulf War.

As the U.S.-led coalition forces proceeded rapidly to destroy the Iraqi army, Saddam faced major rebellions from the Kurds in the North and the Shiites in the South. In a tragic miscalculation, Kurdish and Shiite leaders had taken seriously U.S. propaganda appeals to challenge Saddam, thinking that the hour of Saddam's fall was at hand.[19] The war's quick finale and President George H. W. Bush's reluctance to push for Saddam's fall by military means, provided the Iraqi leader with an unexpected opportunity to unleash his defeated troops against Shiite and Kurdish insurgents that resulted in mass atrocities. By mid-April 1991, 400,000 Kurdish refugees were en route to Turkey escaping Saddam's genocidal phalanxes.[20] While the Shiites were left to suffer the full brunt of Saddam's fury, the Kurds were belatedly extended a helping hand. In April 1991, the European Union approved a plan to provide a UN safe-haven to protect the Kurds under a no-fly zone north of the 36th parallel. The launching of this plan, known as "Operation Provide Comfort," was backed by 21,000 U.S.-led forces and strong U.S. pressure to force Iraqi withdrawal from the Kurdish region.

For the first time in Iraqi history, the Kurdish minority was empowered to organize its own government without the threat of annihilation. The May 1992 elections marked the founding of the Kurdistan Regional Government that sought to unite the Kurdistan Democratic Party (KDP) and the Patriotic Union of Kurdistan (PUK). Despite the outbreak of fighting in May and December 1994, these two parties managed to co-exist under a power-sharing agreement brokered by the United States.[21] During the last decade, the two-party coalition has succeeded in fostering economic development and democratic governance while defending the autonomous region from Iraqi, Turkish, and Iranian machinations.

George W. Bush's ascent to the U.S. presidency and his determination to overthrow Saddam Hussein opened up new opportunities and challenges for Kurdish survival and self-determination. Despite their first preference for total independence, the Kurdish leaders were pressured to join the U.S.-sponsored Iraqi regime, on the condition that the new constitution recognize the full autonomy of the Kurdish region, which they define as including the oil-rich city of Kirkuk. The ongoing Sunni-Shiite civil war and the stratagems of the Kurds' antagonistic neighbors—Turkey, Iran, and Syria—portend a volatile milieu requiring skilled diplomacy and plenty of good luck.

Kurdish Genocide in Turkey

The Republic of Turkey, the successor state to the polyglot Ottoman Empire, was symbolized by a fierce Turkish nationalism under its founder, Gen. Mustafa Kemal Atatürk. As a great modernizer, Atatürk decreed ambitious programs of linguistic and social reform and secularization aimed at the disestablishment of Islamic traditions and lifestyles. Thus, secular Turkish nationalism became the state's official ideology and the only legitimate framework of identity for its citizens. Although the state recognized Christians and Jews as religious minorities, all Muslim citizens were officially classified as "Turks" regardless of their diverse ethnic identities. This all-inclusive label of "Turkishness" did not fit the Kurds, by far Turkey's largest Muslim minority residing mostly in the southeastern provinces.

The Kurds, representing over one-quarter of Turkey's population, came to be known as "mountain Turks"—the only appellation permitted by the government in the public discourse on the Kurds. With their long history that predated the Turks' arrival in the Middle East, the vast majority of Kurds were reluctant to accept the imposed identity of "mountain Turks."[22] Soon after the birth of the Republic in 1923, the stage was set for a protracted conflict between the Kurds and the Turkish state.

In keeping with the autocratic model of European nation-building that promoted national unity based on social homogeneity, the Turkish state pursued three complementary policies toward the Kurds: strict prohibition of all symbols and practices of ethnic identity such as teaching the Kurdish language and history, observances of Kurdish holidays, and cultural practices; systematic Turkification of the Kurdish population through education, indoctrination, and historical revisionism; and use of massive force by the military, police, and special security units to crush any and all manifestations of Kurdish nationalism or separatism. The combined use of these policies by Turkey's powerful state apparatus helped contain the Kurdish "problem" and postpone its dramatic reemergence until the 1980s. In essence, since the Dersim Massacres of 1937–1938, Turkey consistently pursued a combination of strategies to resolve the Kurdish problem—de-Kurdification, Turkification, and mass repression—which would rise to the level of cultural genocide and politicide. The cumulative impact of these policies was the alienation of the Kurdish population, the emergence of political groups pushing for Kurdish civil rights, and the rise of militant separatists challenging the lethal power of the Turkish state.[23]

Another factor contributing to the Kurds' alienation was their impoverishment brought on by the state's developmental failures and the violence pervading the Kurdish region. In search of economic betterment and security, many Kurds joined the great urbanizing trek to the cities to become a part of the *lumpenproletariat*—the restive underclass—a source of growing instability and violence for the beleaguered regime of Prime Minister Suleiman Demirel.[24] In September 1980, the Turkish military overthrew the civilian regime and took direct control for the third time in recent history.

The return of the military to the forefront of Turkish politics marked the reinitiation of hard-line measures against the Kurds—a policy that lasted over two decades. As the military regime launched a repressive campaign in the Kurdish provinces, a 1983 law prohibited the use of the Kurdish language in any form of communication. The next year saw the outbreak of a Kurdish revolt led by the PKK—the Kurdish

Workers Party, a Marxist guerrilla force led by Abdullah Ocalan. As a totalitarian organization led by a supreme leader, the PKK's ideology and operational mode resembled those of the Tamil Tigers (Sri Lanka), Baader-Meinhoff (West Germany) and Sendero Luminoso (Peru).[25] In the mid-1980s, paramilitary forces were used along with regular troops, armored vehicles and helicopters to target the Kurdish population as a whole without differentiating between PKK members and non-combatants. Countless Kurdish villages were raided and destroyed and the villagers arrested and tortured before being driven homeless into the countryside. According to Human Rights Watch, by the mid-1990s, 3,000 villages had been destroyed and 378,335 villagers left homeless, having lost all their possessions and means of livelihood.[26] The strategic aim of the military's campaign was the systematic depopulation of Turkey's Kurdish-populated border regions near Iraq and Syria—a huge "ethnic cleansing" project designed to separate the Kurds in Turkey from their kinfolk in Iraq and Syria.[27]

Emboldened by the non-interference of its NATO allies and Iraq's 1991 defeat, Turkish troops repeatedly invaded the Kurdish safe haven in northern Iraq in pursuit of PKK insurgents. After the 1993 breakdown of a cease-fire with the PKK, the regime even turned against the Kurdish political parties and politicians in Parliament who had opposed PKK's violence and who had pushed for a peaceful settlement of the Kurdish issue. Between 1991 and 1994 over fifty members of the Kurdish parties were killed, and in 1998 the Constitutional Court closed down the Democratic Kurdish Party despite its rejection of separatism and terrorism against the Turkish state. In February 1999, PKK leader Abdullah Ocalan was captured in Kenya and given a death sentence in Turkey, later commuted to life imprisonment under European pressure.[28] In gratitude, Ocalan ordered the PKK to observe a permanent cease-fire from his prison cell, as the regime began to soften the severity of anti-Kurdish measures in preparation for its quest to secure membership in the European Union. In August 2002, the Turkish Parliament passed laws abolishing the death sentence and lifting the bans on Kurdish education and broadcasting. Additional laws were passed in mid-2003, relaxing restrictions on the use of Kurdish, and in June 2004 Turkish television, for the first time, aired a brief broadcast in the Kurdish language.

These reformist measures, adopted at the urging of Turkey's Islamist prime minister, Recep Erdogan, were resisted by the ultra-nationalist factions allied with Turkey's military establishment which fiercely oppose democratic reforms, EU membership, and any policy changes to minimally accommodate the Kurdish constituency. As the Erdogan regime continued to push for liberalizing reforms in mid-2005, the military had begun to undermine the regime by restarting its repressive campaign in the Kurdish provinces. In response, the PKK announced plans to end its cease-fire in May 2005, followed by a resumption of bombings and interactive violence within and outside the Kurdish areas. Should the violence continue, PKK is likely to return to its first preference—an independent Kurdistan—that contrasts with the first preference of the mainstream Kurdish parties—cultural and political autonomy within Turkey. Although it may tolerate a minimal degree of Kurdish cultural rights, the Turkish military oligarchy, also known as the "Deep State," is not expected to agree to any scheme involving Kurdish political and cultural autonomy. Threatened by the success of the Kurdish autonomous state in northern Iraq, the Turkish military could well undertake a new campaign of Kurdish repression in Turkey. Such a move could become a prelude to a Turkish invasion of Iraqi Kurdistan should the latter opt for independence from a disintegrating Iraqi state.

Any resumption of the Turkish military campaign against the Kurds, accompanied by the loss of their newly gained civil and cultural rights, is likely to result in violent outbreaks and atrocities. A limited Turkish invasion of PKK outposts in the mountains of northern Iraq could involve confrontations with the *Pesh Merga* units of the Kurdish autonomous state in one of several worst case scenarios for U.S. forces stationed in Iraq. Next to the Israeli-Palestinian conflict and the looming Sunni-Shiite struggle, the Kurdish future remains the most intractable and explosive issue in Middle East politics. Should a U.S.-sponsored Iraqi state become a success, the inclusion of the Kurdish autonomous region would be at least a partial and temporary solution to the Kurds' dilemma. This accommodation, should it become reality, cannot resolve the existential problems of Kurds in Turkey, Iran, and Syria. In fact, even a quasi-autonomous Kurdish entity within the Iraqi state might be a model to emulate by the Kurds living in the three neighboring autocracies. In the absence of such a democratic solution for Kurds living in Iran, Turkey, and Syria, the Kurdish quest for independence is likely to persist as a destabilizing factor in Middle East politics.

Genocide in Rwanda

In many ways, the 1994 genocide in Rwanda was without precedent. It was perpetrated by a weak regime with alarming rapidity, and a very high kill ratio, before the eyes of an unheeding global audience. Within a short period of one hundred days, 800,000 Tutsis and Hutu moderates were put to the sword by extremist Hutus who had taken control of the state. In one swoop, humanity's fervent hope of "never again" became destined to the dustbin of history.

Historical Background, 1959–1990

The roots of the Rwandan tragedy are found in the tribal demographics and imperial geopolitics of East Central Africa. The Tutsi—a tribe of cattle-herders—migrated south several hundred years ago settling in the contiguous regions of Rwanda, Burundi, Eastern Zaire, and Uganda, that were populated by Hutu farmers. A tall, thin people, the Tutsi intermarried with the Hutu population, which, over the centuries had come to share a common language, religion, and culture. Yet despite these commonalities, several factors caused the separation of the two groups, reinforced by the impact of European imperialism.[29] Under German (1889) and Belgian rule (1916–1961), the Tutsi minority became an upper class ruling over Hutu serfs. The Tutsi were favored with regard to access to higher education and positions of authority that contributed to their wealth vis-à-vis the poorer Hutu.[30] These differences were exacerbated by ambitious leaders seeking to maximize their personal interests in gaining and keeping power.

As Belgian rule came to an end, the power relationship between the Tutsi and Hutu was reversed, leading to a succession of inter-tribal pogroms and massacres. Since the beginning of their mandate over Rwanda-Burundi, the Belgians had governed through Tutsi kings. However, as the Tutsi elite agitated for independence in the 1950s, the Belgians began to favor the Hutu majority by replacing Tutsi chiefs with Hutus.[31] During the painful transition in 1959–1961 from Belgian to Hutu rule, up to 100,000 Tutsis were killed and many took refuge in Uganda.[32] In 1961, Rwanda and Burundi were separated and in 1962 the Belgian trusteeship was terminated, making the two countries independent entities. In the ensuing strategic dilemma, there were two new states led by opposing tribal groups—Hutu in Rwanda and Tutsi in Burundi—caught in the inexorable dynamics of a lethal relationship. In 1963, 20,000 Tutsis were killed in Rwanda, following a Tutsi incursion from Burundi. In April–July 1972, in order to prevent a Hutu takeover, the Tutsi-controlled Burundi regime massacred over 100,000 Hutus in a nation of 3.5 million.[33] A year later, Tutsis were massacred by Hutu "Public Safety Committees" in Rwanda.[34]

The cycle of inter-tribal killings was temporarily halted as Hutu Major General Juvenal Habyarimana took power in Rwanda on July 5, 1973. With the help of a small military junta and his own relatives (*akazu*), Habyarimana dominated the country for the next two decades in the midst of growing domestic and regional challenges. In 1988, Burundi's military government decreed the killing of 20,000 people, mostly Hutus, and 50,000 Hutus were forced to escape to Rwanda. In October 1990, Rwanda was invaded from Uganda by the Rwandan Patriotic Front (RPF)—a powerful force of Tutsi exiles who had escaped the

1959–1961 massacres.[35] The ensuing inter-communal war provided the immediate crisis milieu for a genocidal outcome, more horrendous than all the previous Hutu-Tutsi mass killings combined. Table 9.2 sets out a chronology of the Rwandan genocide.

The Prelude to Genocide, 1990–1994

Investigation of the period preceding the act of genocide is crucial because it could reveal signs of the coming cataclysm. The usual indicators of the genocide's prelude may include growing insecurity, assassinations, small-scale attacks, violent demonstrations, hateful propaganda, and specific preparations to commit acts of mass violence. All of these critical signs of trouble were manifest in the five months leading to the start of mass killings on April 7, 1994. The international community did not need a miraculous "writing on the wall" to discover the requisite preconditions of genocide in Rwanda that were being nurtured, energized, and manipulated by key players—the predominantly Hutu power structure of Rwanda led by President Habyarimana, the Hutu power block of the Liberal Party, and other extremist Hutu groups.[36]

After almost two decades in power, the president was facing growing opposition at home and his first and only preference was to extend his term in office. To accomplish this objective, Habyarimana had developed a multi-pronged strategy to put extremists in positions of authority and maximize his support among the Hutu by exponentially magnifying the Tutsi threat.[37] The president's perverse stratagem received timely reinforcement from the Tutsi-led RPF attack in October 1990. Now the president's men began a systematic campaign to dissolve the bonds of marriage and culture that had been forged between Rwanda's Tutsi and Hutu communities. In order to polarize the citizenry, the Hutu regime subjected the Tutsis, moderate Hutus, and citizens of mixed parentage to brutal propaganda attacks, accusing them of being "collaborators" with the RPF. Radio Mille Collines and the press effectively demonized and dehumanized the Tutsi as the regime prepared lists of prominent Tutsis and Hutu moderates slated for killing.[38] In order to test its genocidal capabilities, the regime organized five pilot pogroms between mid-1990 and 1994 that massacred hundreds of Tutsis. In early 1992, the president's partisans began to train a youth militia, the Interahamwe, for the express purpose of targeting Tutsi and moderate Hutu.[39] The Tutsi could be easily identified because all citizens were legally required to register by stating their ethnic origin, and because in some cases, they were distinguished by physical appearance.

Two key events in 1993 contributed to the acceleration of Habyarimana's genocidal agenda. In February 1993, advancing RPF forces were threatening the Hutu's hegemonic position as well as the president's

TABLE 9.2   Rwandan Genocide, 1916–2001

Date	Event	Death Toll/Outcome
1916	Belgian forces occupy Rwanda	Germans evacuate, losing territory in World War I
1923	Rwanda-Burundi under Belgian mandate; indirect rule through Tutsi kings	Hutu opposition
1957	Hutu majority demands change in Rwanda's power structure	Belgium makes concession to Hutu
1959	Tutsi king and thousands of Tutsis forced into exile in Uganda after interethnic violence in Rwanda	100,000 Tutsis killed
1961–1962	Rwanda becomes an independent republic under Hutu president	More Tutsis leave the country
1962	Rwanda and Burundi separate	Hutu ruled Rwanda and Tutsi-ruled Burundi
1963	Tutsi rebels from Burundi attack Rwanda	20,000 Tutsis killed in Rwanda
1972	Burundi Tutsi regime massacres 100,000 Hutu people	
1973	Military coup led by Hutu General Juvenal Habyarimana overthrows President Gregoire Kayibanda	Habyarimana stays in power until his assassination in 1994
1978	New constitution; Habyarimana elected president	
1988	Burundi's Tutsi military regime kills 20,000 mostly Hutus; 50,000 escape to Rwanda	
1990	Rwandan Patriotic Front (RPF) rebels invade Rwanda from Uganda	
1991–1993	Habyarimana organizes pilot pogroms to kill Tutsis and moderate Hutus and begins training Interahamwe	
Feb. 1993	RPF advances toward the capital threatening to overthrow Hutu hegemony in Rwanda	Habyarimana's power in Rwanda strengthened by Hutu supporters fearing massacre by Tutsis
Oct. 1993	Hutu president of Burundi killed by Tutsi soldiers	
Aug. 1993	Habyarimana signs Arusha Accords with RPF to create broad-based government	Habyarimana delays implementation, fearing loss of power
Nov. 1993	UN Peacekeeping forces (UNAMIR) arrive under General Dallaire to oversee Arusha Accords	Habyarimana fears overthrow
Apr. 1994	Hutu presidents Habyarimana of Rwanda and Cyprien Ntaryamira of Burundi killed as their plane is shot down in Kigali	Attack blamed on Tutsis and used to justify killings

Apr.– June 1994	Hutu militia and Rwandan military massacre Tutsis and Hutu moderates	800,000 killed in 100 days
1995	RPF takeover of Rwanda	Hutu militias and 2 million Hutus flee to Zaire
1995	UN appoints international tribunal to try Hutu perpetrators of genocide in Tanzania	
2001	Gacaca courts established for ordinary Rwandans to judge their peers	

hold on power. In late October 1993, the newly elected Hutu president of neighboring Burundi was killed by Tutsi soldiers, leading to the massacre of thousands of Hutus and Tutsis. The RPF invasion and the Tutsi takeover in Burundi helped expand and solidify President Habyarimana's Hutu following, which he hoped would help him defeat the RPF and keep himself in power—priority objectives which were militarily supported by the French government.[40]

In mid-1993, the RPF's offensive had placed Habyarimana in an untenable situation. On August 4, 1993, the Rwandan president was forced to sign the Arusha Accords, a peace settlement with RPF, to allow the return of refugees and the creation of a broad-based power sharing transitional government.[41] In November 1993, the UN dispatched peacekeeping forces to start the implementation of the Arusha Accords. Headed by Canadian Major General Romeo Dallaire, the United Nations Assistance Mission in Rwanda—UNAMIR—was destined to play a key role in the unfolding tragedy.

The implementation of the Arusha Accords, backed by growing pressure from the UN and the RPF, was seen by Habyarimana and his associates as an existential threat to their leadership position and to Hutu dominance. In all likelihood, the RPF would not accept the president as partner in the coalition regime prescribed by the Arusha Accords, given his many acts of mass murder and treachery against Tutsis. Indeed, the new regime could even try and punish Habyarimana's henchmen for their past misdeeds. These circumstances led the president to pursue a dual strategy—to stall by all means the implementation of the Arusha Accords, while strengthening his domestic Hutu following through military training, illegal import and distribution of weapons, and anti-Tutsi propaganda.[42] By postponing negotiations with RPF and mobilizing the home front for war and genocide, Habyarimana may have hoped to achieve one of the following objectives:

1. resist and reverse RPF's military gains by military means as a first preference; and if that failed,
2. use the threat of a Tutsi genocide as a bargaining tool to force RPF to retreat and negotiate a new settlement more favorable to the Hutu elite than Arusha, that would accord the president's circle a major role in the coalition regime or at least protection from persecution; or as a last resort
3. proceed with the planned genocide as a last act of mass revenge against the Tutsi as his regime collapses or he suffers an uncertain fate.

Given Habyarimana's pattern of decision-making until April 1994, his first and second preferences appear to represent close approximations of his strategic logic. However, the third preference is pure speculation because the Hutu president was killed in a plane crash on April 6, 1994. All that is certain is that he had meticulously planned for genocide but died before he could proceed with or desist from its implementation.

Failed Prisoner's Dilemma

The four final months leading to the Rwandan genocide may be best characterized as a prisoner's dilemma game between the Habyarimana regime, RPF, and the United Nations represented by UNAMIR under General Dallaire. The central problem in the triangular interaction was the indecisive role of the UN and the uncaring reluctance of Security Council members to strengthen UNAMIR, which had been permitted to deploy only 2,500 soldiers as peacekeepers.[43] Meanwhile, the Rwandan government had repeatedly interfered with UNAMIR's mission, postponed the negotiations to form a coalition government, and continued to train and arm the Interahamwe, the Presidential Guard, the National Police, and other Hutu vigilante militias expressly tasked for mass killing. When constrained by the shortage of small arms, the regime imported and distributed machetes to civilians to ensure large-scale Hutu participation in the planned atrocities, which would maximize Tutsi deaths in keeping with the motto "Hutu should stop having mercy on Tutsi"—one of the "Ten Commandments of Bahutu," published in 1990. In summary form, this racist document prescribes a strict code of behavior for all Hutu:

1. Hutu men should desist from any contact with Tutsi women;
2. Hutu men should only marry Hutu women;
3. Hutu women should be vigilant and bring their husbands, brothers, and sons back to reason;
4. Hutu should refrain from any form of business dealings with Tutsi because they are distrustful and only seeking supremacy for Tutsi.

5. Hutu should hold all strategic positions—political, administrative, economic, military, and security.
6. The majority of teachers and students in schools should be Hutu.
7. All military forces should be exclusively Hutu.
8. Hutu should stop having mercy on Tutsi.
9. Hutu must maintain unity and solidarity against Tutsi within and outside Rwanda and remain vigilant against the common Tutsi enemy.
10. The Hutu ideology must be taught to every Hutu, and any Hutu opposing the propagation of this ideology is a traitor.[44]

Repeated requests by General Dallaire for authority to disrupt arms distribution, stop incendiary radio broadcasts, and deploy more soldiers were denied by UN Secretary General Butros Ghali. His assistant, Kofi Annan, told General Dallaire that UNAMIR's mission was one of peacekeeping—a passive role that did not involve seizing arms. As a result UNAMIR and the UN lost credibility; they could neither play an effective mediator's role nor use their power to prevent escalation of the conflict and provide the necessary mix of incentives and threats to push for a negotiated coalition government.[45] Rwanda was not a priority for the members of the UN Security Council. At the core of UN's reluctance was American opposition to armed intervention. After the 1993 debacle in Somalia, the Clinton administration sought to minimize external entanglements, even if these involved low-risk humanitarian intervention.[46]

By late February 1994 the regime's coercive measures had intensified, forcing Tutsi to seek refuge in religious centers and UN agencies. In March 1994, it was clear that the Hutu president was pursuing his second preference as reflected in the regime's mouthpieces: "If RPF resumes the war, Tutsi of Kigali will be exterminated" and "if Arusha is implemented, Tutsi will be liquidated."[47] On March 28, 1994, the president again declined to participate in ceremonies to install the transitional regime—a move that compelled the international community to make concessions on the inclusion of extremist Hutus in the new government. It is possible that, having won concessions to revise the Arusha Accords, Habyarimana was ready to discuss a final settlement when he journeyed to Tanzania for a meeting with leaders of the neighboring states. Whether or not he intended to reach a final settlement would remain an open question because of his unexpected death.

Genocide on Autopilot

Responsibility for the downing of the President's plane on April 6, 1994, was never established. Among the likely culprits were Habyarimana's Hutu rivals and opponents within and outside the regime who sought to replace him or were afraid that the president was ready to make a deal with RPF under a revised Arusha settlement. Regardless of the real culprit, the Hutu regime blamed the shooting down of the president's plane on the Tutsi and used it as a pretext to launch the genocide. In any case, Habyarimana and his henchmen had carefully prepared the milieu to trigger the genocidal process on short notice. In the immediate aftermath of his death two factors could have prevented the mayhem: a determined UN military intervention; and hesitancy and disagreements among the president's successors to launch genocide. Tragically, neither impediment to genocide was to play a role—the international community showed no interest in humanitarian intervention and the vacuum of power created upon the president's death was quickly filled by leaders bent on mass murder. Less than a week after Habyarimana's demise, the genocide had been placed on autopilot by the president's clan and close associates, including the Presidential Guard and Col. Theoneste Bagosora's followers.[48]

Colonel Bagosora's initial attempts to monopolize control over the state apparatus were resisted by some moderate Hutu leaders who had hoped to get backing from the foreign military contingents present in Rwanda. However, the quick exit of the diplomatic corps helped by French, Belgian, and Italian troops emboldened Bagosora's associates to expand their power to reach beyond Kigali. The colonel unleashed a brutal campaign killing and purging moderate Hutu politicians and uniting disparate Hutu factions for "self-defense" against the "common enemy"—the Tutsi minority, and their RPF kinsmen that had gone on the offensive after Habyarimana's death. By mid-April, Bagosora's office functioned as an interim government, the epicenter of control, coordination, and implementation of Tutsi victimization.

Totalitarian Efficiencies

Success in the execution of mass killing projects is largely contingent on the strategic orientation of the leadership and the organizational structure at its command. As amply demonstrated by previous genocides—Armenian, Jewish, and Cambodian—the essential preconditions of genocide necessitate a ruling elite bent on making genocide its ultimate preference based on an ideology of victimization, and in command of a centralized totalitarian state apparatus. By quickly moving into the power vacuum after April 6, Colonel Bagosora adroitly used the existing instruments of ideological propaganda, the military and police forces, the civilian bureaucracy, and various civilian vigilante groups to exterminate over 800,000 Tutsis and moderate Hutus. The fact that most of these killings were accomplished in less than one hundred days reflected a level of efficiency unmatched even by the Nazis. Box 9.2 dis-

---

Box 9.2
Weapons of Genocide

In Kigali in the early days, the killers were well-equipped government soldiers and militiamen who relied mainly on automatic weapons and grenades. In the countryside, where the slaughter gradually spread, the killing was done at first with firearms, but as more Hutu joined in the weapons became increasingly unsophisticated—knives, machetes, spears, and the traditional masu, bulky clubs with nails protruding from them. Later screwdrivers, hammers, and bicycle handlebars were added to the arsenal. Killers often carried a weapon in one hand and a transistor radio piping murder commands in the other.

Source: Samantha Power, *A Problem from Hell: America and the Age of Genocide*
New York: Harper Perennial, 2002, 334.

---

cusses some of the unsophisticated weapons used in the Rwandan genocide.

As Colonel Bagosora took control, the killing had already begun. His first targets were moderate Hutu and Tutsi leaders who had opposed the late president's policies. The next step was to expand the scope and facilitate the process of mass killing by forcing Tutsis into government buildings, churches, schools, and public places for extermination. Subsequent stages focused on comprehensiveness—to kill the elderly, priests, women, and children—and hunting Tutsi in hiding or those protected by Hutu friends. The progressive defeats suffered by the Hutu military regime from RPF forces, combined with growing international criticism, prompted Colonel Bagosora to resort to clandestine efforts to target Tutsis in smaller numbers. Tutsi women were made a special target of Hutu revenge—they were raped, mutilated, and then murdered. In May–June 1994, the colonel's genocidal government began to collapse, amid internecine fighting among Hutu factions. Yet there was no sign of outside intervention to stop the Hutu murder machine. In the end, the Rwandan genocide was halted by the victorious RPF forces led by Gen. Paul Kagame.[49]

Humanitarian Intervention?

The Rwandan genocide, even more than Cambodia's, could have been easily stopped even after the start of massacres on April 7, 1994. In view of the weakness of the genocidal regime, there was no need to mount a major campaign requiring the redeployment of forces in the midst of an ongoing world war that would have been necessary to save Armenians in 1915 or Jews during the Holocaust. The stark reality was that the international community or any of its member states did not even make a credible threat to intervene, which might have scared off some of the marauding Hutu bands. Indeed, the representatives of the UN and some of its leading member states were present at the creation and execution of the genocide.

The reasons for the failure of the United States and others to intervene have been amply documented by Samantha Power. The Clinton White House had lost interest in humanitarian intervention after the Somalian expedition. Also, it faced a recalcitrant Congress and a difficult Republican challenge in the November 1994 elections. Except for France and Belgium, Rwanda had no strategic value in anyone's calculations of self-interest. In Washington there was no one to lobby for Rwanda, and the leadership of the African American community mostly remained quiescent. In mid-May 1994, a concerted move by Senators Paul Simon and James Jeffords to seek UN authorization for intervention met rejection at the White House. Meanwhile, a proposal by General Dallaire for a contingent of 5,000 UN troops was postponed because of Pentagon opposition until July when the slaughter had ended.[50] Only in late July did President Clinton authorize the dispatch of U.S. forces to Kigali and the refugee camps in Zaire to oversee humanitarian relief, but not for peacekeeping.

As former colonial powers, Belgium and France were more deeply involved in Rwandan affairs than the distant Americans. The actions of both countries contributed to the onset and continuation of the genocide. To be sure, initially Belgium had supported a strengthened UNAMIR and contributed 440 troops to the force. However, the Belgian posture quickly changed after Hutu soldiers killed ten Belgian peacekeepers on April 7, in a strategic move to force their withdrawal from UNAMIR. This calculation brought immediate payoffs when the Belgian government ordered the withdrawal of its contingent from UNAMIR and joined the United States in pushing for the total evacuation of the remaining troops. After the departure of the Belgians, General Dallaire faced a desperate situation in trying to protect and save small groups of Rwandans with his depleted force of 500 soldiers.[51]

In sharp contrast to the heroic role of Dallaire's beleaguered soldiers, France played an ominously complacent role in the genocidal process.[52] As Habyarimana's main European ally, France had given the Hutu leader large-scale military aid and political support, particularly in efforts to defeat his rivals at home and fight the Tutsi-led RPF invading armies. As its Hutu allies under Colonel Bagosora faced defeat, France quickly dispatched 2,500 troops on June 23 to southwest Rwanda where they saved Tutsi lives while refraining from targeting the Hutu leadership.[53] This maneuver represented a belated attempt to save face after France's pro-Hutu policies and to reassert itself as a power broker in the Great Lakes region. The remaining members of the Security Council showed no inclination to become involved in Rwanda, while other states waited for the great powers to take a leading role that never came. In the final analysis, stopping the butchery of thousands of black Africans in a remote land was not a priority item in the UN's global agenda and irrelevant to the self-interests of its member states. It was not until June 10, 1994, that under great pressure, the U.S. State Department reluctantly used the term genocide to describe the mass slaughter in Rwanda.[54]

Guilt, Punishment, and Remorse

It is ironic that despite the enormity of the crime of genocide, most of its perpetrators escape punishment. To establish guilt and mete out punishment is a daunting task requiring unwavering commitment to achieving justice, international administrative oversight, large-scale funding, and competent personnel. In Rwanda and elsewhere, it was imperative that the perpetrators be brought to justice under the dictates of morality and international law in a decisive manner, which would send a clear signal to potential perpetrators about the consequences of such criminal acts.

In November 1994 the UN Security Council established the International Criminal Tribunal for Rwanda (ICTR) to try persons for the crime of genocide and crimes against humanity. Headquartered in Arusha, Tanzania, with a branch in Kigali, the tribunal had a slow start plagued by shortages in funding, mismanagement, recruitment of qualified personnel, protection of witnesses, and organizational inability to deal with an immense workload. Rwandans were critical of the tribunal's lengthy deliberations, demanding quick trials without due process. The situation improved in 1998–1999 as some top officials were tried and sentenced. Meanwhile, the new Rwandan government had begun to rebuild the country's legal system to try thousands of suspects it had imprisoned. In the vengeful milieu of the genocide's aftermath, the new regime faced the difficult task of distinguishing between the Hutu perpetrators and Hutus who had abstained from participating in the slaughter. Many of the trials fell short of international standards due to unfair procedures, incompetent judges, lawyers and prosecutors, and a threatening political environment.[55] In April 1998, the regime executed twenty-two people charged with participation in the genocide. For lesser criminals, the law provided for voluntary confessions in exchange for reduced sentences and provisional releases to reduce the prison population. A decade after the genocide, the task of bringing justice to the guilty and giving compensation to the survivors remains a challenge of major proportions, especially for an impoverished and bloodied country like Rwanda. Yet justice and compensation are basic ingredients for building a tolerant Rwandan society in which the genocidal dialectic between Tutsi and Hutu is never resumed. Despite the partial successes of the Kagame regime, Rwanda remains a risky place because of its perilous past and the continuing Hutu-Tutsi violent strategic interaction in the neighboring countries. With a less autocratic leadership, reinforced by international economic aid and political oversight, there might be a chance that Rwanda will emerge as a model of inter-communal reconciliation for its neighbors to emulate.

In the final analysis, the Rwandan genocide was a rational act by President Habyarimana's Hutu political elite designed to perpetuate their hold on power.[56] In order to realize this objective, they decided to employ genocide to reduce or remove the possibility of domestic support for a victorious Tutsi RPF regime; destroy the infrastructure and economic resources a new regime would need in order to rule effectively; and set the stage for a Hutu resurgence under the new regime. Thus, the genocide was carried out by a regime facing an existential crisis with the tools and organizational capacity to quickly mobilize its constituency by exploiting its historically based fears of massacre. In the words of Rui de Figueiredo Jr. and Barry Weingast, the genocide resulted from the failure of the Arusha Accords, which "left weak leaders in power, granting them the opportunity to raise the stakes and gamble for resurrection."[57]

Notes

1. David McDowall, *A Modern History of the Kurds* (London: I. B. Tauris, 1996), 21–27.
2. Donald Bloxham, *The Great Game of Genocide: Imperialism, Nationalism, and the Destruction of the Ottoman Armenians* (New York: Oxford University Press, 2005), 40–41; and McDowall, *A Modern History of the Kurds*, 88–101.
3. Kuper, *Genocide*, 117–118.
4. Kevin McKiernan, *The Kurds: A People in Search of their Homeland* (New York: St. Martin's, 2006), 93–94.
5. For historical details see Edmund Ghareeb, *The Kurdish Question in Iraq* (Syracuse, NY: Syracuse University Press, 1981), 28–86.

6. Human Rights Watch, *Iraq's Crimes of Genocide: The Anfal Campaign against the Kurds* (New Haven, CT: Yale University Press, 1995), 3–4.
7. Gareth V. Stansfield, *Iraqi Kurdistan* (London: RoutledgeCurzon, 2003), 85–87.
8. Ghareeb, *The Kurdish Question,* 87–113.
9. Human Rights Watch, *Iraq's Crimes of Genocide,* 22–23.
10. Ghareeb, *The Kurdish Question,* 156–160.
11. *Ibid.,* 171–172.
12. *Ibid.,* 176; and Human Rights Watch, *Iraq's Crimes of Genocide,* 24–25.
13. Shireen T. Hunter, *The Future of Islam and the West* (Westport, CT: Praeger, 1998), 143.
14. Human Rights Watch, "Genocide in Iraq: the Anfal Campaign against the Kurds," http://hrw.org/reports/1993/iraqanfal/ANFAL2.htm.
15. Human Rights Watch, *Iraq's Crimes of Genocide,* 68–2.
16. McDowall, *A Modern History of the Kurds,* 357–361; and Hewitt, *Defining the Horrific,* 325–326.
17. This psycho-political profile is derived from the author's unpublished study of Saddam Hussein completed in September 1997.
18. Fred Halliday, *Islam and the Myth of Confrontation: Religion and Politics in the Middle East* (London: I. B. Tauris, 2003), 77–78.
19. Power, *"A Problem from Hell,"* 237–238.
20. *Ibid.,* 240.
21. McDowall, *A Modern History of the Kurds,* 385–389.
22. *Ibid.,* 184–211.
23. *Ibid.,* 395–408.
24. *Ibid.,* 409–415.
25. McKiernan, *The Kurds,* 89–91.
26. Human Rights Watch, "Still Critical: Prospects in 2005 for Internally Displaced Kurds in Turkey," 2005. http://www.hrw.org/reports/2005/turkey0305/turkey0305.pdf.
27. On the interactive terrorism between the PKK and Turkey see McDowall, *A Modern History of the Kurds,* 418–449.
28. McKiernan, *The Kurds,* 226.
29. Bill Berkeley, "Road to Genocide," in Nicolaus Mills and Kira Brunner, eds., *The New Killing Fields* (New York: Basic, 2002), 103–105.
30. On the history of ethnic divisions in Rwanda see Human Rights Watch, *Leave None to Tell the Story: Genocide in Rwanda* (New York: Human Rights Watch, 1999), http://www.hrw.org/reports/1999/rwanda/Geno1-3-09.htm#P200_83746; and Jerard Prunier, *The Rwandan Crisis, 1959–1994: History of a Genocide* (New York: Columbia University Press, 1995), 16–17.
31. Stephen R. Shalom, "Genocide in Rwanda," in William Dudley, ed., *Genocide* (San Diego: Greenhaven, 2001), 43–45.
32. Patricia Marchak, *Reigns of Terror* (Montreal: McGill-Queens University Press, 2003), 200.
33. Shalom, "Genocide in Rwanda," 45.
34. Human Rights Watch, *Leave None to Tell the Story.*
35. Marchak, *Reign of Terror,* 206–207.
36. Human Rights Watch, *Leave None to Tell the Story.*
37. Mark Huband, "Rwanda—the Genocide," in Roy Gutman and David Rieff, eds., *Crimes of War: What the Public Should Know* (New York: Norton, 1999), 312–313.
38. For more on the impact of Radio Mille Collines see Power, *A Problem from Hell,* 330–331, 371–372.
39. Marchak, *The Reign of Terror,* 209.

40. *Ibid.,* 211; and Agnès Callamard, "French Policy in Rwanda," in Howard Adelman and Astri Suhrke, eds. *The Path of a Genocide* (New Brunswick, NJ: Transaction, 1999), 157–183.
41. Bruce D. Jones, "The Arusha Peace Process," in Adelman and Suhrke, eds., *The Path of a Genocide,* 131–156.
42. *Ibid.,* 148–153.
43. Power, *"A Problem from Hell,"* 335–346.
44. For details see *ibid.,* 338–339.
45. Turid Laegreid, "U.N. Peacekeeping in Rwanda," in Adelman and Suhrke, eds., *The Path of a Genocide,* 231–251.
46. On U.S. policy see Human Rights Watch, *Leave None to Tell the Story;* and Power, *"A Problem from Hell,"* 358–385.
47. Human Rights Watch, *Leave None to Tell the Story.*
48. *Ibid.*
49. Joan Kakwenzire and Dixon Kamukama, " The Development and Consolidation of Extremist Forces in Rwanda, 1990–1994," in Adelman and Suhrke, eds., *The Path of a Genocide,* 80–81.
50. Power, *"A Problem from Hell,"* 370–377
51. *Ibid.,* 366–370.
52. On the French role see Agnès Callamard, "French Policy in Rwanda," in Adelman and Suhrke, eds., *The Path of a Genocide,* 157–183.
53. Gérard Prunier, "Operation Turquoise: A Humanitarian Escape from a Political Dead End," in Adelman and Suhrke, eds., *The Path of a Genocide,* 281–305.
54. Power, *"A Problem from Hell,"* 364.
55. George Packer, "Justice on a Hill," in Mills and Brunner, eds., *The New Killing Fields,* 129–148.
56. Rene Lemarchand, "Rwanda: the Rationality of Genocide," *Issue: A Journal of Opinion* 23, no. 2 (1995): 8–11.
57. Rui J. P. de Figueiredo Jr. and Barry R. Weingast, "The Rationality of Fear: Political Opportunism and Ethnic Conflict," in Barbara F. Walter and Jack Snyder, eds., *Civil Wars, Insecurity, and Intervention* (New York: Columbia University Press, 1999), 293.

Further Reading

Bird, Christiane. *A Thousand Sighs, a Thousand Revolts: Journeys in Kurdistan.* New York: Ballantine, 2004.

Chaliand, Gerard, ed. *A People without a Country: The Kurds and Kurdistan.* Olive Branch, 1993.

Des Forges, Alison. Human Rights Watch. *"Leave None to Tell the Story": Genocide in Rwanda.* New York: Human Rights Watch, 1999.

Human Rights Watch. *Genocide in Iraq: The Anfal Campaign against the Kurds.* New York: Human Rights Watch, 1993.

Kuperman, Alan J. *The Limits of Humanitarian Intervention: Genocide in Rwanda.* Washington, D.C.: Brookings Institution Press, 2001.

McDowall, David. *A Modern History of the Kurds,* 3d ed., London: I. B. Tauris, 2004.

Melvern, Linda. *Conspiracy to Murder: The Rwandan Genocide.* London: Verso, 2004.

The Organization of African Unity. *Rwanda: the Preventable Genocide,* 2000.

Taylor, Christopher. *Sacrifice as Terror: The Rwandan Genocide of 1994.* New York: Berg, 1999.

Yildiz, Kerim. *The Kurds in Turkey: Past, Present, and Future.* London: Pluto, 2004.

Future Terror: New Forms, Trends, and Antidotes

FORECASTING THE FUTURE is a risky endeavor at best, and political scientists and other analysts are hardly prophets in disguise. Any attempt to look into the future requires assessing recent developments and projecting them onto likely scenarios of political conflict. This prognostication will focus on the evolving forms and methods of political violence and the causal triggers that propel such violence. The game theoretic framework used throughout this book will serve as the conceptual foundation informing the analysis below.

Global Determinants of Future Conflict

Since acts of political violence have causes and objectives, and since actors behave according to their preferences, our task is to ascertain and assess the dynamic forces that may be shaping the near-term global political milieu. At the global level, most of the presently discernable factors and trends point to an uncertain future—a world beset by growing imbalances of power, wealth, resources, and capabilities which portend a rise in the incidence and lethality of political violence in its different forms. Among the interacting factors most likely to promote global instability, ten are readily apparent:

1. Rapid population growth, particularly in the poorer countries, amid decreases in population growth rates in the richer countries;
2. Drastic increases in inequality, marked by the maldistribution of wealth within and among the rich and poor countries;

3. Large-scale population movements across state boundaries from poor to rich countries, triggering ethnic, cultural, and economic tensions and reconstituting the demographics of many states;
4. Imbalances between exponentially growing populations, and finite economic and natural resources, such as food, energy, water, and habitable space;
5. Transnational challenges to the nation-state system from religious extremists, criminal gangs, drug cartels, and other nonstate actors;
6. Internal challenges to nation-states from indigenous movements, ethnic separatists, religious extremists, and economically marginalized classes;
7. The impact of globalization—economic, cultural, technological, and political—eroding state authority and national and subnational identities;
8. The growing economic power of China, India, and other rapidly developing countries and the corresponding decline of the U.S. economic base and growing U.S. indebtedness to China, Japan, India, Britain, Germany, South Korea, and the oil-producing states;
9. Quantum advances in science, technology, and communication and their impact on the modernization of the means of combat, repression, mass killing, and the production of weapons of mass destruction; and
10. Decline in America's hegemonic position as the world's sole superpower and the consequent disequilibrium in the global balance of power.

These destabilizing factors are based on current world conditions and trends, although the list is not meant to be exhaustive, and unforeseen events may change the course of future developments. These could include changes in political leadership and state policies, new discoveries and scientific breakthroughs, and the rise of new ideologies and social movements, all of which could either exacerbate or mitigate the crisis conditions that are likely to face the state system and humankind as a whole in the coming decades.

What is certain in this prognosis is a complex future of multiple challenges that could well result in violent outcomes, including the possibility of inter-state war. Given the great cost and unforeseeable consequences of conventional inter-state warfare, it is more likely that unconventional forms of violence will continue to be used by both states and nonstate antagonists. The category of unconventional political violence, as defined in this book, includes various types of terrorism by individuals and groups against states and by states against domestic and foreign antagonists as well as by groups against each other.

An analysis of the ten crisis factors singly and in combination points to the future likelihood of several types of unconventional violence that could be carried out by a range of political actors. These forms of terrorism may emulate old techniques and patterns or modify and create new methods of unconventional violence.

Ethnic/Indigenous Violence

Ethnic nationalism remains a powerful factor in fueling terrorism against states. The quest for ethnic identity, civil rights, self-rule, or independence can be expected to persist in about two dozen countries, some of which remain engaged in interactive violence, while others face imminent outbreaks of violence. These conflicts are exacerbated by the threatened erosion of ethnic identities under the impact of state policies and the economic and cultural forces of globalization. The revival of ethnic identity and political consciousness has been particularly notable among the indigenous peoples of Central and South America, who have begun to challenge the mostly white ruling elites for a share of power and wealth. Now that indigenous movements have started to use the electoral system to bring to power their preferred candidates—most recently in Bolivia, Venezuela, and Ecuador—the continuing marginal status of indigenous peoples in the rest of Latin American could evoke violence. The following list includes some countries currently beset by ethnic violence or likely to experience such violence in the near-term future.

Afghanistan	Iraq	Rwanda
Bolivia	Israel	Somalia
Bosnia	Ivory Coast	South Africa
Burundi	Kosovo	Spain
Chad	Liberia	Sri Lanka
China	Mexico	Sudan
Congo	Myanmar	Turkey
Cyprus	Nigeria	Uganda
Georgia	Pakistan	
India	Russia	

The Bolivian case amply demonstrates the feasibility of the electoral alternative to violence. The availability of the ballot box combined with government restraint from the use of force could well neutralize the threat of violence from ethnic/indigenous groups. A case in point is the Zapatista movement in Chiapas, Mexico. To the extent that the Mexican authorities have decreased their use of coercive responses and reigned in attacks by vigilante militias, the Zapatista rebellion of January 1994 increasingly assumed a peaceful character by joining the quest for a political solution.

The presence of democratic mechanisms of conflict resolution does not always guarantee peaceful outcomes. Despite a substantial decrease in violence, the Basque issue remains contentious, and Spain faces demands of greater autonomy in Catalonia. In Iraq, the electoral framework outlined in the new constitution has failed to curb the protracted civil war among Sunnis, Shiites and Kurds. Russia's federal system that grants considerable autonomy to its ethnic and sectarian minorities has proven dysfunctional in dealing with the Chechen resistance and other problems of ethno-sectarian unrest. In Turkey, the presence of electoral mechanisms has failed to provide a constructive modality to address the demands of the restive Kurdish minority for autonomy, cultural rights, and economic betterment. As a result, the traditional reliance on coercive means by Turkey's powerful military elite has had a detrimental impact on the Kurdish population and has led to the reemergence of interactive violence between the military and the Kurdistan Workers' Party (PKK), particularly with its militant faction, the Freedom Falcons. Indeed, the century-long Kurdish quest for independence will remain one of the most destabilizing problems at the heart of the Middle East affecting four countries with large Kurdish minorities—Turkey, Iraq, Iran, and Syria.

The other major unresolved ethnic conflict in the Middle East is the Israel-Palestine standoff, a persistent trigger of violence between Palestinians and Israelis and a destabilizing influence that transcends the region to fuel the widening struggle between Islam and the West. The victory of Hamas in the Palestinian elections of January 2006 complicated the search for a solution. In view of the refusal of Hamas to recognize the legitimacy of Israel's statehood, and the continued expansion of Israeli settlements in the West Bank, this low-intensity war may well escalate by transforming an ethnic struggle into a larger sectarian war reaching beyond the Palestinian/Israeli territories and involving outside powers.

Ethnic violence will continue to beset several African states due to the prevalence of tribalism across state frontiers and the divisive influence of despotic ruling elites. The most lethal of these is the civil war in the Congo, and the cross-border inter-tribal violence affecting Uganda, Rwanda, and Burundi. Another theater of ethno-tribal terror is West Africa. While Liberia's civil strife seems to have ended with the election of Ellen Johnson-Sirleaf, inter-sectarian bloodletting continues to threaten the Ivory Coast, fueled by a tribal controversy over the presidential succession. Similar inter-tribal/racial conflicts persist in some East and Central African countries, the most deadly being in Sudan's

Darfur province. Since 2003, the violence between Sudan's Arab government and the restive ethnically African tribes of Darfur has reached genocidal proportions. The regime's combined use of military forces and allied Janjaweed vigilantes has devastated the Darfur region, claiming over 250,000 lives despite the peacekeeping forces deployed by the African Union.

The interactive violence between tribe and state in Darfur has been duplicated across the border in Chad where President Idriss Diby has been facing a rebellion by tribes opposed to the hegemony of his Zaghawa minority tribe. Consequently, the Chad-Sudan borderlands have become killing fields at the confluence of tribal rebellions and clashing state interests. Chadian rebel militias based in Darfur are supported by Sudan, while Zaghawa-led Darfur rebels are aided by Chad's Zaghawa dominated regime. Thus, the conflicting strategies of the Sudanese and Chadian regimes have been to displace or eliminate the population of the borderlands in order to neutralize their respective tribal insurgencies. Since 2005, cross-border attacks have created new waves of refugees—an ominous prelude to a possible general war between the two states.

Among the most volatile of Asia's ethnic conflicts are those of Sri Lanka, Pakistan, India, and Georgia. The violent confrontation between the Hindu Tamil Tigers and the Buddhist Sinhalese government reignited in late 2006 in defiance of Norwegian and Indian attempts at conflict resolution. Meanwhile, India is beset by several ethno-sectarian conflicts, in particular, the seemingly intractable violence in Kashmir. The clashes between Kashmiri Muslim separatists and India are an integral part of the larger Indian-Pakistani military standoff that in the 1990s began to assume a sectarian coloration. After a period of heightened terrorism by Islamist extremist groups like Lashkar-e-Taiba in India and Kashmir, there was a diminution of violence resulting from concerted efforts by India and Pakistan to settle their differences through negotiations. In 2005–2006, Indian prime minister Manmohan Singh and Pakistani president Pervez Musharraf made some progress in normalizing relations which were jeopardized by continued violence in Kashmir and the July 2006 train bombing in Mumbai, reopening the grim prospect of a shift toward religious terrorism.

A half-dozen multiethnic countries can be classified as high-risk because of dormant or low-intensity conflicts that have the potential to become violent. One such case is Kosovo, a remnant of the bloody breakup of Yugoslavia. Since Kosovo's liberation from Serbia's repressive rule in 1999 by a U.S.-led military coalition, the Albanian Kosovar Muslim majority has pressed for independence—an outcome that would threaten the security of the Serb minority and the historic Christian shrines revered by the Serbian people. A revival of violence cannot be precluded should the NATO-sponsored negotiations between the Kosovar Albanians and the Serbian government fail to produce a mutually acceptable settlement. Two other high-risk ethnic conflicts have been brewing in the South Caucasus. Georgian president Mikhael Saakashvili has taken an increasingly aggressive stance to regain the ethnic enclaves of Abkhazia and South Ossetia, which fought to separate themselves from Georgia after the demise of the Soviet Union. This effort has led to periodic clashes that could bring in Russian military intervention to defend the Abkhazians and the Ossetians from Georgian invasion. Equally dangerous is the standoff between Armenia and Azerbaijan over the Armenian-populated Nagorno-Karabakh enclave. Azerbaijani president Ilham Aliyev has repeatedly threatened war to bring Nagorno-Karabakh under his control. His efforts have been resisted by Armenia, which sustains the current autonomous existence of Nagorno-Karabakh economically and militarily. Should oil-rich Azerbaijan decide to invade Nogorno-Karabakh, the resulting war with Armenia could involve some neighboring states and disrupt the flow of oil from the region.

A case of low-intensity ethno-tribal conflict that has shown signs of escalation is Afghanistan. Despite U.S.-led efforts to unify and secure the country under President Hamid Karzai's regime, Afghanistan's ethno-tribal social structure remains unstable in the context of rivalries among the Tajik, Uzbek, Pashtun, and Hazara minorities and a growing insurgency by Islamist Taliban forces. Since September 11, 2001, the protracted efforts of U.S. and NATO forces, backed by substantial economic aid, have failed to pacify the country, particularly the provinces bordering Pakistan. In contrast to the weak Afghan regime is neighboring China with a powerful autocratic government that has effectively suppressed separatism in Tibet, Inner Mongolia, and Xing Jiang province. Among these, the Uygur Muslims of Xing Jiang or East Turkestan have engaged in low-intensity conflict with the Chinese authorities, who rule the province with a heavy hand.

Two North African ethno-tribal low-intensity conflicts are the Polisario Front's struggle against Morocco's annexation of the Western Sahara and the demands of the Berber minorities in the North African Arab countries for cultural autonomy. Although the Polisario movement has been effectively neutralized by the Moroccan military, the Berber minority's quest for autonomy remains a potential trigger of interactive violence, particularly in Algeria, where a repressive military-backed regime holds sway. An even greater risk of ethno-tribal violence is found in Nigeria—one of Africa's largest and most powerful states. In 2005–2006, low-intensity inter-tribal fighting and anti-regime terrorism disrupted Nigeria's oil production, pushing up oil prices in a tight world market. Should President Olusegun Obasanjo's federal government fail to contain the incipient turmoil, a reversion to the inter-tribal/sectarian wars of the past cannot be ruled out—a truly devastating outcome for Nigeria's ethno-religious social fabric, oil industry, and the very viability of the state. Not to be forgotten is the Lord's Resistance Army, formed in 1987 to liberate Uganda's Acholi tribe, which has committed mass atrocities for over two decades, often using children as soldiers. Led by Joseph Kony, a self-proclaimed prophet, the genocidal capabilities of this terrorist group have been weakened but not eliminated by the joint military forces of Congo and Uganda.

Ideological Violence

Several of the ten destabilizing global trends point to growing bifurcation between rich and poor both among and within countries. Exponential population growth in the less developed countries that are also beset by government corruption, oligarchic misrule, and mass unemployment, could hasten the rise of class-based ideological movements challenging state power. Under such circumstances, leftist groups are the most likely sources of terrorism, although the possibility of right-wing extremism cannot be discounted.

A key question is whether the leftist ideological groups that emerge will be similar to those of the twentieth-century, such as the Italian Red Brigades, the German Baader-Meinhof/Red Army Faction, the Japanese Red Army, and Peru's Sendero Luminoso. In general, economic deprivation and mass poverty are a constant source of class polarization and violence. However, in rapidly developing countries, class polarization intensifies when the benefits of new wealth bring about a sharp maldistribution of income between the new rich and the rest of society. In such cases, the newly affluent class, usually connected to the political elite, engages in public displays of conspicuous consumption while the bulk of the lower classes receives only incremental benefits from the trickling down of the country's growing wealth. This situation, described by Ted Robert Gurr as one of "relative deprivation," is seen as a potent trigger of leftist or rightist violence.[1] When the heightened aspirations of the masses for dramatic betterment are thwarted, the widening economic gap could readily translate into political unrest and anti-state violence. The obvious remedy to curb class-based violence is the material improvement of socioeconomic conditions that many governments are unable or unwilling to carry out due to lack of strategic foresight, selfish greed, political ignorance, and corruption. The destabilizing impact of relative deprivation is expected to become more acute in the context of globalization, where even well-meaning governments may be unable to take effective remedial action to reverse the destabilizing consequences of gross inequalities.

Among the foremost examples of relative deprivation is China, where unbalanced growth has opened up great class cleavages in the world's most populous country. Despite China's official adherence to communist ideology, it is hardly a classless society. Great inequalities between the wealthy coastal regions and the poorer interior provinces have introduced enormous strains in the body politic, exacerbated by official corruption, difficulties of central governance over a very large and populous country, and the rampant quest for material excess by the new rich working in tandem with members of the ruling elite. It is no accident that the regime has had to forcefully suppress a succession of peasant protests, demonstrations, and outright resistance, which are likely to grow in size and frequency in the near-term future. In February 2006, the Chinese government acknowledged the seriousness of the looming class conflict and promised to take measures to improve the impoverished condition of the peasantry.

A situation similar to China exists in India—Asia's second emerging giant. The exponential growth of India's economic power, second only to China's, has been based on developing advanced technology industries such as computers, electronics, and services. This strategy has left behind most of the urban and rural poor belonging to the untouchables and other lower castes. Yet, in contrast to the past, these lowly classes are in the midst of a surge of expectations that could generate unrest if left unfulfilled. The Naxalites are a leftist revolutionary movement that has challenged the Indian state for over fifty years. Emerging as a faction of the communist party of Indian in the 1960s, the ideology of Naxalism is an Indian version of Mao Zedong's revolutionary thought that advocates the mobilization of peasants and lower classes to overthrow the government. Centered in Chhattisgarh province, the Naxalite guerrillas include up to 10,000 fighters who, in 2005 alone, killed over 600 people and displaced many more. Unless the government addresses the economic needs of these impoverished tribal people, Naxalite violence is likely to spread throughout India's mineral-rich tribal belt from West Bengal in the north to Karnataka in the South.

A prime factor causing relative deprivation in over a dozen countries is maldistribution of proceeds from their oil and gas resources. In view of the world's rapidly growing energy demands, there has been a massive infusion of wealth into the treasuries of oil and gas producing countries, resulting in their accelerated development and modernization. However, in many cases, energy-derived wealth has been a mixed blessing because government mismanagement and corruption promote sharp inequalities in income distribution, growing social injustice, and manifestations of opulence that go against the grain of traditional cultures. Oil-induced relative deprivation can become a prelude to class-based terrorism and insurgencies unless the ruling elites institute socioeconomic policies and mechanisms to share their wealth with the deprived sectors of society. Although the Arab monarchies of the Persian Gulf—Kuwait, Oman, Bahrain, Qatar, United Arab Emirates, and Saudi Arabia—have instituted "cradle-to-grave" policies of development, much remains to be done in the less-developed African oil-producing countries such as Nigeria, Gabon, Chad, Sudan, Angola, Cameroon, and the Congo, which already face domestic instability. A parallel situation exists in four former Soviet republics with energy resources—Azerbaijan, Uzbekistan, Turkmenistan, and Kazakhstan—where autocratic rule and relative deprivation are a ready-made formula for instability as shown by repeated public protests, which have been put down by force. Even the stridently Islamist regime of Iranian president Mahmoud Ahmadinejad is expected to be vulnerable to growing socioeconomic disparities at a time of major increases in income derived from oil and gas production. It would be instructive for the current Iranian leadership to remember that it was the combined effect of autocratic misrule, corruption, and relative deprivation that brought down the shah's monarchical regime in 1978–1979. In this context, the attempts of Venezuelan president Hugo Chavez to redistribute oil-derived income may ameliorate class cleavages in South America's largest oil-producing country.

While there is a high probability that conditions of economic deprivation would trigger anti-state violence, it is difficult to predict the ideological coloration of such insurgencies. In keeping with past patterns, some future insurgencies in Latin America and Asia are likely to adopt leftist ideologies, such as Maoist and Castroist variants of communism. In the Himalayan country of Nepal, King Gyanendra's autocracy has faced the growing threat of a Maoist insurgency—a pattern that could be adopted by the incubating rebellions in Myanmar and Thailand. However, in a historic reversal of ideological polarities, certain situations of relative deprivation might well produce anti-state violence from rightist groups with fascist or neo-Nazi doctrines.

Ironically, the critical triggers that could cause the emergence of right-wing manifestations of violence reside in Europe's democratic and quasi-democratic countries and in one of the world's largest democracies—the United States. The confluence of cultural and economic factors driven by the multifaceted forces of globalization are likely to provide the impetus for the reemergence of right-wing nationalism, particularly in Germany, Italy, France, Spain, Russia, and in the former communist states of Eastern Europe. Given the prevailing economic trends, these countries may be forced to curtail their welfare-state policies, which would alienate the lower and lower-middle classes already competing for jobs with a growing number of Middle Eastern, African, and Asian immigrants. This economic crisis is likely be exacerbated by the cultural clash between the indigenous Europeans and the newcomers whose religious, ethnic, or racial identities are found incongruent with Western cultural norms and practices. The violent protests against the Danish cartoons of the Prophet Muhammad, the riots of Muslim youth in France, and the deadly attacks against trains in Madrid and subways and buses in London might produce a right-wing backlash from European whites, whose feelings of economic deprivation are reinforced by the perceived threat to their national-cultural identity and sense of security and superiority. The confluence of these factors could well produce an explosive mix that the existing democratic governments may not be able to manage. In such a negative scenario, one might expect a proliferation of Europe's right-wing groups, expansion of their constituencies, and increased violence against immigrants as well as the authorities.

The European pattern of right-wing resurgence could be paralleled in the United States with some modifications. Because most legal and illegal immigrants to the United States are Latin American Christians, the opposition against them is likely to take an ethno-racial coloration that would lack the anti-Muslim fervor of European right-wing extremists. True to tradition, American right-wing extremism is likely to be dominated by white supremacists mostly from economically marginalized small towns with few venues of upward mobility except military service. Driven by hatred toward blacks, Jews, immigrants, and the federal government, the white supremacists are likely to meld with the Christian identity groups, as in the past, and become part of the nebulous militia or patriot movement. Given the trend toward outsourcing of jobs and the pressure of competition with cheap immigrant labor, the right-wing constituency can be expected to increase in numbers in the foreseeable future. An additional factor that could contribute to the ranks of the militia/patriot movement is the huge phalanx of U.S. soldiers returning to civilian life should the wars in Iraq and Afghanistan wind down. Unless the U.S. government makes a concerted effort to create employment for these veterans, some are likely to be drawn to right-wing extremist causes and groups, fueling their potential to engage in political violence.

Another potential source of domestic unrest is the growing urban ghettos in the United States. The dramatic increase of immigrant populations during the last two decades, combined with existing problems of racial discrimination, class segregation, and unequal access to basic services, have placed heavy economic and social burdens on urban governments, particularly in education, housing, health, and employment. Given the declining capabilities of the educational system to socialize the newcomers into America's democratic culture, there would be islands of ethnic, sectarian, or cultural groups for whom the legitimacy of the country's political and legal framework is alien or even unacceptable.

Despite the great flexibility of America's multicultural system to accommodate diversity, there is a clear risk of alienation leading to inter-group or anti-state violence particularly in times of economic decline. Examples of urban inter-ethnic violence include fighting among rival street gangs and between Hispanic, African American, and white inmates in the prisons of Southern California and other locations. Aside from inter-group violence, the crowded ghettos contain many of America's poor people, estimated at thirty million—about ten percent of the total U.S. population. Living in poverty in the midst of super-affluent city skyscrapers, hotels, and luxury apartments, the urban poor exist in a state of extreme relative deprivation that could engender not only criminal behavior but periodic outbreaks of mass rioting, looting, and arson. Outbreaks of urban violence reminiscent of the rioting of the 1960s and 1990s cannot be discounted, given the complex interaction of socioeconomic forces in the inner cities and their wealthy periphery. There is a high risk that incidents of urban violence, such as the 1992 Los Angeles riots, or natural disasters like New Orleans just after hurricane Katrina, could evolve into situations of mass anarchy that defy the control capabilities of local police agencies necessitating intervention by national guard units and even the federal government.

Religious Violence

Political violence motivated and sanctioned by religious belief is likely to remain one of the most common and lethal types of inter-group and anti-state conflict in the foreseeable future. The root causes of this phenomenon appear to reside in the human tendency to turn to religion when faced with crisis situations that threaten the physical, cultural, psychological, and/or economic security of the individual or collectivity. The contemporary widespread upsurge in political religiosity appears to be a natural development after the mass human sufferings of the nineteenth and twentieth centuries, brought on by the clash of imperialisms and ideologies in two world wars, the Cold War, and the many bloody conflicts in between.

This return to religion commonly takes the form of revivalism, a return to puritanical roots of faith that usually translates into a salvational movement seeking to impose its truths on the larger social fabric—a quest ultimately requiring control of the levers of state power. The puritanical impulse has the potential to politicize religion to become the means for the leading exponents of the revivalist movement to take over the political sphere.

Virtually all the major religions experienced the revivalist impulse during the twentieth century, in varying degrees. In the 1960s, Liberation Theology emerged among Latin American Catholics as a leftist revivalist movement against economic inequality and repressive regimes. In the United States, Christian revivalists became a powerful right-wing force within the Republican Party in the 1980s and the Jewish messianist/settler movement succeeded in having a formative influence in the rightward trend in Israeli politics. In India, Hinduism experienced a powerful political resurgence directed against Muslims, Christians, Sikhs, and other religious minorities, and helped the Baharatiya Janata Party (BJP) to come to power. Yet only Islam among the great religions underwent a deep and comprehensive revivalist transformation resulting in significant politicization and radicalization in response to multifaceted crises that the Muslim people had experienced. By all indications, these crisis factors continue to sustain the twin dynamics of Islamic revivalism—politicization and radicalization. The first, the politicization of Islam, involves transforming Islam into a political ideology (political Islamism) to justify efforts to take power in Muslim countries. When political Islamism is radicalized, jihadists use it to justify violence against the West and its Muslim allies.

The twin trends of Islamic politicization and radicalization have acquired new momentum since the end of the Cold War. As the international system was reconfigured after the Soviet demise, the century-long crisis conditions besetting the Muslim world intensified, at least in the perception of many Muslims. These crisis conditions included economic underdevelopment, social injustice, repressive governments, Western domination, a sense of insecurity, and feelings of victimhood. These perceptions and feelings were further deepened by the actions of the United States and its allies after September 11, 2001—actions that were ostensibly directed at al-Qaida jihadists, but resulted in more profound alienation among the Muslim mainstream which pushed more Muslims toward political Islamism and radicalization. Instead of curbing these powerful trends toward extremism, the U.S.-led "war on terrorism" contributed to further radicalization of the Islamic ethos. The ill-conceived invasion of Iraq was viewed by the world's Muslims as an ambitious strategic scheme to establish military bases at the heart of the Arab/Islamic world in order to project U.S. hegemonic power over the region and its energy resources. The use of military power and declarations to force Iraq and the neighboring autocratic states to conform to U.S. policies backfired. Instead, the overthrow of Saddam Hussein's regime empowered the Shiite Islamists in Iraq and throughout the region, strengthened Iran's ideological and political influence, and angered Sunni majorities in the other Arab countries and the larger Muslim ummah. In addition to the Iraqi imbroglio, Israel's continued expansion of settlements in the West Bank and use of massive force against Palestinian provocations, resulting in the death of many civilians, has fuelled widespread anger in the Muslim world and provided ready reference for the violent rhetoric of jihadist terrorism.

The confluence of these critical factors clearly points to continuing Islamist violence against the United States and its Western and Muslim allies from al-Qaida and its affiliates within and outside the Muslim world. Although the full blowback from the 2003 Iraq war is too early to assess, there can be no doubt that it has greatly contributed to increases in the size, training, and commitment of Sunni jihadists, both within and outside al-Qaida's umbrella. After their Iraqi exploits, these new jihadists may well return to undermine the regimes of their home countries or to engage in terrorism against the West, in keeping with the precedent established after their role in the 1980s insurgency in Afghanistan. However, "the law of unintended consequences" could open up new possibilities with unwelcome results for the West and allied Muslim regimes. The Bush administration's rhetorical promotion of "democracy," accompanied by its half-hearted support for elections, has had the effect of discrediting and destabilizing a number of Arab autocratic regimes, some with close ties to the United States. In view of the growing strength of political Islamist movements, the availability of the electoral option provides a peaceful venue for the establishment of Islamist theocratic regimes, without resort to the revolutionary terrorism of al-Qaida and similar jihadist groups. Why shed blood when political Islamists, such as the Muslim Brotherhood, control growing grassroots constituencies that are ready and capable to vote Islamist regimes into power? In January 2006, the spectacular victory of Hamas over the secular al-Fatah in Palestine could presage the future. Similarly, the impressive showing of the Muslim Brotherhood's candidates in Egypt's 2005 elections, despite the government's coercive constraints, pointed to the possibility of their victory in a fair election. Should Islamists be permitted to prevail through electoral means, there is likely to be a string of Islamist theocracies which would not automatically adhere to U.S. / Western policy dictates, and might refuse to allow further democratic elections that could threaten their hold on power. Should Sunni Muslim governments refuse to provide electoral opportunities for the political Islamists' quest for power, and continue to suppress them, these regimes risk the rise of anti-state terrorism from the political Islamists who will move toward more radical expressions of their Salafi ideology by undertaking jihadism against their governments and the Western powers supporting them.

Sunni political Islamist movements aspiring for power against secular regimes are usually affiliated with the Muslim Brotherhood and share its ideology and agenda to establish an Islamic order. In about a dozen countries, it is likely that the growing grassroots support of Islamist movements represents an existential challenge to secular autocratic regimes beset by declining legitimacies. In open and fair electoral contests the Islamist groups could either win majorities or constitute large minority blocs opposing the authorities. Among the countries potentially facing Islamists challenges in the next decade are Egypt, Syria, Morocco, Tunisia, Pakistan, Algeria, Jordan, Libya, Bangladesh, Indonesia, Somalia, and some Central Asian and Persian Gulf states. Should the authorities continue to deny electoral participation to the Islamist groups or refuse to cede power after Islamist victories, the outbreak of violence will be virtually inevitable. The ominous precedent is the ten-year Algerian Islamist insurgency triggered by the regime's cancellation of phase two of the 1992 elections after the victory of the National Salvation Front (FIS) in phase one. In such insurgencies, home-based Islamists fighting their governments are likely to be joined by foreign jihadists supported by al-Qaida or its ideological kinsfolk representing the global jihadist/salafi confraternity. Unlike Algeria in 1992, it would be difficult to contain these conflicts because they are likely to involve external jihadists as in the Sunni insurgency after the 2003 U.S.-led invasion of Iraq. In the event that political Islamists come to power, there could be a decline in jihadist violence within individual states and, possibly, against the West.

Multicausal Violence

The three-fold classification of anti-state terrorism—ethnic, ideological, and religious—should not obscure the causal convergence between these categories. The reason for ethnic violence against the state may be that the ethnic group is politically suppressed as well as impoverished. Where class divisions based on incomes are cross-cutting, vertical ethnic or sectarian divisions may remain relatively stable. In other words, the likelihood of violence decreases when class divisions are present more or less equally among all ethnic groups in a multiethnic society. On the other hand, should class divisions reinforce ethno-sectarian divisions and one group become disproportionately richer than the others, the situation might produce a violent outcome driven by ethnic as well as class differences. Examples of mutually reinforcing ethnic and class cleavages that generate opposition to the richer ruling ethnic group are the conflict over Northern Ireland and the struggles between the poor indigenous people of Latin America and governments dominated by rich white Europeans and mestizos.

Other situations of anti-state violence could be driven by class differences that assume religious coloration. The single most powerful factor fueling Islamist violence against authoritarian regimes is the absence of social justice. Thus, the concentration of wealth in the hands of ruling elites and their affiliates could trigger grassroots violence led by Islamist groups calling for regime change in the name of socioeconomic justice. The intensifying economic deprivation, the growing gap between rich and poor, and the geometric increase in the poorer segments of the population are potent motivations to embrace political Islamism and the major catalysts for recruitment of future jihadists.

Inter-Sectarian Violence

Under the general rubric of religious violence, attention should be given to violence among opposing sects—a phenomenon that has assumed special significance in recent years. This category of interactive terrorism includes violence between two different sects within a single religious tradition, or between two different religious traditions, particularly in countries where one sect controls the levers of governance. In recent years, over a half-dozen countries have experienced incidents of sectarian violence.

Iraq. Since the U.S. invasion of Iraq and the overthrow of Saddam Hussein's Baath regime, there has been escalating interactive terrorism between militant elements of both Sunni and Shiite sects. Saddam's overthrow replaced the dominant Sunni Arab minority (18 percent) with a U.S.-backed regime consisting primarily of Shiite Arabs (60 percent) and Kurds (18 percent). Having lost power to their former Shiite and Kurdish subjects, the Sunni Arabs mounted a massive insurrection against the new Shiite-led regime and the U.S.-led coalition forces. In 2005–2006, the Shiite-Sunni struggle became a civil war with the participation of non-Iraqi jihadists from al-Qaida's affiliates. The destruction of the al-Askariyah Mosque of Samarra in February 2006, one of the holiest Shiite shrines, triggered wholesale attacks on Sunni mosques and killings by Shiite militias. Not only did this protracted conflict in Iraq weaken the U.S. position in the Middle East, but also threatened to bring about a full-scale Sunni-Shiite war that could draw in the neighboring states, with Iran in support of the Shiites versus Jordan, Syria, Egypt, and Saudi Arabia coming to the aid of the Sunnis.

Pakistan. Interactive terrorism between the dominant Sunni majority (80 percent) and the Shiite minority (20 percent) has persisted for over two decades. The root cause of the conflict is the progressive radicalization of Islamist ideology as a consequence of Pakistan's sponsorship of the anticommunist Afghan mujahidin (1980–1989) and the use of Sunni Islamist discourse as a legitimizing device by successive Pakistani governments. The resulting rise of militant Islamist political parties and clandestine terrorist groups has polarized the sectarian divide leading to cycles of uncontrolled mutual terror. Extremist Sunni vigilante groups have repeatedly targeted Shiite mosques and individuals whom they regard as infidels and rejectionists of true Islam. These attacks and killings have evoked Shiite violence against Sunnis albeit on a much lesser scale. While the Pakistani authorities under President Musharraf have sought to curb Sunni extremism, the Shiites remain in a highly vulnerable position in a milieu where the legitimacy of their faith is put under question by the large Sunni extremist constituency, which has come to share al-Qaida's rejectionist position toward the Shiite Muslims. Given the ongoing spread of Sunni militancy at the grassroots and among the tribal peoples of the Northeast Frontier, both the Shiite minority and the regime itself face an uncertain future.

India. Since its founding in 1947, India's secular government has faced multiple episodes of intersectarian strife, mostly involving the Hindu, Sikh, Muslim, and Christian communities. The rise of Hindu extremism in recent decades has led to attacks against India's small Christian population as well as its huge Muslim minority, the largest in the world. Hindu-Muslim clashes hark back to the bloody population transfers of the 1940s between India and Pakistan. There was a revival of sectarian violence after the 1992 destruction of the Ayodha Mosque by extremist Hindus. Over the next decade, Lashkar-e-Taiba and eight other jihadist groups supported by Pakistan attacked Indian military and civilian targets in and outside Kashmir, killing hundreds of people. In December 2001 the attack on the Indian parliament and low-intensity fighting in Kashmir threatened the outbreak of full-scale war that prompted a U.S. diplomatic initiative to bring the two sides to the negotiating table. Despite the parallel resurgence of both Hindu and Islamist extremism, and Pakistan's sponsorship of Islamist terrorism, the Indian government has largely succeeded in containing Hindu-Muslim sectarian violence in the context of its secularist federal system. However, periodic bombings attributed to Lashkar-e-Taiba targeting Indian cities and Hindu holy shrines continue to claim many lives.

Lebanon/Syria. Since the 2003 U.S. war in Iraq, there has been a heightened risk of sectarian violence both in Lebanon and Syria. Lebanon's fine-tuned consociational system, where stability is maintained by a delicate balance among seven major Christian and Muslim sects was destabilized as the United States and France pressed for the withdrawal of Syrian forces that had arrived in 1976 to pacify the country. Syrian resistance to withdrawal polarized Lebanon's political life, leading to the assassination of former prime minister Rafik Hariri in February 2005—an act blamed on Syria by UN investigators. While denying complicity in Hariri's killing, Syrian president Bashar al-Asad quickly withdrew his forces, leaving behind a dangerous power vacuum in which Lebanon's Maronite Christian president and the Shiite Hizbullah and Amal parties remained allied to Syria and Iran. The subsequent assassination of several anti-Syrian public figures and U.S. threats to target Hizbullah and the Syrian regime revived long dormant sectarian enmities and fears of a new civil war. These sectarian conflicts were exacerbated after Israel's July 2006 attack on Lebanon in an unsuccessful bid to neutralize Hizbullah's power.

More ominous is the prospect of sectarian conflict in Syria. Since 2003, Syria's government has been progressively weakened by the U.S. intervention in neighboring Iraq and by U.S. efforts to undermine the secular regime. Despite its opposition to Saddam's Baath party and cooperation with the U.S. war against al-Qaida, Syria was severely criticized by the Bush administration even before Hariri's murder because of its support for Palestinian militants and its failure to stop the flow of jihadists across its long border with Iraq. Syria's Baath regime is led by the Alawite minority (about 15 percent), a small sect affiliated with Shiism, that is rejected by extremist Sunni Islamists who fought and lost a six-year bloody insurgency in 1977–1982. U.S. pressure to "democratize" or otherwise undermine the Syrian regime could backfire should a new Islamist insurgency backed by the Sunni majority assume power in Damascus, in another demonstration of the law of unintended consequences paralleling the rise of Hamas in Palestine. The emergence of a Sunni Islamist regime in Damascus could have serious consequences for American interests in the Middle East by having a destabilizing impact on Lebanon, Iraq, Egypt, and the Israeli-Palestinian imbroglio.

Shiite versus Sunni in the Gulf Region. The empowerment of the Iraqi Shiites after Saddam's overthrow, combined with the growing geopolitical influence of Iran's Shiite theocracy within and beyond Iraq, have generated serious concerns among many Sunni Muslims and governments. It is feared that the confrontational assertiveness of President Ahmadinejad, backed by Iran's large energy resources and quest for nuclear power, could radicalize the Shiite minorities in the Sunni Arab monarchies of the Persian Gulf and lead to sectarian conflicts. However, given their common interests in stable oil markets, neither Iran nor the pro-U.S. Arab monarchies seem prepared for a return to the violent confrontations of the 1980s and the Shiite terrorism sponsored by Ayatollah Khomeini's revolutionary regime. To be sure, in recent decades, the Shiites in the Arab states of the Persian Gulf have made substantial progress in the political and economic spheres and have no incentive for engaging in conflict, unless the whole region is thrown into a war between Iran and the United States.

Nigeria. A major oil exporter to the United States, Nigeria has experienced repeated ethnic and sectarian violence since independence in 1960. The most lethal divide is between the tribes of the Muslim North and the Christians and other tribes of the South, where the oil wealth is concentrated. The human losses in the tribal/sectarian violence before and after the 1969 Biafra war of secession reached genocidal proportions. After two decades of quiescence under President Obasanjo, the factional conflicts of yesteryear reemerged in the 2000s, driven by situations of extreme economic deprivation in a large and socially diverse country. In recent years, the Ijaw People's Movement for the Emancipation of the Niger Delta and other armed ethnic militias have fought for a fairer distribution of oil income in one of Nigeria's poorest regions. In 2006, attacks on Royal Dutch Shell oil platforms and on foreign contractors reduced oil production by 20 percent causing the loss of large revenues for a poor country. It is feared that such incidents of ethnic versus state violence could expand to other regions and serve as the impetus to another country-wide armed struggle between the major sects and tribes.

Indonesia. Since the economic downturn of 1997, Indonesia has been roiled by the overthrow of President Suharto's military regime and the rise of Islamist groups, some of which share al-Qaida's jihadist ideology and tactics. The largest of these radical Islamist groups is al-Jamaa al-Islamiya, which has been blamed for hotel bombings in Bali (2002, 2005) and Jakarta (2004) because of its vehement opposition to the Western lifestyles and tourism that these places foster. Also, the trend toward militancy has had a negative impact on the lives of Indonesian non-Muslim minorities, i.e., Christians, Chinese, Buddhists, and others. Rioting, mob attacks, and killings in the late 1990s forced many Chinese to flee the country. In the 2000s, armed Islamist bands have repeatedly targeted the Christian minority, causing sectarian strife, particularly in the country's remote islands. The government's failure or unwillingness to protect the minorities testifies to the growing political strength of militant Islamism in Indonesia and its potential to fuel sectarian and anti-Western terrorism.

Emerging Threats and Modalities of Terror

The world's political landscape is in constant flux brought on by the clash of old and new social forces, national interests and transnational movements. Thus, analysts and students of political violence need to engage in systematic scanning of the global arena in order to identify emerging causal factors that could produce violent outcomes, and the specific agents and modalities of such behavior. Among the new groups challenging state authority are anarchists, ecoterrorists, narcoterrorists, cyberterrorists, and international criminal gangs.

Anarchists

Anarchism, as a revolutionary ideology and movement, reached its apogee in the nineteenth century, leaving behind a bloody path of terror against leaders and governments. Anarchist violence reappeared in the 1960s as a driving force in various student protest movements in the United States, France, West Germany, and other countries. At the fringes of the student movements were extremists employing terrorist tactics against the state and society. While these protest movements soon fizzled out, they left behind a legacy of challenging state authority that devolved into leftist terrorism in Europe, with groups such as the Baader-Meinhof/Red Army Faction in West Germany and the Red Brigades in Italy. There was a parallel development in the United States as the student movement disappeared after the cancellation of the draft and the end of the Vietnam War. Yet the anarchist legacy of the 1960s anti-war movement persisted in quietist form and reemerged in the 1990s as a mostly peaceful challenge to globalization.

There are several types of anarchists—leftist, rightist, violent, and pacifist. Most anarchists are opposed to state power, hierarchy, and private property. American anarchist groups are mostly pacifist, oppose materialism and multinational corporations, and live together in self-governing communes away from urban areas. Although leftist in ideology, most anarchists reject Marxism. Other anarchist groups are activists in confronting the state and its symbols of authority in demonstrations and even through acts of violence. In the 1990s, the Clinton administration's advocacy of economic globalization galvanized the anarchist community as it joined the mass demonstrations in the December 1999 "Battle of Seattle." These protests caused the cancellation of the WTO meetings as well as some damage to businesses and property. Similar mass protests in Europe, Asia, and Latin America against globalization have brought together a multinational confraternity of anarchists that could evolve into a transnational anarchist movement, with some fringe groups advocating rioting and violent tactics.

A more likely source of violence is rightist anarchism in the United States and Europe. The rightist anarchists share the strongly anti-state stance of the leftist and mainstream anarchists, as well as their passionate opposition to globalization. Yet the rightist opposition to state power and globalization extends to the rejection of all foreign influences and preservation of white supremacy. Right-wing U.S. anarchists such as the skinheads, KKK, Aryan Nations, and the German neo-Nazis do not share the humanism and pacifism of left-wing anarchists, which makes their resort to violence more probable in the next decades.

Ecoterrorism

Ecoterrorism represents the extremist fringe of the environmental movement. Its roots go back to the British Earth First movement and its activist offshoot—the Earth Liberation Front (ELF), which in 1997 began to operate in the United States in tandem with the Animal Liberation Front (ALF). The ideology of these allied groups is to attack the "earth's enemies," consisting of the wealthy capitalists, and lumber and construction companies responsible for unrestrained urban expansion and killing animals for profit and in laboratory testing. The ELF/ALF partnership claims a passionate commitment to "nonviolent destruction," i.e., taking care that humans are not harmed in the course of their acts of violence by sabotage and arson. The most notable acts of ELF/ALF terrorism include arson attacks on a ranger fire station (1996) and horse corral (1997) in Oregon, a ski resort in Vail, Colorado (1998), a laboratory at Michigan State University (1999), a lumber company office in Monmouth, Oregon (1999), expensive homes being built in Long Island, New York (2001) and San Diego (2003), and damaging and torching of SUVs at a Southern California car dealership (2004). The FBI's estimates of total damages caused by ELF/ALF exceed $100 million. Ecoterrorists consist of small underground cells, without centralized leadership or organization, making it difficult for police or the FBI to detect and detain their members.

Narcoterrorism

Violence associated with the production, export, and sales of illegal drugs and narcotics, such as marijuana, cocaine, and heroin, has become pervasive in the exporting, trafficking, and consuming countries. In recent decades, the growing demand for illegal drugs in the United States, Europe, and other rich countries prompted the expansion of cultivation, production, and exportation of drugs in Afghanistan, Myanmar, Turkey, Peru, Mexico, Colombia, Guatemala, Jamaica, and other Asian and Latin American countries. These multi-billion-dollar enterprises have been controlled and operated by powerful drug cartels, drug barons, and warlords, whose capabilities for violence and financial power transcend national boundaries. In some Latin American countries like Peru and Colombia, the drug cartels have worked in tandem with both rightist and leftist terrorist groups to weaken or subvert the authorities and even to control the levers of state power in order to facilitate narcotics operations. Although U.S.-sponsored programs in the 1990s did succeed in weakening the Medellín and Cali drug cartels in Colombia, the drug trade has continued unabated, along with its violent and destabilizing impact on both the exporting and consuming countries. Notably, much of the cocaine trade in Colombia is controlled by right-wing paramilitary forces, with ties to the government, and the leftist Revolutionary Armed Forces of Colombia (FARC). Usually, narcoterrorism flourishes in poor countries where there is a power vacuum because of the weakness of state authority. Given present conditions and trends, narcoterrorism is certain to become a growing threat at the national and global levels.

Criminal Gangs

The meltdown of central authority in the 1990s created a power vacuum in the former Soviet republics and many Third World countries. The resulting environment of lawlessness has been a breeding ground for a plethora of transnational criminal gangs which operate regionally and globally in defiance of national governments and the international system. Transnational drug cartels are but one example of such activity that target police and government officials and terrorize thousands of common folk. In Mexico alone, over 1,500 people were murdered in 2005 by drug trafficking cartels. Other criminal gangs specialize in illegal immigration across the seas and national borders, money laundering, piracy on the high seas, transfers of weapons and technology, slavery, or some combination of these. The abduction and trafficking of women and children has been a growth industry that governments have been unable or unwilling to dismantle. The trafficking of women for prostitution and servitude has flourished in Eastern Europe, Asia, and the Middle East. Aside from conventional slavery, thousands of children have been abducted and trained as terrorists or soldiers by the Tamil Tigers in Sri Lanka and the Lord's Resistance Army in Uganda.

Biological and Chemical Terrorism

The use of biological, chemical, and nuclear weapons by subnational and transnational terrorists as well as by state authorities represents an existential threat to all humanity. These means of killing are classified as weapons of mass destruction (WMD) because of their potential to cause mass killing, maiming, and environmental destruction. Chemical and biological toxins have been used periodically in conventional warfare since the Peloponnesian War (425 B.C.). In World War I, both sides used tear gas, chlorine gas, anthrax, phosgene, and chloropicrin. In the interwar years, biological and chemical weapons became a means of imperial conquest, used by Spain against the Riff rebels (1922), Italy in Ethiopia (1936), and Japan in China (1940). During the Cold War, some of these agents were employed in three self-defeating military campaigns by Egypt in Yemen (1963–1967), the United States in Vietnam (1965–1975), and the Soviet Union in Afghanistan (1980–1989). Belated attempts by the United States under President Nixon to outlaw the manufacture and use of biological and chemical weapons had limited success because a growing number of smaller powers began to develop these weapons as a substitute to nuclear arms to deter more powerful antagonists. Among these states was Iraq, which developed an offensive biological and chemical capability and employed it against Iran (1980–1988) and in the Anfal campaigns against the Kurds culminating in the massacre of Halabja (1988).

Fortunately for humanity, the employment of biological and chemical weapons in mass killing by governments has not been matched by anti-state or transnational terrorist groups. Among the possible reasons are the difficulty of acquiring such weapons from the states which possess them, groups' lack of scientific expertise and materials to build them on their own, and the tactical problems involved in the delivery of such weapons on specific enemy targets without causing collateral damage extending to friendly populations near the target regions. The major exceptions were the anthrax attacks in September and October 2001 in the United States by perpetrators whose identities remain unknown, despite extensive investigation. Anthrax is a highly lethal bacterium that has great potential as a bioterrorism agent. On September 18 and October 9, 2001, letters containing anthrax powder were sent from Princeton, New Jersey, to NBC, ABC, American Media International, and to Senators Tom Daschle and Patrick Leahy with threatening notes that attempted to scapegoat al-Qaida. Of the eighteen confirmed cases of anthrax poisoning, five died, setting off a mass scare from New Jersey to Florida and an extensive investigation that failed to establish authorship or any ties to al-Qaida. The anthrax scare and a wave of sniper attacks carried out by a Gulf War veteran and his young protégé in October 2002 contributed to the climate of fear, which was manipulated by the Bush administration in the run-up to war in March 2003.

Nuclear Terrorism

The possession of nuclear weapons by subnational terrorists, "rogue" states fearing existential threats, or countries with psychologically unstable leaders constitutes the greatest potential threat to life on this planet. Despite the nonproliferation accords to limit the acquisition or development of nuclear arms and delivery systems, a growing number of states are bound to join the nuclear club in the next few decades.

Even if "rogue" states with authoritarian regimes succeed in acquiring nuclear capability, they can be deterred from using such weapons because this would ensure their own destruction, assuming that their leaders are sane and able to clearly perceive their self-interests. A far greater danger is the possession of nuclear materials by subnational or transnational terrorist groups that may not be easily deterred by conventional means because of the nihilistic or apocalyptic nature of their ideologies or the absence of a return address—a well-defined territorial base and clearly identifiable leadership apparatus that can be attacked and destroyed without causing massive collateral damage.

The threat potential of nuclear terrorists depends on the kinds of nuclear materials available to them and their own in-house technological capabilities to configure and deploy a nuclear weapon against an enemy target. Given the highly technical nature of nuclear materials, potential terrorist groups would need a level of scientific expertise that would be difficult but not impossible to acquire. There are two well-documented cases of terrorist organizations that have made concerted efforts to possess nuclear capability—al-Qaida and Aum Shinrikyo of Japan. In the early 1990s, Aum Shinrikyo developed a two-pronged outreach to Russia to acquire nuclear material and scientific expertise by offering huge monetary incentives along with recruiting converts to its apocalyptic religious cause. It was Aum's failure to get Russian nuclear materials and its inability to develop an in-house nuclear capability that prompted Asahara to fall back on his second preference—the use of sarin gas in 1995 to attack the Tokyo subway system. Similarly, documents captured in Afghanistan after the Taliban's overthrow revealed al-Qaida's plans to develop nuclear capabilities. Notably, both Aum Shinrikyo and Islamist extremist groups sharing al-Qaida's ideology had succeeded in attracting some scientific talent to their ranks—a worrisome prospect that negates the assumption that highly educated, middle/upper middle-class scientists and engineers are immune to the calls of cultic or religious extremism.

Nuclear terrorism could involve two modalities—radioactive material to make a "dirty bomb" by embedding it into a shell of conventional explosives or an improvised or government-manufactured nuclear bomb. Placing radioactive materials in crowded areas could expose hundreds of people to potentially lethal radiation. Exploding a dirty bomb would spread radiation to a larger area and cause greater contamination if the source of radiation is powerful. Although these methods can be expected to cause great public fear and panic, their lethal impact is likely to be limited to a small number of people, in contrast to the devastation caused by a nuclear device. However, it is considered highly unlikely that terrorist groups will be able to gain access to radioactive materials or nuclear technology because of tight national and international controls. Nuclear trafficking increased after the Soviet demise but, under President Putin, controls over nuclear materials and weaponry have been greatly strengthened. Still, the possibility of access to dispersible radioactive elements or even a dirty bomb cannot be discounted. Least likely is the willingness of states to transfer nuclear bombs or even the capability to make improvised nuclear devices to terrorist groups unless there is a sudden dissolution of central authority, a conspiracy within the leadership or in the military ranks, or officials ready to sell such weaponry for financial gain. The focus of such scenarios was post–Soviet Russia in the early 1990s, and Pakistan after September 11, 2001. Yet, in the foreseeable future, the risk of nuclear terrorism remains low if states and international agencies remain vigilant. As for terrorists, they are likely to prefer the many cheaper and low-tech methods of violence over the complexities of nuclear weaponry.

Cyberterrorism

Cyberterrorism represents one of the newest forms of attack against national and international agencies, institutions, and the web of global interactions. The main instrument of cyberterrorism is a computer used by hackers working alone or in groups to disrupt the operations of key governmental, economic and infrastructural targets—intelligence agencies, military command networks, banks, police agencies, electrical grids, communication networks, nuclear power plants, air traffic control centers, and corporations. Most hackers are amateurs "having fun" while causing widespread misery by sending destructive viruses through the Internet or by penetrating the secret files of businesses and governments. Perhaps more damaging are professional hackers—self-employed or working for corporations and foreign governments. Some self-employed hackers steal money from bank transfers or blackmail banks and companies into paying protection money, while others are lured by corporations to spy on rival companies to gain access to their trade secrets. Finally, a highly professional class of hackers is employed by governments tasked to penetrate the computer systems of other governments, intelligence agencies, defense systems, and communication networks. Devising computer security systems to defend against foreign penetration has been a persistent challenge for the Pentagon and other U.S. government agencies. Some ideologically motivated hackers wage propaganda campaigns against targeted governments and attack their websites and communication networks. The most dangerous computer hackers are those working for terrorist groups who use the Internet to propagandize their cause, recruit followers, communicate across long distances, and target enemy regimes and organizations with the goal of causing chaos, injuries, or death on a large scale.

Suicide Terrorism

The growing incidence of suicide terrorism has been a prominent feature of the contemporary milieu of political violence. The motivational propellant of suicide terrorism is the readiness to die for a chiliastic cause, in return for worldly and/or heavenly rewards. Suicide terrorists are unlike ordinary combatants—soldiers, paramilitaries, guerrillas, and terrorists—fighting for or against the state. While the commitment of such fighters to their cause involves degrees of self-sacrifice and even death, there is no uncertainty about the outcome of a suicide attack in terms of making the ultimate sacrifice—one's life. This totality of commitment and the absolute certainty of the sacrificial outcome make suicide terrorism the single most potent modality of attack and among the most difficult to defend against or prevent. The mix of psycho-political reasons that propel suicide terrorism varies depending on the conditions prevailing in different crisis environments. Yet, several commonly shared motivations can be readily identified—alienation from humanity and material life, deep anger against the oppressive state, a primal compulsion to take revenge, a sense of humiliation and hopelessness, a desire to end a purposeless life with a purposeful act, and the need to reaffirm one's identity as a true believer. Whatever the mix of motivations, suicide terrorists are deployed to further their group's strategic objectives in pursuit of possible gains in material compensation for their families, worldly fame as martyrs, or heavenly rewards for their sacrifice.

As a method of strategic violence, suicide terrorism has evolved over the years because terrorist groups have learned from each other's techniques and incorporated new technologies in the building and delivery of more lethal devices. Hizbullah's 1983 truck bombings of the U.S. embassy, the marine barracks, and French troops in Beirut set powerful precedents for emulation by later terrorists. In time, car and truck bombings perpetrated by one or two people transformed into al-Qaida's "collective martyrdom" operations characterized by the hijacking of planes to be used as missiles, as was done in the attacks on September 11, 2001. In that sense, the relatively low-tech suicidal attacks of September 11, 2001, upstaged the use of high-explosive packs, vests, and belts by the Tamil Tigers (LTTE) in Sri Lanka, PKK Kurds in Turkey, Chechens in Russia, Palestinians against Israel, Islamist extremists in Jordan, Egypt, Pakistan, Afghanistan, and Britain, and Islamist and nationalist insurgents in Iraq. Since the second Palestinian intifada (2000) and the wars in Afghanistan (2001) and Iraq (2003) suicide terrorism has become a preferred tactic of political violence, particularly among jihadist groups. According to Scott Atran, there have been more suicide

TABLE 10.1   Suicide Terrorism, 1980–2005

Country	Organization	Number of Attacks
Afghanistan	Taliban/al-Qaida	6
China	East Turkistan Liberation Front	2
Colombia	FARC	1
Egypt	al-Qaida affiliate	4
Europe	al-Qaida affiliate	3
Iraq	al-Qaida (Zarqawi)/ Sunni Baathists	537
Israel/West Bank/Gaza	Hamas/Islamic Jihad/Aqsa Brigade/PFLP	158
India	Lashkar-e-Taiba/various Islamists	82
Indonesia	Jamaa al-Islamiya/al-Qaida affiliates	3
Jordan	al-Qaida affiliate	3
Kenya	al-Qaida	2
Lebanon/Israel	Hizbullah	30
Morocco	al-Qaida affiliate	12
Pakistan	al-Qaida affiliates	10
Phillippines	Abu Sayyat	2
Russia	Chechens	25
Saudi Arabia	al-Qaida affiliate	12
Sri Lanka	Tamil Tigers (LTTE)	77
Tanzania	al-Qaida	1
Tunisia	al-Qaida	1
Turkey	PKK/ al-Qaida Affiliate	16
United States	al-Qaida	4
Uzbekistan	Islamic Movement of Uzbekistan	6
Yemen	al-Qaida	1

Source: These estimates are based on Pape (2003), Atran (2006), and various newspaper sources.

attacks since 2003 than in the previous twenty years combined.[2] Table 10.1 lists the numbers of recent suicide attacks.

The strategic utility of suicide terrorism should not be underestimated. According to Robert Pape, suicide terrorism is used strategically, as part of a larger campaign against occupying powers to force them to make territorial concessions or achieve national self-determination. Pape states that the rate of suicide attacks increases because it pays— that is, such attacks have succeeded in coercing countries to make some concessions. However, he expects that more ambitious suicide attacks would backfire and prompt the targeted states to refuse to make further concessions.[3] While these conclusions, which are based on extensive empirical analysis, are basically sound, they do not explain the psychological motivations of a growing number of volunteers for suicide operations, particularly in certain Arab and Muslim countries. Could it be that these volunteers are driven to suicide terrorism because of their desperation and sense of powerlessness against seemingly implacable and powerful enemies? The fundamental logic of suicide terrorism could well be that having nothing else to lose, the suicide terrorist sacrifices life to gain several payoffs:

1. a sense of pre-mortem satisfaction from imposing maximal harm on a hated enemy;
2. demoralization and weakening of the enemy's resolve to maintain its offensive position or policy;
3. bringing praise and honor to oneself and one's family in the community as a hero-martyr.

If the volunteer for suicide terrorism (*intihariyah*) is an Islamist, the payoffs listed above will be supplemented by rewards expected in the afterlife.

Women in Political Violence

There is a public misperception that women are less likely to engage in political violence because they are "naturally" more peaceful and less aggressive. Is it so strange that women living amid the perils and deprivations of the modern world have increasingly resorted to terrorism as men have done for so long? Indeed, women have always played a role in violent conflicts particularly in the provision of logistical support—food, supplies, intelligence, medical care, morale, and sex. In the context of the progressive emancipation of women in the West and in many non-Western cultures, women have assumed more combat-related roles as soldiers fighting for the state as well as insurgents opposing the state. In the foreseeable future, female involvement in terrorist activity is expected to increase as political conflicts exert increased pressure and exact higher costs on women. As more leaders call for women to fight for their cause, women's increased motivation to commit violence and proven effectiveness in terrorist operations could result in women playing an ever more lethal role in violent strategic interactions.[4] Table 10.2 lists percentages of women in insurgent groups.

The emergence of leftist revolutionary movements in the 1960s and 1970s provided unprecedented opportunities for women to participate and even assume leadership roles. Women were particularly active in Latin American insurgencies, constituting up to 50 percent of Peru's Sendero Luminoso, 30 percent of Nicaragua's Sandinistas, and 30 percent of the Farabundo Martí National Liberation Front (FMLN) of El Salvador.

Equally significant was the growing role of women terrorists in the 1980s in conservative non-Western cultural settings, such as Sri Lanka, Chechnya, Morocco, Lebanon, Palestine, Egypt, Turkey, and Iraq. In these patriarchal societies, joining a revolutionary organization has been an important venue of liberation for women—a means to demonstrate their equal commitment to a common cause alongside men.

TABLE 10.2   Women in Insurgent Movements

Terrorist Group	Percentage	Country
Farabundo Martí National Liberation Front	30%	El Salvador
Red Army Faction/June Second Movement	30%	West Germany
Revolutionary Armed Forces of Colombia (FARC)	30%	Columbia
Sandinista National Liberation Front	38%	Nicaragua
Sendero Luminoso	50%	Peru
Tamil Tigers (LTTE)	50%	Sri Lanka
U.S. right-wing movements	25%	United States

One of the first terrorist groups to encourage women's participation was the LTTE. Facing the depletion of male fighters killed in operations against Sri Lanka's Sinhalese regime, Tamil women were enlisted to join the struggle. The Tamil leader, Velupillai Prabhakaran called upon women to liberate themselves from "the shackles of oppression" by becoming Tigers. The first female recruits worked in support services, and in 1983 they began entering the warrior ranks in the Women's Front of the Liberation Tigers, ultimately joining LTTE's suicide battalion, the Black Tigers, and its women's wing, the Birds of Freedom. Two of the most prominent victims of the Birds of Freedom were Indian prime minister Rajiv Gandhi (1991) and Sri Lankan president Premadasa (1993). Driven by nationalist fervor and ideals of women's liberation, these female bombers were also motivated by strong feelings of revenge against a regime and army that had killed their relatives, committed mass atrocities, and engaged in hundreds of rapes, bringing dishonor upon them. The immense rage felt by these women made them effective instruments of terror—a model soon to impact terrorist tactics in Muslim societies.

The application of the Tamil model of female suicide terrorism had even greater social and cultural implications when implemented in Islamic settings. Although both the Muslim and Tamil societies are strongly patriarchal, the Tamil Tigers constitute a fundamentally secular, ethnic nationalist organization. In contrast, female aspirants for revolutionary violence in Muslim settings have had to overcome the cultural impediment of patriarchy as well as the religious constraints of Islam.

In some Muslim insurrectionary groups, female participation is readily accepted regardless of the constraints of patriarchy or religion. The Kurdish PKK, a leftist, ethnic nationalist movement, has employed several female suicide bombers in its separatist struggle against Turkey. The Chechen separatists fielded up to twenty-eight Black Widows in five major suicidal operations against Russian civilian and military targets in 2002–2005. Notably, the Kurdish and Chechen cases resemble the

Tamil Tigers in their secular ethno-nationalist configuration and significant parallel development; the increase in women's participation in terrorist organizations is a consequence of the desperate need for recruits brought on by the heavy human toll of the ongoing conflict with government forces.

In the Palestinian case, there was a modicum of female involvement in the 1970s in PLO's secular leftist organizations. The first intifada (1987) brought women into direct participation in protests and demonstrations against the Israeli occupation. Yet it was the second intifada that propelled Palestinian women into the vortex of terrorism. In his quest to match the suicide bombings of Hamas and Islamic Jihad, PLO leader Yasser Arafat, in a January 27, 2002, speech, called upon Palestinian women to engage in "martyrdom all the way to Jerusalem." Arafat's call for female martyrdom (*shahidah*) created an important precedent. Soon after this speech, Wafa Idris became the first *shahidah* in a suicide operation organized by Al-Aqsa Martyrs Brigade, the military arm of the Fatah movement. The Arab world praised and glorified Wafa Idris as the first *shahidah*, which prompted Hamas leader Shaikh Ahmad Yassin to issue a *fatwa* legalizing the role of female suicide bombers under Islamic law. In the next three years, six more women performed martyrdom suicides on behalf of Hamas, Islamic Jihad, and al-Aqsa Martyrs Brigades. The lives of all seven *shahidat* had been disrupted by the Israeli occupation and the killing of family members or relatives, causing the women personal anguish, debasement, and humiliation.[5]

The Islamists' legitimation of women's participation in terrorism including suicide bombings is likely to have widespread repercussions. In March 2004, two Uzbek women exploded themselves in separate attacks in Tashkent, Uzbekistan. In October 2005, a female suicide bomber attacked an Indian military convoy. Finally, several *shahidat* have been deployed against the U.S. military and other targets in Iraq in 2003 and 2005 by Zarqawi's al-Qaida fighters, a group also responsible for a terrorist outreach to Jordan in which a failed female bomber was captured after her husband died in the bombing. Iraq's violent milieu has been a magnet for European Islamists, including women converts such as Muriel Deganque of Belgium who died in a suicide attack against an American military patrol. The growth of suicide bombings by women could have an unprecedented destabilizing impact on Muslim regimes and societies and become a threat to the internal and external security of the United States, EU, and allied Muslim regimes. In addition, the impact on women's lives from their participation in political violence remains unknown both in terms of addressing the social disadvantages of patriarchal societies and their continued participation in political activity outside the violent realm.

Antidotes to Political Violence

A peaceful world has long been the dream of humankind. Humanity's aspiration for global peace resonates as a central theme in the great religions and secular ideologies, each containing specific prescriptions for a world without conflict. Yet, after several millennia of civilized existence, peace on earth remains a utopian dream. The exigencies of human nature, conflicting values, beliefs and cultures, and inequalities of wealth and power, define the contours of a global society where conflict remains universal. In such a world, the challenge becomes how to ameliorate, contain, manage, and resolve conflicts, to prevent or minimize violent outcomes resulting in human and material losses. This immense task would require a powerful supranational entity with sufficient authority and resources to engage in ongoing monitoring of conflicts and employ diplomatic or military means to limit their lethal potential and even reach a settlement. However, no such supranational agency exists in today's world system of sovereign states. The United Nations is not empowered to perform effectively as an agency of conflict regulation and resolution, except in cases when the five permanent members of the Security Council are fully united and ready to provide the necessary financial and military resources for the task. Such unity of resolve has been infrequent given the conflicting agendas of the Council's permanent members. Hence, the task of "global regulator" or "world policeman" often has fallen on America's shoulders with mixed results, often detrimental to the United States and the parties involved in the conflict in need of resolution. In order to function as an effective world watchman, the United States would need, at a minimum, enlightened leaders backed by strong public support and massive funding. Yet, during the second half of the twentieth century, all of these were in short supply. Only in the 1990s, after the Soviet demise did America emerge as the world's only superpower, capable of settling conflicts, but mostly failing because of internal partisan disputes, a lack of presidential initiative, strategic missteps, and the sheer complexity of the global political milieu. President Clinton refused to intervene to stop genocide in Rwanda, intervened only belatedly but effectively in the Balkans, and failed to forge an Israeli-Palestinian settlement due to the recalcitrance of the antagonists and his own hesitance to compel both sides to compromise. In many instances, Clinton used U.S. power through a multilateral framework, in conjunction with European and other allies. The situation changed radically with the Bush administration's adoption of a more offensive and unilateralist strategic rationale that became official doctrine after the 2001 attacks. The Bush doctrine emphasized the global projection and use of U.S. power on a unilateral basis, combined with preemptive action against perceived enemies, the overthrow of unfriendly regimes, and pressuring of allies to conform to America's will. A retrospective look at the Bush administration's record reveals a mixed picture in terms of U.S. achievements, vulnerabilities, and capabilities. One of the two major U.S. achievements under the Bush administration was the overthrow of the Taliban theocracy and its replacement by an elected multiethnic regime that has had to rely on U.S. and coalition forces to maintain stability, particularly in facing a resurgence of Taliban forces in the borderlands with Pakistan. The second major achievement was the capture or destruction of large segments of al-Qaida's leading cadres and disruption of its funding networks and channels of communication with the help of allied governments, degrading its short-term capabilities to mount major attacks on the American homeland.

These successes were outweighed by major failures arising from the U.S. invasion and occupation of Iraq as well as foreign policy miscalculations in other areas such as North Korea, Iran, and counterterrorism operations. These missteps have entailed immense human and material costs, and have triggered developments detrimental to United States and world security. These major costs and negative developments include:

1. a weakened U.S. military capability under the strains of personnel and material shortages and repeated deployments in war zones;
2. a weakened U.S. economy incapable of supporting an offensive global strategy because of the growing burden of indebtedness in excess of nine trillion dollars;
3. the empowerment of pro-Iran Shiite Islamist parties in Iraq and the ascendance of Iran as a major force in Middle East affairs demanding recognition for its new role;
4. the destabilization of pro-U.S. autocratic Muslim regimes because of the widespread anti-American sentiments of their citizens and the rise of oppositional elements emboldened by the Bush administration's rhetoric on building democracies as a means to prevent terrorism;
5. the U.S. refusal to directly engage North Korea in diplomacy, combined with threatening rhetoric culminating in the failure to limit North Korea's nuclear ambitions;
6. inattention to humanitarian crises, incipient genocides, and future threats to peace such as the genocide in Sudan's Darfur region, the civil war in Somalia, the Kurdish problem in Turkey, unrest/narcoterrorism in Mexico, and the destabilizing consequences of increasing poverty at home and abroad;
7. the weakening of the United Nations and U.S. multilateral relations with key allies such as Germany, France, Britain, and other NATO countries, which has created obstacles in the struggle against global terrorism;

8. the negative consequences of U.S. unwillingness to limit violence and press for a settlement of the Israeli-Palestinian conflict;
9. the continuing increase in anti-American anger in Muslim countries, which translates into growing phalanxes of recruits to the jihadi cause and the proliferation of radical groups sharing al-Qaida's violent creed. Over thirty such extremists groups have emerged since September 11, 2001.

Clearly, these negative "blowbacks" from U.S. policies and initiatives since September 11, 2001, require major policy changes and readjustments to reduce the growing threat from Islamist and other sources of terrorism against the United States at home and abroad. It should be recognized that making policy changes is not easy for a superpower and even if implemented, most of their consequences may not be known in the immediate future. Certainly, anti-U.S. violence will remain an amorphous and persistent threat in the long term future. However, it might be possible to take some steps to reduce the magnitude and duration of this threat:

1. Return to multilateralism as a comprehensive strategic framework, particularly in fighting and defending against terrorism.
2. Reduce foreign exposure by adopting a lower U.S. military profile worldwide, particularly in the Muslim countries, where widespread anti-Americanism will continue to trigger violence against U.S. targets and pro-American indigenous regimes.
3. Refrain from pushing for "regime change" rhetorically, electorally, or by clandestine means because interference in the domestic politics of other states increases the likelihood of revolutionary mass violence and the probability that the new regime will be less democratic than the old one. In the Muslim countries, "regime change" is most likely to result in the establishment of anti-U.S. Islamist theocracies. Encouraging democratic movements should follow the logic of gradualism, as democracy usually cannot be imposed from the outside through pressure or conquest.
4. Reduce the U.S. military presence in Iraq gradually as a prelude to total withdrawal in an orderly manner leaving to Iraqis the ultimate responsibility for their security. The longer the United States remains in Iraq, the more prohibitive the human and financial costs will become and the greater the number of jihadists being recruited, trained, and deployed from Iraq worldwide. The maintenance of U.S. bases and forces in Iraq and in other oil/gas-producing countries is likely to be dysfunctional since it does not guarantee access to energy sources, protect the safety of production facilities and pipelines, or ensure the longevity of a friendly regime.
5. Initiate a definitive effort at conflict resolution in the Middle East based

on regional multilateralism by involving a select number of relevant neighboring countries to resolve two of the region's main sources of political violence—the Iraq war and the Israel-Palestinian conflict.

6. Strengthen key U.S. domestic vulnerabilities by implementing comprehensive air-cargo and ship-container inspections, effective policing and control of borders, and better detection equipment at key points of entry. Undertake broad-based reform of immigration laws to ensure that potential terrorists do not succeed in entering the United States.

7. Reorganize and strengthen the U.S. intelligence agencies to maximize the collection, analysis, and use of actionable intelligence, while minimizing inter-agency conflicts and bureaucratic impediments to the flow of information;

8. Sign the treaty accepting the jurisdiction of the International Criminal Court and lead the campaign to establish a multinational force to intervene quickly and effectively to prevent or stop genocides.

9. Strengthen U.S. democracy at the grassroots by investing heavily in humanistic education and the development of morally and strategically enlightened political leadership while promoting public debate and mass participation in the political process.

Spectrum of Terror: A Synopsis

This book sought to analyze the phenomenon of political violence in its nonconventional forms from two interrelated theoretical perspectives. First, it set forth a spectrum of political violence organized along a two-dimensional continuum that defined types of violence according to perpetrators and magnitude. These types ranged from assassinations to subnational and transnational groups challenging the state, to instances of state violence including repression, politicide, and genocide. Second, it depicted political violence as a strategic interaction between different subnational actors and nation-states within a modified game theoretic framework. Here political violence was seen as an interactive process of action and reaction by parties in pursuit of their interests defined by history, crisis milieu, culture, psychological predispositions, and leadership. In each case study, the strategic interaction was guided by the goal-oriented behavior of rational actors leading to violent outcomes, some intended, many unintended.

This modified game theoretic approach was applied to over a dozen case studies of individual, subnational, transnational, and state violence, which have yielded a number of important findings. Leaders of states and non-state groups considering the use of violence should weigh the short-term and long-term consequences of their choice given the propensity for such violence to result in blowback, which could be detrimental to the objectives they are trying to pursue. Furthermore, since subnational conflict can readily lead to genocide if left unresolved, it is imperative for leaders to recognize the full magnitude of the risk involved in perpetuating the cycle of violence for minimal gains or in hopes of total victory for their side. Notably, the quick evolution from micro-level interactive violence to politicide and genocide does not always require a powerful state or stable leadership. Indeed, many genocides have occurred at times of relative weakness during state formation or dissolution. Given this tendency for conflict to grow in magnitude over time, efforts at resolution should be undertaken at an early stage in the evolution of the conflict. To maximize their chances of success, these efforts must take into account the preferences of the antagonists by providing incentives and disincentives for the conflicting sides to accept lesser preferences and move toward an equilibrium of peace. All too often, the parties to a conflict are unable to achieve such an outcome by themselves, thus necessitating intervention by a third party "jailer-mediator." In pre-genocidal situations, the willingness of outside parties to intervene could have salvational consequences for the subordinate group. However, it should not be assumed that outside intervention in a prisoner's dilemma situation is guaranteed to succeed. If not properly pursued, outside intervention may exacerbate the conflict and contribute to greater lethality.

Unfortunately, any sober assessment of the global political milieu suggests that various forms of political violence are likely to persist for the foreseeable future. It is hoped that this book contributes to a deeper understanding of the dynamics of violent strategic interactions and the mechanisms of conflict resolution.

Notes

1. Ted Robert Gurr, *Why Men Rebel* (Princeton, NJ: Princeton University Press, 1970).
2. Scott Atran, "The Moral Logic and Growth of Suicide Terrorism," *The Washington Quarterly* 29, no. 2 (2006): 127–147.
3. Robert Pape, "The Strategic Logic of Suicide Terrorism," *American Political Science Review* 97, no. 3 (2003): 343–361.
4. Karla J. Cunningham, "Cross-Regional Trends in Female Terrorism," *Studies in Conflict and Terrorism* 26 (2003): 171–195.
5. Terri Toles Patkin, "Explosive Baggage: Female Palestinian Suicide Bombers and the Rhetoric of Emotion," *Women and Language* 27, no. 2 (2004): 79–88.

Further Reading

Guelke, Adrian. *The Age of Terrorism and the International System.* London: I.B. Tauris, 1998.

Howard, Russell, James Forest, and Joanne Moore. *Homeland Security and Terrorism.* New York: McGraw Hill, 2006.

Jones, David Martin, ed. *Globalisation and the New Terror.* Northampton, MA: Edward Elgar Publishing, 2004.

O'Neill, Bard E. *Insurgency and Terrorism: From Revolution to Apocalypse,* 2d ed., Washington, D.C.: Potomac Books, 2005.

Palmer, Monte, and Princess Palmer. *At the Heart of Terror: Islam, Jihadists, and America's War on Terrorism.* New York: Rowman and Littlefield, 2004.

Stern, Jessica. *The Ultimate Terrorists.* Cambridge, MA: Harvard University Press, 1999.

Whittaker, David J. *Terrorists and Terrorism in the Contemporary World.* New York: Routledge, 2004.

Subnational and Transnational Organizations: A Profile of Case Studies

Name of Group	Motivation	Target State	Date Founded	Group Membership	Group's First Preference	Leadership Type	Key Leader(s)	Tactics	Killed in Interactive Violence
al-Qaida	Religious	U.S. and allied Western and Muslim regimes	1988	20,000 (est.)	Rollback of U.S./Western hegemony by global Islamist struggle	Charismatic	Osama bin Ladin, Dr. Ayman al-Zawahiri	Suicide attacks, small arms, bombs, rockets, IEDs	10,000+
Aum Shinrikyo	Religious	Japan	1987	2,000	Ruling Japan or world destruction	Charismatic	Shoko Asahara	Chemical weapons	Around 50 killed; over 6,000 injured
Basque Homeland and Liberty (ETA)	Ethnic	Spain	1959	300	Independence	Collective	Alvarez Txillardegi	Bombings, assassinations	800
Chechens	Ethnic	Russia	1994	800	Independence	Charismatic	Aslan Mashkadov, Shamil Bashayev	Bombings, assassinations, suicide attacks, hostage taking, airplane hijacking	100,000
Hamas	Religious	Israel	1987	Mass party	Islamic state in all of Palestine	Collective	Shaikh Ahmad Yassin, Abd al-Aziz al-Rantisi, Ismail Haniya, Khalid Mishal	Bombings, suicide attacks, shootings, stabbings, kidnapping	6,870
Hizbullah	Religious	Israel/United States	1982	Mass party	Israeli withdrawal from Lebanese territory; protection of Shiite community	Charismatic	Hasan Nasrallah	Truck bombs, suicide attacks, rocket attacks, snipers, guerrilla tactics	18,000

Irish Republican Army (IRA)	Ethnic	Britain/Unionists	1919	2,000	Unification with Ireland	Collective	Gerry Adams	Assassinations, bombings, marches, hunger strikes	3,500
Kashmiri separatists	Religious	India	Mid-1980s	Several thousand	Independence or unity with Pakistan as an Islamist state	Collective	Hafez Muhammad Said, Maulana Masud Azhar	Massacres, car bombs, assassinations, ambushes	80,000
Liberation Tigers of Tamil Eelam (LTTE)	Ethnic	Sri Lanka	1976	8,000	Independence	Charismatic	Velupillai Prabhakaran	Bombings, suicide attacks, assassinations	64,000
Patriot/militia movement	Ideological	U.S. federal government and minorities	1970s–1980s	50,000	Establish white supremacist regime in United States	Decentralized	William L. Pierce, Rev. Richard Butler	Shooting, bombing, robbery	200
Sendero Luminoso	Ideological	Peru	1979	1,000	Take state power	Charismatic	Abimael Guzman	Bombing, assassinations, murder	27,000

Subnational and Transnational Organizations: Timeline of Violent Interactions

Date	Event	Location
Mar. 44 B.C.	Marcus Junius Brutus and Gaius Cassius Longinus assassinate Julius Caesar in the Roman Senate	Rome
Jan. 661	Abd al-Rahman ibn Muljam (Kharijites) assassinates Ali ibn Abi Talib	Arabia
May 1812	John Bellingham assassinates Prime Minister Spencer Perceval	Great Britain
April 1865	John Wilkes Booth assassinates President Abraham Lincoln	United States
July 1881	Charles J. Guiteau assassinates President James Garfield	United States
Sept. 1901	Leon Czolgosz assassinates President William McKinley	United States
June 1914	Gavrilo Princip (Young Bosnia / Black Hand) assassinates Archduke Franz Ferdinand	Austro-Hungary
1915–1922	Genocide of 1.5 million Armenians in the Ottoman Empire	Turkey
Mar. 1921	Soghomon Tehlirian (Dashnaks) assassinates Mehmet Talat Pasha	Germany
July 1936–Apr. 1939	General Francisco Franco defeats the Republicans and occupies Basque land; more than 300,000 killed and 250,000 displaced	Spain
1939–1945	Six million die in the Holocaust under the Third Reich	Throughout Europe
1947–1949	First India-Pakistan war; Kashmir divided at cease-fire line	India
1948–1956	Ceylon (Sri Lanka) gains independence from Britain; Sinhalese majority monopolizes power	Sri Lanka
Jan. 1948	Nathuram Godse assassinates Mahatma Gandhi	India
July 1951	Mustafa Shukri Usho (Arab Dynamite Squad) assassinates King Abdullah ibn Hussein	Jerusalem
1954–1955	Pakistan joins U.S.-led Western coalition against communist bloc; India sponsors establishment of the Nonaligned Movement, a coalition of Third World states opposed to taking sides in the Cold War	India
1956	Elections followed by communal violence; 150 killed (mostly Tamils)	Sri Lanka
1959–1960	Genocide of 1.2 million Tibetans in China	China

Date	Event	Location
July 1959	Basque Homeland and Liberty (ETA) founded	Spain
Sept. 1959	Prime Minister Bandaranaike assassinated by Buddhist monk opposed to Tamil recognition	Sri Lanka
1962–1963	Pakistan signs border treaty with China; India loses border war with China; Pakistan–China relations and India-Soviet Union ties strengthened	India
Nov. 1963	Lee Harvey Oswald assassinates President John F. Kennedy	United States
1965	Second India-Pakistan war starts with Pakistan's offensive in Kashmir and Indian counterattack on Lahore; UN-sponsored ceasefire followed by mutual declaration to solve disputes peacefully	India
Aug. 1968	ETA assassinates police chief Melitón Manzanas	Spain
1970	Hardline Sri Lanka Freedom Party (SLFP) takes power and limits education for Tamils and Sinhala/Buddhism given priority in the constitution	Sri Lanka
1970	Abimael Guzmán Reynoso establishes Communist Party of Peru-Sendero Luminoso (PCP-SL)	Peru
1971–1976	Militant Tamil youth organize attacks and bank robberies; TULF pushes for an independent Tamil Eelam	Sri Lanka
1971	Third India-Pakistan war as the secessionist Awami League wins election in East Pakistan, triggering genocidal massacres by the Pakistani Army that prompt Indian intervention and defeat of Pakistan. East Pakistan declares its independence from Pakistan as the state of Bangladesh	India
1971	Genocide of 1.5 million Bengalis in East Pakistan/Bangladesh	India
May 1972	Arthur Bremer attempts to assassinate Governor George Wallace	United States
1973	Establishment of al-Mujamma al-Islami by Shaikh Yassin as a branch of Muslim Brotherhood in Gaza	Israel
Oct. 1973	Syria and Egypt attack Israel (Yom Kippur/Ramadan War)	Sinai/Golan Heights
Dec. 1973	ETA bombers assassinate Admiral Carrero Blanco in retaliation for execution of Basque militants	Spain

Date	Event	Location
1974	India detonates underground nuclear weapons	India
Sept. 1974	A bomb kills 12 in a cafeteria in Madrid	Spain
1975–1979	Genocide of two million Cambodians under the Khmer Rouge	Cambodia
1975–1989	The separation of East Pakistan and defeat by India in 1971 were cataclysmic losses for Pakistan; Pakistan seeks to counteract India's growing strength	India
Mar. 1975	Prince Khalid bin Musaid assassinates King Faisal bin Abdul Aziz	Saudi Arabia
Nov. 1975	Francisco Franco dies; King Juan Carlos frees 15,000 political prisoners	Spain
1976	Liberation Tigers of Tamil Eelam (LTTE) founded	Sri Lanka
1977	UNP wins election; TULF forms the opposition; anti-Tamil violence breaks out; hundreds killed	Sri Lanka
1978	LTTE outlawed after killing of a police inspector in Jaffna	Sri Lanka
Apr. 1978	ETA political party, Herri Batasuna, founded	Spain
1979	Basque Autonomy Statute approved/ratified	Spain
Mar. 1979	IRA splinter group Irish National Liberation Army (INLA) kills Airey Neave, Conservative MP	Britain
Aug. 1979	IRA bombers assassinate Lord Louis Mountbatten	Ireland
May 1980	Sendero's first attack; arson on voter registration office in Chuschi aiming to disrupt elections	Peru
May–Dec. 1980	Sendero's "Initiation Plan"	Peru
July 1980	Sendero attacks on electrical grids in Lima; bombings in Cagallo and Huancapi	Peru
Jan. 1981– Jan. 1983	Sendero's "Deployment Plan"	Peru
Mar. 1981	John Hinckley Jr. attempts to assassinate President Ronald Reagan	United States

Date	Event	Location
Oct. 1981	Shukri al-Islambuli (Tanzim al-Jihad) assassinates President Anwar al-Sadat	Egypt
June 1982	IDF attack on and invasion of PLO bases in Lebanon	Lebanon
Sept. 1982	Maronite phalangist militia allied with Israel massacres Palestinian and Shiite civilians at Sabra and Shatila refugee camps	Lebanon
Apr. 1983	Islamic Jihad (Hizbullah) suicide truck bombing targeted at the U.S. Embassy in Beirut kills 63	Lebanon
May 1983–1986	Sendero's "Plan to Conquer Bases"	Peru
July 1983	LTTE ambush kills 13 soldiers in Jaffna; anti-Tamil riots kill hundreds of Tamils and displace over 200,000	Sri Lanka
Oct. 1983	Islamic Jihad (Hizbullah) suicide truck bombing kills 241 U.S. Marines and 56 French soldiers in Beirut	Lebanon
Nov. 1983	Hizbullah car bomb targeted at IDF kills 50 in Tyre	Lebanon
June 1984–June 1985	A series of Hizbullah bomb attacks targeted at IDF posts kill 46	Lebanon
Oct. 1984	IRA bombs Brighton Hotel during Conservative Party Annual Conference	Britain
Sept. 1984	Islamic Jihad (Hizbullah) suicide truck bombing targeted at the U.S. Embassy Annex in Beirut kills 24	Lebanon
1985	LTTE massacre of 150 Sinhalese worshippers at a Buddhist shrine in Anuradhapura	Sri Lanka
July 1985–May 2000	Hizbullah versus Israel/SLA; series of interactive attacks, mostly bombings, abductions, and assassinations, kill more than 200	Lebanon/Israel
June 1986	250 Sendero prisoners killed in military massacre in Frontón Prison	Peru
July 1986	Car bomb targeted at Civil Guards on microbus kills 12 and injures 50 in Madrid	Spain
Dec. 1986–July 1989	Sendero's "Plan to Develop Bases"	Peru

Date	Event	Location
1987–1988	Genocide of 100,000 Kurds in Iraq	Iraq
1987	Shoko Asahara establishes Aum Shinrikyo, a messianic cult	Japan
May 1987	Fighting breaks out between IRA and British Special Air Services (SAS), killing eleven IRA members	Great Britain
June 1987	Car bomb at a supermarket in Barcelona kills 21 and injures 45	Spain
Nov. 1987	Britain intercepts the *Eskund*, a ship full of Libyan arms for the IRA; IRA bombs Enniskillen in Northern Ireland, killing 11	Great Britain
Dec. 1987	Outbreak of first intifada in Israel and the occupied territories; establishment of Hamas as Mujamma's fighting force; 1,230 killed through Sept. 1993 on both sides	Israel
Dec. 1987	Car bomb targeted at Civil Guard in Zaragoza kills 11 and injures 40	Spain
1988–1991	Demonstrations, rock throwing, and sporadic attacks by Palestinian Islamic Jihad on civilians and security/military personnel in Israel	Israel and the occupied territories
1988	Al-Qaida founded	Afghanistan
Mar. 1988	Three IRA members killed in Gibraltar, suspected of planning attack on British garrison; Loyalist gunman kills three Catholics; two British soldiers abducted and killed	Great Britain
1989	Asahara establishes Shinrito (Truth Party) to compete in elections	Japan
Aug. 1989–Aug. 1992	Sendero's "Great Plan to Develop Bases and Serve the Conquest of Power"	Peru
Sept. 1989	Eleven British army bandsmen killed in Deal, Kent, by IRA bomb	Great Britain
1990	LTTE ends ceasefire killing hundreds of police officers and Muslims as regime allies with other Tamil groups in fighting LTTE; hundreds are killed and over 120,000 displaced	Sri Lanka
July 1990	Alberto Fujimori assumes presidency; program of state terror undertaken by Vladimiro Montesinos, head of National Intelligence Service	Peru

Date	Event	Location
July 1990	Conservative MP Ian Gow, strong Unionist supporter, killed by IRA bomb in Sussex	Great Britain
Aug. 1990	Iraq invades Kuwait	Kuwait
1991–1994	Ongoing war between government and LTTE marked by massacres, assassinations, bombings, and ambushes; thousands are killed	Sri Lanka
1991–1995	Osama bin Ladin in exile in Sudan training jihadists	Sudan
May 1991	"Strategic Equilibrium" apex of Sendero power	Peru
May 1991	Thenmuli Rajaratnam (LTTE) assassinates Prime Minister Rajiv Gandhi	India
May 1991	Car bomb targeted at Civil Guard in Barcelona kills 10 and injures 28	Spain
Nov. 1991	General Dzokhar Dudayev declares independence of Chechnya	Chechnya
1992–1995	Genocide of 200,000 Bosnian Muslims in Yugoslavia	Yugoslavia
Feb. 1992	IRA kills seven Protestant workers in County Tyrone	Great Britain
Feb. 1992	An Israeli assassinates Sheikh Abbas al-Musawi, secretary-general of Hizbullah; eight are killed, and Hasan Nasrallah is chosen as successor	Lebanon
Mar. 1992	Hizbullah suicide bombing targeted at the Israeli Embassy in Buenos Aires kills 38	Argentina
Apr. 1992	Alberto Fujimori carries out *autogolpe* (self-coup)	Peru
Apr. 1992	IRA bomb near Baltic Exchange building in London kills 3	Great Britain
Sept. 1992	Abimael Guzmán Reynoso captured by GEIN in Lima	Peru
Feb. 1993	Islamist attack on World Trade Center in New York	United States
Mar. 1993	IRA bombs in Warrington, Cheshire, kill 2 children	Great Britain
Apr. 1993	IRA Bishopsgate bomb at N.W. Tower in London kills 1	Great Britain
May 1993	LTTE suicide bomber assassinates President Ranasinghe Premadasa	Sri Lanka
July 1993	"Operation Accountability" launched by Israel	Lebanon

Date	Event	Location
Sept. 1993	Oslo Accords mediated by President Bill Clinton and signed by Prime Minister Yitzhak Rabin and Palestinian Authority chairman Yasser Arafat in Washington, D.C., leading to increased violence by hardline opposition groups on both sides	Israel and occupied territories
Oct. 1993	Loyalist gunmen kill 8 people in bar in Greysteel County, Londonderry; IRA bombs Shankill fish shop, killing 10	Great Britain
Dec. 1993	Joint Declaration of Peace signed by Irish and British prime ministers	Great Britain
1994	Genocide of 900,000 Tutsis in Rwanda	Rwanda
June 1994	Sarin nerve gas attack targeted at judges trying Aum Shinrikyo case kills ″ and injures 270 in Matsumoto neighborhood	Japan
July 1994	Hizbullah bombing at Jewish Cultural Center in Buenos Aires kills 95	Argentina
Aug. 1994	IRA ceasefire	Great Britain
Sept. 1994–Feb. 1995	One journalist and twenty dissidents are killed and over 250 civilians are njured in Aum Shinrikyo attacks	Japan
Oct. 1994	Loyalist ceasefire	Great Britain
1995	Violence resumes as peace talks fail; LTTE evacuates Jaffna and the Sri Lankan army occupies the city creating a massive humanitarian crisis	Sri Lanka
Mar. 1995	Sarin gas attack on the Tokyo subway kills 12 and injures 5,499	Japan
Apr. 1995	ETA attempts to assassinate Partido Popular leader José María Aznar, killing one bystander	Spain
Apr. 1995	Timothy McVeigh bombs the Murrah federal building in Oklahoma City, killing 168	United States
May 1995	Shoko Asahara arrested	Japan
July 1995	Charles Ray Polk's plot to bomb IRS building in Austin, Texas, foiled when he is arrested purchasing weapons from undercover police	United States

Date	Event	Location
Oct. 1995	The Sons of Gestapo orchestrate the derailing of Amtrak passenger train in Hyder, Arizona, killing 1 and injuring many	United States
Nov. 1995	Yigal Amir assassinates Prime Minister Yitzhak Rabin	Israel
Nov. 1995	Oklahoma Constitutional Militia's plot to bomb Southern Poverty Law Center, gay bars, and abortion clinics foiled	United States
Nov. 1995–Aug. 1996	First Russian-Chechen war	Chechnya
Dec. 1995	Car bomb targeted at a military van kills 6 in Madrid	Spain
Dec. 1995	Joseph Bailey's attempt to bomb the IRS building in Reno, Nevada, fails	United States
1996	LTTE fights back, attacking soldier and bombing Colombo; state of emergency declared	Sri Lanka
Jan. 1996	A string of bank robberies by the Aryan Republican Army ends in shootout with FBI in Ohio	United States
Jan.–June 1996	A series of suicide bombings targeted at Israeli civilians and soldiers (in reaction to Israeli killing of Hamas bomb maker Yahya Ayyash, "the Engineer")	Israel
Apr. 1996	Larry Wayne Shoemaker kills a black man in Jackson, Mississippi, in a racist murder based on *Turner Diaries*	United States
Apr. 1996	"Operation Grapes of Wrath" launched by Israel, resulting in the deaths of hundreds	Lebanon
May 1996	Sudan regime expels Osama bin Ladin; he takes refuge in Afghanistan	Afghanistan
June 1996	IRA bombing destroys Manchester's Arndale Center	Great Britain
July 1996	Unionist Orangemen march at Drumcree sparks clashes between Catholics and Protestants; bombing of hotel in Enniskillen causes many injuries	Great Britain
July 1996	One person is killed and over 100 are injured by Eric Rudolph's bombing at the Atlanta Summer Olympics	United States
July 1996	Washington State Militia's plot to attack government is foiled	United States
Oct. 1996	The Phineas Priesthood orchestrates two bank robberies and four bombings	United States

Date	Event	Location
Oct. 1996	IRA bombs Lisburn Barracks, killing 1 soldier	Great Britain
1997–1998	Government carries out major offensive against LTTE and war escalates LTTE bombs Temple of the Tooth, Buddhism's holiest shrine, and commercial areas in Colombo	Sri Lanka
Jan. 1997	Eric Rudolph bombs an abortion clinic in Sandy Springs, Georgia, injuring 7	United States
Feb. 1997	IRA sniper shoots British soldier in Armagh	Great Britain
Apr. 1997	National Alliance member Todd Van Biber accidentally explodes pipe bomb and is arrested for plot to bomb and rob banks	United States
Apr. 1997	IRA bomb hoaxes cause havoc on Britain's highways	Great Britain
Apr. 1997	Explosion of weapons cache leads to capture of Montana Freemen's massive arsenal in Yuba City, California	United States
May 1997	Sons of Liberty commit arson on IRS building in Colorado Springs, Colorado	United States
July 1997	Second IRA ceasefire	Great Britain
July 1997	Third Continental Congress's plot to attack U.S. military base in Ft. Hood, Texas; 7 arrested	United States
July 1997	ETA kidnaps and assassinates Miguel Angel Blanco, Basque Councillor; six million Spaniards demonstrate against the ETA	Spain
1998	Good Friday Agreement signed after negotiations and violence; disagreement on timetable for decommissioning IRA's weapons; attacks by "Real" IRA and other extremist IRA splinter groups	Great Britain
1998	World Islamic Front brings together four jihadist groups under al-Qaida's umbrella, resulting in a fatwa calling for the killing of Americans	Afghanistan
Jan. 1998	Eric Rudolph bombs an abortion clinic near Birmingham, Alabama, killing one and injuring another	United States

Date	Event	Location
Aug. 1998	Truck bombings targeted at the U.S. embassies in Kenya and Tanzania kill 224 and injure 4,500	Kenya and Tanzania
Sept. 1998	ETA announces ceasefire	Spain
Oct. 1998	Dr. Barnette Slepian, gynecologist, assassinated by sniper James C. Koppe in Amherst, New York	United States
May 1999	Meeting between Spanish government and ETA in Zurich, Switzerland; negotiations fail	Spain
July 1999	World Church of the Creator member Benjamin Smith goes on a killing spree in Illinois and Indiana, targeting minorities and ultimately killing himself	United States
Aug. 1999	Aryan Nations member Buford Furrow kills a Filipino mailman and opens fire at a Jewish community center in San Fernando Valley, California, killing 1 and injuring 5	United States
Dec. 1999	President Chandrika Kumaratunga injured in an assassination attempt	Sri Lanka
1999–2002	Second Russian-Chechen war	Chechnya
Apr. 2000	Richard Baumhammers commits five racially based murders	United States
May 2000	Israel withdraws from South Lebanon; SLA collapses; Hizbullah declares "Liberation Day"	Lebanon
Aug. 2000	Car bomb in Bilbao kills 4	Spain
Sept. 2000	Massive Palestinian demonstrations mark the start of the second intifada after Ariel Sharon visits al-Aqsa/Temple Mount in Jerusalem	Israel
Oct. 2000	Al-Qaida suicide boat bombing targeted at the USS *Cole* kills 17 U.S. soldiers	Aden, Yemen
Mar.–Nov. 2001	Series of car bombings and assassinations throughout Spain kill about 50	Spain
May 2001–Mar. 2004	Hamas/PIJ/Al-Aqsa Brigades launch over 50 suicide attacks and other assaults throughout Israel and Palestinian lands	Israel and Palestinian lands
July 2001	LTTE bombs airport killing twelve	Sri Lanka
Sept. 2001	Al-Qaida suicide plane bombings of the World Trade Center and Pentagon kill over 3,000 in New York City, Washington, D.C., and Pennsylvania	United States

Date	Event	Location
Oct. 2001	United States attacks Afghanistan to destroy al-Qaida bases and oust Taliban regime	Afghanistan
Dec. 2001–Mar. 2003	Government crackdown on ETA, including arrests, financial seizures, ban on Herri Batasuna, and newspaper closure	Spain
Dec. 2001	Jewish Defense League Chair Irving Rueben and Earl Krugel arrested for conspiracy to bomb office of Representative Darrell Issa and King Fahd mosque	United States
Feb. 2002	Government and LTTE sign a permanent ceasefire with Norway's mediation	Sri Lanka
Mar. 2002	Prime Minister Ariel Sharon launches "Operation Defensive Shield"	Israel
Apr. 2002	Al-Qaida suicide bombing of a synagogue in Djerba kills 19	Tunisia
Oct. 2002	Suicide bombings by Jamaah Islamiyah (al-Qaida affiliate) targeted at nightclubs in Bali kill 202	Indonesia
2003–present	Genocide of 150,000 members of Darfur tribes in Sudan	Sudan
Apr. 2003	LTTE suspends peace talks citing unfair treatment	Sri Lanka
May 2003	Suicide truck bomb targeted at a Chechen government building kills 59; two female suicide bombers unsuccessfully attempt to assassinate Chechen president Ahmad Kadyrov, killing 16	Russia
May 2003	Al-Qaida ground attack and bombings targeted at Riyadh foreign nationals' compound and U.S. office kill 34	Saudi Arabia
May 2003	Suicide bombings by Salafiyah Jihadiyah (al-Qaida affiliate) targeted at Spanish restaurant, hotel, Jewish center, and Belgian consulate kill 45 (including 12 attackers) in Casablanca	Morocco
May 2003	Car bomb targeted at police officers in Navarre kills 2	Spain
June 2003	Female suicide bombers targeting a military base in Mozdok, North Ossetia, kill 20; two suicide bombers targeting a rock music festival in Mozdok kill 15	Russia
Aug. 2003	A truck bomb targeted at a military hospital in Mozdok kills 50	Russia

Date	Event	Location
Aug. 2003	A suicide bombing targeted at a hotel in Jakarta kills 12 and injures 150	Indonesia
Nov.–Dec. 2003	Thirteen ETA members captured by Spanish and French police	Spain
Dec. 2003	A suicide bomb targeted at a passenger train in South Russia kills 44; a female suicide bomber kills 6 near the Russian Parliament in Moscow	Russia
Dec. 2003	Suicide bombings of synagogues in Istanbul kill 23 and injure 300; bomb attacks by al-Qaida affiliates targeted at British consulate and bank in Istanbul kill 27 and wound 450	Turkey
2004–present	Al-Qaida suicide attacks targeted at U.S. forces, Iraqi government, and Shiite opponents kill several thousand	Iraq
Feb. 2004	A suicide bomber in a subway kills 41 in Moscow	Russia
Mar. 2004	Ten bombings by al-Qaida affiliate in Morocco targeted at four trains in Madrid kill 191 and injure 1,800; bombings initially blamed on ETA	Spain
Mar. 2004	Hamas leader Shaikh Ahmad Yassin assassinated by Israeli airstrike; 10 others are killed	Gaza Strip
Apr. 2004	Aryan Nations member Sean Gillespie firebombs Oklahoma City synagogue; makes film to inspire others	United States
May 2004	Al-Qaida shootings targeted at foreigners kill 22 in Al Khobar	Saudi Arabia
May 2004	President Ahmad Kadyrov and 6 others are killed by a bomb in Grozny	Russia
June 2004	Ingush/Chechen assault on Russian forces in Ingushetia kills dozens	Russia
Aug. 2004	Two female suicide bombers targeting two airlines in South Russia kill 90	Russia
Sept. 2004	Chechen terrorists take hostages at a school in Beslan, North Ossetia, killing 330	Russia
Nov. 2004	Yasser Arafat dies in Paris	France
Dec. 2004–Mar. 2006	Bombs in gas stations, bars, cafes, and other public areas (planned to prevent injuries and killings) explode throughout Spain	Spain
Feb. 2005	Former Lebanese prime minister Rafiq Hariri assassinated in Beirut; 23 killed	Lebanon
Feb. 2005	Prime Minister Ariel Sharon and President Mahmoud Abbas agree on a ceasefire	Israel

Date	Event	Location
Mar. 2005	Aslan Mashkadov killed by a bomb in Chechnya	Russia
Apr. 2005	Syrian forces leave Lebanon	Lebanon
June 2005	A bomb targeted at Russian soldiers in Daghestan kills 10	Russia
July–Dec. 2005	Islamist groups resume attacks with rocket launchings and four suicide bombings aimed at Israeli citizens	Israel
July 2005	Suicide bombing by al-Qaida affiliates targeted at three trains and one bus kill 52 and injure 700 in London	Great Britain
July 2005	Train and bus bombings by al-Qaida affiliates targeted at hotels kill 64 and injure 200 in Sinai	Egypt
July 2005	A bomb targeted at Chechen police in Grozny kills 10	Russia
Aug. 2005	Israel removes settlements from Gaza	Gaza Strip
Oct. 2005	Al-Qaida suicide bombings in tourist areas in Bali kill 22	Indonesia
Oct. 2005	An assault on government buildings in Nalchick, Kabardino-Balkaria, kills dozens	Russia
Nov. 2005	Suicide bombings by Zarqawi/al-Qaida of Mesopotamia targeted at hotels in Amman kill 57	Jordan
Jan. 2006	Prime Minister Ariel Sharon suffers massive stroke and goes into coma; Hamas wins Palestinian elections by a surprisingly wide margin	Gaza Strip and West Bank
Mar. 2006	Ramzan Kadyrov is elected prime minister	Russia
Mar. 2006	ETA declares a permanent ceasefire	Spain
Apr.–Aug. 2006	Interactive violence restarts after rioting breaks out in Trincomalee; both sides join in land and sea battles with government carrying out airstrikes and the Tamils undertaking bombings and other violence; hundreds killed, tens of thousands displaced	Sri Lanka
June 2006	Palestinian militants capture an IDF soldier	Gaza Strip
June–Dec. 2006	Israeli military undertakes massive operations in Gaza including airstrikes, tank attacks, and arrest of Hamas leadership, killing more than 300	Gaza Strip
July–Aug. 2006	Israel invades Lebanon after Hizbullah captures two IDF soldiers, killing ~,100 Lebanese and 160 Israelis	Lebanon

Web Resources for Further Research

Amnesty International
www.amnesty.org

BBC Special Reports Page (includes Quick Guides on al-Qaida, Chechnya, Northern Ireland, Sri Lanka, etc.)
http://news.bbc.co.uk/2/hi/in_depth/default.stm

B'Tselem
www.btselem.org/index.asp

Cato Institute Terrorism Web Page
www.cato.org/research/terrorism/index.html

Center for Defense Information Terrorism Program
www.cdi.org/program/index.cfm?programid=39

Centre for the Study of Terrorism and Political Violence at the University of St. Andrews
www.st-andrews.ac.uk/academic/intrel/research/cstpv

Combating Terrorism Center at West Point
www.ctc.usma.edu

Council on Foreign Relations
www.cfr.org/issue/135/terrorism.html

CQ Press in Context: Terrorism
www.cqpress.com/incontext/terrorism_links.html

Genocide Studies Program, Yale University
www.yale.edu/gsp

Genocide Watch
www.genocidewatch.org

"The Greedy Terrorist: A Rational-Choice Perspective on Terrorist Organizations' Inefficiencies and Vulnerabilities," by Jacob Shapiro, *Strategic Insights,* vol. IV, issue 1 (January 2005)
www.ccc.nps.navy.mil/si/2005/Jan/shapiroJan05.asp

Human Rights Watch Counterterrorism Page
www.hrw.org/doc/?t=ct

Institute for Counter-Terrorism
www.ict.org.il

Memorial Institute for the Prevention of Terrorism
www.mipt.org

Middle East Research and Information Project
www.merip.org

"The Moral Logic and Growth of Suicide Terrorism," by Scott Atran
http://jeannicod.ccsd.cnrs.fr/docs/00/05/99/38/PDF/TWQ06spring
_atran.pdf

Open Source Intelligence Center's Terrorism Web Page
http://osint.isria.com

PBS *Frontline*'s Foreign Affairs and Defense Reports
www.pbs.org/wgbh/pages/frontline/programs/categories/1.html

RAND Corporation's Terrorism and Homeland Security Web Page
http://rand.org/research_areas/terrorism

Shoah Visual History Archives, University of Southern California
www.usc.edu/libraries/archives/arc/libraries/sfa

Social Science Research Council's Online Terrorism Essays
www.ssrc.org/programs/gsc/themes/terrorism.page

South Asia Terrorism Portal
www.satp.org

"The Strategic Threat from Suicide Terror," by Scott Atran
www.aei-brookings.org/publications/abstract.php?pid=410

Terrorism Research Center
www.terrorism.com

United States Holocaust Memorial Museum
www.ushmm.org

U.S. Department of State Country Reports on Terrorism
www.state.gov/s/ct/rls/crt

United States Institute of Peace Terrorism/Counter-Terrorism Web
Resource Page
www.usip.org/library/topics/terrorism.html

Web Pages of Terrorist and other Insurgency Organizations

Tamil Eelam homepage
www.eelam.com

Alleged official Web site of the Sendero Luminoso (Spanish-language
only)
www.geocities.com/pcp_bandera_roja

Aum Shinrikyo's official Web site
http://english.aleph.to

Hizbullah's official Web site (with English translation option)
www.hizbollah.org

Hamas's alleged official Web site (English translation doesn't function)
www.palestine-info.cc

Index